The Sierra Adventure

The Sierra Adventure
The Story of Sierra On-Line

Shawn Mills

The Sierra Adventure: The Story of Sierra On-Line

Published by Shawn Mills
164 Gair Street
Frenchville 4701 QLD Australia

Cover Illustration by Bruce Brenneise
www.brucebrenneise.com

Edited by Jack Allin and Emily Morganti

Second Printing

Portions of this book are adapted from a series of Sierra retrospective articles written by the author and published by AdventureGamers.com between May 2017 and December 2017 and are reprinted with permission.

ISBN: 978-1-716-86706-4

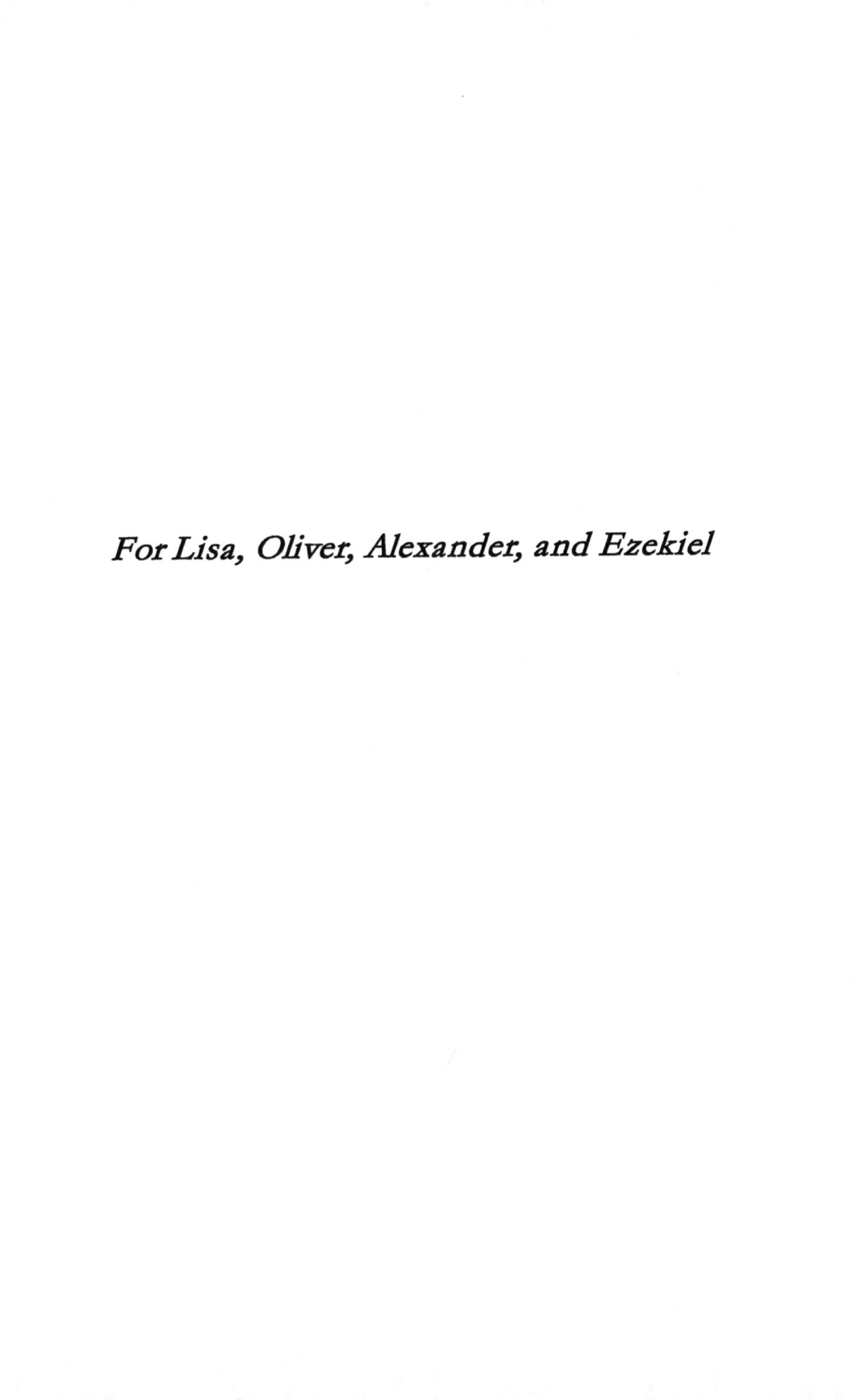

For Lisa, Oliver, Alexander, and Ezekiel

Table of Contents

The Sierra Adventure 1

Foreword by Josh Mandel 13

Introduction (or, "Where I apologize for missing your favorite game") 17

Chapter 1: The Perfect Storm 21

    First Thread of Survival (or, "Al Lowe and the Disney License") 26

    Second Thread of Survival (or, "*King's Quest* and the IBM Deal") 33

Interlude: Hints 39

Chapter 2: First Steps 41

    Full Steam Ahead 47

    One Massive Adventure 50

    The On-Line Dorm 52

Interlude: The RPG Market 55

Chapter 3: Two Guys and Two Sequels 59

    Enter the Two Guys 60

    Making a Sequel 63

    Heading into Space 65

    Return of the Prince 68

Interlude: Journey to the East 71

Chapter 4: Leisure Suits and Police Uniforms 75

    Call the Police! 80

    Return to Space 82

    AGI's Final Outings 84

Interlude: The Producers 89

Chapter 5: New Technology 95

    A Princess's Quest 98

    Larry's Back 99

    Space Rock 102

A Hero Arrives..105

Interlude: Music to the Ears..113

    MIDI Music..117

Chapter 6: Trying (Mostly) New Things...................................121

    Mystery!...121

    Secret Agents, Submarines and Tropical Islands...................124

    The Holy Grail..127

    The Final Larry...130

Chapter 7: A New Creative Direction..135

    Creatively Directing..136

    The Graphics of Sierra...141

    The Conflicts of Change...144

Interlude: Buying Power..153

Chapter 8: Old Favorites, New Tech..157

    The End of EGA...157

    Return of the King..161

    A Real Pantload..166

    Exit: Sonny Bonds...171

    They Really Did Skip *Larry 4*...172

Interlude: Edutainment...177

Chapter 9: Colorizing Old Movies...183

    Fans to the Rescue..187

Chapter 10: A Bandit, a Detective, and a Detour.....................191

    "Let's Get *Laura Bow 2* Done"..194

    A Detour Into War...198

Interlude: The *Hoyle* Connection...201

Chapter 11: The Golden Era...205

    A Dynamix Space Quest...207

    A Pharmacist for a Hero 209

A Fresno Experience 212

After a Detour, Darkness Arrives... 214

Chapter 12: Continuing Success 219

A Knight to Remember.. 221

Rodney King's Quest... 223

Princeless.. 225

Chapter 13: The Sierra Network................................ 231

Card Games and RPGs 235

Bad Behavior.. 241

Selling ImagiNation.. 243

Interlude: The Buyout... 245

Chapter 14: Changing Adventures 247

A DOOMed Sale 248

Adventures in the First Person 250

Adventures in Full Motion Video.. 254

More FMV Sequels 259

Sierra's Return to Online Gaming.. 261

Interlude: A Larry Platform Game........................... 265

Chapter 15: All Good Things 269

One Last Mess to Clean Up 269

Out with a Bang!.. 273

Chapter 16: . . . Must Come to an End................... 279

Heavy Is the King's Crown 279

A Final Visit to Daventry... 285

Sierra's Final Damned Adventure 290

Interlude: Theme Songs and Academy Awards 295

Chapter 17: Game Over... 299

The Gradual Decline of Oakhurst.. 302

Different Genres.. 305

It All Came Crashing Down... 311

Epilogue 1: The Shoulders of Giants..315

Epilogue 2: Why Sierra Matters 321

    Serena Nelson 321

    Luke Jensen 323

    Christopher Brendel...326

    Jason Mical...328

    Michael Della Pia 329

    Craig Harman 330

    Reverend Paul Miller..331

    Chris McGee 333

    Shawn Jones 334

    Michael Martin 335

    Alastair Mclellan..337

    Paul Marzagalli 338

    Stuart Feldhamer 339

    John-Thomas Foster..340

    Jeremy Hedges 342

    Brad Herbert 343

    Konstantin Grusha..345

    PushingUpRoses*..347

Acknowledgments...351

Kickstarter Backers 353

Appendix 1: Systems Developed For...359

Appendix 2: Internal Development Systems 361

Appendix 3: Games 363

Foreword by Josh Mandel

If you were fortunate enough[*] to have worked at Sierra On-Line, whether in its earliest incarnation (as On-Line Systems) or its final one (arguably Sierra Entertainment, Inc.) – or, for that matter, at any time in between – there is a high probability that someone, some time, has said to you, "You oughta write a book about it."

I think everyone always assumed such a book would be written by one or both of the co-founders, Ken and Roberta Williams. Roberta obviously has shelves of her fiction from her days as the company's preeminent designer, and Ken has written several sailing-related books since his Sierra days. They're both writers. A book from either of them about the Sierra days would, you would think, be the most comprehensive and revealing.

Truth is, we have all fallen down on the job. None of the ex-designers, directors, producers, programmers, artists, composers, marketers, administrators . . . nobody has accepted the challenge. Maybe it seemed like too overwhelming a task. Maybe some have started and never finished to their satisfaction. Maybe some people are averse to telling tales out of school. And no doubt some feel too much animosity about their time in the company, about Ken or Roberta or someone else, or about how it all ended up.

About that. As you read through this book, you may well get a sense of how frequent and intense the disagreements were. Naturally, any company is going to have its daily dramas and disagreements. But some unique circumstances combined to make Sierra a particularly volatile place to work. For one thing, you had best friends working side by side. You had siblings working together, and cousins, and parents and their children (and the occasional grandparent), significant others, fiancés and newlyweds. You also had interoffice politics as people vied for more recognition and responsibility in a culture that was, to put it mildly, managerially deeply dysfunctional. Experienced managers were

---

[*] Not everyone came away feeling fortunate. Believe it or not.

eventually brought in, but by then tremendous damage had already been done and the collapse of the company seemed inevitable.

Add to all of this the fact that Oakhurst was a tiny town, so your co-workers were also the people you were liable to encounter constantly during your off-hours, creating precious little breathing room between your work life and your social life. Another complicating factor was that Oakhurst was, and still is, a very redneck, suspicious little town – I vividly remember the KKK proudly marching on the local Planned Parenthood office.* Meanwhile, the artist community created in the process of building the company was expectedly progressive, so there were frequent culture clashes.

There were, of course, the expected tensions among employees of any company. Programmers versus artists, artists versus other artists, programmers versus other programmers, designers versus teams, teams versus managers, and so on. One should also keep in mind that not everybody working at Sierra was there because they loved the company and/or the product. Some of us definitely were (I was thrilled to be one of those), but others were there simply because they needed the work. A good percentage of those were locals with no prior experience in the gaming field.

We were under constant pressure to create a million-seller – or at least be profitable. On game after game, we were told that the project we were working on would have to sell at least umpteen thousand units, otherwise there would be layoffs.

And to top it off, we had Sierra's very public persona as a Disneyesque, one-big-happy-family place to work, as encouraged by the Sierra newsletter (which eventually became *InterAction* magazine). There was always a gentle pressure to maintain that carefully crafted image.

If I sound like I'm griping, I'm really not. I loved my years at Sierra. I learned a great deal and made lifelong friendships. I cherish the memory of those years and the feeling that we were creating something of true value.

So, when one contemplates the notion of writing a book about Sierra, it seems like it would be a pretty colossal undertaking, with so many threads to pick up and weave into the picture.

Now along comes Shawn Mills, who accomplishes the seemingly impossible by delivering a beautifully comprehensive overview of Sierra, talking to dozens of interested and involved parties, culling the smaller, less interesting stories (which are legion) but touching on pretty much

---

* Nobody at Sierra, to my knowledge, was involved with the KKK.

every major development the company went through from start to finish. You'll find in-depth looks at many of the major games and some of the larger conflagrations and conflicts. Basically, this is the book that people have been asking for all these years, and it's an astonishing and loving tribute.

I am eternally grateful to Shawn for putting this history together, because now when people tell me, "You oughta write a book," I can say, "Hey, it's been done."

FINALLY!

Josh Mandel
Albany, New York
October 2019

Introduction (or, "Where I apologize for missing your favorite game")

When I was an early teen, my dad worked as a trainer for Australia Post. After being away for work in another city for a couple of weeks, he came home with a surprise: the first computer to enter our house. It was state of the art at the time. For the nerds in the room, it was a 286AT, 16 MHz with a 40 MB hard drive and a full megabyte of RAM. No mouse, but it did have a cool "turbo" button that lowered the CPU speed. Now, I was only twelve, so to be perfectly honest, the only thing I cared about were the two games that came with it: *Hero's Quest* and *Thexder*.

I remember playing *Hero's Quest* with my dad and brothers, solving the mystery of the missing baronet, fighting evil goblins and brigands, learning where it was safe to sleep. I recall mapping out the Valley of Spielburg. Talking to the Healer. Finding Erana's Peace. Hearing that cool *Hero's Quest* fanfare for the first time.

It was the first computer game I ever played and the memory of that game – the magic of that world – has stayed with me all these years.

As I grew older I fell in love with the *Space Quest* series, then the *Police Quest* games. I probably have the same story as thousands of other people about *Leisure Suit Larry*: I played it without my parents' knowledge, my pirated copies of the first and third games copied into the DOS directory and the executable file renamed to begin.com. Sneaky!

The other major series followed as I worked my way through Sierra's vast catalog. By the time I was in my mid-teens, I was able to buy games for myself and the first one I purchased with my very own money was *Freddy Pharkas: Frontier Pharmacist*, a game that I considered then (and still believe today) is about the best one Sierra made. The second was *King's Quest VI* (the white box version on 5.25-inch disks). I still have both.

I've had a lot of interests in my life, and as with most people they've only lasted a season, but Sierra's games have always stuck with me and I've continued to love them and play them through the decades since I first tried *Hero's Quest*. Like a good book, they're something I return to over and over.

Loving these games and realizing that I really wanted to know more about Sierra, I started searching for any information I could find. But there wasn't much out there. Early on, I managed to get a copy of Steven Levy's *Hackers*, which is a brilliant read that gave me some insight into the earliest days of the company, but it stops at about 1983 and all the games I really loved came after that.

Over the years I've read bits and pieces about Sierra. Interviews with Ken Williams, Al Lowe, Scott Murphy, and so many others related little pieces of the story, but I never had a clear picture of the whole thing. Why adventure games? Who orchestrated the changes to VGA and point-and-click? How did they design games? All these questions and more niggled at the back of my mind.

It seemed that the only way I could get an answer to these and all the other questions I had was to research and write a book myself. So that's what you're reading right now.

This is the story of Sierra On-Line, told mainly through the words of the people who worked there themselves. A *lot* of people were employed by Sierra over the years, so it would be impossible to interview them all, but I've spoken to what I hope is a good cross section of the company. People with interesting stories to tell. All the quotes in the book are from my own original interviews, except where indicated. I should also point out that sales data for games in the era being discussed are incredibly unreliable. Most of the figures referenced are therefore not from official sources but based on the recollections of those who worked for Sierra at the time.

Sierra On-Line was a fascinating company. But it's also more than that. It's really a microcosm of the history of computer games themselves. Sierra's rise and fall as a developer coincided with the ascendance and evolution of the gaming industry as a whole. There's so much to the story of Sierra that it's virtually impossible to fit it all into a single book.

This is the part where I apologize to the hardcore Sierra fans out there. This book doesn't cover every single aspect of the company, nor does it include every single game they produced or published. It also stops at 1999, when they closed their internal development studios. Honestly, there's just too much to go through in detail. I also only lightly touch on Sierra's subsidiary companies, since they're a story in their own right. I would love to write that history of Dynamix and Bright Star (in particular) but those are tales for another day.

One obstacle I experienced was that I simply couldn't get people to talk on the record about some games released in the mid to late nineties, as it seems there are nondisclosure agreements still in place regarding their production. Read into that what you will. Others, I just couldn't find room to explore. If I missed your favorite game, I am sorry. I missed a few of mine, too.

Another significant problem I encountered stems from a narrative point of view. Particularly with pre–*King's Quest* titles, many early games involved a single programmer sitting in front of a computer and making the game. While they might have been pivotal for the company at the time, there's not actually much to say beyond that. This isn't to disparage them in the slightest, just a reflection that I can't say much about someone working on an Apple II computer for twenty hours a day writing a game.

What is very important to me is the story behind *why* Sierra was so successful. I know there are probably going to be people who don't agree with me, but the answer to that question, at least in my mind, is innovation. What I've tried to do is cover the important parts of Sierra's history as well as the interesting stories and anecdotes I uncovered in my research. I am certainly proud of what I've managed to bring together, and I hope you enjoy reading it.

Chapter 1: The Perfect Storm

The hardest thing I have ever done in my life is to lay someone off.

Ken Williams, Founder and CEO

The previous three years had been successful, and there was no reason to believe that this one would be any different. In his strategy outline for 1984, Ken Williams was highly optimistic about Sierra's prospects:

"We believe the home-computer market to be so explosive that 'title saturation' is impossible. The number of new machines competing for the Apple/Atari segment in 1983 will create a perpetually new market hungry for winning 1982 titles. We will exploit this opportunity."[1]

Unfortunately for Ken and Sierra, title saturation proved to be a real, and near-fatal, thing.

It wasn't too many months after the strategy outline was released that Ken, not yet thirty years old, was sitting behind his desk in his Oakhurst, California office at Sierra On-Line, a company he and his wife Roberta had built from the ground up into one of the biggest computer software developers in the country, trying to salvage his business.

That morning, Sierra had 140 employees. By the end of the day, he had laid off two-thirds of his staff.

"The hardest thing I have ever done in my life is to lay someone off," Ken confesses. "There are people who bought homes, who moved their families, whose lives were destroyed by being laid off. It tore me apart to think that my actions might destroy someone else's life.

"I justified it via the knowledge that if I didn't do what had to be done, no one would have a job. Ultimately, if you make smart decisions, which sometimes means conforming spending to revenues, the company will grow, and if you don't, it will be game over."

Al Lowe, designer of the *Leisure Suit Larry* series, was one of those people Ken had to let go that day. Al says that although Ken was forced to lay him off, he also offered him an alternative:

"It was a tragic blow. A lot of those guys were given the same offer I was given, which was, 'You're not going to get a salary but I will pay you advances against future royalties. As you finish parts of the game, bring it in and we'll give you more advances.' Just like a book author would do. You get an advance up front and additional checks as you go along, and you finish it. A lot of those guys that got laid off like that just went home and didn't work, just took the time and watched soap operas or smoked dope or something. But I didn't. I went home and worked my ass off. There were several other guys that did too."

Although the most affected people were the staff Ken was forced to let go, the impact was felt throughout the entire town. John Williams, Ken's younger brother and Sierra's marketing manager at the time, remembers the effect it had on the whole community:

"In little Oakhurst, that had repercussions that went well beyond the company. We had been a primary employer in the town and our people had been throwing a lot of money around. Suddenly rents on apartments weren't getting paid and people were just packing up and leaving town. People were angry at us."

Another challenge Ken and Roberta faced was paying for the new building they had recently moved into, which was custom-built by the developers for Sierra. Ken had agreed to a long-term leasing arrangement that cost around $25,000 per month in rent. Desperate, he approached the owners about a decrease in rent until the industry turned around, even offering them a share in the company, but they would only agree to subletting part of the building as a way to offset the costs.

Chuck Benton, who was working as a contract programmer for Sierra, visited the office around that time and was surprised at what he found: "I remember the last time I was out there doing the *Donald Duck's Playground* stuff. They'd created this new huge office building and three-quarters of the building was empty."

Someone else who remained after that fateful day was Mark Crowe, who was working on graphics for some of Sierra's adventure games.

"I survived all that," Mark recalls. "I seem to remember all that happening just prior to us starting to work on *Space Quest* because I remember we had just moved into this fabulous building, the famous redwood building. It was kind of eerie because it was almost too nice; you know, 'We don't deserve this place!' It was so expensive because the company was growing and was planning to grow. Then this happened and suddenly the place was a ghost town and it was like everybody was off-world and we had the whole place to ourselves."

So, what caused things to collapse almost overnight?

The Atari Video Computer System (renamed to the more commonly known brand of Atari 2600 in 1982) was released in 1977, and in the six ensuing years it first created and then eventually dominated the home gaming market. It was, by 1983, the biggest video game platform in America, but the emergence of other game systems would coincide with the end of its life cycle before long.

New options followed quickly – the Intellivision, the ColecoVision, Tandy's TRS-80, the Commodore 64 – all of which absorbed a portion of the gaming market.

Commercial giant IBM released the IBM Personal Computer in August 1981, a system that, while solid and dependable, failed to make much of a splash mainly due to its high price in a market dominated by Apple Computer, Inc. While they followed up with a few alternatives such as the XT (the first PC to come with a hard drive as standard) and the PCjr (their entry level option), none of these were massive hits and hadn't bitten into Apple's sales to any great degree.

Meanwhile, an ongoing price war between Commodore and Texas Instruments (TI) hit new heights in 1982. The former cut the cost of their Commodore 64 computer almost in half to only $300, rocking the fledgling game industry and butchering Commodore's own Vic-20 sales. Customers suddenly wanted a full computer system, not just a game console, and could now get one for a similar price.

With all these consoles and computers on the market, companies began acquiring rights for games, particularly arcade games, for their respective systems. Some, like Sierra, not only acquired these sorts of rights, they also expanded production of their original titles. Using a variety of media such as disks, cartridges, and tapes, Sierra made plans to publish one hundred products in 1983.

John Williams was managing Sierra's marketing department when the crash happened and claims that it was mainly due to an oversupply of low-quality video games on the market.

"The crash of '83/'84 wasn't so much about computers, though they got swept up in it, as about video games. It was a perfect storm of sorts," John explains. "The Atari Video Computer System was at the end of its life. The ColecoVision and Mattel Intellivision had hit [the] market with great fanfare and just enough early sales to get everyone in the software business really excited. Texas Instruments released their TI-99, which they billed as a computer but was priced and sold like a game machine; it got some traction but then seemed to fall by the wayside."

Texas Instruments' TI-99/4A personal computer was an early casualty of the price war and was discontinued in 1983. As well as the price reduction of the Commodore 64 hurting TI's sales, another factor was TI's aggressive entry into the video game market. But according to John, they committed a crucial oversight:

"Texas Instruments was a big, big company when they entered the video game space. They had pretty much owned the early calculator business – which probably doesn't sound like much, so as background, I got my first ever pocket calculator in 1978 and I was one of the first people in my school to actually own one. At the time, it cost about $230. By the end of 1979, just about every kid in high school had one, and just about all of them were TI calculators and the same was true for colleges and middle schools.

"At that point in time, they were sitting on a ton of cash and a reputation as a quality technology company with consumer experience. People remember that they launched their personal computer / video game system to compete against the ColecoVision, Apple II, Atari, etc. and that the machine was actually very well priced and powerful.

"What they perhaps don't remember is how much Texas Instruments had invested in snapping up the cartridge rights to just about every hot game they could find, then actually hiring some of the biggest of the big video game publishers to create games based on them. Name a hot video game title from that year of release and they probably held the cartridge rights to it on not just their own machine, but also on [the] Atari 8-bit computer, Atari 2600 console, Coleco / Coleco Adam, TRS-80 and other game machines."

The crucial oversight, as John explains, was TI failing to purchase the diskette rights, which were instead acquired by smaller developers. "Sierra and a few of the other 'little guy' computer game publishers had purchased the diskette rights, which TI probably didn't even think about or they would have snapped them up too," he says. "We small publishers all knew once those cartridges got out there, our publishing rights would be worth a lot less."

The decision was made by some of these smaller publishers to flood the market with their diskette versions of major titles. Instead of their rights becoming useless, they planned to turn the tables and get to market quicker, hurting TI and other major publishers instead.

Rumors also abounded that some developers helped people burn EPROM (erasable programmable read-only memory) versions of cartridge titles once they were released – in essence, pirating game console cartridges.

John goes on to detail his plan to beat the cartridge producers to market and fill it with Sierra's diskette versions: "We knew we couldn't just drop the retail prices – price fixing and predatory marketing were illegal even back then – but we could do elaborate 'buy two, get one free' type promotions both to retailers, meaning they got a free boxed game with every two they bought, and again to consumers, meaning the gamer got a free game when he bought a few games.

"You could get diskettes to market much faster than cartridges because cartridges took two to three months to manufacture at the time. We all rushed our titles out and just did crazy deals – stuffing the market. By the time TI and their big-name trade partners in publishing like Activision, Parker Brothers and Intellivision got their cartridge titles to market, we had scorch-earthed the marketplace.

"TI, Parker Brothers, Activision and the others probably sold 10% of what they had projected, and all took a huge hit financially."

Unfortunately, while effectively stopping the sales of cartridges from their larger competitors, Sierra had also created a problem. They had sold so many copies of these licensed titles that sales of their own games were drying up. John describes another marketing plan that was devised to overcome this new hurdle.

"We had our own problems with the amount of stock for these big titles that we had placed at retail, but we offered retailers a one-for-one stock balance and traded out their overstocks on the big titles for our lesser-known titles, which gave us lots of shelf space and games people hadn't already played. Suffice to say that we totally blocked those big guys at a time when it looked like they had just bought themselves into the market by snapping up all the big titles. Those big companies, all public, had to announce huge losses to shareholders and some of those stocks lost 50% or more of their value quickly."

Between the failure of the TI-99, the low performance of the IBM PC range, and this flood of new games, the market quickly became oversaturated. With few quality controls in place, a string of high-profile flops such as Atari's infamous *E.T. the Extra-Terrestrial* followed.

Then it all came crashing down.

"It was like an industry that had been moving at light speed all hit a wall at once," John Williams recalls.

The computer industry in general, and the game industry in particular, were new markets, and some businesses saw them as a trend that had already passed.

"Those game machines were all cartridge-based and the cartridges were expensive. If I remember, it was around ten dollars a cartridge; that was what we paid for them when we bought twenty thousand at a time. The primary sales channels were places like Toys"R"Us and Sears, mass-market channels where the game companies had zero leverage," John explains.

"It was this simple. The retailers said, 'Well, video games were a fad and it's over now. We're canceling our orders and returning what we have on the shelf.' Hundreds of thousands of dollars of inventory was being returned to us, wiping out sales we thought we already had completed and hundreds of thousands of dollars more in cartridge inventory that suddenly we had no place to sell. Those cartridges couldn't be reprogrammed either; they were just dead plastic."

Entire companies were folding with warehouses full of now-worthless Atari, Vic-20 and Coleco cartridges. Atari famously took truckloads of their unsellable cartridges and consoles to a New Mexico landfill site, dumping over 700,000 unsold and returned cartridges.

"It was backbreaking and a lot of the game companies of the time didn't survive or were mortally wounded. Software companies that had private financing saw their credit lines pulled. Companies that needed capital to finish games they had been working on suddenly had no money to pay programmers. A lot of games that had been in development for the game machines were canceled and the teams laid off," John recalls.

"It was just ugly."

First Thread of Survival (or, "Al Lowe and the Disney License")

Sierra survived, as Ken Williams puts it, because "Roberta and I were literally funding the company off of our credit cards, and by borrowing money against our home."

One of the decisions Ken was forced to make was to refocus the company's output and, necessitated by having to lay off so many of their staff, he decided to reduce the number of games to only a couple of titles. What had always consistently worked for Sierra were adventure games.

"It was a return to what had worked historically. And my recollection is that we didn't have a lot of choice. We had to scale back to the one or two projects which looked most promising," Ken recalls.

One of those projects to survive the crash was *The Black Cauldron*, a game based on Disney's new animated movie. Prior to the collapse, Ken had used the opportunity of Texas Instruments pulling out of the game market to purchase TI's license to create computer games based on Disney characters. Acquiring the license allowed Sierra to bypass the usual up-front licensing payment Disney required, instead only having to pay royalties on sales.

The Black Cauldron was being designed by Al Lowe, who also took on some of the programming duties in the small team. Al had joined Sierra a year or so earlier, having previously moved from playing saxophone professionally to a career as a schoolteacher, then to writing games for his own company Sunnyside Soft.

Al had developed a love for music at an early age, although he admits not a lot of thought went into his choice of instrument. "When I got old enough that music classes were offered at school, I asked my parents and they said, 'We can't afford to buy a horn, but your older brother has a saxophone. It's still down in the basement and you can play that.' I said, 'Okay, I'll play that.' Literally that was exactly the amount of thought and preparation and research that went into my decision. 'Hey, there's a horn in the basement, you get to play that.' It's worked out well," Al laughs.

As he moved into junior high school, the early beginnings of his music career began to form. After starting out playing with a large school band, something Al didn't particularly enjoy, he was picked along with six other bandmates to form a small combination.

"I had a teacher that put together a small combo and we were supposed to play for some music assembly or something like that. And it was a lot of fun! I liked it a lot more than playing concert band music and stuff with a fifty-piece band that wasn't very good. She took the seven best people from the band, and that was a lot better!

"So one of the guys knew somebody who wanted cheap music and said, 'Get those kids to play; nobody really cares! It's not important; just get some kids.' So they hired us. We played this performance at school and that summer we got together and had an actual gig and I think we got five dollars apiece as I recall. Which was cheap for him but it was fun for us. I was like, 'Wow, I can just play music and have fun and make money.'

"Then all through high school that's what I did. During that time I probably worked five or six nights a month, every Saturday night mostly; a few Fridays and some other gigs along the way. I never had a job during high school; I always put myself through playing music. Then when I got to college I continued doing that too. I never really had a regular job doing anything until halfway through college when I had a summer off and I ended up working in a factory. Which convinced me all the more that music was a hell of a lot more fun than making corrugated paper boxes."

As well as his musical leanings, Al was also a self-professed tech geek from an early age. "I was always a geek. I started off when I was in seventh grade; I had a tape recorder. A reel-to-reel tape recorder," he recalls. "You've got to remember this was 1958. A tape recorder was very esoteric. The size of a microwave oven and it recorded about fifteen minutes of music on a five-inch reel of tape and it weighed about fifty pounds. This was pretty advanced stuff. All through high school I was always the kid wiring the PA system, building the speakers and soldering cables. I was always that guy. Fixing the movie projector. All kinds of skills that are no longer needed in school.

"When computers came along, this just seemed like something I had to do. I had no training and I didn't have a math background, but when the Apple II came out and Steve Jobs lied to us and said how easy it was to program and all the wonderful things that you could do with it someday, maybe, when you figured out how, I bought the story. I convinced my wife we should spend a full month of both of our salaries to buy this box that would sit on my desk and actually do nothing. So that was actually a pretty big leap. I said I would make it pay for itself and eventually I did! It took a while but eventually it paid for itself and much more."

Before he bought the computer – mail order, because the only computer shop in town wasn't interested in assisting him – he bought two Sierra games, one of which was On-Line's early adventure game *Cranston Manor.*

Al loved it.

Making good on his promise to his wife Margaret that the computer would pay for itself, he taught himself to program and developed three games, *Dragon's Keep, Bop-A-Bet* and *Troll's Tale*, then set up Sunnyside Soft to sell them, primarily at educational trade shows.

"We went out on a limb, because we took our games to a small show in California that was for computer-using teachers. It was called the CUE Conference (Computer Using Educators) and since we wrote educational games we took them there. Rented a table on the gymnasium floor at this high school, set up a computer and had the games running. They were a big hit; people raved about them and said they were wonderful and very professional. We thought, maybe this isn't crap after all; maybe somebody will buy this.

"So we sold a bunch that weekend; we got a bunch of orders and it gave us enough courage to tackle a bigger show, which was Applefest in 1982. That was the last big Apple II conference. Everybody who was anybody in the Apple world was there. Every publisher of any note whatsoever; there were lots and lots of peripheral people. We decided to spend a lot of money for us and rent a booth in that show with the hopes of selling more software. But what we actually did was put ourselves on display before every major publisher in the business. They all came by and said, 'Oh, you don't want to publish these games. You should let us publish them, then [you'd have] time to make more games. You should be game designers and game makers. You don't want to be putting disks in baggies and sticking them in boxes and waiting for the UPS truck. You want to be a designer,'" Al remembers.

After talking with a number of publishers, Al received an offer from Ken Williams to buy Sunnyside Soft and publish his games. Al accepted and went to work for Ken for the next sixteen years.

Since Al was still working as a teacher, it wasn't until summer break that Ken finally convinced him to join Sierra full time. Ken asked Al to come up with a number of proposals they could go through and consider.

"I came up with a lot of ideas for games, and somewhere along there he got the rights to the Disney characters, so several of those games became Disney games," Al says.

Sierra had the rights to create four titles for Disney and put into production *Mickey's Space Adventure*, *Winnie the Pooh in the Hundred Acre Wood*, *Donald Duck's Playground*, and *Goofy's Word Factory*, the latter being canceled before release.

Al recalls working on all three released titles. "I did *Winnie the Pooh* and wrote music for *Mickey's Space Adventure*, and I was really proud of *Donald Duck's Playground*, which won educational game of the year."

Although Sierra had counted on high sales, the reality was different and the educational titles were quietly pushed aside for other games. *Donald Duck* sold a few thousand copies, not an insignificant number for the time but not up to the expectations that having the Disney name and characters attached had brought. "It was a good game, it really was," Al remembers. "So that was disappointing. But it was a fun experience."

Disney had no prior experience with computer games. The industry was barely a few years old, after all, and not being sure how games fit into their structure, Disney assigned their educational department to act as liaison with Sierra. The department, whose usual work was in educational film strips and workbooks for schools, was not a natural fit and struggled to understand what Sierra was creating.

"They had these two former elementary school teachers who had no clue what a computer was and they were assigned as our liaisons. Everything we did went through them," Al scoffs.

Both *Mickey's Space Adventure* and the unreleased *Goofy's Word Factory* became bogged down in the interactions between the production team and their Disney counterparts. Every time the team showed their updates for approval, they received a new list of changes required.

As composer on *Mickey's Space Adventure*, Al watched the process unfold. "They wouldn't make improvements or even have good suggestions. They would just say, 'Do this differently or make this a different color.' It was just so that they had some input into the development process. Basically, it wasted our time."

John Williams agrees that working with Disney wasn't easy, and certainly not profitable enough in the early days. "They were hard to work with and therefore game development was very expensive and frustrating. Their royalty per game was high, something like 20% right off the top, and while the Disney name certainly had cachet, most of these games were still education titles and had limited sales potential, so the volume of sales per title was really not that big.

"In the end, it just seemed like we had our very best people working on the products and they ended up being our least profitable projects and we didn't even own or benefit from the intellectual properties we were working with."

When it came to designing *Winnie the Pooh in the Hundred Acre Wood*, Al worked on his design by reading the books by A. A. Milne and synthesizing what he could. He then created a map of the Hundred Acre Wood and worked out the story and puzzles for the game. Then he decided to take a different tack in working with Disney's liaisons: "I just went ahead and did the entire *Winnie the Pooh* game, got it finished and then showed it to them.

"They said, 'Can you change this or can you do that?' and I replied that if we did that it's going to get behind and I have other projects that I have booked ahead, so I don't know how. I just kind of rammed it through; I did an end around [on] them and scored. I knew I had Ken's ear and I knew Ken would support me on it because he was interested in shipping the game and selling copies. He wasn't interested in futzing around with this guy's shirt color and that person's feet color and stuff. I basically said, 'Here it is, wanna sell it?' So they did. They took the money."

It worked. Disney was satisfied enough with the success of the three games that they offered Sierra the opportunity to create a game based on their new animated movie, *The Black Cauldron*.

Al Lowe and Roberta Williams were to design the game, and the team accepted an offer from Disney to visit their studios and view an early cut of the film. Seated in a private theater, Al was impressed with the movie and could imagine creating a game based on it.

"I got to see *The Black Cauldron* when it was the midst of production. Parts of the scenes were gorgeous finished and finalized stuff. Parts of it were pencil sketches. Parts of it were just a backdrop hanging on a piece of pipe in a basement. Literally you could see the pipe and a piece of wall and they zoomed in on it because it was going to get replaced with the final product. They would pick classical or some other sort of music and play a record behind it. The dialogue was all in, though. So I got to see the film ahead of time and I said, 'Yeah, I can work on this.'"

Mark Crowe was involved in some of the Disney games and remembers the thrill of being able to work with characters he had always cherished.

"That was exciting times," Mark says. "We got to go down to Disney studios and sit in the screening room and watch a half-baked animated film in the process of being made. Just getting shown around the hallways where nine old men created Disney magic. Priceless. Then being given the responsibility to create a game with those cherished Disney characters. I was very excited and proud to have worked on those games."

After watching the movie, Al was sent to the archives, expecting to see something grand and opulent like the national archives in Washington, DC. Instead he went down a set of exterior stairs to a door where he rang the doorbell and was led into a basement hallway by the archivist.

Al recalls, "As I stepped inside she said, 'Oh hang on, the phone's ringing and there's nobody else here. I'll go get it; just wait here.' So I stood in the doorway there waiting to start our conversation, and leaned my hand against the wall. I looked over and my hand was on the original pencil drawings for *Sleeping Beauty*. I was like, 'Oh my God! Seriously?!'"

In this basement hallway, with sewer pipes, water lines and sprinklers overhead, sat open industrial shelving with original drawings for every movie from Mickey Mouse's first cartoon, *Steamboat Willie*. With no protection other than manila folders, the pencil drawings were stored on a steel shelf, so it was an easy process getting access to *The*

Black Cauldron to take back to the production team for use in the game. Al took away copies of Elmer Bernstein's original score and some pieces of background art.

Al also remembers his great surprise when he was taken to a gigantic mound of poster boards, each with an original background watercolor from *The Black Cauldron*. "They were just thrown in a giant heap and I said, 'So, what's with this?' and she said, 'I have to go through this and decide which ones to keep.' I said, 'You don't keep them all?' and she replied, 'Oh no! We'll throw 98% of this in the garbage.'

"That was my introduction to Disney. But working on *The Black Cauldron* was fun. It was a fun project. There was very little oversight from anybody down there. We pretty much made the game that we wanted to and it was a really fun project to do."

Mark Crowe didn't get to visit those archives himself, but was amazed at what they were allowed to use. "Unfortunately, I didn't get to go into the archives firsthand; that was Al. Roberta got to go in there because she was doing *The Black Cauldron* design, but a lot of that stuff got to come back to our studio, which still to this day amazes me they let that out the door. It just boggles my mind and I'm sure that would never happen today."

Still working at a reduced scale after the video game crash, the team worked out of the study at Ken and Roberta's house. A large, relatively empty room, it had a shelf that sat about desk height and ran for close to thirty feet around the room.

According to Al, "We just all kind of moved in there and worked on that shelf. That became our desks. We sat in their house every day and night. Because I lived down in Fresno, they just gave me a guest room at their house. I'd work until I couldn't stay awake anymore and I'd go and have a lie down upstairs and come back and do it again. That was how we wrote that game!"

The *Black Cauldron* team, which also included Ken Williams and Scott Murphy, worked hard to keep each other's spirits up. One thing that stands out to Al about that time was the people involved. "Chris Iden, Bob Heitman [both programmers], Mark Crowe, Scott Murphy, myself and a few others, we became in essence the basis of the new Sierra. The phoenix that rose from the ashes of the Atari 2600 crash."

While *The Black Cauldron* marked the end of Sierra's relationship with Disney, with Sierra moving on to concentrate on their own properties and Disney developing their own computer games, Al still has a reminder of those days on his home office wall.

"I ended up becoming a big Lloyd Alexander fan. He's the guy who wrote the *Chronicles of Prydain*; they're five kind of youth novels, I suppose you'd call them. But boy, they're really good books and good writing. One of my favorite things on the wall here, I have a signed letter from Lloyd Alexander talking about how much his nieces and nephews enjoyed my game. Pretty cool."

The Black Cauldron was a moderate success for Sierra, but certainly enough to help see the company through their troubled times. Though, as Al recalls, it was another title that mattered more. "Sierra was in a precarious place. I think *Black Cauldron* made a big difference, but the bigger difference was *King's Quest*."

Second Thread of Survival (or, "*King's Quest* and the IBM Deal")

In 1981, IBM released their IBM PC into the home user market dominated by Apple and Commodore. Already firmly established in the corporate sector, the PC made some headway into the home market but due to the high cost of the PC in comparison to its more established competitors, IBM began to look at a cheaper option. After all, everyone anticipated all the big revenue growth to be in personal computing in the future.

Knowing they needed a low-cost version of the PC to continue their massive expansion, IBM started development on the PCjr and approached Ken Williams and Sierra to help produce software that would take advantage of their newest system. John Williams believes there were a number of reasons Sierra (which was known as On-Line Systems until 1982) was contracted by IBM.

"First off and most importantly, On-Line Systems and Ken were highly visible in the early Apple community, and so IBM identified Ken as a person who could help champion the new machine they were creating. Also, Ken was an ultimate networker and pretty much knew everyone in the young industry and had business relationships of some sort all over the industry," John recalls.

"Finally, and it sometimes gets lost in this, is that Ken had a hell of a resume for a guy his age, and so his reputation kind of preceded him. He was a programming thoroughbred and I think that made a difference in the IBM hallways."

IBM asked Ken to develop two products for the PCjr that would take full advantage of the new system's capabilities, HomeWord (a word processor) and *King's Quest* – a move John says "allowed us to stay alive and fund development." IBM also put up some of the development costs of *King's Quest*, Sierra's most expensive production to date.

What appealed to Ken and Roberta was being at the forefront of what appeared to be a new evolution of computers. It was easy to see that the new technology would be a huge advantage for the type of games they wanted to produce. The PCjr increased both the graphics and sound capabilities of the original IBM PC. Graphically, the PC could only produce 320x200 resolution with 4 colors and 640x200 in monochrome mode, but the PCjr blew that away by producing 160x100, 160x200, and 320x200 displays, all with 16 colors. The sound capabilities were also increased substantially, from a single sound on the IBM PC to three tones to be played simultaneously through the PCjr's internal speaker. Other factors, such as easily upgradable memory, cartridge slots for games and educational software, and compatibility with MS-DOS (which accounted for 70% of the PC market) made the PCjr a sure hit.

Two brothers, Ken and Doug MacNeill, worked on *King's Quest* and Doug tells of how they ended up working on one of the most influential games in computer game history. "My brother Ken was a flight instructor at the airport [in] Fresno and Ken Williams started taking lessons from him to become a pilot," Doug says. "Ken Williams respected my brother Ken and they got to become friends. My brother had a degree in computer science and Ken Williams asked him if he wanted a job up there at Sierra. He was taken on to the *King's Quest* team, and they got him to work on some of the utilities and development of the early stages of the game."

Knowing the team needed a graphic artist, Ken MacNeill had the perfect person in mind. "They needed a graphic artist and my brother Ken mentioned to the manager of the project that I was able to do graphics," Doug recalls. "I drew some sketches up and my brother took them up there. I got interviewed and got the job doing graphics for *King's Quest*. That was my first assignment. I didn't have any experience in computers at all. I didn't even like computers. I didn't play computer games. I didn't want anything to do with it. I drew pictures on paper and ended up starting to digitize them into the game, and then when I got that done they wanted me to start on animated objects. By this time I was starting to get into the computer stuff. I did it and it turned out I had an aptitude for it, and I think I did really good for the day. Nowadays it wouldn't be anything anyone would be excited about. In those days we were pioneering it, so everything was new and exciting."

When Doug joined the team, though, he recalls they didn't even have the basic technical specifications worked out. What resolution was the game going to be made in? How were they going to have a three-dimensional look? From what he saw, the game was at a standstill, but the decision was soon made about resolution and the idea of "priorities" was developed to give that much sought-after 3D appearance.

The concept of priorities was a unique idea. A part of the screen – a tree, for example – could be designated as an area that could be walked behind. If King Graham went behind that tree he would disappear, making it look like he was really behind it, and he would reappear only when the player walked him further out. If Graham's coordinates were below that tree, he would simply appear in front of it. It sounded simple, but the reality was nobody knew how to make it work.

"I had to get moving on it, so one night I spent time just drawing a grid on paper with pen and ink," Doug remembers. "I drew it out. I drew the resolution that we were going to use, and I drew the priorities we would use for the background. I worked all night on that. I brought that in in the morning and I heard, 'You earned your pay this month!' We then had a grid we could photocopy and I could draw on top of, and we could easily figure out how the 3D animators would get the 3D animation to work.

"So I drew all those pictures on paper and we had a digitizer, which was a piece of hardware that looks like a tablet but a bit bigger, and inside it has a cursor that knows its location relevant to itself. Anywhere you place the cursor, it knows its location on that tablet. It's like a connection to the real world. My brother Ken actually made the utility for digitizing pictures. I could put my drawing on there and you would start off by setting the color, then the priority and giving it either a command line or point or circle or arc or whatever. It was real simple. You would set color one, which was red or whatever priority, and you would start digitizing. But you had to do it efficiently, because our memory restrictions were so difficult back in those days.

"That's how I drew all those pictures. You could draw an outline you could fill in, but it would always miss things. Every picture had to be very detailed because even though the resolution wasn't very good (it was low resolution), you had to use every color and every pixel to make it look that good. In *King's Quest I* it didn't look that good, but by the time we got to *King's Quest III* and *Gold Rush!* we were actually making decent pictures, I think."

What was unique about the development of *King's Quest* for Sierra was the intense secrecy involved. Ken Williams and all the staff had to sign nondisclosure agreements and were required to work out of a separate office, locked and secured away from anyone not directly involved in the project. Sierra was using prototype computers and IBM didn't want their plans to leak before the PCjr was released.

Doug MacNeill remembers the secrecy around the entire production. "Every office IBM set up, they told the people there that this computer was going to be called a certain name – I think they told us it was Pickle, they told another office it was Peanut. These were all IBM secure offices; we couldn't tell anyone we were there. We couldn't tell anyone anything about the machine at all!"

When the leak did occur it wasn't from Sierra, as Doug recalls. "It ended up in the news being called the Peanut. IBM knew who leaked it because of the name it came out with."

King's Quest was released shortly after the PCjr launched and it fulfilled all the promises Sierra had made. It was the first fully colored 3D adventure game, with animated characters instead of then-standard static images. It was also replayable – another request of IBM's – with different ways of completing tasks.

Al Lowe says the IBM deal was the saving grace of the company due in large part to the contract Ken signed. "When Ken negotiated the deal with IBM to make the first game for the PCjr, he was smart enough to ask the guys at IBM if he could keep the engine. They said, 'Yeah, we don't care. As long as you get a game done for the opening and it's gotta be a game that can't be moved to the Apple.' It had to take advantage of the PCjr's additional memory and additional colors and sound chip and show all that stuff off. And that was the deal they ended up with."

John Williams says that it wasn't only the development of the PCjr that helped Sierra, but a change in attitude in the industry that came with it: "It's hard to point at a single game and say 'this saved the company' because what happened was a bit bigger than that. What we found was a new lease on life when IBM came along and brought some legitimacy to a business that had been labeled as yesterday's news.

"A lot of computer stores didn't stock games in the early days. ComputerLand, perhaps the biggest chain of the time with several hundred stores, wouldn't stock them at all. The attitude was, 'We're trying to sell businesses these very expensive pieces of equipment.' They didn't even want to hint that employees might use them to waste time. It was a real attitude out there – the salespeople in those stores looked down on anything that wasn't professional and expensive.

"When IBM suddenly joined Apple and said, 'Yes, there is a home market and yes, it's worth building a market in,' it really changed the face of retail and opened up new avenues for us. High-end computer stores that wouldn't have touched our products started stocking the IBM offerings and when they started selling in large numbers, those retailers opened up shelves to companies like Sierra. It probably tripled our distribution inside of a short time. So yes, in a way *King's Quest* was a big winner and helped keep the doors open, but it wasn't so much the game itself as the change of attitude it represented at retail that saved the company and made us viable again."

Ironically, the PCjr turned out to be a massive failure, regularly heralded as one of the biggest flops in personal computing history. The reasons were many, but chief among them was price. While the PCjr was indeed a cheaper model than the standard IBM PC, it was still more expensive than the Apple II, and twice the price of the budget-friendly Commodore 64 and Tandy TRS-80.

Another issue was that the promised backward compatibility wasn't exactly true. While some new PC software titles were compatible with the PCjr, others weren't. At a time when the PC held 70% of market share, resulting in a massive catalog of software already on the market, PC compatibility was essential and the PCjr was hit or miss. Applications such as MicroPro's WordStar, the industry leading word processor at the time, and Lotus's 1-2-3 spreadsheet software, also an industry standard, wouldn't work on the PCjr. The perceived crossover from business to home that IBM anticipated didn't come to fruition and hurt the PCjr's sales extensively.

The biggest factor hurting the PCjr, however, was a terrible keyboard that couldn't be used by touch typists due to the key design. The standard layout was replaced with a smaller version, with spaces between the keys to allow developers to include keyboard overlays. Meanwhile, the numeric keypad was removed, with function keys assigned a secondary use for numbers. (Instead of pressing F5 to save your game in *King's Quest*, you had to hold Function and press the number 5.) Another issue was the wireless functionality of the keyboard, which promised a six-foot range but only delivered three feet in most situations and drained the AA batteries in only a matter of hours. Small issues individually, but combined they caused major headaches for IBM.

It was less than two years before IBM canceled the PCjr.

In the meantime, Tandy was looking to create a replacement for its TRS-80. Seeing the massive amount of software on the market for the IBM PC, and the technical upgrades of the PCjr, they decided to make a system that was compatible with both. In November 1984, the company released their Tandy 1000 with a $1,200 price tag –

significantly lower than the PCjr. Sold through Tandy's RadioShack storefronts, the Tandy 1000 was a major hit.

King's Quest did save Sierra, but it wasn't because of the PCjr. It was because of the Tandy 1000 and the contract Ken Williams signed with IBM to develop the game.

"At the time, IBM was under a lot of government pressure and was afraid they might be broken up as a monopoly, although it's hard to imagine now!" Ken explains. "Even though IBM paid for the development of *King's Quest*, they asked me to sign agreements promising that we'd also sell [*King's Quest*] to their competitors. It was totally screwy! And a great thing for us. Even though the PCjr bombed, RadioShack launched a similar machine and we made a fortune selling the IBM-funded product on their competitor's machine."

The IBM deal paid off again when *The Black Cauldron* team used the engine behind *King's Quest*, named the Adventure Game Interpreter (AGI), to create their game. "That became the basis of the company for five years, that engine they created for the original *King's Quest* on the PCjr. That was the saving grace, as it were, for the company," Al Lowe says.

At this point, Sierra wasn't the company that Ken and Roberta had envisioned back when they got their start in 1979, but after the successful releases of *The Black Cauldron*, and more importantly, *King's Quest*, things were looking brighter. Sierra would survive.

Interlude: Hints

The earliest game hints were given to players by Roberta Williams herself. With *Mystery House* and her other early titles, On-Line Systems would include a slip of paper with Ken and Roberta's home phone number on it, advising players that if they were stuck, they could ring. Players, of course, didn't expect the designer of the game herself would answer the phone!

When the company set up shop more officially in Oakhurst, those calls were routed to the receptionist until a full-time position was created solely to give out game hints. Ultimately, an entire department was formed to service players' need for clues about what to do next.

Printing hint books wasn't something that Roberta and the other designers at Sierra wanted. What was the point of giving away all the answers to the puzzles? Wasn't working out how to proceed the fun of playing the game in the first place? Eventually, though, it became clear that there was money to be made in hint books, and Sierra pioneered what is now yet another industry standard (although they tend to be called strategy guides now).

Originally royalties were paid to the hint book writers, according to Corey Cole, who co-designed the *Quest for Glory* series with his wife Lori: "Sierra paid about 3% royalties on game design and they paid 15% royalties on hint books because you were doing everything. You were doing all the writing for it," he says.

It wasn't long before Ken Williams realized these books were making a lot of money for Sierra. "They decided that hint books were far too lucrative, so for our first game Lori got a 15% royalty," Corey continues. "For the second game she got a fixed $5,000; by the third game they decided it was just part of the designer's job and they would not pay for the hint book. They gradually welched on it. The same with the game royalties. We negotiated variable royalties on the second or third game, depending on sales, that would go up to a higher number depending on the number of copies they sold. They brought those back down to 3% again after a couple of games."

Although not initially happy with the concept of hint books, Roberta was eventually won over by both the demand for them and the revenue they could generate. She did have a stipulation, however: the books weren't just to be a list of directions for completing the game. Instead, they needed to drip out clues in a progressively more obvious manner. To do this, at first the hint books were printed with invisible ink that only revealed itself when colored in with the special marker included. This technique was later dropped in favor of a card with a red cellophane window that could be held over the obscured clues to reveal them.

Another feature of Sierra's hint books was the addition of fake clues – small jokes that the writer would put in both to amuse players and to hopefully stop them from reading things they didn't need to. Al Lowe, when writing the original *King's Quest* hint book, took great pleasure in writing clues that sounded legitimate but weren't, such as "Now that I'm riding on the alligator's back, how do I make him fly?"

While the scope of later hint books expanded to include interviews with the creative teams and more stylized maps, the basic premise remained the same: drip-feed clues to the player to maximize their gaming experience.

One interesting note about the hint books was that for a lot of their games, Sierra sold more hint books than they did copies of the game.[2]

Chapter 2: First Steps

I got a mysterious package from Ken . . . Inside the box I found about twenty ziplock baggies, each stuffed with a piece of paper, printed in single color, and something I would learn was a 'floppy diskette' for a computer.

John Williams, Marketing and Distribution Manager

It was 1972 and nineteen-year-old Roberta Heuer had just married eighteen-year-old Ken Williams. They had met during high school when she was seeing a friend of Ken's and they had a double date together with their respective partners. At first Roberta wasn't too interested in Ken, finding him shy and insecure, but over time she came to see that he was a lot different than the other guys who were around. He was intelligent and very driven to succeed, both virtues that Roberta found appealing.

After high school, Ken enrolled at a trade school called Control Data Institute where he would learn the basics of programming and data processing on the big mainframe computers of the time.

In the seventies, the Williams family was a lot like any other at the time. Ken worked long hours to support his growing family – eldest son DJ was born in 1973, with his younger brother Chris coming along in 1979 – while Roberta stayed home and raised their children.

It was a hectic decade. They moved at least a dozen times, each time with Ken taking a new job that was slightly more difficult but also paid a little more. Ken's younger brother John says that by the end of the seventies, Ken had become a really great programmer. "He had worked at Informatics when they developed some pretty key business tools that were probably as big in their day on the mainframes as spreadsheets are on the modern PC."

Ken had a strong entrepreneurial spirit and a belief that computers were where the next fortunes would be made. So, along with his regular job at Informatics, Ken consulted after hours on as many other projects as he could fit in.

"At the time I was working in Los Angeles for a wide variety of companies," Ken recounts. "I had a full-time job but also had a number of clients for whom I was working nights and weekends. I was somewhat of an expert on the 'online operating systems' for mainframe IBM computers (IMS and CICS). I was working virtually nonstop and rarely home. What I most wanted was to start some sort of business that would allow me the freedom to quit Los Angeles and move to the woods. I remember Roberta and I looking at a house in the middle of twenty acres of property. We had this idealistic notion that we could live out in the woods happily ever after!

"I am not sure if my strong motivation to become an entrepreneur was born out of a desire to be rich, or if it was to escape Los Angeles. Really, it was probably both. I remember telling people that I wanted to retire by the time I was thirty. I hated driving in Los Angeles traffic and just wanted out of there. Thus, I was constantly coming up with ideas for businesses that I could start."

It was in January 1980 that Ken scraped together the money to purchase an Apple II computer, recognizing that this was going to be the next big thing in computers. He was right, but at that stage he was thinking that the money would be made building tools, so he set out to do just that.

In the meantime, he had given up his job at Informatics and went out on his own as an independent consultant. During this time, while working on an income tax program on an IBM mainframe, he discovered a text game called *Adventure* (sometimes known as *Colossal Cave*). It only interested him for a short time, but he knew Roberta would love it, so he brought home a terminal and convinced her to play it. For someone who wasn't interested in computers, it ended up changing her life. She loved *Adventure* and finished it within a month.

Having completing *Adventure*, Roberta bought all the other adventure games she could find, mostly from Scott Adams and Infocom. She enjoyed them but felt like she could design something better. Roberta was a storyteller. She loved telling stories and had done so since childhood, so this new medium seemed perfect for her.

Roberta sat down at her kitchen table and wrote the story for what was to become her first game, *Mystery House*. It was a simple enough game, a murder mystery influenced by Agatha Christie's *And Then There Were None* as well as the board game Clue. The player had to solve the mystery of who the murderer was or risk becoming the next victim.

At this stage, Ken wasn't interested in games and it took some convincing by Roberta to get him involved. Ken and Roberta both agreed that their game needed a different edge to separate it from the competition, and Roberta wanted pictures in addition to text. Up until *Mystery House*, no adventure game had graphics – that was the key to making their game stand out.

"I had started a Fortran compiler for the Apple computer when Roberta talked me into programming *Mystery House*," Ken says. "I remember thinking it was only a few days of coding and that afterwards I'd return to the Fortran compiler. But once I started talking to retailers, none wanted Fortran and they all wanted more games."

The problem was, nobody had done graphics in an adventure game before, so there was no roadmap. Ken wasn't deterred and worked out how he could store all the data required for the graphics, with practically no disk space, by only storing coordinates for each line and writing a routine that would make the computer draw the line at runtime.

In the short space of only a month, Ken had programmed Roberta's first game.

After taking *Mystery House* to distributors, who offered Ken and Roberta only a 25% royalty, and having not heard back from Apple about distributing through them, they decided to self-publish. They'd written the game; why not reap all the rewards? Ken decided that they should present more than a single game to be more attractive to retailers, so he offered a royalty payment to a friend of his who wrote a small arcade game for the Apple II called *Skeet Shoot*. They now had two games to sell.

Over the next few months they took *Mystery House* around to computer stores, selling as much as they could, but only after placing an advert in *Micro* magazine did things really take off. They were suddenly selling five hundred, one thousand, two thousand copies a month by mail order. It was great money, and it was all a second job for Ken as he was still running his consulting business. He worked during the day and programmed at night while Roberta raised the children, copied disks, posted orders, and – most importantly – answered the phone. They had put a hint line phone number in the paperwork that came with the game and the calls went straight through to their kitchen, where Roberta would give out hints and talk with their customers.

Wanting to expand their reach even further, Ken shipped some copies of *Mystery House* to his brother John in the Midwest with instructions to see if he could sell the game there.

"It was early 1980," John recalls. "I was living in Wheaton, Illinois then, still in high school, in fact, and got a mysterious package from Ken, who was living in Southern California at the time. Inside the box I found about twenty ziplock baggies, each stuffed with a piece of paper, printed in single color, and something I would learn was a 'floppy diskette' for a computer."

John had never seen a floppy disk before, his only experience with computers at that point being with cassette tapes, punch cards and teletype terminals.

"I also found a note from Ken asking me if I could take these things around to something called a computer store to see if they would sell them," John explains. "I looked up 'computer store' in the yellow pages and found out there were about ten of them in the greater Chicago area. I learned from Ken's brief note that these floppy diskettes went in something called an Apple II computer, so I called a few stores to find one that sold the Apple on the fourth try."

Displaying an attitude that was all too common at the time, the first few retailers John talked to told him that they sold "real" computers, not toys, and one of them actually referred him to a Toys"R"Us location. Eventually he found a retailer who would help and instructed John to drive the twenty miles up the freeway and he'd help boot up the disk.

"I arrived on a Saturday to find the store full of people, and the retailer was a bit irked because this was a big sales day for his little store, but [he] decided to help me out anyway. He pulled the diskette out of the baggie and helped me boot it up, and what appeared on-screen was a game called *Mystery House*. I had seen text-based adventures and in fact had spent a summer playing them on a mainframe terminal with Ken and Roberta a few summers before, so I quickly got the hang of how to play the game.

"I drew an immediate crowd around the small green screen. Almost as an afterthought, I told the retailer I had some copies, and would he be interested in selling them. Before I left that day, we had sold all ten copies at about $25 a copy, and I had gotten through about 10% of the game. After I discovered that retailers liked what Ken had to offer, I made it a habit to visit computer stores as often as I could. In fact, over the next months I pinballed everywhere I could reach, like Wisconsin and Indiana, and that summer I started south and didn't stop until I hit ocean, then went west and got as far as Denver. Before the summer was over, I'd hit eleven states."

Mystery House was a massive success, and by the end of 1980 Roberta had written and Ken had programmed two more games in what they were now calling their Hi-Res series. To simplify the game-making process, Ken had created a new interpreter for adventure games called Adventure Development Language (ADL). Why reinvent the wheel every time you started programming a new game? Even early on, Ken saw the value in having a system in place to quickly get their products to market.

While *Mission Asteroid* was a simple adventure game, designed quickly and as a way of introducing new players to the genre, it was with *Wizard and the Princess* that Ken and Roberta again pushed the boundaries of what was possible. *Mystery House* had introduced graphics, but *Wizard and the Princess* would implement something even more remarkable: color.

Within the small amount of disk space available, Ken devised a system that not only stored the pictures in that very small space, but could also generate them in color. "Computers in those days had very little memory and virtually no disk space. I think the Apple II had only 16 KB of RAM and the floppy drives were only 80 KB," Ken explains. "You couldn't do much. There also wasn't much for graphics. The graphics cards we see today, which function independently of the processor, didn't exist.

"Color graphics had never really been planned for the Apple II. I don't know if it was deliberate, or an accident, but the Apple II would do only six colors [orange, blue, purple, green, black and white]. Even these colors were somewhat wonky. I forget exactly how it would work, but it was triggered by bits in memory. Two bits in a row that were lit were white, and two bits off were black. Meanwhile, a bit alone on an even row was orange or blue, whereas a bit alone on an odd row was green or purple. I may have that wrong, but it was something archaic like that. I remember hearing that painters blend multiple paints to achieve various colors, and I wondered if there were some way to blend colors on the Apple II.

"I did some experimenting and found I could produce dithered patterns of color that could somewhat look like color. Then I came up with the idea of recording endpoints of lines to produce outlines. I used vectors and endpoints, with color fill points, to describe pictures. This resulted in a horrible-looking picture, but it was a picture! In color! And on a device with virtually no memory or disk storage. People were amazed, though now we look at those games and they are not very impressive."

By the end of 1980, Ken and Roberta had decided that this new career of software development and distribution was what they wanted. And they had earned enough money to buy that house in the woods they both desired, in the little California town of Coarsegold.

"Roberta and I had this naïve notion that if we brought our kids up in the woods, they would escape all the crime and drugs of Los Angeles. I think we had watched too many episodes of *Lassie* and *Andy Griffith* or something!" Ken says. "But we really did see it as a small-town, back-to-nature life. The complete opposite of life in Los Angeles. We would have been happy with any forest away from civilization, but chose Coarsegold because Roberta's parents had an apple ranch nearby, so we were familiar with the area."

It was around this time that Ken, who had been distributing the games himself under the name Robwin Computing, decided to give up distribution and concentrate all his energy on development.

"I did start Robwin Computing, which is a name come up with by a friend, Bob Leff. I'm not sure where he got the name. Bob and I had worked together somewhere and shared an interest in finding some entrepreneurial project to start. When I started making games, I started selling them to computer stores and also selling games from my competitors," Ken says. "As the business started going, I turned over the selling to my father-in-law John Heuer, who I remember selling games from the back of his car.

"Almost immediately, it became clear that the distribution business was a distraction and I sold the inventory to my friend Bob Leff. He focused on selling software and created Robwin, which he later renamed to Softsel. He did very well with it, turning it into a very large company."

Now the Williamses had a company, some very successful computer games, and their own office. John Williams was one of their earliest employees, getting a call from Ken to join them just before Christmas that year.

"I moved to Coarsegold and started working in the first On-Line office, which was a small single room over a print shop," John explains. "At the beginning, I just copied disks, picked up the phone to take orders and give out game hints. We worked all the time, often until midnight or more. It was something to do in a small town. We would also take the day off and go skiing, firstly snow then water skiing as 1981 progressed, and slowly but surely began to expand. First by adding people to pick up the phone and then by adding programmers."

Full Steam Ahead

The next two years were a heady time for On-Line Systems. On the one hand, the antics within the company quickly became that of a college frat house, while on the other hand there was constant game development. A steady stream of arcade-style games were either produced or published while Roberta continued to develop her adventure games, each one pushing the boundaries a little further.

The Apple II was the machine that seemed best suited to arcade games, and Ken developed this line into one of the most profitable for the company. With titles like *Crossfire*, *Lunar Leeper*, *Cannonball Blitz* and *Threshold* all turning profits, it seemed like the success would never end.

Early on, John Harris joined On-Line Systems and developed a *Pac-Man* clone called *Jawbreaker*, which became one of their most successful games to date. Ken was impressed with John's programming skills and, having the home computer rights, offered him the chance to create a *Frogger* port.

John worked hard on *Frogger* but took a long time to complete the project, much to the annoyance of Ken, who wanted a quick turnaround. Eventually John finished, wherein he packed up both the game and his toolset and left for a trade show. It was there that all John's disks were stolen and he was forced to rewrite the game from scratch in only a few weeks. In spite of this challenge, *Frogger*, like *Jawbreaker* before it, was a massive hit for the fledgling company.

Unfortunately, it wasn't long before Atari, who owned the home computer rights to *Pac-Man*, realized that *Jawbreaker* was a nearly identical clone and decided to pursue legal action. Atari applied for an injunction that not only would have stopped the company from working on or selling *Jawbreaker*, it would also ban them from owning or using any of the tools used for further development. This meant that every computer within On-Line Systems was to be seized by the sheriff's department until the court case had been heard or the injunction was lifted.

Hearing the news of what had been ordered, John Williams and other On-Line staff moved quickly. If their computers were seized, the company would fold almost overnight, which was likely Atari's plan all along. So they grabbed as much of the computer gear as they could get hold of and left.

"When the cops came with the warrants, they walked out with a few computers that we considered throwaways and expendables," John Williams recalls. "The good stuff we used to keep the business afloat had been dispersed all over Oakhurst by the time the sheriffs came to seize our machines. I guess that could be called obstruction of justice; maybe the most serious crime I ever committed. I don't even think I was twenty-one yet when that all happened."

The court case was eventually won by On-Line Systems and business returned to normal, although Ken always believed the win was a mixed blessing. Now people would be free to steal his ideas!

Another game that caused controversy, although not legal issues this time, was a small text adventure that Ken had gained the rights to publish.

"I'm in a sleazy bar!" In 1981, not many games started with a line like that, but for Chuck Benton, creator of Sierra's only text adventure *Softporn Adventure*, it seemed like a good place to start. "I was in my twenties and wrote a game about what I liked. Girls and partying," Chuck admits.

Working in the field engineering office of a small flight simulator manufacturer, Chuck wanted to enhance his skills by learning to program on the newly released Apple II computer and went about convincing his employer to buy him one. Chuck says, "I sold them on the idea when I said I could automate their paper-based systems."

It was during the process of teaching himself how to program the new computer to streamline many of the mundane tasks of his job that he decided instead to write an adventure game. It made sense: create something that wasn't important in order to learn the finer points of programming, and then use those skills to write the business software he wanted to.

And so *Softporn Adventure* was born. Chuck thought it was a fun little game and showed it to a few friends, who encouraged him to sell it. He printed a thousand copies of the game, but his self-publishing efforts as Blue Sky Software weren't a success and he only managed to sell one hundred units.

Chuck's lucky break in the game industry came when he rented a booth at a computer trade show and a representative of On-Line Systems bought a copy of his game and took it back to show Ken Williams, who loved it.

It wasn't long before Ken had bought the rights to *Softporn Adventure*, offering Chuck a massive 35% royalty on the gross profit and offering him more contract work converting the company's other games to different systems.

On-Line Systems was the right fit for *Softporn Adventure*, and its release seemed to be a relatively simple exercise. While Chuck supplied

On-Line with his Apple II version, another version for the Atari 8-bit computer, a popular computer system at the time, was also produced. "It was a text adventure – extremely easy to port from the Apple to the Atari format," claims John Williams. Otherwise, as the game was already made, all On-Line needed to do was to package it and advertise.

The advertisement Ken Williams proposed was to become a controversial and famous marketing campaign.

Using the Williamses' own redwood-paneled Jacuzzi, three semi-naked women sat drinking champagne and eating an apple while a waiter served them. Those three women – On-Line's production manager Diane Siegal, the company bookkeeper Susan Davis, and Roberta Williams herself – stared into the camera for an afternoon while a local photographer took picture after picture. All three happened to be involved with men who worked for the company. According to John, "Ken, Larry Bain and Bob Davis were as thick as thieves back then, and so the idea that their wives made up the rest of the threesome makes sense."

As John explains with a laugh, "It can't be disputed that Ken was the instigator of the famous photo shoot that was the face of the game. It was his company and his hot tub. It was not something someone from marketing came up with. Can you imagine anyone going up to the president or their employer with a line like, 'Hey, can we take naked pictures of your wife and put them on the cover of a game?' This was a classic Ken move."

The hot tub ad first ran in the September 1981 issue of *Softalk*, a specialist Apple II magazine in which On-Line advertised extensively. Chuck believes that particular advertisement was the main reason behind the large increase in sales. "It was a wonderful marketing tool. I do have to give the Williamses credit; they seemed to just have a magic touch for figuring out how to get free promotion, and all publicity is good publicity."

Controversy quickly followed, of course, both within the pages of *Softalk* and in the wider market. Even *Time* magazine covered the new game, something which took Chuck by surprise. "I remember getting a phone call for the interview on that and wondering why the hell somebody from California was calling trying to sell me a *Time* subscription. I didn't realize they were calling to interview me."

Due to the ongoing controversy, *Softporn* was withdrawn from stores after only a few months, but that didn't stop it from selling. In 1982, the computer game industry still wasn't heavily represented in traditional storefront retail space, so a lot of *Softporn*'s sales occurred through other channels. "We did a lot of direct by mail and phone sales then, and it did brisk business as a mail-order product," John Williams explains.

Sales of *Softporn Adventure* were only helped by all the positive and negative publicity. The game sold an estimated fifty thousand copies within a few months, and Ken Williams estimates that those sales helped drive a near doubling of the company's total sales to that point. It was an especially impressive feat considering that only one hundred thousand Apple II computers had been sold by Apple at that time.

One Massive Adventure

"You are out taking a stroll in the field surrounding your house one day. While walking, you encounter a strange pulsating metal cylinder. Upon entering it, you discover it to be a time machine. By fiddling with the dials and levers, you quickly learn how to control the machine. With this, your journey through history begins . . ."

These words from the manual of On-Line's 1982 release *Time Zone* perfectly describe what Roberta was trying to do with her fourth Hi-Res adventure. She wanted a game that wouldn't end, or at least would take a long time to finish. And she wanted to continue to push boundaries. This time, the boundary was the game's sheer size.

At a time when most games took up a single side of a 5.25-inch floppy disk, *Time Zone* took six double-sided disks. While *Mystery House* had about 60 rooms (On-Line always referred to each discrete location as a "room"), *Time Zone* had over 1,400 divided into zones that were each the size of a standard adventure game.

While the premise was simple enough – discover and solve the major quest in each particular zone, then complete the final zone – the production was anything but. The majority of the work fell upon two people.

Terry Pierce was a local eighteen-year-old artist On-Line had hired straight out of high school, and his job was to draw each of the 1,400 rooms Roberta envisioned onto graph paper. Each of these images would then be traced, filled in with color, and transferred into the game where the descriptions and actions would be added.

The other important person was Bob Davis. Bob – who first met Ken Williams while working at a local liquor store – had been with On-Line for about a year, quickly working his way up to become a designer and programmer using Ken's ADL toolset. During this time, he and Ken became quite friendly and wrote another Hi-Res hit together,

Ulysses and the Golden Fleece, which released in 1981. Bob's role on *Time Zone* was to keep the game's production running efficiently – something that was rapidly becoming impossible.

The whole project became a burden for everyone involved. While Bob Davis was well liked, he wasn't capable of keeping this unwieldy project on track. As the programming team stitched together the different zones into playable areas, Bob lacked the programming skills to modify the ADL toolset and unite these separate areas. And the pressure didn't let up, with Ken demanding a Christmas release, even though it was looking more and more unlikely.

Terry Pierce was at his wits' end. Unable to keep up with the pressure of drawing that many pictures, he gradually broke down. It wasn't just the daunting number of backgrounds required, it was also the agonizing tedium of the task. For every useful background in the game, there were dozens of empty rooms: forests, deserts, and city streets that served no purpose except to showcase that On-Line was making the biggest game ever. While Terry ended up finishing the game, it was his last effort in the computer industry.

Time Zone's saving grace was a new employee, Jeff Stephenson. With experience from a previous job at Software Arts and a steady and conservative nature, Jeff joined the team and soon brought a sense of order to the chaos, assigning everyone specific jobs and making sure everything that needed to be done was getting done.

He also quickly realized that he needed to make some major modifications to Ken's ADL engine to get the different zones tied together, and he convinced Warren Schwader, another programmer at On-Line, to entirely rewrite Ken's graphic rendering system, dramatically decreasing the time it took to load each background.

As John Williams noted in the game manual, "To make *Time Zone* fit in memory, it required a complete restructuring of our adventure programming procedures. New graphic routines had to be written and a new procedure had to be developed to accommodate for the movement of information from one scenario disk to another."

Time Zone was eventually released in 1982, missing the Christmas release window Ken had wanted. With a price tag of $99.95, it was almost double what On-Line had been charging for their other games, and became the company's first commercial failure.

The On-Line Dorm

While the staff at On-Line Systems worked hard, they also partied hard. Alcohol, drugs and wild parties were common, with practical jokes always high on the agenda.

"There was a feel to the place then that was much like a big college dorm," John Williams recalls. "Lots of working and studying, but also a lot of fooling around. It was just what happens when you put a lot of young people in a place together."

Chuck Benton also remembers those days fondly: "It was a great party atmosphere; kind of amazing that everything got accomplished that did. I was still on a contractor basis but I lived out there for about six months at one point, and my wife came out with me. We ended up living with Larry Gain and Diane Siegal; she was one of the girls on the *Softporn Adventure* hot tub cover. We lived at their house. There was a lot of partying, lots of wild times."

Chuck also spent a lot of time with Scott Murphy and his wife, recalling a close friendship at the time. "[Scott] hadn't started authoring anything yet. I think he was working in customer support but he was married to a gal called Shelley. I hung out with the two of them an awful lot. They were my best friends in that time period. Scott certainly had a great sense of humor."

According to Chuck, the partying, drugs and alcohol weren't unique to On-Line Systems. "I wouldn't even say it was just an industry thing. I think part of it was just the age I was. But it was when cocaine was all the rage and so on."

Sometimes the fun crossed the boundary into work, especially when it came to the suit-and-tie professionals and sales people who would come to town with their tailored attire and expensive briefcases, trying to sell to On-Line Systems. Ken Williams would often have more than a bit of fun with them.

"One day, a guy selling something came to town and did a big presentation to Ken and then invited him and Roberta to dinner, where they made sure the guy drank too much," John Williams says. "They poured him into the back of Ken's big pickup and announced they were going to go create some mayhem, and drove around the mountain country roads, picked a house seemingly at random, and then broke into a garage.

"As I understand it, the sales guy was kind of panicked about it all, but we represented a big account, so he played along but was clearly terrified. Ken took some pink paint out of his truck and they all painted big pink polka dots all over the little green sports car they found in that garage, laughed like fools, and left.

"I don't know if the salesperson ever found this out – to this day he probably thinks the head of a successful software company took him out to randomly participate in the breaking and entering and malicious destruction of a vehicle – but that car actually belonged to me. So not only did Ken and Berta prank this poor sales guy, but in the morning when I went to get in my little green sports car, I found it decorated with big silly polka dots. I had to drive it into town that way, and in a small town everyone knows you and knows everything."

On another occasion, John had been on vacation in Thailand and was completely out of contact with everyone back at On-Line. "I was basically out of touch unless I wanted to call in, but intercontinental land lines were like $15 a minute then. Ken finalized the lease on a new building while I was out of town, and as the building was empty they told Ken he could move right in, so he moved the whole company but had them leave my desk and chair. So when I got back from vacation, the entire company (probably twenty-five to thirty people at that point) was gone, as was everything else down to the walls. No one had told me, so when I went to work there was my desk and chair but the rest of the office was empty. The phone lines hadn't been moved completely yet, so I had to go to the local liquor store and ask around to find out where everyone was."

Although there were lots of fun times, Chuck Benton also remembers being rocked once. "There was an earthquake at one point when we were out in a town called Coalinga, which was a reasonable way away. This was at the time that On-Line was sprinkled between a strip mall and some other buildings. I was out there and I was in a room with fifteen software guys, and all of a sudden everything started shaking and everybody in the office turned to look at me, the guy from New England who'd never been in an earthquake before. I remember looking at the plate glass window that looked like it was shimmering, like it was made out of a liquid. Nothing broke; everything ended up being okay."

While they were fun times, they had to end, says Mark Crowe, who joined Sierra around the end of this era. "I think that had to happen; they had to grow up a little bit to be in that world. From the frontier days."

Interlude: The RPG Market

Fans of Sierra's adventure games may think Lori and Corey Cole's *Hero's Quest: So You Want to Be a Hero* marked Sierra's move into the roleplaying game (RPG) genre. But the company's first foray into the RPG market began six years earlier, in 1982.

Ken Williams had seen the massive success of *Ultima*, a breakout hit created by a young college student named Richard Garriott, and he had managed to negotiate a deal with Garriott to publish the sequel.

Ultima II, like its predecessor, was an enormous hit.

While Garriott had secured a massive 30% royalty from Ken Williams, much higher than the usual amount offered, the contract gave the company total distribution rights to the game. Unfortunately for Garriott, there was a major issue. No royalty rights were specified in the contract for an IBM PC version. It was an unavoidable situation, of course, as the IBM PC didn't exist when the contract was drawn up.

This put Garriott in the position of not being able to shop a PC version to other distributors, although a new deal was eventually reached with Sierra. The whole royalty situation, as well as the need to negotiate a new contract for future sequels, helped persuade Garriott to start his own company, Origin Systems.

Marketing manager John Williams remembers that management at Sierra didn't believe [the *Ultima* series] would continue to be published by the company in the long term. "I don't think we were ever part of Richard Garriott's long-term plans. Richard was a big personality with his own orbit. He was a lot like Ken; he drew people to him and created his own opportunities. Richard had his own standards and a real vision for what he wanted from the game and everything surrounding it."

Losing subsequent *Ultima* games left an RPG-sized hole in Sierra's catalog that came to be filled by another young college student.

Christopher Crim was like a lot of fledgling game designers in the early eighties. He became interested in computers, and in particular the Apple II, through his high school. The highlights of the Apple II were titles like *Ultima* as well as Sierra's Apple II arcade and adventure games.

Eventually getting his own Apple II, the next logical step was to start writing his own games.

His first project was a text adventure. "You're walking around a world where things are just described to you," Chris explains. Showing the game to his close friends and family, he was pleased to discover that they actually enjoyed playing his creation, giving him a great sense of fulfillment.

Having played the first three *Ultima* games, he decided to take things a step further by making his own graphical game, inspired by the visual look of Richard Garriott's series. In his game, the four kingdoms of the once-peaceful realm of Deledain descend into war, ravaging the world and allowing the evil Denethenor to rise up and become dominant. The player character is a scoundrel intent on capitalizing on this war-torn land by looting and pillaging the countryside, eventually leading to a confrontation with Denethenor.

Chris started working on this game, eventually called *Wrath of Denethenor*, while in high school but didn't complete it until his first year of college. At first a one-man production, it soon expanded to a team of two when his friend Kevin Christiansen offered to help. "I gave him the routines to do the rendering on-screen," Chris says.

It was a fun time for Chris, having a friend to work with and bounce ideas off, but being in college made the process more difficult. "It was really awkward when we went off to school because we went off to two different parts of the country. We were having to send letters back and forth, which is funny to say because it wasn't email, right? Postal mail, sending things back and forth. We had to send each other disks of updates of what we'd done so far."

They didn't always wait for each other, each having their own parts of the game to work on, but it was an exercise in coordination. The game took eighteen months between 1984 and 1985 to complete, with finishing high school, starting college, holding down jobs, and living in different parts of the country all taking their toll on production.

Convinced they had made a great game, Chris decided to deal with publishers directly about getting *Wrath of Denethenor* released. Unsure of how to approach them, or whether he should visit in person or not, he simply packaged up the game and mailed it to his three chosen publishers.

"I had a whole user manual that explained the deal and the story, and a walkthrough if they wanted to quickly play through it. I sent it to three different publishers. Electronic Arts was one of them and Sierra

On-Line was another. It was unsolicited; I just sent it to them," he recalls.

He didn't hear anything back from EA or the third publisher. Fortunately, "somebody at Sierra contacted me. John Williams was definitely my primary contact there. They flew me up to visit and have a chat. Having played Sierra On-Line games before, and especially *Ultima II*, it was pretty exciting. It was a short flight because I was in Orange County; just an hour or two."

Chris admits, "I was pretty nervous because it was all new ground for me. My jobs before that were a paper route and working at a fast-food restaurant. I didn't have any experience in the games business at all. They handed me a fat contract which I didn't know how to read."

Soon after, he signed that contract and Sierra had a replacement in their catalog for *Ultima II*.

Part of the deal required Chris to create a version of his game for the Commodore 64, a system he didn't know anything about. Sierra sent him the computer and gave him some time to get to know the new system. It turned out to be an easier task than he first imagined: "I didn't know what to expect, but I checked it out and apparently it's the same processor [as the Apple II]. Things were a little bit different, but I could reuse our code and just sort of fix it. I had to redo [Kevin]'s graphics routine, as that's the major difference between the Commodore 64 and the Apple II. The Commodore 64 version is actually entirely my work."

One stipulation Chris asked for in the contract was regarding the price of the game. "My friends and I were always frustrated at how expensive the games were at that time. We suggested that if the prices were less, it would help stop how people were always pirating games."

Sierra agreed, although looking back Chris doesn't know why. They put a note written by Chris in the box explaining that this was a trial to see if a lower-priced game would sell well, and *Wrath of Denethenor* was released for nearly half the normal retail price.

One thing that sticks out to John Williams about it was the box. "I loved the box on that game, the little pewter game characters and the black box with the inside flap."

It wasn't the hit that either Sierra or Chris hoped, selling only a few thousand copies each quarter – nowhere near the numbers that *Ultima II* had achieved only a few years previously.

John says there are a number of reasons the game wasn't particularly successful: "It was at the end of the Apple II era, and distribution on Apple games was faltering, but we thought it deserved a release. Christopher Crim was a good kid and pretty realistic about what to expect. We put a box around it and sold some – not too many. It wasn't a winner."

Chris believes there wasn't much effort put into promoting the game, saying, "I did get a little annoyed . . . You'd see all the stuff they were pushing for *King's Quest* and so on all over the place. I think one time they published an advertisement in a major computer gaming magazine, but they didn't really seem like they were putting a lot of effort into it for some reason.

"Maybe it was because of Richard Garriott, I don't know. I do believe Garriott was upset when he saw it. I remember them saying that he was annoyed that they did what he saw as an *Ultima* rip-off," he explains. "I was obviously inspired by the *Ultima* style and how it's rendered, but of course the story is unrelated. Except I guess the idea that you're wandering this world and there's these people you talk to. But that's more mechanics and pretty much describes all exploratory adventure games."

John Williams remembers it slightly differently. "People create a lot of myths about that game. About how it was a 'screw you' to Garriott or something. That really wasn't the case. It was simply a game we found and enjoyed and tried to get out there."

Even with disappointing sales, the making of *Wrath of Denethenor* is a good memory for Chris and he still receives fan mail about it.

"To see people talk about this world that I created; it's a completely imaginary space," he shares. "It must be a little bit like for authors, for fans to get absorbed in their world and write to them about the characters that are in it. This game of mine didn't have the kind of depth of characters you get these days, but it's still neat to hear people describe the experiences they had, the surprises and the fun they had with it. That's always fun to receive and every so often someone will look me up on the web and say some nice things about it. That's just really cool, that it had that much of an impact on people."

Wrath of Denethenor was Sierra's last Apple II game, and their last RPG until the successful *Hero's Quest* a few years later.

Chapter 3: Two Guys and Two Sequels

I had this Batmobile coming out of the cave and I snuck that into the game. I don't think Roberta was too happy with me on that, but everybody thought that was pretty funny.

Mark Crowe, Artist, King's Quest II

Sierra is probably best known for their six major *Quest* series: *King's Quest. Space Quest. Leisure Suit Larry. Quest for Glory. Police Quest. Gabriel Knight.*

These games, and many more, were conceived in Sierra's Oakhurst, California studios and later their Seattle studios during a hectic period between the 1983 debut of *King's Quest* and 1999, when the company stopped internal development.

What held Sierra together during these busy years were a few principles Ken had learned during their frantic Apple II days, and from the crash that nearly destroyed the company. Concentrating primarily on adventure games might have started out as a necessary step, post-collapse, but it proved to be a winning formula that established the foundation for major growth and innovation in both the genre and the wider gaming industry.

Although Sierra's strategy evolved over time, Ken Williams adhered to some basic core beliefs about pairing niches that had limited competition with designers who were passionate about those niches, and about reducing costs. The two main expenditures were development and marketing. Ken focused the company on leveraging their existing code base into new products, while also utilizing existing profitable brands to reduce those marketing and development costs.

Sierra's *King's Quest* series was the crown jewel in their catalog from its debut until its final installment fifteen years later. As designer Josh Mandel puts it, *"King's Quest* was the golden-haired boy!"

The first *King's Quest* – which was redubbed *King's Quest: Quest for the Crown* after its initial release – ended up being a major seller after its slow start, and a sequel was put into production almost straight away.

King's Quest II: Romancing the Throne used the same code base as the original game and the same main character, King Graham, which saved on art and animation costs. More importantly, though, this time Sierra wasn't reimagining the entire adventure genre from the ground up.

Roberta Williams again designed and wrote the game, while Doug MacNeill oversaw the art. Al Lowe composed the soundtrack.

In addition, fledgling designers were given a chance to prove themselves to Ken and Roberta on *King's Quest II*, a practice that became common for the flagship series. It was on this project that Mark Crowe and Scott Murphy got an opportunity to showcase their talents.

Enter the Two Guys

In 1982, a young Mark Crowe was unemployed. After leaving school a couple of years previously, he had been working as a graphic designer at a label printing business in Fresno, thirty miles south of Oakhurst. Constantly looking for a job in the area, Mark says, "I lived a number of years in the Oakhurst area. I always spent my summers up there as a kid camping and everything. It was always a dream to live up there someday. My folks lived nearby Oakhurst in a small town called North Fork."

Knowing he was looking for work, Mark's mother-in-law tipped him off to a relatively new company in town. "She lived up there in Oakhurst and sent me a clip from a local newspaper about this computer game company called On-Line," Mark says.

"I didn't know anything about personal computers; I had no exposure to them at all. I didn't really know what that was about. My only exposure to video games at that point was walking into a coin-op arcade. I put together a portfolio, I got hold of the art director there, called him and said I was interested in coming up. They said, 'Yeah sure, come on up.' I had an appointment there the next day."

After driving up to Oakhurst, Mark interviewed for a position in the marketing division. "I met with the art director [Greg Steffen], then I met with [John] Williams and showed him my portfolio and he seemed impressed. I got walked around and shook hands with Ken but that was my entire interaction at the time," he recalls. "This was in the art department where they were generating labels for disks, documentation, and box art and all that stuff. That was fine with me; I thought that was awesome."

Not wanting to waste the trip to Oakhurst and being familiar with the area, Mark used the opportunity to organize another appointment, this time with a local pizza shop. "I was looking at making some money and I knew Danny Wheeler, the owner of the Pizza Factory chain before it was Pizza Factory. Oddly enough, it was in that same newspaper that had the Sierra article that there was a write-up about Danny starting to franchise his business. It said it was going to be called Pizza Factory and everything.

"I took it upon myself to, totally on spec, design this logo for him. It was the day I happened to be up there interviewing for Sierra and I dropped in on him. I didn't know him too well personally. I was a patron; I'd go in there and buy pizza. I said, 'Hey, I heard you were franchising your business. I took it upon myself to design you a logo if you're interested.' He said, 'How much do you want for it?' I said, 'I dunno, fifty dollars?' He cut me a check for fifty dollars and said I was going to be sorry I sold it to him for only fifty dollars!"

That logo is still used by Pizza Factory across their multiple franchised stores.

It wouldn't be the last time Mark's knack for designing logos would prove to be significant. Another logo he did a few years later became equally well known, or at least it was during the eighties and nineties: the Sierra On-Line Half Dome.

"Apparently it's a little-known fact, but I'm the one who designed the Sierra logo," Mark reveals. "That was back when they had the old Sierra On-Line logo and they wanted a new logo. They hired this advertising agency, paid them this outrageous amount of money to come up with some designs for a new logo. We all felt slighted in the art department. Why didn't they come to us to come up with something new?

"They paid all this money and the advertising company came back with, I kid you not, a green triangle. That's all it was. The Sierra logo. This green triangle. I guess it was supposed to be an icon of a tree. No Half Dome, none of this. That's when I went to work and came up with several different logo designs and pitched them internally. They picked mine." Mark called his design "the AT&T hybrid Half Dome" due to its similarity to the striped orb used by the phone company. "I wanted to keep the Half Dome but wanted it to look high tech. It's something I'm proud of."

That never would have happened if he hadn't landed the job, because back in 1982 Mark was just interested in getting regular work. Fortunately he soon received a call from John Williams offering him a position at On-Line Systems. "I went home, then I got a phone call the next day saying they wanted me to go to work."

In the art department, Mark undertook a number of different tasks for some of Sierra's earliest titles, including making disk labels for *The Dark Crystal* (based on the Jim Henson movie of the same name). "That was before desktop publishing so that was cut and paste of artboards and everything. Nothing exciting about that at all or to brag about. But it was fun."

Mark wanted to move into working on the games instead of their packaging, so he enlisted the help of fellow artist Doug MacNeill in learning Sierra's Adventure Game Interpreter (AGI) toolset. "Doug taught me how to use the tools to do those vector graphics. Knowing what a hair-pulling experience it was working with those tools and trying to get decent-looking art out of that stuff, man, I have a ton of respect for that guy. Definitely took some passion."

Doug MacNeill also remembers showing Mark the ropes on *King's Quest II*: "He wasn't interested in doing the computer work at first; he was a pure painter, an artist, but he got into it. Then he went on to do other games. He became pretty much hardcore in the industry!"

Working on a number of projects, Mark was eventually put to work on *The Black Cauldron*, where he struck up a friendship with programmer Scott Murphy.

Scott had been living in Oakhurst and working as a cook at a local restaurant when he met Doug Oldfield, who worked with Scott's wife Shelley in a different diner in town. After a fire destroyed that diner, Doug applied and was hired for a programming position at On-Line Systems, which had opened in town a few years earlier.

Not knowing anything about computers but knowing he hated restaurant work, Scott had hounded Doug Oldfield and On-Line's management until they eventually offered him a position in dealer returns.

With the company still small at the time, Scott quickly moved from returns to customer support, eventually managing the support department. What he wanted, though, was to work on the games themselves, so he convinced Ken Williams to let him learn how to program on their internal AGI engine.

Working from five in the afternoon until three in the morning, he learned the AGI system from Ken Williams and Al Lowe, programming on the Disney title *The Black Cauldron*. Alone one night and very tired, Scott programmed in a crude response message to a puzzle that he thought would amuse his co-workers in the morning. Little did he realize that this particular build would be sent to Disney for review and his message would be read, and not appreciated.

Although he got into trouble with management over the joke, something clicked for him. Seeing his own words appear on the screen during a game had inspired him.

Scott Murphy wanted to write his own games.

Making a Sequel

With the company still in a perilous position financially, employees had to double up on projects. Mark and Scott were both assigned to work on *The Black Cauldron* at night and to help with *King's Quest II* during the day.

One guiding principle for Ken Williams and the *King's Quest II* development team was to innovate, and the group was determined to push boundaries even further. With the introduction of story-driven cutscenes and a linear progression where the environment would change as the player advanced toward their goal, the world of *King's Quest II* felt alive, at least by the standards of the time.

Writing in the *King's Quest Collection Series* manual in 1994, Roberta talked about how the story developed: *"King's Quest II* reminded me a little of *Wizard and the Princess*. We saw how previous games (*Mystery House* and *King's Quest I*) were received by the public, and I was anxious to try my hand at a bigger story right away.

"Graham would be king by now. What quest should a lonely king go on? What should he see through the magic mirror? A maiden in distress! I started to foresee a family for Graham in the future. I couldn't fit some ideas into *King's Quest I*, so I was happy to get a chance to include King Neptune, Dracula, everyone from Little Red Riding Hood, and that infamous rickety old bridge you could only cross so many times."[3]

Doug MacNeill fondly recalls the group of programmers toiling on that game. "Working with Jeff Stephenson, that guy was such a professional; Greg Steffen – the team was just great. Jeff was so steady; without him [*King's Quest II*] probably wouldn't have happened. He was the one who came in at the same time, worked the same amount; he just kept going. He was so effective at what he did. Bob Heitman, too; he wasn't there for the first [*King's Quest*] game but after that he was the one who worked on the utilities like the picture editor and object editor. When he came to work on that, it became a lot easier to work on the graphics. He deserves a big shout-out. The rest of us were all goofballs."

One surprising addition to the *King's Quest II* team was Ken Williams himself, who joined the existing group of programmers to help complete the game. Ken was the person Doug saw the most.

"Every day he would come down to see me. My inspiration wouldn't always come; I couldn't just force it. The pictures would come and I would get them done, but it was a slower pace than what Ken Williams wanted," Doug recalls. "Every day, and you could set your watch by it, he would come to my office and ask how it was going. Trying to keep me moving. Then he would leave me alone all day after that. But every day it was the same thing."

While Ken might have visited him daily to prod him along, Doug remembers he was also great to work for. "He was really good. He was a really fair guy. One of the things I always remember about him is he would always say, 'Are you having fun?' He thought people should have fun in their work. We would say, 'We're working on this or working on that or doing this or doing that,' and he would inject [what we'd said] into the conversations. I thought that was pretty thoughtful. He had a good respect for Roberta, too; he really trusted her ability to design games that were fun. He also told us he didn't trust himself [to know] whether a game was fun; he couldn't tell if it was fun or not. He trusted her for that."

While Doug mainly worked on the background art, Mark Crowe was assigned to help with the animations. "The first thing I animated was this fish jumping out of the lake; the fish would jump up, do a little wiggle and land back in the water," Mark recalls. "Then I got brave and did this Batmobile. I had this Batmobile coming out of the cave and I snuck that into the game. I don't think Roberta was too happy with me on that, but everybody thought that was pretty funny." Mark's Batmobile stayed in the game as an Easter egg.

Production went very smoothly, partly because of the team members' experience, but mainly because of the established code base they utilized. "I remember *King's Quest II* seemed to be the one that was the easiest to do; it just stayed on schedule and wasn't difficult," Doug MacNeill recalls. There were also some fun times. "They had a party at a fancy restaurant in Oakhurst and I couldn't tie a tie. I showed up and Ken Williams tied my tie for me. We had a good dinner there. There were some good parties we had there; the *King's Quest* team was a really good team. We had a good time."

Heading into Space

As Mark Crowe recalls, production on *King's Quest II* had wound up and *The Black Cauldron* was being finalized when he and Scott Murphy put their heads together and came up with a new concept for a game: "[We] wanted it to be kind of a sci-fi spoof that didn't take itself too seriously. We approached Ken with the idea and he said, 'Yeah, sure, make me a couple of test rooms, a demo.' They actually set us up in an office and we kind of went crazy. We did a couple of scenes. Just real quick demo scenes of a couple of corridors with an elevator that went up and down between them."

"I remember them doing a small mockup of what the game could look like, and that I was blown away," Ken Williams remembers of the prototype Mark and Scott created. That test demo turned into the opening scenes of what would become *Space Quest: Chapter I – The Sarien Encounter.*

"We showed that [demo] to Ken and he loved it and said, 'Yeah, okay, it looks like you guys know enough about what you're doing [that] you could probably design a whole game map. Go do that.' We basically started designing a full-fledged game as far as progression and storyboarding go."

Originally titled *Star Quest* during development, the name was changed to the now-familiar *Space Quest* when it turned out that *Star Quest* was already trademarked.

Mark and Scott's original intent was to make a game that was different from everything else in Sierra's catalog: a space comedy. A far cry from the sword and sorcery fantasy that had made Sierra famous.

"Any game that can make you chuckle is fun," Mark says. "We didn't want a game that took itself too seriously; we were ready to have fun. Poke fun at all our sci-fi tropes. That's what we set out to do from the beginning. We wanted to make ourselves laugh, so that's where we had a lot of fun, doing stuff that cracked ourselves up. We knew other people would like that."

Like other designers at the time, Scott and Mark negotiated a royalty rate with Ken based on the sales of their game. According to Mark, "Ken offered us a percentage – he did our initial negotiation – and I said how about double that with both of us working on the game, and he said sure. I don't pretend to be a hardball negotiator when it comes to that sort of thing. At the time I felt we were worth what we were asking for. It wasn't a *King's Quest* ransom."

The early games at Sierra were generally two- or three-person productions, and *Space Quest* was no different, with Scott programming while Mark designed and drew the graphics. According to Mark, "I was doing all the visual stuff. We'd brainstorm together, then I'd go off and design and whip out a couple of scenes. Scott did all the programming; he knew the game language and knew how to script all that. He was able to take all my art and animation and put all that together and that would spawn other ideas. It was a lot of fun working together in those days because we were able to just come up with stuff off the cuff and make it happen on-screen."

Sierra was still recovering from the aftereffects of the console crash, and with time running out as they got closer to the 1986 holiday release season, Ken Williams stepped in to help program parts of the game. Even Ken wasn't able to resist the opportunity to put jokes in, adding a number of *King's Quest* references aboard the spaceship Deltaur in the final portion of the game.

One thing Mark had in mind for *Space Quest* was a particular theme song, but he found he wasn't able to relate what he intended to the team, so in the end he composed it himself. "I had bought a little four-track synthesizer. I was a wannabe musician; I had some musical ability from back in school. I had this tune in my head and I wasn't able to communicate with anybody how I wanted it to sound. So I just started working it out and programming it into this keyboard. Then I was given the tools to convert that to PC sound. That was kind of the birth of the original *Space Quest* theme."

As the game was being completed, attention turned to marketing and promotion. John Williams was in charge of the marketing department at the time and credits Mark and Scott with the game's memorable promotional campaign.

"Marketing on *Space Quest* was an easy gig. Scott was a very good friend of mine and had a great sense of humor. Mark had worked in my art department and was incredibly creative. I knew and trusted them both," John remembers. "The only thing I really had to do was just make sure I didn't get in the way. They had great ideas! I just made sure my people let them have free rein and did everything possible to let them go wild."

The usual practice at Sierra was to put a photo of the designers on the box, but neither Scott nor Mark was extremely keen for that to happen. "I felt kind of uncomfortable about it actually," Mark says. "We didn't know how the game was going to do! Did we really want our faces on it and that sort of thing? In keeping in the spirit of the game, we thought of making ourselves these alien characters. At the time there was a pizza franchise across America called Two Guys from Italy, so we thought, 'Let's just call ourselves the Two Guys from Andromeda' and that was our alias. We agreed to that.

"When it came time to get our picture on the box, it must have been near Halloween, because I went down to a costume store and bought a bunch of stuff to make these two alien getups. I bought these two Mohawk wigs and these Spock ears and these little pig nose things. 'Let's just throw these on and we'll wear our Hawaiian shirts so it looks like we're on vacation,' and we just drove up to Yosemite Valley, which is just an hour up the highway, and had our picture taken up there in front of the Half Dome. In fact, I still have the 35 mm slide of that laying around somewhere. We just got a good laugh out of it and thought that would be that."

The idea of the Two Guys took hold, and each game in the series had bigger and more elaborate videos, commercials, photo ops, and even public appearances of these strange, pig-nosed aliens.

John Williams refuses to claim any credit for the success of marketing *Space Quest*, saying that Mark and Scott took control of the advertising campaign as well as the game production itself: "About the only thing I ever really contributed was that I loaned them my sports car once when we were filming one of their silly sales videos. Mark and Scott played off each other well for those first few games, and their attitude was infectious. When it came to promoting their product, it was their world and we just lived in it. I wouldn't say I really did anything there that contributed other than providing them with the access to our marketing vehicles. Any success that product had belongs to them and I wouldn't claim a bit of the credit."

It was at one of those marketing events that John got his only taste of being one of the Two Guys.

"I think Scott was sick or something, so I got to wear the red and silver suit with the neon orange Mohawk and elongated pig nose. I had the time of my life," John says. "A big secret to that big phallic nose was that if you inhaled quickly, the rubber appendage would wiggle about in a very lewd way. It made men laugh. We never put it into a video – it was just too obscene – but I can tell you it was a total chick magnet.

"We did get a nastygram about it once after the Two Guys were in a local parade. An old lady thought it was incredibly pornographic and wrote us to tell us so. I actually took the time to write her back and let her know we totally agreed with her and we were sorry we offended her. She wrote back and said she wasn't offended. She just wanted to point out that it was really lewd in case we hadn't noticed. I had that letter on a wall in my office for a long time."

Space Quest I turned out to be a hit for Sierra, believed to have moved over one hundred thousand units – something only the *King's Quest* games had previously done – but it wasn't without its problems. Some of the parody was deemed too close to the truth by Toys"R"Us and the rock band ZZ Top, and changes to those elements of the game were required in later updates, with the band removed from the bar and Droids R Us renamed to Droids B Us.

Space Quest was also a favorite of Ken Williams, who says, "I was never much of a gamer but I did like silliness. *Space Quest* was hilarious and outrageous. A truly great series."

Return of the Prince

In production at the same time as *Space Quest I*, Roberta Williams's third *King's Quest* game was yet again pushing the envelope. This time Roberta wanted a more complicated game with a deeper story and more memorable characters – a goal she approached by replacing the series' protagonist, King Graham, with a slave boy name Gwydion.

As she wrote in the *King's Quest Collection Series* manual: "My earlier games, from *Mystery House* to *King's Quest II*, were great games, but they couldn't have the deep complex plots I wanted due to memory and space limitations. Basically, they were treasure hunts with lots of simple goals (you go from here to there) and fun puzzles to add challenge. *King's Quest III: To Heir Is Human* had to push things a little farther. The designs had to be more complicated, the plots better and longer, and the characters more developed with personalities and more dialog.

"First I'd start with a mystery: 'Who's that character? Where's King Graham?' Then I'd add the pressure of an evil magician watching your every move, ready to kill you for any mistake. The puzzles were focused on helping you struggle to escape the wizard and right an old wrong you knew nothing about, to tie up everything with a climactic ending. Rosella was introduced toward the end of the game; seeing her on the screen for the first time, I suddenly saw her on her own adventures in a sequel."[4]

In *King's Quest III*'s final scene, after Gwydion is revealed to be King Graham's long-lost son Alexander, Graham throws his adventurer's cap into the air for one of his two children to catch. This first cliffhanger ending to a *King's Quest* game was picked up in *King's*

Quest IV: The Perils of Rosella, when Princess Rosella ends up going on the next adventure.

Al Lowe amusedly recalls the origin of *King's Quest III*'s cliffhanger ending slightly differently than Roberta's account: "[Roberta] was going to have Alexander catch it. I said, 'No, the two of them are there; why not leave it spinning up in the air like a cliffhanger and you can start the next game and have it be a woman.' She always took credit for that idea!"

The production of *King's Quest III* was a smooth process, with Doug MacNeill and Mark Crowe again supplying the artwork and Al Lowe as the main programmer, along with Bob Heitman and Bob Kernaghan. "I didn't have much involvement with Mark and Doug because I was working with Bob Heitman; we had our office together," Al Lowe recalls. "Bob [Heitman] and I would interface with Roberta a lot, but I think we would call Mark Crowe and he would say, 'Oh, okay!' The backgrounds would just show up; Doug would do those."

Even then, they knew they were working with restrictions due to AGI's low screen resolution and 16-color palette, with Al recalling one particular situation where it caused an issue with the intended design. "We laughed because Roberta said, 'Can you make his clothes look more tattered?' and it was like, 'There's only one pixel here and it's got to be one color or another. You can't change part of his pant leg.' That was how low the resolution was."

With Al moving to programming on this game, a new composer was brought in: Al's wife Margaret. "She wrote the music on the piano and I believe by then I had a synthesizer and sampler and a Macintosh computer hooked up to a keyboard, and I had a music workstation," Al says. "I think she probably played the music into the synthesizer at that point. We used MIDI to record but it was then stored in a program on the Mac called a sequencer, then you could move those files around and stuff. I would say she probably produced a file that we then ran through a converter program that would convert it to something that [Jeff Stephenson]'s interpreter could read and use it to play back music. You could only play back on the PCjr and the Atari ST, and I think the Amiga probably had sound capabilities back then. All of the others had just one-voice tweakers."

When *King's Quest III: To Heir Is Human* was released in October 1986, fans were divided. Was this really a *King's Quest* game? Where was King Graham? Who was this slave? It wasn't until later, after people finally finished the game, that these questions were finally answered. *King's Quest III* was another bestseller.

With *King's Quest* and *Space Quest*, Sierra now had two massively successful series, and a third was just around the corner . . . wearing a leisure suit!

Interlude: Journey to the East

It was 1986 and Sierra had emerged from the great video game crash intact and profitable. But the only way to maintain that strength was to expand, and Ken Williams saw an audience in Japan that was open to buying Western products, one that had barely been targeted by the American computer game industry.

Ken formulated a plan, traveling overseas to meet with some technology companies for the purpose of selling Sierra games in the Japanese market. "When I scheduled my first trip to Japan, my intent was to set up methods of selling Sierra products there," Ken said in 1990. "I quickly realized I (and American software publishers in general) had a lot to learn."[5]

The market in Japan was very sophisticated, but what Ken hadn't realized was that unlike in the United States, where IBM clones were prevalent, the Japanese market was dominated by the Famicom.

The Famicom, more popularly known elsewhere as the Nintendo Entertainment System (NES), had a market share that simply dwarfed anything Sierra was doing. Over four million homes had the console. Ken was impressed with the quality of the graphics and sound, as well as the fact that children not only loved games like *Super Mario Bros.* but were almost obsessed with them. As Ken recounted of his first look at a Japanese game in 1990, "I was hooked. There was a multi-voice stereo soundtrack and an elaborate cartoon to start the game, and the animation and graphics were simply incredible. I couldn't believe what I was seeing. This wasn't programming – this was an artform!"[6]

Ken left Japan without selling any of his games, but he had a lot of ideas to share with his programming team – some of which made their way into Sierra's new SCI programming language. He also left Japan with a game, *Thexder*, and an NEC PC-88 computer to run it on.

"We managed to wire the NEC to run on U.S. electrical current, and the Sierra programming department ground to a halt for weeks," Ken admitted. Indeed, *Thexder* was such a hit within the programming team that much of the other work was set aside to play the new game. "I think I decided to acquire *Thexder* from Game Arts [the Japanese publisher] for two reasons: I thought it would be a good game and I desperately hoped that after debugging the game for IBM, [Apple] IIGS, etc., the programmers and quality assurance people might get so sick of seeing it that they would get back to 'work.'"[7]

Thexder was unique in the American market. It was an arcade game, but it did things that hadn't been seen on the personal computer before, such as offering the smoothest scrolling graphics achieved to that point. After Ken signed the deal for Sierra to acquire the rights to publish *Thexder* in the United States, it was ported to the IBM PC, Tandy Color Computer 3, Apple II, Apple IIGS, Macintosh, and Tandy 1000 computer systems, going on to become Sierra's best-selling title over Christmas 1988. By 1990, it had sold over one million copies.[8]

With the success of *Thexder*, Sierra and Game Arts struck a long-term publishing deal to release each other's games in their respective countries. Sierra put in place their own ambassador for Japan, Ed Nagano, and hired Mickie Lee and Akiko Skjellerup for the programming department specifically to work on the Japanese titles. As a bonus, Sierra staff was treated to Japanese language classes.

The next Game Arts title to be published was *Silpheed*, released in 1990. It was touted as a sequel to *Thexder* and became another runaway hit for the company.

Josh Mandel was in charge of the Game Arts products for Sierra when he arrived as a junior producer in 1990, and explains how the deal was originally constructed: "I know it was supposed to be a very mutually beneficial relationship. We would send a game to them, they would send a game to us. I don't know if it was really a one-for-one switch but that was the idea."

It wasn't an easy position for Josh. As he explains, "It was an area where I felt really uncomfortable and really out of my depth, because I had no managerial experience in any way whatsoever and here I was being told I need to interface with these people in Japan. You need to observe proper protocol because it's very important when you're dealing with [Japanese people], and you need to make the calls during their business hours, which was a little weird sometimes for me.

"I really felt out of my element and I didn't like that aspect of my job, but of course when I went [to Sierra] to be a junior producer I had my heart set on being a designer, so I hoped that I wasn't going to have to do too much of that paper-pushing kind of work."

Josh was assigned the next two games in the Game Arts deal, *Zeliard* and *Fire Hawk: Thexder – The Second Contact*, both of which Sierra released in 1990, although he only had a minor role in both games. "I would go over the translations, most of which were done by Bridget and Marti McKenna, who were just wonderful. They had done translations on the earlier Game Arts games that had been done before I got there," Josh says.

"Although I was sort of interested in handling the translations myself, because that really appealed to me as a writer, I was working hard on the *King's Quest I* remake and they knew what they were doing, so I just let them continue and changed very little of their work. They're both published authors and they knew their way around the game world and how to rub two words together, so they didn't need much input from me. So that was really just a paperwork kind of a job, those games."

Along with *Sorcerian*, a Japanese title from publisher Nihon Falcom, both *Zeliard* and *Fire Hawk* were released in 1990 primarily for MS-DOS but also other systems. While *Fire Hawk* was another great success for Sierra, neither *Sorcerian* nor *Zeliard* was a big enough seller to warrant more Japanese imports (although Sierra did release a remake of *Thexder*, called *Thexder 95*, as part of its first wave of Windows 95–compatible products).

Not every game was a hit in the US, but Sierra had brought Japanese games to the American market before most other companies, yet another example of the forward thinking that drove the company to the top of the industry.

Chapter 4: Leisure Suits and Police Uniforms

I could make fun of guys' sexual problems, which was all we talked about anyway, pretty much.

Al Lowe, Designer, Leisure Suit Larry

Five years is a long time in the computer industry.

By 1987, Sierra had gone through its major downturn brought on by the video game crash a few years earlier. They had acquired venture capital as a way of increasing the size of the company and ensuring they wouldn't have to live hand-to-mouth as they had in the past, and then dealt with all the changes and ramifications that entailed. They launched two massively successful series, *King's Quest* and *Space Quest*, and had started to move out from under the financial stresses they had been experiencing.

During that time Al Lowe had created his own games, worked on the Disney range of products, created music, and headed up programming on *King's Quest III*, but it was time for a change.

"I had worked on *King's Quest III* and watched Roberta go through the whole process from beginning to end. [I worked] with Bob Heitman on that game; he was one of the engine writers but he also ended up working with me coding that game, then a couple of other guys joined. The company was very small then," Al recalls.

As work on *King's Quest III* wound down, Al and Ken Williams started discussing his next project, and one thing was firmly in Al's mind. "The big difference was I wanted to do a game that is not like anything else out there. To me, I thought that people like books that are funny, movies that are funny, and TV shows that are funny. Comedy has a niche in all those markets. Why isn't it in computer games? I could make fun of guys' sexual problems, which was all we talked about anyway, pretty much.

"It seemed like I could do a game that wasn't like all the other games on the market. That was really the niche we were going for back in the eighties. We were trying to expand the marketplace and do games that were unlike any other games out there."

Knowing he wanted to do something funny, and something a little more adult-oriented than what Sierra had been producing, Ken suggested Al look at one of the company's earlier successes. "Ken said, 'Softporn Adventure was a huge hit. Maybe you could do a remake of that? Bring that up, use the modern interpreter, graphics and sound and all that stuff we were doing then and move it six years into the future.'"

After his experiences working on Donald Duck's Playground and a number of ports for different titles, Chuck Benton had moved on from making computer games. By then he had sold the rights for Softporn Adventure to what was then On-Line Systems, so he was surprised to receive a phone call from Ken Williams about it in early 1987. "I remember Ken calling and testing the waters and seeing if I was amenable to there being a graphic version of the game created," Chuck says.

"I said go for it. At the time I was still in the 'I'm not doing any more video games' mode. He offered me a 1% royalty or $5,000." For Donald Duck's Playground, Chuck had chosen a royalty over the fixed fee. "It ended up being a really bad decision; the game didn't go anywhere financially. So I looked at this and said, 'I'll take the cash, thank you very much.' If I had taken the 1% I'd be retired, which I'm not!"

Al hadn't played Softporn Adventure for years, so he played it again and wasn't impressed with what he saw. "I took it home and played it and came back and said, 'You're kidding. This game is so out of touch it should be wearing a leisure suit.' Which literally came to me out of the blue. I didn't plan that line or anything but I got a big laugh from the other guys in the room. So I thought, 'Oh, leisure suits are funny!' I said, 'I think the only way I could do a version of this game is if you let me make fun of it.' Ken said, 'Fine, go ahead.' So I went home and did it."

Al made some major changes to Softporn Adventure when designing Leisure Suit Larry in the Land of the Lounge Lizards. Chuck's game had no main protagonist, instead referring to the player as "master," but Al wanted a defined character so he created Larry Laffer, named after Arthur Laffer, one of then–US president Ronald Reagan's economic advisors. And in keeping with his joke, he put Larry in an outdated leisure suit.

The overall structure and puzzles of Softporn Adventure were kept, but all the text was rewritten from the point of view of Larry and the omnipotent narrator. (Only one line of text survived: "The peeling paint gives the roaches something to watch," a description of a room in the bar in which Larry starts his adventure.) Due to his plans to make the game more comedic, Al decided to make fun of Larry and the situations he was in through the use of the narrator, whom Al thought of as himself talking to the player about Larry.

One challenge for Al was working with the type-in interface, since all his previous games had used a simplified interface where the player selected an option. "I hadn't done a game that had a parser, so the parser was the big challenge for me on that project. I watched what Roberta had done on *King's Quest III* and learned how she assigned synonyms and so forth to make the game more intelligent."

Leisure Suit Larry has three designers credited, an unusual situation for the time. Al was the primary designer, writing the vast majority of it as well as programming and composing the soundtrack.

Chuck Benton was also cited as a designer but reveals that he didn't do any work on the game. "The first *Leisure Suit Larry* was basically *Softporn Adventure* converted into a graphic game. So I was credited for it because I was essentially the story author. But then all the subsequent ones I had nothing to do with."

The third designer credit goes to Mark Crowe, who not only singlehandedly created all the artwork but also offered insight on puzzle design and came up with some of the gags in the game. "With a lot of the gags, we couldn't show them doing things so I came up with a clever thing and covered them with a black box, then animated the black box. Your imagination was able to run wild with that. It was a lot of fun doing that game. It's pretty mild by today's comparison, but back then there was always a little tinge of, 'Should I be doing this?'"

Mark was already working full-time with Scott Murphy on their debut *Space Quest* game when Sierra assigned him to *Leisure Suit Larry* for four weeks to create all the art. It was a tight schedule, and working with the graphics tools was always difficult, but it was all finished on time. "I think by then we had worked out a lot of the kinks in our system and I was comfortable enough with the tools to knock stuff out fairly quickly," Mark claims.

"I think I was procrastinating and procrastinating on that stuff, and finally I lit a fire under myself and got it done. After thinking and thinking about it, you spend too much time thinking about stuff, then it's time to execute and you just go crazy. I definitely had a fire under me to get it done and get on with the animation, which is what I really loved to do. That was the fun part for me."

Although Al was happy with *Leisure Suit Larry in the Land of the Lounge Lizards*, he still wasn't confident in his ability to program a parser-driven game. The solution? Beta testing, something he had seen done for other products but never for a game.

After receiving Ken's approval, Sierra advertised for beta testers on CompuServe, the first major online service provider in the United States and a place where the hardcore gamers of the eighties met. Asking for a 100-word essay on why they should get a free game, Sierra was inundated with applications that they ended up whittling down to a dozen testers.

In the game version he sent testers, Al added a small program that saved to a file every time the player attempted an action that came back with a generic response. Using those log files, he then wrote hundreds of responses into the game, making it a more immersive experience for the player and one of the better parser-based games of the period.

Leisure Suit Larry in the Land of the Lounge Lizards was released in July 1987 and initial sales were poor. Moving only four thousand copies in the first month according to Al Lowe, *Leisure Suit Larry* was the lowest selling debut game Sierra had released. Al, figuring he had wasted three months of his life, took a position as the lead programmer on *Police Quest* when it became available.

While the game received a large number of good reviews, there were also some savage ones, as well as protests about the product and hate mail to Sierra. *Leisure Suit Larry* was given an adult rating in some countries, severely limiting sales potential, and South Africa banned the game outright. One retailer, when sent a promotional copy of the game, sent it back sawn in half. There wasn't a note attached but the message was clear.

Inside Sierra, the occasional issue arose as well. When interviewing for a position with the company, one prospective employee stated that he refused to work on *Leisure Suit Larry* or any potential sequels, resulting in him not being hired even though he was fully qualified.

After its slow start, however, the game started selling. Each month sales doubled until, by Christmas, Sierra had another hit on their hands. *Leisure Suit Larry* went from being the company's worst product launch to its second biggest success, surpassed only by *King's Quest III*.

Marketing the game had been a challenge for John Williams and his team, and there was a reliance on public relations and word of mouth over more traditional advertising. The former seemed to be the most important factor in driving sales, and the demographic of the gaming audience matched neatly with the adult subject matter. "By the time that *Larry* was ready to ship, the dominant buyer demographic was an adult male, mostly married, and with kids," John says. "It was a demographic that was likely interested in a game like *Leisure Suit Larry*, but retailers held a skepticism that these married dads would actually pick it up, take it to the register and then home to their wives."

Sierra was also having cash flow issues when *Leisure Suit Larry* was released, something John Williams says is a major reason they concentrated on PR more than advertising. "We were at an odd point as a company. Sierra was having some money problems, so our ad spend was low and we had suspended some of our pricier promotional vehicles like [Sierra's in-house magazine] and slowed our distribution of catalogs."

The main goal of Sierra's advertising plans at that stage was to make sure the products that were stocked on shelves were sold, as they had to refund the retailer for any returned products, something that had nearly broken the company a few years earlier. "The problem was that the retailers were not ready for a game like *Larry* and a great many of them took a pass on it," John claims.

"We [had] lots of problems getting the original *Larry* onto retail shelves. A lot of retailers just wouldn't touch it, especially the newly powerful mall-based chains, and we were not at a place as a company where we could spend a lot of money promoting a product that wasn't on shelves."

Reflecting further, John claims, "It was a different era then, and to really understand *Larry* you have to put it in context of the time. Movies like *Fatal Attraction* and *The Witches of Eastwick* seemed pretty edgy then, but could probably be shown pretty much uncut on network television today. On the radio, Michael Jackson and Lionel Richie were tearing up the charts along with hardcore headbangers like Bryan Adams, Peter Gabriel and Bruce Hornsby, all of which would be played in elevators now.

"Where the game did get on shelves, it sold through mostly because of that almost obscenely pink box with submerged orbs, and [because of] the public relations program we had in place to promote *Larry*."

Like walking a tightrope, that PR plan was a cross between, "Yes, it's naughty! It's being banned!" and "It's no worse than what's in movies or on television!" The marketing team managed to garner some major coverage in the biggest gaming magazines of the era. In *Computer Gaming World*, John wrote a three-part series about adult-themed games and why they were acceptable, arguing that at the end of the day, if people wanted that style of game they would buy them.

"We were looking for controversy to sell the game, much as *Softporn* had sold a few years earlier. We were also hoping to avoid the backlash that we had gotten for having the word 'porn' in the title of the original text adventure game. That word had gotten us in a lot of trouble!" John remembers. "Like a lot of things from that era, it was a lot of creative writing. I think we did a good job playing the hand that we were dealt with this product."

Positioning *Leisure Suit Larry* in the market had been a tricky process, but the results spoke for themselves and *Larry* became a major success, later spawning five sequels that were always on Sierra's bestseller lists.

Call the Police!

Looking for another new niche the company could make their own, Ken Williams started thinking about a police game. Cop movies were all the rage in Hollywood at the time, and an adventure game series in the same vein seemed like a sure winner.

It was around this time, in 1985, that Ken met Officer Jim Walls.

Jim lived in the Oakhurst area and had worked for the California Highway Patrol (CHP) since December 1971, starting as a CHP officer in the town of Van Nuys. Over the next thirteen years, Jim filled a number of CHP positions across southern California – until one incident changed everything.

Out on a standard patrol, Jim spied a car traveling over the posted 55 mile-per-hour speed limit and started pursuing. The driver eventually slowed down, so Jim was about to let him go, considering he hadn't been too far over the limit in the first place, when the vehicle suddenly sped up again and swerved across two lanes and up an off-ramp. Jim gave chase.

Eventually cornered in a parking lot, with the two vehicles facing each other, the driver of the other car jumped out with a loaded .357 Magnum. Jim ripped off his seat belt and leapt out of the car just before the driver shot out his windshield, aiming directly at Jim. Fortunately, he was distracted by his car starting to roll.

The driver got away, although he was picked up and arrested later. His car had been filled with drugs that night.

Jim was alive, but from then on, his love for the job had left him. He quickly realized that he was surrounded day in and day out by the dregs of society, and the only good people he saw in the line of duty were people he'd occasionally pull over for speeding. A year later, Jim took administrative leave from the California Highway Patrol.

Jim's wife Donna worked as a hair stylist in Oakhurst and one of her customers was Ken Williams. Sitting in her salon one day, Ken started talking about his ideas for a police-based adventure game, aware that Donna's husband was a CHP officer. Wanting a cop involved in the design in order to capture the essence of being a police officer, Ken gave his card to Donna to pass onto Jim.

A phone call later, Jim was invited to play racquetball at Ken and Roberta's home – his first experience with the sport. Jim was thoroughly beaten, but on retiring to the game room for drinks, Ken outlined his ideas for a police adventure. He sought someone with experience to be involved and Jim was the person he had in mind.

A process quickly developed over the following weeks. Jim detailed some of his experiences on paper and Ken would go over the work, offering suggestions and comments. Jim would return a few days later with more detail and Ken would again make comments. Eventually, they had the story for *Police Quest*.

Soon enough, Jim resigned from the California Highway Patrol and assumed a game designer position with Sierra. A team was put together, with Mark Crowe and Gerald Moore on graphics; Margaret Lowe on sound; and Greg Rowland, Ken Williams and Scott Murphy as programmers. Al Lowe later joined the programming team as well.

The main story elements were taken from Jim's personal experiences as a cop, as well as those of friends who had worked undercover. The plot was simple enough: follow young police officer Sonny Bonds as he uncovers a major drug ring working in his once crime-free town, infiltrate the gang and take down the bad guy. But Jim wanted to give the narrative a realistic approach to police work, so it was decided that to successfully complete the game would require a focus on following correct police procedure.

"There's a lot of tedium, and a lot of rules we have to follow. If we don't, lives can be lost, or arrests can be bungled. But there's a lot of headwork and excitement, too," Jim shared in a 1987 interview.[9]

While Jim was nervous in the beginning about being a game designer, he was helped along by his veteran team, with Mark Crowe being given a role greater than just the graphics he was credited for.

"Jim was a lot of fun to work with because he was a real character," Mark reveals. "It was a little challenging, for sure, because I was put with Jim and basically told to teach him how to design a computer game because he had zero experience with developing games. He was a brilliant storyteller and had a lot of great material, but I kind of had to work with him on the story and say we can probably do this and probably can't do that. Basically, design what he wanted to see happen on-screen and work closely with him on that. At the same time, I educated him with what was possible in our system."

Jim learned fast. *Police Quest: In Pursuit of the Death Angel* was completed smoothly and released in 1987 to much acclaim.

Something the team at Sierra hadn't expected was real police using the game to promote the value of following procedure. In 1988 an officer in Michigan related the positive effect the game had achieved at his precinct to *Law and Order* magazine, which was reprinted in an issue of the *Sierra Newsletter*.

"I also observed that squad room conversation between officers was now less concerned with fishing and more oriented toward discussing proper procedures. These topics were raised by *Police Quest*. It is very unsettling to see yourself in the persona of Sonny Bonds getting blown away because he did one thing wrong. The fact that our officers were interested in such things – without waiting for one of our officers to actually get hurt – was very encouraging."[10]

Police Quest: In Pursuit of the Death Angel was another success for Sierra and marked the beginning of their fourth major adventure game series. But the company wasn't resting on its laurels, and 1987 was a busy year. Along with launching both *Police Quest* and *Leisure Suit Larry*, they had also put into production the first sequel in the hit *Space Quest* franchise.

Return to Space

"Heroes come and heroes go, and people soon forget. Your celebrated herodom slowly fades, leaving you, once again, a janitor."[11]

Space Quest II: Chapter II – Vohaul's Revenge doesn't so much pick up from the end of its predecessor as start the story over again, returning Roger to his former career as a space custodian. "It's a reset for sure," according to Mark Crowe. "I remember thinking we would do the one game and that would be it and it never really entered our minds we would be doing a sequel. At the time we felt it would be a one and done kind of thing. But it sold so well for them, obviously, it made sense to do another one. But that wasn't on our minds at the time.

"When Ken did approach us to do a sequel we thought, 'Oh crap! What are we going to do? How can we make a sequel out of that; continue the story?' Because we had pretty much put a button on the end of that one and didn't leave much room for, at least in our minds, a sequel."

Mark goes on to share that the production was started quickly and the whole creative process was instigated by Ken cramming Mark and Scott Murphy together in close proximity: "Put us in an office together and put us in the can and shake us up and see what we can come up with. I just remember that being a lot of pressure for us."

With the majority of *Space Quest I* set on the desert planet of Kerona, a significant change suggested by Scott was to place the sequel on a jungle planet. A flimsy tie-in to the original game was devised, with the bad guy from *Space Quest II* being the developer of the weapon in the first game who wanted to exact his revenge.

This villain, Sludge Vohaul, also offered a chance to riff on the creation of a rival game company. Mark admits, "Vohaul was obviously inspired by Darth Vader. That was always a big influence, I'm not ashamed to say. The first time we saw Darth Vader without the helmet on is obviously the influence for our Vohaul character design. It was also kind of our way of parodying Lucasfilm."

These elements were tied together in a story involving, of all things, insurance salesmen. "At the time I was starting to get a little money coming in from [*Space Quest I*] and putting a little money away. I was talking with financial advisors and life insurance people and that sort of thing. I found it very annoying. I was definitely influenced by that and I thought, 'I want to have a life insurance salesperson as the evil person in the next game.' Because I thought they were inherently evil," Mark laughs.

"They were just tenacious people. This person I worked with was very aggressive as a salesperson. That was very off-putting; it definitely stuck with me. That manifested itself as the characters in *Space Quest II*."

Scott was enthusiastic about the idea, as Mark had given his phone number to his insurance agent and she had been hounding him as well.

Space Quest II was once again a small production, with the majority of work being done by the Two Guys from Andromeda and Al Lowe joining later to provide additional assistance on the music. It was also, according to Mark, a fast process during which they were under a lot of pressure to complete the game.

One aspect of its completion that stood out was the box design. Having done a number of boxes for Sierra already, Mark worked up the cover art for *Space Quest II*. Using cardstock to design the title letters, he colored then textured them using car parts and pieces of models he had lying around, including some from *Star Wars*. The insurance salesmen on the cover are also borrowed from popular culture, with Mark dressing Mattel Ken dolls in suits and ties and placing them in glass cases.

Space Quest II met with similar success to the first game and Ken Williams immediately commissioned a third, this time using Sierra's new game engine.

AGI's Final Outings

Since *King's Quest I*, all of Sierra's adventure games had been made with AGI. By 1988, its use was dwindling in favor of the Sierra's Creative Interpreter (SCI) engine. The company developed four titles in 1988 and 1989 that used the AGI toolset. Three of these, *Manhunter: New York*, *Manhunter 2: San Francisco*, and *Gold Rush!*, pushed AGI to its limits.

Back in 1983, before Sierra shifted its focus to adventure games, they published *Sierra Championship Boxing* for Evryware, a software development company co-founded by Dave Murry. Seeing the success of Dave and his brother Barry's *Ancient Art of War* series, which had been published by Brøderbund in the mid-eighties, Ken Williams approached the brothers about producing another game for Sierra.

Using Sierra's AGI toolset, the Murrys crafted a unique adventure game: *Manhunter: New York*. With no type-in input, no character dialogue, and a postapocalyptic story that was far removed from anything Sierra had previously published, the Murry brothers and their sister Dee Dee delivered a hit that sold more than one hundred thousand copies – a gold standard in 1988. The next year they followed up with *Manhunter 2: San Francisco*, the last game released using AGI, before parting ways with Sierra and moving on to work with other publishers.

King's Quest III, meanwhile, had wrapped production in 1986 and the team split up and dispersed onto different projects. Al Lowe had *Leisure Suit Larry*, while Mark Crowe and Scott Murphy had *Space Quest II*. Roberta Williams turned her attention to *Mixed-Up Mother Goose*, a children's game based around the stories she loved as a kid. That left brothers Doug and Ken MacNeill without a project.

"Ken Williams asked us if we wanted to do a game and I had the idea to do a Roaring Twenties game; my wife might have had that idea. We had a couple of different, funny things we could base a game on," Doug remembers. "Ken [MacNeill] had an idea about the gold rush era. We were going to do a quick game, knock one out on the [California] gold rush, and then we were going to do that other game we were talking about."

That quick game, *Gold Rush!*, ended up being a massive project.

"It turned out that *Gold Rush!* grew and grew and grew and turned out to be the maximum AGI could produce," Doug says. "It was maxed out. The last AGI game [developed internally at Sierra] and we had a good finale for that. I don't know why we let it get so big; there was a lot of content in that game. Lots of pictures, lots of animated objects. We just let it get too big!"

Gold Rush! had a two-man team: Ken MacNeill programming, Doug MacNeill in charge of the artwork, and both brothers designing the game. It wasn't an easy job. "We also decided that was the last game a two-man crew could do," Doug recalls. "After that, all games got bigger teams than that. We really pushed it to the limit to get that done; it was rough."

At the start of the project, neither brother was living in Oakhurst. "My brother Ken was working for the [Federal Aviation Administration] in the Bay Area; he actually quit his job, it got so difficult. Once Ken quit his job, I moved from Washington and we both lived away from home. I refer to it as the gold rush of '88. We actually lived the way the forty-niners lived; they left their wives and families and moved to California to do their gold thing. We did the same thing. We left our families and we lived in a motor home in the [Sierra] parking lot," Doug recollects.

"We worked out of a warehouse. [Sierra] had a building up on Highway 49; we just worked out of that. It got kind of cold up there," he continues. "I had a PS/2 [IBM computer], which was one of the first floor-mounted computers; it just got caked in dust. I had to clean it up once in a while. We developed the game out of there and then later Sierra built the metal building on the Talking Bear Road out on Highway 49. In that metal building we had a little spot where we could work. We were still in the motor home out the back, but we could work out of that office."

Most productions at the time took no more than a year, but the MacNeills spent nearly two developing *Gold Rush!* "We were under such pressure to get it done, but we were friends with everyone there," Doug remembers. "We liked everybody, they all liked us. We put signs up that said Do Not Disturb outside our cubicle, but people would think that didn't apply to them and they would still come in and talk to us. Every half an hour somebody would come in and talk to us!

"We had big boxes that had stuff in them from shipping; we actually moved those boxes in front of our cubicle two or three layers deep and put the Do Not Disturb signs on top of that. Then the people who thought they were such good friends with us, they would come and move all the boxes out of the way and come into our cubicle even after all that! They wouldn't understand we were under such pressure to get that done," he laughs. "We just marveled. We were just, 'Wow!' People would be straining to move these boxes to get into our cubicle, even past the sign!"

Production was slow, which frustrated management. Although Ken Williams got along with the MacNeills, he was also a savvy businessman who wanted results. "He was always a nice guy, but he also had [general manager] Rick Cavin. He let Rick Cavin do the dirty work, I think, then he could stay the nice guy," Doug reveals. And yet, "Ken was really very strong in the business. He wasn't afraid to say things the way he thought they were.

"[My brother] Ken went to a trade show with Ken Williams; my brother was the pilot. They took a twin-engine prop plane to Las Vegas. While [they were] at the show, someone who had a booth there had forgotten some very critical stuff they needed for their presentation. Ken Williams told them, 'I've got a pilot and a plane here; I'll fly it back and get your material for a certain amount.' It seemed like a very high figure to my brother Ken and I. The guy said, 'How about this much?' Ken just turned around. It was his number or no number. So the guy paid the amount of money and my brother flew back and got the stuff.

"That showed he was a good businessman and his business side. There was no negotiating. Once he decided it was fair, that is what it was. And he was really strong that way. He made sure he held the cards. That's how he did it. I wouldn't want to be a competitor of his, that's for sure."

While Ken Williams was a strong businessman, his relationship with Ken MacNeill helped smooth the rough development of Gold Rush! "I think what it came down to was the respect Ken Williams and Ken MacNeill had for each other was so strong that nothing would break that completely," Doug surmises. "I think that Ken Williams respected me too. I don't know why exactly, just because we were so respectful to him and he returned it to us."

The MacNeill brothers both realized that they needed to finish their game soon, and Doug also knew this would probably be his last with the company. The stress of getting Gold Rush! finished was enormous, and living away from his wife for such a long stretch of time wasn't easy.

"The truth of it is, Gold Rush! was going fine. Ken Williams liked it; it was going good. Then somebody said something negative about

Gold Rush! and that got Ken Williams thinking about it, and all of a sudden he wasn't that excited about the game anymore. After that it was very difficult to overcome anything that happened. Rick Cavin became our archenemy, basically; made our life miserable and we had to get it done. With all the politics in that, and Sierra didn't kind of keep their agreement on some things and tried to pay us less in the end. That's basically how it finished for us."

Following its arduous production, *Gold Rush!* was finally released in 1988 and it performed well. With its accurate portrayal of the gold rush period, it sold particularly strongly in the educational market. But while sales were solid initially, like all the AGI games, *Gold Rush!* didn't sell well over the long term. With Sierra's move to SCI, coupled with the development of 256-color graphics a few years later, *Gold Rush!* soon looked antiquated to customers and eventually it was removed from the Sierra catalog and effectively from sale.

It was after this that the MacNeills decided it would be worth trying to sell the game themselves, so they approached Ken Williams about getting the rights. "I went to his Bellevue office," Doug remembers.* "I think I went there one time before to get the lay of the land before I was going to ask for the rights. I get into the elevator and who gets into the elevator with me except Ken Williams himself. I just said I was here to check it out."

On the day of the actual meeting, Ken Williams was more than happy to give *Gold Rush!* to the MacNeills, providing Doug with all the original assets and source code. Many years later, after various changes of management, all the original assets of Sierra's vast catalog were destroyed except for a few pieces saved by individuals. *Gold Rush!* is possibly the only game with all its original assets still surviving.

"He gave me the rights to the game. Ken said, 'I don't think there's any more money in it, but if you want it, you can have it.' He told the art department to give me everything, so I have it all now. It's all preserved, like the cover art, the map art, everything from it," Doug says.

Ken's only stipulation was that the MacNeills make it clear the product no longer had anything to do with the company. "I asked Ken if he wanted me to take Sierra's name off of it but Ken said, 'I don't think it's possible to modify this, so leave it the way it is, but put a note on the box that this work is no longer related to Sierra On-Line.' He

---

* Sierra headquarters moved to a new office in Bellevue, Washington, near Seattle, in 1993.

gave me a quote and we put that on there. It turned out that Ken [MacNeill] and I still had our old computers and I got my old tablet out again; it was a miracle to get it all working again. We went through and took out all mentions of Sierra," Doug says.

While they were at it, Doug explains, "We redid a lot of the graphics because there were little things we'd heard over the years that made it difficult to play. We changed a lot of the messages and brushed it up. That version I sold under the Software Farm name is actually a different version [from] the Sierra version. It's actually a really clean version. It's called *Gold Rush! Classic* now."

Ken Williams remembers that meeting with Doug and says he was glad to give the MacNeills the game. "If I had thought I could make money on *Gold Rush!* I would have kept it within Sierra," he admits. "But my perception was that the market was too small and the product would receive no attention within the company. Whereas, for the MacNeills, with all of their attention on it, they could make some nice money for themselves. They were good guys and I wanted to see them succeed, and it didn't cost Sierra anything. The product would have rotted within Sierra."

AGI had been a revelation for Sierra: an engine that could be used on all their adventure game titles, meeting Ken's requirement to reduce production costs. But with *Gold Rush!* it had reached the end of its lifespan. Between the release of *King's Quest I* in 1983 and *Gold Rush!* In 1988, fourteen games had been created using AGI, but now Jeff Stephenson and his team of programmers had developed a new engine that would take the company even further.

Interlude: The Producers

As Sierra positioned itself more centrally around the graphic adventure genre, a field that Roberta had created with *Mystery House* and then followed up with the hugely successful *King's Quest* series, it became evident that her creative vision for the company required help overseeing all the games Sierra was now producing.

Guruka Singh Khalsa was living in Ohio, running a residential yoga center while also working at the local university, when he first discovered gaming. He quickly devoured all the Infocom text adventures and moved on to Sierra's graphic adventures. Highly enthused by them, he wrote to Sierra with his thoughts about the games, suggestions, and reports of any bugs or problems he found.

"I started sending feedback back to Sierra," Guruka recalls. "I would just write to [general manager] Rick Cavin about the games and stuff and he said, 'Would you be willing to test a game we haven't released yet and give me your ideas?'"

Intrigued by the notion, and happy to play a game that wasn't yet publicly available, Guruka agreed and soon had an early copy of *Gold Rush!* Loading it up from the 5.25-inch disks it came on, Guruka wasn't impressed. "The game was just dead. There just wasn't interest in any of the screens or puzzles. I wrote Rick back at length about what was wrong with the game and what I thought could be done about it."

About a month later, Guruka received a follow-up call from Rick. "He said, 'How would you like to come out here and work for us?' I said, 'I can't do that. I'm the director of a yoga center here. There's hundreds of students; I work at the university,'" Guruka recalls.

Rick Cavin offered to pay for Guruka and his wife to fly out to California and the couple spent three days there, meeting with Rick, Ken and Roberta Williams, and other staff at Sierra. Although they loved the area, and the job sounded exciting, they weren't sold on the notion and had decided to turn it down, but Rick asked them to think about it more before giving their final answer.

"I was down in Florida in January and my spiritual teacher said, 'What's new?' I said, 'Not much,' and he said again, 'No. What's new?' 'I was offered a job in California but I'm not going to take it.' He said, 'How much are they paying you?' I told him how much and the stock options and all that and he said to take the job. That's how we moved to Coarsegold. I came to Sierra in the winter of '89 and left in spring '92. I wasn't there for very long. But the time I was there I got to work on a ton of fun projects."

After working in quality assurance for a short time, Guruka was soon promoted to the newly formed role of producer, and quickly became the executive producer as he employed other producers to help him. "My job was to head up the creative teams, so I got to work on everything: story design, puzzle design, resolving arguments between the writers and the programmers," Guruka recalls.

One of the first producers Guruka hired was Josh Mandel. Josh had started working for Sierra as a beta tester and Guruka Singh Khalsa was his main contact with the company. According to Josh, "He was the producer there, the only producer, so he had all of these projects going on under his auspices and he was the one I connected with, and I think all the beta testers would connect with, so he was a very central figure during the golden years."

Josh believes his beta testing led to him being offered a position as junior producer with Sierra. "I think one of the inciting incidents that led them to offer me a job was when we were working on *Codename: ICEMAN*. I was living in Chicago; I had a job in advertising but I was beta testing for Sierra and I found a crash bug in *Codename: ICEMAN* and no one at Sierra was able to duplicate it.

"So in order to do so, I had to play through the game with programmer Mark Hood on the line with my telling him every single thing that I did and him doing it as well there, until I ran across the bug. And it took hours and hours and hours and then finally I got the bug and he said, 'I got it! I got it!'"

It was soon after this that Josh received the phone call from Guruka that altered the course of his career. "He's the one who called me up one day and said, 'Look, there's too many games here for me to handle. You're a great beta tester; would you be interested in a junior producer position under me?' So I owe a huge debt of gratitude to Guruka, because he changed my life."

Josh's interview at Sierra was a unique experience, one that he cherishes and believes demonstrates the family atmosphere at the company during that period. "It really reinforced the image I had from *InterAction* [Sierra's promotional magazine] and from the game content itself of Sierra being a very friendly place.

"I took the flight from Chicago to get to Fresno and I drove through the mountains up to Oakhurst. I'm looking at the building and I'm thinking, 'This must be it, I'm following the directions.' As I'm pulling into the parking lot, a man comes out of the building and he walks towards the car as I'm getting out and I didn't recognize him at first," Josh remembers. "He sticks out his hand and says, 'You must be Josh Mandel. You're here for the interview?' I said yes; he said, 'I'm Ken Williams' and I'm like, 'D'oh! How could I not have recognized him?' He led me in and took me to [creative director] Bill Davis's office and then he took off. But I thought it was absolutely the most charming thing in the world to be greeted in the parking lot by the owner of the company and somebody I admired incredibly."

Robert Holmes, probably better known as the composer of the *Gabriel Knight* games, was also the producer for that series. Although the producer's role was mainly to manage the business side of a production, while the designer handled the creative side, Robert also contributed to the game's development. "The best ones – Josh Mandel is a great example and there were several at Sierra – were really great producers," he says. "Sabine [Duvall], who took over *The Beast Within* after I left the project, was another great producer. A lot of these people were really good at supporting teams and having that producer role be a service role to that team.

"I was producer on a few projects before I was assigned to Jane [Jensen] and some of it was very traditional, in as much as being a sounding board for the designer and be somebody to help maintain Sierra quality standards. Very often you'd have the designer, the art director and the producer working early on to really define the standards and quality and the point of view," Robert explains.

Josh Mandel worked as both a producer and designer and has unique knowledge of both sides of the process. He says the two most important roles – the lead programmer, and the art director or lead artist – would be filled first.

"Once the designer had some definite ideas about what the game was going to entail, they would meet with the lead artist and discuss the style of the game," Josh says. "They might also meet with the lead programmer and talk about the larger issues of the game. Was it going to need any special programming sequences? Would it use the in-house (SCI) engine?"

Most games at that time did use SCI, as utilizing the same engine kept development costs down, though a team of programmers were constantly adding to what it could produce.

According to Al Lowe, "The problem with those tools, SCI and AGI before it, is they were constantly changing. You have to have the set of tools that were used to create the game if you're going to rebuild the game, because they weren't backwards compatible or forwards compatible."

Al goes on to say that there was no effort made for compatibility. "It was, 'Hey, we've got a new idea. We'll make this now. All your stuff is crap; rebuild it all.' That was the way it worked back then. Compatibility wasn't an issue."

As well as assigning a lead programmer, the producer also assigned an art director. The art director's job was also extensive and required a lot of preparation, as Marc Hudgins, who held that role on *Quest for Glory IV*, explains: "You're basically given the design document, whatever shape it was in at the time the project was spun up. It was usually a list of what we used to call rooms – you know, screens – and a rough outline of the progression through the game.

"Part of it is like, 'Well, what are the environments here? What needs to be designed? What's the tone of this? What's the visual approach to take to this? What characters need to be designed?' And then breaking out animation lists. I'd started out as an animator so that was always a big thing for me; [a] very animation-focused approach. I think it was different because a lot of the previous lead artists were more illustrators who did the backgrounds. As an animator, my concern was making sure the backgrounds supported the animation, and not the other way around. So I would try to compile as much as I could about every scene, what the animation needs were, and stage that, and sketch out background designs that would accommodate the action that needed to be supported."

As the designer progressed further along with their game, the producer would work with them to refine the number of staff required to create it. Josh Mandel says, "You'd have a record of all the programmers and a guide to when each one was expected to come off of whatever project they were currently on. You looked to see who was going to be available around the time you were going to need them. They might not be available when the team was being formed, but they might come on later. The same thing for the artists and the musicians."

Once all the pieces were in place, production of Sierra's games followed a fairly standard process. The designer would develop a section of the game and the artists would create the background artwork and animations to present it. These assets would be delivered to the programmers, who would implement them into the game, again using the design document as a guide. This same process would be repeated for the musicians and the writers.

With so many moving parts, everything didn't always go as planned and there was constant pressure for producers and designers. Josh says the possibility of layoffs was a constant. "It was normal for every team to be told that if we don't pull this in on schedule and on budget, we're going to have to lay people off. That was always the threat that was hung over us to keep things on track."

Things were almost never on track.

"There was constant juggling of personnel. If things had gone too far off schedule, then the programmer I had working on the game, they might pull him off and say, 'Nope, you gotta work on the next game now.' That would just increase the delay of my game," says Josh.

Eventually, however, a game would be finished and all the stresses forgotten, or at least set aside.

Josh Mandel describes one of his best memories from his time at Sierra. It was at the end of production on *Freddy Pharkas: Frontier Pharmacist*, his first design credit, and he vividly recalls watching the finished product being constructed.

"Watching the boxes of *Freddy Pharkas* coming off the assembly line, filled and shrink-wrapped and put in cases to be sent out. That memory is the one that comes to mind above almost everything else because I wasn't getting enough sleep for the duration of the project or at least the crunch time. I have never felt such a strange and powerful mix of emotions. What a sense of accomplishment and dread that now it was out of our hands. They were going to go out and the first person who bought it was going to get a crash bug that everyone else was going to get. So there was abject horror, there was pride, and sleepiness and confusion. I really cherish the vibrancy of that memory."

Getting a game's direction right was important, and despite some bumps along the way, by the early nineties Sierra had established a winning roadmap for the new era.

Chapter 5: New Technology

Wouldn't it be crazy if we made ourselves game characters? Put ourselves in there and introduce Ken and all that. It fit in with where we were trying to take Roger Wilco in that storyline.

Mark Crowe, Designer, Space Quest

The AGI engine had served Sierra well for fourteen games, but times and technology had progressed, and more was needed. Instead of tweaking the old system, lead programmer Jeff Stephenson developed an entirely new one. Sierra's Creative Interpreter (SCI) was to serve as the basis for the majority of the company's output from 1988 until 1995, going through several major changes over the years.

SCI was built knowing that changes to the way they were making games would be needed. The major difference between AGI and SCI was one the player never saw. The language moved from a procedural one (where every action and response is individually coded) to being object-oriented (a system that allowed for small functions to be repeated over and over, saving space and runtime memory). This huge change allowed for much greater flexibility in scripting and much smaller code. The other major modifications – the kinds players would actually notice – were added support for sound cards, an increase in resolution from AGI's 160x200 to 320x200, and a parser input that was no longer always visible but appeared on the game screen when a word was typed.

Mark Hood, who started with Sierra right around the time the switch was made, explains the rationale behind the move: "The main reasons for the change from AGI to SCI were tech-related. I believe a lot of the programmers had wanted Jeff Stephenson to do an updated AGI, but OOP [object-oriented programming] was big, and in my opinion, perfect for the kind of games we were doing. AGI needed to be completely revamped, and when Jeff did that, he decided to add the OOP language to control it all."

It wasn't an easy transition for most programmers, as Mark explains: "Jeff Stephenson basically wrote the language. It was intended to be used as an object-oriented language but most of the programmers there were used to AGI, very much a procedural language. Jeff really wanted it to be object-oriented, and the guys who had been there forever wanted to use it like a new AGI."

A procedural language is made up of defined procedures within the code that specify all the steps the computer must take to complete the desired function. It is a very rigid structure and any possible actions have to be programmed in individually, making the process of coding a game a massive task.

An object-oriented language like SCI instead focuses on the data and how it interacts with other data, divided into categories called classes. By making SCI object-oriented, classes and objects could be defined and transferred between games and objects. For instance, the ability of a character to move from left to right on a screen would only have to be programmed once as a class and then attached to the objects that needed that functionality (such as characters that needed to move).

Al Lowe used the SCI engine for a lot of his games and became very familiar with the engine and how to use it. "It wasn't a very complicated language, but it was a lot of hard work. For example, we had a list of verbs and that was kept in a file called 'verbs.h,' a header file that . . . contained an ASCII number, a tab, and some letters that described a word. The next line would be number 2, then there would be another word, then line 3 would be a third verb. There might be a comma and another verb. Well, those two words would be synonyms, so if you used 'take' or 'get' that would just be changed by the computer to a number 3 and it would go through the code looking for anything that said, 'If somebody typed in 3 . . .' It was incredibly simple. On the other hand, it took a lot of work to figure out how to do all that. It was nontrivial, but on the other hand you can explain it and it's understandable."

Al laughs when he remembers finally getting rid of his last 5.25-inch disk drive around the turn of the millennium, and deciding to back up all the tools and source code he had kept for years in boxes on his top shelf.

"I copied all those disks that I could to a hard drive. Maybe I could burn a couple of DVDs or something to store this massive box after box of floppies. It turned out that the whole damn thing, ten years of my life, was 35 MB in a zip file. It's amazing. All the source code, all the source drawings, the music, all the sound files, everything, the tools and such. All that stuff was added together as 35 MB."

The parser interface was initially a large part of SCI, and Mark Hood remembers how much work went into making it intuitive. "Pablo Ghenis had just been hired from PARC to help with the natural language parser, but he was a real Smalltalk guy.* I really liked the object-oriented stuff and started to write a bunch of classes, with Pablo's guidance, to help make the game [*Codename: ICEMAN*].

"A lot of the classes ended up being used, so after we finally shipped the game eighteen months later, they made me 'class librarian' to teach new programmers and evangelize the class system we had so everyone didn't need to rewrite everything from scratch on every game."

Corey Cole was also a programmer familiar with object-oriented languages and says he had to create a lot of classes for the *Quest for Glory* series.

"We had to do the same thing, as far as roleplaying, because there was nothing to do with stats or character development or skill checks or all that stuff. SCI was designed as an object-oriented language, so I was able to build that on as a layer of classes that did things. It's amazing we fit all that stuff into 64 K [of] memory. That's all we had to program, 64 K of memory at any given time."

As a programmer himself, Ken Williams would at times look in to see what the programming team was working on, something that caused Corey and the other team members to come up with a system to always show him something new.

"Ken is a win-of-the-day person," Corey explains. "You might not see him in the programming area for a month or two and then you might see him three times in one day. The rule was, you had to have something new and different to show him when he showed up. Even if it was three times in the same day. So you never showed him everything, you only showed him one feature and said, 'This is what I've been doing.' And if he showed up again two hours later you'd say, 'Here's this different feature and here's what I've been doing.' The flipside – the good side for us – is he really did leave us alone to be creative and he trusted us to know what we were talking about and know what we were doing."

---

* An object-oriented programming language developed by Xerox PARC.

A Princess's Quest

The first game to use this new SCI toolset was *King's Quest IV: The Perils of Rosella*. It was the first time Sierra featured a female protagonist and Rosella was one of the first female leads in any computer game. Sierra was again blazing a trail for others to follow.

In 1994, Roberta spoke about how she was initially worried about having a woman star in *King's Quest IV:* "I knew the female lead is just fine for women and girls who play the game, but wasn't sure how it would go over with some of the men. And you know what? It wasn't as controversial as I expected. However, it was real strange at first designing the game; quite a different point of view."[12]

One thing Roberta didn't want was gender being a determining factor in the puzzle solutions. Puzzles in Roberta's games were about problem solving, logic, and thinking of the best – and usually nonviolent – solution. None of these things had anything to do with the character's sex.

Roberta also wanted to enhance her storytelling, and one of the primary things she planned to implement was a sense of urgency for the player. She decided early on that King Graham would have a near-fatal heart attack at the start of the game, and this would be the impetus for Rosella to begin her quest. What she hadn't expected was for word to leak to fans of the series. The rumor was that he died of the heart attack and fans wrote to Roberta and Sierra en masse, trying to get him saved. The plan, though, was never to kill Graham but to tell the story of Rosella saving his life.

That sense of urgency was created by setting the entire game within a very short time span. "I wanted *King's Quest IV* to have some pressure applied to you; a timed game, taking place over a 24-hour period, so you could roam around during the day and eventually it turns to night. I don't remember other games using the same scenes at night; it looked creepy," Roberta said.[13]

As she had done with each previous installment, Roberta once again wanted to improve the narrative by making her characters more believable. The key this time was in the new SCI engine's increased graphics capability. Instead of standardized or similar-looking animations for characters, finally they had the opportunity to give each character their own. As the animators described it, they gave the characters "body language."

As well as the increased resolution, *King's Quest IV* was also the first computer game to use an independent sound card. Knowing that sound was the next big step, Ken Williams had made contact with musical equipment giant Roland at a trade show and arranged a great deal. For Sierra, this meant they had access to Roland's state-of-the-art MT-32 MIDI synthesizer, which had the ability to play up to thirty-two sounds at the same time, a vast step up from the single-noise PC speaker or even the Amiga's sound capabilities, which were much more advanced than what the PC offered.

King's Quest, as Sierra's flagship series, would be the first game to use this technology and Roberta wanted something special, so she looked to Hollywood. William Goldstein, famous for his work in TV and movies such as *Fame, The Miracle Worker* and *Shocker*, was asked to compose a soundtrack for the game and went on to create more than seventy-five pieces for it, including a unique theme song for each of the thirty-five characters.

While Sierra was at the cutting edge of technology and always wanted to innovate, they also believed a lot of their existing customers wouldn't necessarily have the latest hardware. To ensure the game was available to those with older computers, a second version of *King's Quest IV* was developed simultaneously.

While the two versions were almost identical apart from a few cosmetic changes, they were entirely separate projects. The second used Sierra's older AGI toolset, and with the vast differences between the programming languages, that meant an entirely different code base was required.

What Sierra hadn't expected was the extremely poor sales of the AGI version. It seemed PC users were staying with the times more than they realized. The SCI version continued flying off shelves and the AGI version was quietly discontinued.

Sierra released *King's Quest IV: The Perils of Rosella* in October 1988 and it wasn't just an instant hit, it was the company's biggest selling title to date. It showcased to the world that Sierra was still the market leader in computer games and set the standard for the next few years, both within Sierra and among their competitors.

Larry's Back

With the first *Leisure Suit Larry* game eventually becoming a big success for Sierra, Al Lowe started working on the sequel, *Leisure Suit Larry Goes Looking for Love (In Several Wrong Places)*. "I assumed because Larry had finally lost his virginity now that he wasn't just looking to get laid. He was looking for love, so that's where the title came about," Al explains. "The title set the theme for the overall game."

A byproduct of Larry's maturation was that the second game had less emphasis on trying to have sex than the first game had, though sometimes less is more. "I don't think there was that much less sex in that one than the first one. In the first one you could only really get laid at the end of the game. I guess the hooker! You could sleep with the hooker," Al laughs.

The original game was designed so that the player kept moving between areas to progress. Due to disk size limitations, different locations were stored on separate floppy disks. At a time when the majority of computer owners didn't have a hard drive, one complaint that kept coming up was the need to constantly change disks while playing. Al agreed, so for the sequel he intended to design a more linear adventure.

"I decided that *Larry II* would be built in a series of areas that would fit, self-contained, on one disk. That was kind of my limiting factor, so we made the area of Los Angeles small enough to fit on one disk, on the first disk, along with the interpreter and drivers and that stuff. We then made the second area small enough to fit on the second disk, and so forth. I kind of built it like they were beads on a string."

Al designed the game intending that the player couldn't leave an area until they had all the items they required to progress, but a few instances slipped through the cracks and created what today are called dead ends, with the player being unable to go back and correct their mistake, or even being aware they had made one.

"I think the idea of not being able to leave an area until you have everything you need from that area was valid," Al says. "The problem was I made some mistakes. I think you could leave Los Angeles without the sunscreen and then you didn't need it until two disks later, and if you didn't have it you were screwed. That was just sloppy work on my part. I didn't mean to do it that way; that was not intentional, it was just the way it worked out."

Programming *Leisure Suit Larry II* would be a learning process for Al. He'd become adept with Sierra's AGI engine, but all their games were now being made with SCI, something that was a big hurdle for him.

"It was horrible! None of us were great programmers to start with; furthermore, none of us knew anything about object-oriented languages," Al confesses. "What we knew, we had learned from BASIC,

C or Pascal. This was very Smalltalk-like [an object-based computer language] and none of us had ever used that.

"What we were hoping for was a more flexible system, but what we got was a completely new ilk; everything about it was different. We had to think in a different way. We had to send messages back and forth between objects. We'd never had objects; we'd had code, we'd had subroutines. Now we had procedures.

"Not only [had] the terminology changed, but the whole construction of the games, everything changed. It was a bitter pill. I remember questioning Jeff Stephenson's sanity for making such a huge change. That said, he put us in the forefront of software at that point. In that sense it was really tough. It was a brutal change for all of us."

Another major factor in the design of the second *Larry* game was jokes. Al had always had a penchant for running gags and built one into the game in the form of hairdressers – each hairdresser you visit gives Larry a haircut, but when finished he looks the same as when he started.

"Gosh, I love running gags! I've always thought running gags were funny in TV shows and movies and I thought it would be nice to have a running gag of sorts, and that's how I ended up with the various barber shop jokes," Al explains.

Taking inspiration from Mark Crowe's drawing of the Larry character in the first game, Al also decided to poke fun at himself in the process: "Mark drew Larry's head balding, so that's funny, and I'm bald so that's an obvious thing to poke fun [at]."

Al looked at the situations he was placing Larry in and considered the comedy that could come from seemingly normal circumstances.

"All those things came about because I had a natural situation and thought, 'How would a guy get out of this; what would you do?' I always stand in the wrong line; you end up at this airport and you stand in the wrong line and the only correct answer is to get out of line and cheat. There was a lot of talk around that time about airport bombings and sneaking bombs onto planes, so that was in the news and in the zeitgeist, so I kind of threw that all in."

One graphic design decision Al made was to include a moment of actual nudity this time. "I wanted to push the bar a little bit and actually have two pixels of nipples. At the very end of the game when you meet the girl . . . If she was *National Geographic*–style, if you met this native girl nobody could complain. *National Geographic* got away with showing nipples for years! I could get away with that too; that's why I put that towards the very end of the game as well. That was kind of fun," Al laughs.

One addition was a minor character who would go on to become a major player in future games. Polyester Patty, later renamed Passionate Patti, appeared as a blonde pianist in this installment, later to return with dark hair.

Leisure Suit Larry Goes Looking for Love (In Several Wrong Places) was released to positive reviews and had less trouble getting shelf space than its predecessor, going on to surpass 250,000 copies sold.[14] Al went straight to work on what he anticipated to be the final game in his *Larry* trilogy.

Space Rock

Meanwhile, in the same way that *Space Quest II* was put into production, *Space Quest III: The Pirates of Pestulon* was commissioned as soon as the previous game was released. Although this time the Two Guys were given a little more time to get the project together.

Sitting together in their office, Mark Crowe and Scott Murphy were wondering how best to continue the *Space Quest* series. Unlike the end of the first game, where everything was tied together in a neat bow, they had left the end of *Space Quest II* open, with Roger being placed in suspended animation and sent off floating through space in his life-support pod.

They eventually decided on two main themes for *Space Quest III*. Firstly, they wanted the player to feel they were in control. They planned to give Roger a spaceship, so the player should be able to freely travel in it. "There was a desire to make the player feel like they could go anywhere they wanted in their spaceship. To make that possible, we needed to make it so the player could backtrack and go back and forth and visit those places," Mark says.

The other idea was a little crazy: to put themselves, as the Two Guys, into the game. "When the third game came along, I'm sure we were just purely out of ideas," Mark laughs. "Wouldn't it be crazy if we made ourselves game characters? Put ourselves in there and introduce Ken and all that. It fit in with where we were trying to take Roger Wilco in that storyline."

Sierra designers were known for putting puns and jokes about their bosses in their games. Al Lowe had put Ken Williams in his *Leisure Suit Larry* games, and the Two Guys were putting general manager Rick Cavin in a scene in this game, but Ken Williams believed that most of their customers wouldn't understand it.

"I liked it personally, but usually fought it," Ken says. "Some of the things in games were hidden because the teams knew I'd make them remove it. As cool as it was, I just don't like what I call inside humor. They are jokes that only we, and a few fans, would get. Our job was to entertain customers, not to crack each other up. Why would a customer want to pay us to tease each other? I just didn't see why I should take [customers'] money to pay for something that would only benefit us."

Another parody in *Space Quest III* was aimed at computing giant Microsoft and its founder, Bill Gates. In one scene, the Two Guys are being held prisoner by Gates lookalike Elmo Pug at a software development business called ScumSoft, Inc. While for Mark and Scott the joke was always aimed at Microsoft, fans quickly began to believe it was instead aimed at Sierra's main adventure game competitor, Lucasfilm Games. Lucasfilm's adventure game engine, SCUMM, seemed too close to ScumSoft to be a fluke!

"We'd been accused of poking fun at their SCUMM game development system. Calling our company ScumSoft, that really wasn't the intent. We didn't even know their engine was called SCUMM at the time. Just a coincidence," Mark insists, dispelling the myth.

With the series moving from the older AGI toolset to the SCI engine, a new opportunity opened up to really improve the sound quality of the game. Sierra had recently introduced support for Roland's MT-32 MIDI system and composer Mark Seibert started to make full use of it, composing sound effects that helped immerse the player in the game world.

"The early days of *Space Quest III* bring back memories of having to figure it all out, and [being] the first to attempt such a thing," Mark reminisces. "Seeing and hearing a computer game come alive!"

Mark Crowe also remembers being impressed with the new sound capabilities but says he didn't think the MT-32 would sell too well and most customers wouldn't get the full effect of Sierra's efforts. "That was all still brand new to us as well. We were blazing some new trails there. I thought it was neat we were doing the MIDI stuff, but at the same time I didn't really see it catching on, because with the MT-32 box, how many people are actually going to go out and spend that kind of money on game music?

"At the time I guess I kind of wrote it off. It was great for us because we had them sitting on our desks and thought, 'This is cool, but how many people are actually going to get to hear this music?' I probably underestimated how much money people would throw into game audio because it was so new and groundbreaking for the time."

One major advantage of the new MIDI capabilities was the ability to compose a much richer soundtrack, and Ken Williams had met just the man for *Space Quest III*: Bob Siebenberg, drummer for rock band Supertramp.

"Ken ran into Bob Siebenberg at a local restaurant in Oakhurst," John Williams recalls. "It wasn't a business meeting; they just happened to live close by and everyone in town knew who Ken was. Bob invited Ken to visit his home [recording] studio since Ken mentioned we were building one at Sierra, and I actually tagged along.

"Bob had this building on his property that looked kind of like an old barn from the outside, and when I say old, I mean it had old vines growing all over it and looked like it was leaning. Inside, though, it was comfortable with lots of equipment and a big sound board. He had his awards and old posters from tours all hanging on the walls, and the place had a kind of lived-in look that told you he really spent a lot of time there. I remember he had a bumper sticker over a doorway that said, 'Use an accordion, go to jail. It's the law,' which for some reason I found funny as hell."

According to Ken Williams, "One of the coolest things about Sierra was that we achieved an amazing amount of fame, and that anyone would return my phone calls. Even though the industry was tiny at the time, there was an understanding in Hollywood that something big was happening. It was an amazing time. I could call anyone and do any deal. Or so it felt!"

Bob Siebenberg agreed to create a soundtrack for *Space Quest III*, and the process was something that everyone involved enjoyed. John Williams remembers him being down-to-earth and normal, not what was expected of a rock star. "Bob was just a regular guy. That I remember. Very calm and unassuming. At the time, Supertramp was still a big group and *Breakfast in America* was still in heavy rotation on my own turntable, so I thought it was all really cool."

As the designer of the game, Mark Crowe also dealt a lot with Siebenberg and enjoyed working with him: "Yeah, that was a trip. I considered myself a big Supertramp fan. I loved their music. I didn't even know [what] the drummer's name was, let alone that he lived at Oakhurst. . . . It was great to meet with him and go to his studio at his little ranch there and work on the music."

Space Quest III was released in March 1989 and went on to become yet another bestseller for Sierra. While Bob Seidenberg's soundtrack was a highlight for fans and developers alike, he didn't end up composing another one for Sierra. The Two Guys were given a small break after

Space Quest III, working on other projects before Ken asked them to deliver the next game in what was now a Sierra staple.

Meanwhile, Ken realized it was time for something new.

A Hero Arrives

In 1986, Sierra had released *Wrath of Denethenor*, an RPG in the style of the popular *Ultima* series, but it had been a sales disappointment. Yet by 1988 Ken wanted to try again. Sierra owned the adventure game market. Why not the roleplaying market, too?

It wasn't a genre Ken particularly cared for, but he knew RPGs were lucrative and believed that Sierra would be able to develop roleplaying games easily enough with their existing tools. Although the management team had been brainstorming ideas about how to fill the RPG void in their catalog, all Ken really knew was that he wanted something new and exciting. And after the mediocre response to *Wrath of Denethenor*, he wanted a hit.

John Williams was involved in those brainstorming discussions but recalls that at the time there weren't many people in the company who understood the genre: "Ken, I don't think, ever really understood the allure of RPG. I remember a bunch of us sitting down early on to try to play *Dungeons & Dragons* and understand why it was building such a following, and Ken was clearly bored playing."

According to John, Ken's desire to produce another RPG wasn't the only, or biggest, factor in greenlighting *Hero's Quest.** Although Ken was always looking for something new, John believes his main reason for commissioning the Lori and Corey Cole project was that they had a good idea Ken believed would work.

"I think Lori and Corey got a game contract because they had a desire to make an RPG with the Sierra toolset and Ken saw that they had a drive to do something good, something different. Ken contracted the Coles to do a game; he didn't go looking for an RPG game just because he wanted one," John says.

Another of the people involved in the RPG brainstorming sessions was Carolly Hauksdottir, lead animator on *King's Quest IV*. The Coles had met Carolly at a science fiction convention and one night they ended up talking about the RPG situation at Sierra. "Carolly said that Ken was looking for an award-winning, championship-professional

---

* *Hero's Quest* would later be renamed *Quest for Glory*.

dungeon master or something like that. We all kind of laughed about the ridiculousness of that notion," Corey remembers.

"Then I stopped and thought about it. Well, I played in a *Dungeons & Dragons* tournament once that I won. Therefore, I'm a prize-winner. I was a published author because I'd published one scenario through Judges Guild*, so I've got that. Finally, Lori and I created a dungeon and ran it at a Timecon (a *Doctor Who* convention) one time. We're tournament-level dungeon masters because we had dungeon mastered at a tournament. We've got every single one of those points, so [we] must be the [people]."

Corey's first telephone conversation with Ken Williams didn't start well. "We called up Ken and he was like, 'Okay, yeah, Carolly said you'd call.' All with this kind of downer tone to it. 'I've got a whole company and every single person here thinks they should be a game designer. Why are you any better?'" Corey recalls Ken asking him.

Startled by the unexpected turn, Corey started outlining his background and experience, but then he said something that caught Ken's attention: "And I know how to work with programmers because I've been a programmer for ten years."

The mood improved immediately. Ken was a programmer at heart. Hearing that Corey was, too, his interest was piqued and he wanted to know more about what Corey was capable of. "My latest thing was this desktop publishing system I'd developed for the Atari ST," Corey says. "And at that point the whole conversation changed. The temperature on the phone went up five degrees. Ken said, 'Ooh, Atari ST!'"

Ken had recently signed a deal with Atari to convert the Sierra catalog to Atari's home computer system, the Atari ST, but the only programmer they had on staff with any knowledge of that system was Bob Heitman, who was crucial to a lot of other projects at the company. Ken ended up hiring Corey as an Atari ST programmer to fill that void. His wife, Lori, was employed a few months later to design what would soon become *Hero's Quest: So You Want to Be a Hero*.

Corey notes, "That's kind of typical of the whole roller coaster ride of Sierra. You come in there because you want to design roleplaying games but you end up interviewing as a programmer."

---

* The Tower of Indomitable Circumstances was published by Judges Guild, a game and module publisher. It was while Corey was playtesting this scenario at a convention that he first met Lori and invited her to join his game.

Mark Hood had recently been employed as a programmer on the upcoming adventure game by Jim Walls called *Codename: ICEMAN*, and clearly remembers his first interaction with Corey.

"I had been at Sierra for just a couple weeks and was commuting to Oakhurst from my dad's house in Fresno. Up and down Highway 41 in the thick fog. As I was headed home one night, I went from the clear above the fog down into it very suddenly and around a corner at probably 55 miles per hour. The next thing I knew, my Chevrolet S-10 Blazer was spinning around on this small mountain road. When it stopped, I got out and saw what happened. I had hit a deer and its antler was in my radiator, with the bulk of its body jammed into my front left wheel well."

As Mark was telling the story of this encounter to his teammates the following day, Corey leaned over from the next cubicle and asked Mark if he thought the skull was intact. Mark replied that he thought so. "I was creeped out a bit and then I heard him call Lori and tell her, 'One of the new programmers hit a deer last night and he thinks the skull is still intact!'" It turned out that the Coles wanted a skull for their ranch house fence, a common feature in the area. "It's not so strange up there, but I was a city boy still, so it was strange to me!" Mark laughs.

While Corey was working on the Atari ST conversions he'd been hired to do, Lori was busy designing *Hero's Quest*. Serving as producer on the game was Guruka Singh Khalsa, someone who was both a great advocate for the game and also brought an understanding of Sierra's development process and budget requirements.

Guruka's job called for him to work through the design document with Lori, figure out how to accomplish her goals, and try different ways to achieve positive results within the limits of the budget. One instance of this concerned the main protagonist.

In Lori's original design, the player was given a lot more customization options for their Hero than ended up shipping in the final game, such as being able to choose the character's gender. There were also four character classes represented by four different races: a human jack-of-all-trades, a gnome thief, an elven magic user, and a centaur archer.

Guruka quickly realized this would require more work than they would be able to afford, so the Hero was made a human male, and the choices limited to three classes of fighter, magic user and thief. Guruka recalls, "The character types, I wanted to keep very basic because it was [Sierra's] first crossover game between linear adventure games and

RPGs. I said, 'Let's keep this simple because our primary market is going to be adventure gamers.'"

Along with the streamlined character creation, the decision was also made to completely remove a large underground goblin maze from the design, although references to it remain in the original release. Another feature cut from the game was the ability for the magic user to obtain a "familiar," a creature that could be summoned and perform certain special functions for the Hero. This time the issue wasn't the budget so much as programming difficulties. They simply couldn't get the idea to work properly.

Programming on *Hero's Quest* wasn't as straightforward as on a traditional adventure such as *King's Quest*, thanks to variable elements such as player statistics that improved based on how you played, health and stamina points that determined fatigue and death, and the requirement for the Hero to eat every day so he didn't starve to death. A function at the end of the game allowed the player to save their character and export him into future games, something Sierra had never done before.

Complicating matters further, a fully integrated day/night cycle required the artists to create different versions of each external background. Although the original plan was to also include dawn and dusk, this idea was quickly dropped for budgetary reasons.

One key element that remained from Lori's original design was the combat system, an integral part of the RPG side of *Hero's Quest*. Along with combat sequences the player had to beat to progress the story, they could also have random encounters with goblins, brigands, and a wide array of fantasy creatures. While these battles gave the experience a sense of depth and immersion that most adventure games hadn't yet achieved, it did cause programming problems for the team. The plan initially called for battles to occur on the current game screen, but memory restrictions forced them to be moved to a separate scene where more animations could be run.

The biggest challenge with combat, and the puzzles in general, was finding the proper balance, something Corey says was tricky to gauge: "It's interesting, because we felt we were making relatively easy beginner games, but we've gotten a lot of feedback from players saying how hard they were. I guess it's easier to build a puzzle than to solve it while playing. A lot of the adventure game players had trouble with the combat and figuring out, 'Oh, you have to build up your skills to do well.'"

Within a few months, *Hero's Quest* was beginning to take shape. "The bones of the game were built. The rooms were built and the game was designed," according to Guruka. Unexpectedly, however, although development was going well, a problem of another kind popped up internally.

David Slayback had been assigned as lead programmer on the game and was working with programmer Bob Fischbach to get the early parts of the game coded. David and Bob worked well together, but David was becoming increasingly uncomfortable with the subject matter. Unable to reconcile his religious beliefs with a game where the Hero could be a thief, he left the project.

Corey himself was unhappy at Sierra, working in the programming department on the engine rather than on games as he preferred. Rather than let Corey get away, Ken offered him the role formerly occupied by David Slayback working alongside Bob Fischbach. "They didn't want to lose me, and Ken said, 'Hey, we need a lead programmer for *Hero's Quest*; how'd you like to work with Lori and do your own game?' Then they offered me stock options and said, 'We really want you to stay here.'"

Although Corey had been converting SCI games to work on the Atari ST, at this stage he had no experience in programming a game in SCI. Bob Fischbach showed him what they needed to do to continue building the game.

"Bob [Fischbach] was a really good guy. He was an ex-roadie and guitarist who had gone along with all kinds of rock bands and some real famous ones. He had no professional programming training; he was self-taught and had an amazing sense of theater and timing. He was the first one to put puns into *Hero's Quest*. Lori had set up the basic map and so on; Bob started to put together the first room and gave a different pun for every tree in the room. Or some sort of funny message.

"Bob was the one who taught me the ropes of programming SCI, because up to that point I had spent my first eight or nine months working on the interpreter and the engine behind the games, but not working on a game. I knew all the theory and I knew all the instructions but I hadn't actually used them. Bob showed me how you actually put together a game, and I looked at the funny messages and thought, well, we were thinking of this as a pretty serious game but if the art is going to be 16 colors and cartoony to start with, it makes more sense to make this game kind of funny. So I basically picked up with what Bob was doing and made that the game."

Corey continues, "Bob Fischbach was absolutely essential to the feel of all the [*Quest for Glory*] games. Really set the tone. Mind you, for years people called me an incorrigible punster. I had a little button that said 'Incorrigible punster. Do not encourage.' I love making word plays so that was right down my alley. Right in my sweet spot."

Lori and Corey came up with a plan to put as many inside jokes and pop culture references into the game as possible. Their reasoning was that no single player would get every single one, but enough players would get enough of them. "We tried to put them in so they would fit in the game and made sense," Corey says.

One example of adapting their own personal experiences was the Spore-Spitting Spirea plant that became an important puzzle in the game. "We had gone to a science fiction convention in Phoenix, Arizona and they had a fountain that would periodically shoot a jet of water toward another section of the fountain, and that section would shoot a jet of water to the next, and so on. It made it look like a continuous jet, and we thought that was really cool-looking and that's what turned into the Spore-Spitting Spirea," recalls Corey. "I wouldn't have called it that, but Lori happens to know something about plants! So everything in there is just life experiences and just reading a lot of science fiction and fantasy."

Development of *Hero's Quest* wasn't always smooth sailing, with the game actually being in danger of cancelation at one point. Producer Guruka Singh Khalsa remembers being called into a meeting with Ken Williams, where he was told that they were considering pulling the plug.

"It wasn't a pure adventure game; it was an adventure game with RPG elements in it. Character creation and stuff like that. Plus it had a branching plot and the early adventure games had a fixed path. You could do things in a different order but things always happened the same way. You could get stuck very easily, and killed very easily," Guruka says. "Lori and Corey brought a lot of humor to *Hero's Quest*, plus all these RPG elements. Ken said, 'I don't think we should do this because the Sierra brand stands for adventure games and we don't want to get confused with the RPG market.'"

Left to him to make the final decision, Guruka returned to Ken and said they should go ahead with it. "I thought the game was so funny. It kind of broke the mold. I went back to Ken and said, 'We have to do this game.' Everyone was happy and we had the most fun."

Lori claims that another important factor in changing Ken's mind about the game was the opinion of someone very near and dear to Ken and Roberta. "It was Ken's son Chris, who had played a build of it and he also said, like Guruka had, 'I love this game!'"

According to Corey, the success of *Hero's Quest* "was a big surprise to the company. They were expecting to move thirty thousand to fifty thousand copies. They had so many preorders and so many reorders that the moment it hit the shelf, it sold out. They moved one hundred thousand copies in a month, and [those were] *King's Quest* numbers. They didn't expect that."

Sierra now had their fifth major adventure series, and the first that blended elements of another genre into the mix. With *King's Quest, Space Quest, Leisure Suit Larry, Police Quest,* and now *Hero's Quest* all taking advantage of the higher graphic resolution and orchestral sound that the new SCI engine provided, it was time for Sierra to branch out.

Interlude: Music to the Ears

Sierra had an unrivaled ability to produce groundbreaking soundtracks for games during the eighties and nineties. "The level of talent they had within the music department was just unbelievable," says Robert Holmes, composer on the *Gabriel Knight* series. "All of these guys in the music department, they were really, really, really good. There just wasn't a slacker in the entire group."

Being part of such a skilled group of musicians helped bring everybody's work up to a higher standard. "The way Sierra would work was, once a quarter there would be a company meeting and everyone would show off a demo or something that was part of their current project," Robert says. "You knew at some point your music was going to be shown as part of that to the whole company, so you really wanted it to be good."

Music teacher turned game designer Al Lowe agrees, but also claims that there were a lot of other talented musicians at Sierra working in other roles: "I know a lot of not only the programmers that worked at Sierra, but also the artists, played music, and some of the guys quite well. One guy that is now a programmer at Sony, he was a trombone player with Maynard Ferguson[*] in the [eighties]. Toured the country and lived on a bus. Made a living as a professional musician. Several other guys there worked professionally."

It was through these people with musical backgrounds that the connection between soundtrack and game design became evident, something that Al puts down to the similarities between the two disciplines.

"I think there's a strong correlation between studying music and software," he says. "I think part of it is, in both cases you're learning to translate some obscure shorthand or symbols and references into another concept. When you look at notes on paper, they don't look anything like music sounds except when a musician plays them. Then

---

[*] Chris Braymen worked as a programmer and musician for Sierra on titles such as *King's Quest VI*, and *Mixed Up Fairy Tales*.

it's like, 'I see what you did; I see how you did that.' And that's the same way with software. You have the same sort of feeling of, 'Well, wait, what's all this gibberish here? Oh, I see, it does this.'"

Another similarity is the logic behind both programming and music. "Logic, I think, is more important than the math itself in programming," Al suggests. "And, obviously, with advanced math study comes advanced logic. I didn't have strong math skills, but I did have strong logic skills and I think that helped me. My difference was, I had the logic half of my brain, which worked pretty well, but I also had the creative side.

"Playing jazz, you are forced to follow a set of rules that are very strict down to fractions of a second, but then improvise something that goes on top of that, which works with those strict rules. I think all that makes a difference. You have a set of chord changes and the chords may change once per second. Well, you've got to play the notes that are correct for that chord at the right second, because if you're half a second late it sounds terrible.

"But I think that cross between improvisation and strict interpretation came in very handy for me with programming games, and particularly with designing games. Because I could understand the problems the software engine had. I could also think as if I was a movie director and figure out how things should move on-screen and timing of jokes and stuff like that. I think all that made a difference."

Ken Allen, composer on many Sierra titles including *King's Quest V*, *The Colonel's Bequest* and *Space Quest IV*, concurs, adding that "there are studies that suggest studying music will make you a better programmer and make it easier to study a second language. Music is a symbolic language that has conditional branching and many other things in common with computer programming. At the same time, the result is very creative. I think studying music stimulates a certain kind of brain function that people might not otherwise get."

While music was a vital ingredient in games, the composers and musicians usually came on board only toward the end of production. For Ken Allen, "Music is often an afterthought in games, so I've been brought into the project late in the process. I have heard of some games where the music was chosen at the beginning and the game was designed around that, but those tend to be games out of Japan."

At Sierra, once a composer had been assigned, they would meet with the designer to get a feel for the project and what the designer had in mind for the score.

Mark Seibert was the company's first staff musician and ran the music department before becoming a producer in later years. It was a far cry from his previous gig with Christian rock band Omega Sunrise.

"I was a touring musician and had been on the road for about three years pretty much nonstop. The record label for the band I was touring with had just gone under and I was looking at what's next. My dad called me and told me I should apply for the music job at a game company that he saw in the paper. I didn't want to do that, as my understanding of games at the time was 'beep, beep, boop, boop.' But he kept after me 'til I finally sent in a tape and resume. I didn't even follow up on it, thinking that would be the end of that, and I started working at the local studio writing jingles and as a studio musician," Mark recalls.

It was a few months later that Mark heard from Sierra about the position of staff musician. "I got a call from Sierra, which I had completely forgotten about, to come for an interview. So I went because I had sent the resume, but I didn't expect much. Wow – was I wrong. They totally blew me away with a soundtrack being written by William Goldstein, and some really cool story called *King's Quest*. It immediately clicked with me that this was something completely new. I was hooked!"

Mark's first assignment was working on *King's Quest IV: The Perils of Rosella*, the first Sierra game to utilize specialized sound cards. When he started working, he realized there was no design format for building a game soundtrack, so developing a system was an early priority.

"Since we were making adventure games, I approached it like scoring a movie. Yes, of course the order in which things happen might be different, and the lengths of each scene might change (or even some of the story elements might be slightly different), but in general we could break it down into a series of events like a story or a movie. So that's where I started with the designers," he says. "Creating this framework helped us understand the big story arcs, and I think it also helped our designers to see their design in a new and different way."

Ken Allen explains that along with understanding the story arc, the composer also needed to intuit what the designer felt the music should be: "I talked with the designers to get a feel for the musical style they imagined, and to see if they had any preconceived ideas for the music in cutscenes, or if they wanted characters to each have a theme. I was looking for the psychology everywhere music is needed."

When the basic outline was in place, the composer would begin listing themes they would be required to create. As Mark explains, "Once we had the framework, then we started talking about the important scenes or moments that the player might experience and how we wanted the soundtrack to support the emotional content we hoped to evoke. From there, we started creating a list of themes that would need to be written, and then from those themes [we created] a list of scene-specific cues that would be written based on those themes. This is the time where we would also begin to develop the sound effects lists and ambient sounds lists."

While working through the game design document looking for the musical cues required – a process called spotting – the composer would also listen to music the designer liked or felt was similar to what they envisioned for a particular scene. This helped clarify for the composer what the designer wanted and why they felt a particular style of music would be appropriate.

Using the information gathered from this spotting process, the composer would then start to develop concept pieces. While sometimes they might have the luxury of a fully designed game with a script for inspiration, their references were usually just sketches, storyboards or scene descriptions.

Ken Allen says he would work on proof-of-concept pieces to make sure everyone was on the same page, while also choosing instrumentation based on emotions the designer wanted to elicit: "If we decided on a certain musical style, the instruments I selected would support that decision."

It was after working at Sierra for about a year that Mark Seibert realized the company needed a specialized team to help produce the music and sound effects required: "As we started building product that first year, it became clear that we needed not only music composed for the product, but we [also] needed composers that understood the very special and specific way in which we needed the music and sound to be developed. This pushed us toward more in-house development, which meant that I needed to hire some other staff musicians.

"As I started doing that, and helping the new hires to work with each individual team, I think management wanted to have a central point for that part of development. Being the music director for the company was not something I sought out, but I think was something that happened [because] I held most of the learned knowledge of how to make everything work. In some ways, I didn't really want that position, as it took me away from composing to do more management, but I was a team player and wanted to do what I could to help. And as I got more into the management part of development, I learned that it could be a very creative and fun experience as well."

One of the new musicians Mark hired was Robert Holmes, who describes a more unique way of composing the soundtrack for the first *Gabriel Knight* game. Robert had become romantically involved with designer Jane Jensen prior to working together on the project. Together, Robert and Jane would take daily walks around Bass Lake in Sierra National Forest and talk about ideas and how Jane envisioned her supernatural series.

"We both watched movies together and talked about various influences, so I had a pretty good sense of what she was attracted to and what she was trying to achieve. And I brought my film music education to the problem and thought about what some of the guys I respected in the film world would do," Robert says. "I think what I was trying to do was make music that was darker, more dramatic, and a little more emotional than had been done in games."

In 2014, Robert Holmes had the opportunity to return to his original *Gabriel Knight: Sins of the Fathers* soundtrack for the *20th Anniversary Edition* remake: "There were parts of it that I still like, and actually it was really interesting to listen to. I hadn't heard some of it in quite a while. I was actually really pleased with some of it and thought, 'Gee, if I had to play that right now, I wouldn't know how to play it.'"

MIDI Music

Composing music for Sierra's early games required a different process for each platform.

Music in games today is generally composed in a similar way to how a band would record a song for an album: the instruments and vocals are recorded on separate tracks that are then mixed together, or layered over each other, to form a complete track. Turn back the clock to the eighties, however, and the situation was vastly different.

Back then, Sierra published its games in a wide variety of formats, the most common being the IBM PC, the Tandy 1000, and the Apple IIGS. As each system had its own technology that wasn't compatible with the others, every game soundtrack had to be recreated for each.

The PC speaker in most IBM-compatible computers was only capable of playing a single beep that could be made to approximate different musical notes, as well as only playing a single track at a time. The Tandy 1000 copied the improvements IBM had developed in their short-lived PCjr by allowing three tracks to be played at once, although these were still system-generated tones. The Apple IIGS was arguably the most advanced of the three systems, as it allowed for digital sampling of sounds to be recorded and played back. This let the composer sample real instruments and compile those samples to make a more layered and realistic-sounding score.

By the mid-eighties, sound technology had further developed with the advent of MIDI (Musical Instrument Digital Interface), which enabled a composer to store commands in a very small file format. These weren't music files like an MP3, but rather a collection of commands that directed a computer's sound card to play a certain sound at a certain speed for a specified amount of time. The most common MIDI cards at the time were the AdLib and later the Sound Blaster.

In his first role at Sierra, Robert Holmes was tasked with converting other composers' soundtracks to different platforms, which helped him learn to use the technology. "While I had had some exposure to MIDI, I really wasn't a keyboard player and I really wasn't well-versed in MIDI," Robert admits. "It took a while for me to really get into that. I never really got to the same level as some of the other guys who were really amazing MIDI composers. It was a good education."

Mark Siebert remembers a gentler learning curve, as he had done some MIDI work previously: "I started working with MIDI in the early eighties as a songwriter and guitar player for a touring band. I think our band was one of the few at that time that was touring with tightly integrated computer-controlled music mixed with live instruments. It was a time when sequencing was done on special devices created by companies like JLCooper, and learning how to make everything work was a lot of trial and error. So going through the early days of programming for a live touring band gave me a lot of experience and confidence to start hacking around on the new hardware we got at Sierra."

Mark goes on to say, "At Sierra I was able to make connections with third-party software developers that helped us build editors for the devices to create new and different sounds. The sound staff at Sierra was very supportive with in-house tools that allowed us to translate that work into a format that was usable in-game."

The biggest advance in MIDI for Sierra came with the release of the Roland MT-32 Sound Module, a hardware peripheral that generated ten MIDI tracks simultaneously. Sierra supported this module, which they believed offered the best listening experience for their games, selling it through their mail-order system with an incentive offer of two free games.

As Mark Seibert remembers it, "We did have a relationship with Roland, but they pretty much created the devices and gave them to us. There was very little additional support from them. That is why I had to develop relationships with other third-party developers to create the editing tools we needed. I think Roland was focused on their business of selling musical devices."

Working with Roland did have some extra benefits for the music department, though, says Mark. "Most of us musicians at Sierra took advantage of being able to purchase their gear at cost during this time. I still have a rack full of old Roland gear in my studio from back then!"

While Ken Williams was a strong advocate for the Roland MT-32, the cost of the device (over $500) was a concern for some of the staff, as Sierra's first producer, Guruka Singh Khalsa, recalls.

"I remember Ken being so excited about the Roland because MIDI was so compact. It didn't take any space on disk to do MIDI code, and the sounds were generated by the Roland box. I said to him, 'People aren't going to spend several hundred dollars on a MIDI box,' and he said, 'We'll include it with every game!'" Ken wasn't serious, of course, but the conversation does show the importance Sierra placed on their music.

On *Quest for Glory II*, Mark collaborated with the programmers to further enhance the music as part of the game. "I recall working with [systems programmer] Stuart Goldstein to create a way for the music to drive animation. We had a scene in the game where a character was supposed to dance to the music. In order to get the animation to move correctly, we built a way for the music to trigger the next frame of animation. By embedding the triggers, I was able to make the character move to the beat of the music."

As technology advanced to the point where realistic sounds could be produced, sound effects also became a major focus, both for Sierra's music team and for the industry as a whole. According to Mark Siebert, "For *Space Quest III*, I started playing around with creating non-musical content by programming new sounds into the devices: wind blowing, atmospheric sounds, sound effects like explosions, laser fire, and the jello gun. I think that was a big change in things for the game industry. Once we opened that can, everything changed. I remember the sounds I had created showing up in other games from other companies. I used to always put my initials on the sounds like 'Wind MS,' or 'Explode MS.' It was amusing to then see those show up in LucasArts games, as well as others."

Chapter 6: Trying (Mostly) New Things

*I always like to look and see what people aren't doing, what
needs to be done to be different, unique, plus areas that people
obviously have an interest in.*

Roberta Williams, Designer, The Colonel's Bequest

Hero's Quest was a first bold step into new franchises, and it was a highly successful one, but by 1989 Ken and Roberta both wanted more. Roberta was growing tired of *King's Quest* and sought to try her hand at a murder mystery, something she had last attempted with her debut *Mystery House* eight years prior.

Ken, also looking for new potential franchises, recruited Jim Walls, who had successfully delivered two *Police Quest* games by then, to design a spy thriller in the vein of James Bond. At the same time, husband and wife team Christy Marx and Peter Ledger were commissioned to create a game based on the King Arthur mythology. Adding these to their plans for existing series sequels, Sierra certainly had a full production schedule to close out the 1980s.

Mystery!

After *King's Quest IV*, Roberta wanted a change of pace. *King's Quest* wasn't the only game – or indeed even style of game – she had made, but it was what most people knew her for. Roberta wanted to work on something different and the thought of returning to the murder mystery genre appealed to her. Murder mysteries were popular in other mediums, and Ken and Roberta liked to find niches that hadn't been explored much and make games that suited them.

"I thought it was time," Roberta claimed in a 1989 interview for *Sierra News Magazine*, the company's in-house publication. "Not just our company, but other companies in our industry are concentrating so much on fantasy stories, fairy tales, dungeons and dragons. Games now are very fantasy oriented, even a lot of science fiction . . . I always like to look and see what people aren't doing, what needs to be done to be different, unique, plus areas that people obviously have an interest in, and murder mysteries, in my opinion, are very popular. If you go into a book store, you see more mystery books on a shelf than you do science fiction."[15]

It had been nearly ten years since she had created *Mystery House*, her last whodunit, and Roberta knew she could radically improve on the formula with the technology available to her now.

Two elements of *King's Quest IV* had stuck with her: a female protagonist and the use of night scenes. Both would be integral ingredients in *The Colonel's Bequest*. This time, though, instead of the usual epic quest of Sierra's adventure games, the experience would be about character development, listening to people, and asking the right questions to obtain clues throughout an in-depth story.

Unique to *The Colonel's Bequest* was its narrative progression accomplished by triggering key scenes, which in turn changed the direction of the game. During the course of events, the other guests would make plans to meet at certain times. This allowed the player to follow them and advance the story, usually when one of those other guests was killed.

"*Colonel's Bequest* is more like a story than a quest, you want to get to the end, and find out the truth," Roberta said in 1989.[16]

The heroine of this adventure was twenty-year-old Laura Bow – a play on the name of 1920s silent film actress Clara Bow – who, at the invitation of a close friend, attends a family gathering where the elderly Colonel Dijon tells those present that he is leaving his vast wealth to all of them, divided equally.* Of course, if any of the guests die before the Colonel does, their share of the inheritance will go back into the pool.

Ken Allen started his game development career at Sierra, and the first two projects he worked on were *Fire Hawk: Thexder – The Second Contact* and *The Colonel's Bequest*. Initially, though, Ken had left school with very different intentions.

"I had gone to college to learn how to be a music teacher," Ken says. "After I got out of college, I took the first educational position that was open and it was at a private school. I had been hired to build their music program but after I got hired, they said, 'We need a math teacher; you're going to teach math and not music.' This was a private school; there was no contract, no union, so I tried my hand at teaching non-

---

* Colonel Dijon's name is another play on words, this time parodying Colonel Mustard from the famous board game Clue / Cluedo.

music topics and I was really bad at it. After the first semester I said to them that I wasn't their guy and I was going to go ahead and leave."

Taking any work he could get, Ken worked at the United States Postal Service for a couple of years and it was there that he saw a job advertised in the local newspaper that appeared perfect for him.

"When I saw the want ad, I had no idea it was Sierra; they didn't have the name of the company on there. The ad said 'Needed: musicians for video games' and I thought, well, that's probably not a real job, and if it is it's probably part-time or temporary or something like that. There's no way that a game company is going to put a want ad in the *Fresno Bee* but on a lark, I'll try it," Ken laughs.

He soon received a surprising call from Sierra, during which he was told that they were impressed with his resume and the sample cassette tape he had submitted, and wanted him to come to Oakhurst for an interview.

Ken felt that the interview went well, and only a week later he received the call offering him a job starting on April 7, 1989.

"I met with Stuart Goldstein and Mark Seibert, and later on with Guruka [Singh Khalsa] and finally Rick Cavin. When I interviewed, I said, 'I [am] willing to come in at a lower salary than what I'm currently making because I want to give you a chance to test-drive my contribution to the company. After ninety days, if you're happy with me, let's move my salary back up to what you have in the budget.' Rick Cavin said, 'Okay, we'll do that,' but I didn't get it in writing," Ken remembers. His salary wasn't raised.

Still, for Ken the job was "a dream come true. My hobby at the time was writing games in BASIC, then my training was in music, so I thought, I get to marry my two favorite things together into a career, music for video games. For the longest time I was very, very happy!"

Ken Allen's first full soundtrack for Sierra was for *The Colonel's Bequest*, and he has nothing but good memories of dealing with Roberta Williams on that and subsequent games.

"Roberta is an absolute delight to work with. For somebody who is a celebrity, she was not pretentious, and I really loved working with her. We just hit it off. She was not demanding, and she certainly could have been because she was the co-founder of the company. She was just a joy to work with."

Roberta wrote the game and shared the directing duties with Chris Iden, who also helped program the game alongside Chris Hoyt. Douglas Herring and Jerry Moore were responsible for the art, while Ken composed the entire soundtrack and sound effects. *The Colonel's Bequest* was in development for nine months, and would be one of the last games Roberta worked on with such a small team.

The game released in 1989 to strong reviews, and Roberta was again master of the murder mystery as well as fairy tales.

Secret Agents, Submarines and Tropical Islands

Another niche Ken Williams wanted to exploit was the spy thriller. James Bond was eternally popular, and when actor Timothy Dalton took over the movie role in 1987, increased hype about the new 007 made Ken realize that this genre was something people loved. Of course, he required a designer.

Jim Walls, in need of a new project after shipping *Police Quest 2*, seemed the right fit. Production on the game had gone relatively smoothly and resulted in another bestseller for Sierra, so Jim expected to be asked to make *Police Quest 3*, but instead Ken wanted him to make a spy thriller.

Jim designed a story that took place during a time of a future global oil shortage, when tensions between the United States and Soviet Union were high. Johnny Westland, a naval officer, is called into action to track down an American ambassador who was kidnapped by the Soviets, along with an agent Johnny had enjoyed a brief love affair with. It was vintage eighties spy fiction.

Jim approached *Codename: ICEMAN* the same way he had his *Police Quest* games, working procedures and protocol into the game design. He wrote the story out and created a basic outline of the game in the design document. This was common in the early days at Sierra, and Jim enjoyed working closely with the programmers and artists to collaboratively put the meat on the outline's bones.

This casual relationship between designer and producer contributed to some big hits for Sierra, but it also caused some problems, as Guruka Singh Khalsa claims happened with this project: "*ICEMAN* was the worst designed game ever. In fact, the rooms didn't make any sense. If you actually mapped out the rooms, there was no way to get from one to another. And it had all kinds of graphical bugs and logic bugs in it."

Josh Mandel says it was simply a symptom of the company's design philosophy at the time. "A designer would get a game and then they would go off and do their own thing. Nobody really checked it over. Nobody said, 'Here's the flaws in your design, here are your dead ends' and so on."

Newly hired programmer Mark Hood wasn't aware of this relationship between designer and production team, so after completing everything in Jim's design document, he went ahead and spent a lot of time designing unique but nonessential features for the game.

"I mostly felt I had time to do this because Jim had only a basic rough outline of a game," Mark recalls. "What most of Jim's game programmers did back then was make the game with him as they went. I basically did what was in the design and created a system for doing the stuff we needed to do within the object-oriented system."

Mark was able to implement several features that were distinctive to *Codename: ICEMAN*, although they were adopted into other games later. One of the more unique ideas was called "sorted features," although it did cause problems.

"Sorted features was an innovation that just didn't work as intended with the design," Mark admits. "In all the games before *ICEMAN*, if you typed 'look' it would say either the same response no matter what you were looking at, or would ask you what you were looking at. We sorted every 'feature' in the room based on which way your character was pointed, and how far away things were. So if you were pointed at a door and typed 'open,' the door would open after the game walked you over there, but if you were standing near a chest and typed 'open,' it knew you meant the chest and would open it. It sounded great technically, but no one knew how to write or design for that, so it was a lot of useless tech."

Another feature was the introduction of eight directions for the main character to walk in, instead of four, with the character "gradually [changing] between them instead of [instantly changing] in one cycle to the new direction, like all previous games. That was my 'gradual looper' class, called 'grooper,'" Mark explains. "There was an animation to change directions while scuba diving too; that was a class called 'smooth looper' or 'smooper.' Those classes became part of the [SCI] system. Jim hated them. It was just code, maybe a couple weeks. Fun to code and I worked with [artist] Cheryl Loyd to get the art needed for them." This movement system became standard in later Sierra games.

The biggest new gameplay element of *Codename: ICEMAN* was the nuclear-powered submarine simulator. Although originally conceived as a more traditional adventure game puzzle, what was created instead was more of a sim that proved extremely difficult for players to use.

"We basically built the sim based on what we all thought [Jim] wanted," Mark explains, "before there was really any design. Then after the sim was basically built in code and art, we got the design of what things he wanted to see happen. You could steer that sub up and down and all around and it was pretty fun as a pure sim.

"He stated the things that would happen, like an adventure game. But in a sim, people could do what they wanted to some extent. So it ended up being a strange hybrid of the artists and [me] trying to make a sim first, then trying to shoehorn in all the events that he listed in the design."

Mark notes that one of the obstacles players would come across in the submarine sequences were icebergs: "[Jim] listed out all the things that happened and where the icebergs appeared from, but it was coded as a sim! You could go on either side [around the icebergs], but that wasn't what he wanted, so we threw up iceberg sprites the way he wanted them to show up no matter what you did with the controls, right or left. We used to joke that it was like [the Autopia race car track] at Disneyland, a real car (sub) that was on rails. So you could turn the steering wheel and make [the submarine] go up and down, but it would only do what the design said it should do."

Another element that Mark put too much effort into, in retrospect, was a sequence at the start of the game where Johnny dances in the bar. "The dancing was also driven by algorithms instead of just pure scripted scenes, so again, we tried to shoehorn in a design *after* we built a 'dancing sim.' No one really liked or appreciated it that way and it didn't really add anything to the game in hindsight."

Codename: ICEMAN fell behind in production and Mark Hood believes that these features were among the main culprits. "[The submarine] and the dancing room at the beginning held the game up. Basically we had very little memory to work with back then, and I actually had to end up stripping out all the debugger code in order to get it to fit in memory without the dreaded 'out of heap space' message.

"I added some debugging code that took up a lot less memory, little print messages like 'got here' with some info on how the code got to where it was. Most of that was removed, of course, before shipping, but I think some of it didn't get removed."

The game was released in November 1989 but failed to make a great impression on the game-buying public. Although Jim had started working on a sequel, *Codename: PHOENIX*, poorer-than-expected sales led to the game being abandoned. The major feedback was that although people enjoyed *ICEMAN*'s story, the submarine portion was unplayable by a lot of people due to computer speed issues.

"That submarine was a class that had all kinds of properties that we could tune and refine to make the performance appropriate for the machine you were on, but machines instantly got like ten times faster the next year, and the code didn't really adjust things the way it should have, so it was hard to control on anything other than the 386-type machines we built it on," Mark reveals. "Had we known up front what [Jim's] design was, we'd have never built it as a sim, even though that's what he had always referred to it as. We'd have just made it like most adventure games, where you clicked on a choice of options at each point and [the game] determined the outcome for you."

Mark chalks this up to "my naïveté about how adventure game development worked as a team all working together to make the game work well. Jim made some great games with teams that understood this. I, far too much in hindsight, was interested in the tech and really just tried to read a design and implement it."

The Holy Grail

Codename: ICEMAN wasn't the only new property being developed at the time, with accomplished writer Christy Marx and her husband, award-winning artist Peter Ledger, also working on their first game, Conquests of Camelot: The Search for the Grail.

"Peter and I were living up in the high desert in the San Gabriel mountains near a small ski resort town called Wrightwood," Christy remembers. "We'd been hit hard by a WGA [Writers Guild of America] strike that kept me from doing WGA writing. At the same time, the animation work and comics work had dried up. Out of the blue, I answered a phone call from a recruiter that Sierra On-Line had hired to find artists who would be willing to move to Oakhurst to work for them. Somehow they found out about Peter. Having listened to their pitch, I asked whether Sierra was also looking for writers. The idea of a writer/artist team appealed to them, so they invited us up to meet with them.

"We had one meeting with Ken and Roberta. By the end of that meeting, we agreed to move to Oakhurst and work for them. On our side, we had nothing to lose, and I've always been eager to move into and learn new fields of storytelling. This felt like an amazing opportunity that came along at precisely the right moment."

Adventure games start with an idea. Sometimes that idea came from the designer, sometimes it came from elsewhere. For Christy, the idea for both of her *Conquests* games came from meetings with Ken and Roberta Williams.

"During that meeting, we discussed what sort of games we might do," Christy says. "Because of my background working in TV, animation and comics, I was sensitive to who would own the intellectual property. Ken and Roberta were definite about owning it, so I indicated that we wouldn't be willing to create something new unless we had some ownership.

"I believe it was Roberta who said they'd been thinking about a King Arthur game. I quickly said that we'd be happy to do that type of game, and we agreed upon that." Ownership of the games would stay with Sierra, and there were no complications over character rights for a product based on the myths of King Arthur.

"Moving to Oakhurst was little different from where we were living. Both were small mountain towns at high elevation in a gorgeous environment. In fact, Oakhurst was significantly bigger than Wrightwood, so we had more amenities than before. We were private people and kept to ourselves, but one of the nice things about small towns like that is getting to know the people at the local stores, bank, etc. We especially liked getting to know Rusty, who ran the tiny local movie theater. He was an interesting character."

Producers like Guruka Singh Khalsa were deeply involved in the early stages of game design at Sierra. He has vivid memories of working with Christy Marx on *Conquests of Camelot.*

"Sitting on the grass. Outside. Under a tree. Christy and I with a legal pad and pen. Sketching stuff out. Talking about puzzle logic and getting really excited about twists we could make in the puzzles. Mapping out the sequence of the character arc in the game and sparking each other creatively. It was very informal," Guruka says. "That was before we did formal storyboards up on the wall. It was the creative game ideas in the early stages where we would answer questions like, 'How can we make this game more fun?' 'How can we make the puzzles more fun?'"

Guruka also remembers how quickly Christy came to understand game design in comparison to her television work. "Christy was totally a story person. New to puzzle design but got it right away and really enjoyed doing it."

According to Christy, "When I first got there, everything was open and free and the creativity flowed. We had a good time making games. We had fun. Nobody knew entirely what they were doing because games were so new, so we got to experiment."

Christy says there was one particular event that made her realize how different the two mediums were: "They're massively different, one being linear and one being nonlinear. With a TV script, the writer is in control and making the story decisions. In nonlinear storytelling, you need to find a way for the player to make the decisions.

"Naturally, I did my research. I played through all the existing Sierra games, studied how they worked, read the design outlines from the other designers, and did my best to understand what a typical gamer's mindset was. As I began work on *Camelot*, some people at Sierra told me I was still being too linear. I didn't think I was, but I didn't truly understand what they were trying to tell me until about halfway through the project. We had the first half of the game working and took it to a small local convention down in Fresno where we let people bash away at it. Watching the totally chaotic way people would play the games, with no logic, no strategy, was what opened my eyes. I had to be prepared for players to do anything in any order and set aside any preconceived notions of what people would do."

The artwork in *Conquests of Camelot* was also unique and highly detailed, something Guruka credits to Peter Ledger: "What I remember about Peter was, at that time we only had a palette of 16 colors. Peter wouldn't work in 16 colors; he said, 'I'm an artist. I can't do art like this.'

"The way I got Peter to do the game — besides the fact he dearly loved Christy, and Christy and I were having so much fun designing the game — he asked if he could put all kinds of ancient druidic iconology in the game. Lots of phallic mushrooms, things like that. I said, 'You can put whatever you want in the game.' So then he got excited about [it], and [had] a lot of fun putting secret Easter egg artwork in.

"Peter was purely an artist. [He and Christy] had a very passionate relationship and the energy of their creative teamwork made that game really unique."

When *Conquests of Camelot* was finished but not yet released, Guruka and a few team members took it to a convention and showcased the game privately to some of the people from their major adventure gaming opposition, Lucasfilm Games.

"We went to GDC [the Game Developers' Conference] in San Jose, and I remember sitting in a room, and we hadn't shown off certain things in *Camelot* yet because the game hadn't been released. And we had a sort of competition night where we each showed off our coolest stuff to the Lucasfilm guys; we showed off the dancing girls with the veils from [*Quest for Glory II*] and stuff like that. Then about two weeks later I got a call from Lucasfilm asking, 'Can you come out here for an interview?' So there was a big rivalry between Sierra and Lucasfilm," Guruka laughs.

Upon release, *Conquests of Camelot* was a big hit for Sierra, and Christy and Peter were asked to work on the follow-up, *Conquests of the Longbow*.

"That game won an award the year it came out," Guruka says. "There were just brilliant people on that game. Christy's brilliant."

The Final Larry

Meanwhile, Al Lowe was given the chance to finish off his planned *Leisure Suit Larry* trilogy. After the titular character lost his virginity in the first game, then found what ended up being a short-term love interest in the second, Al decided to finish up the story of Larry Laffer by having him find true love and settle down.

"I didn't know of any other series of books or games or movies that had gone more than three. I thought that three was kind of the balance, the tradition. So I needed to end this somehow, tie it up somehow with a ribbon, put a bow on top of it. So that's what I did. I had him find true love and get a house on a lake," Al says.

By *Leisure Suit Larry III: Passionate Patti in Pursuit of the Pulsating Pectorals*, the production team had expanded to include an internal quality assurance (QA) team. Robin Bradley was the head of QA for *Leisure Suit Larry III* and remembers it being an enjoyable and collaborative experience.

"Sierra hadn't peaked yet and teams were small. Al would toss parts at me to test as he was developing them. It was a more cohesive experience and much more intimate [than Al's later work]. Though the projects were always storyboarded, there was always room for improvisation when working with Al," Robin explains. "I am most proud of the work I did on *King's Quest VI* but I had the most fun when working with Al Lowe. I just want to add that I never 'worked' a day in my life when I was working with Al Lowe!"

Al's early career working with teenagers had taught him the importance of building a cohesive team. "I was a high school music teacher and collaboration is part of that game," he recalls. "You've got to have the kids on your side and you've got to build the team. That was just the way I always operated. It wasn't a strange thing."

His convictions served him just as well at Sierra. "I remember we had meetings; the rule was that anything that anyone came up with that made everybody else laugh, we had to figure out a way to put it into the game."

Regardless of where a joke came from, Al tried to incorporate it. Al Eufrasio later worked as an animator on the final *Leisure Suit Larry* game and says that this collaborative attitude lasted all the way through the series: "Al Lowe's philosophy was always: you don't cut funny. If something's funny, you try to include it."

Carlos Escobar was soon added as a programmer on the project, working at Al Lowe's home in Fresno a lot of the time. Al had designed and programmed the first two *Larry* titles from home, only going into the Sierra studio periodically to check on the progress of the games. But *Leisure Suit Larry III* would need a larger team, and space was at a premium in Oakhurst with the company now renting multiple buildings to house their staff. Ken Williams made the decision to open an office near the Fresno airport for Al and Carlos, along with art director Bill Skirvin and QA lead Robin Bradley.

Working at the Fresno office was a productive and fun time for Al, and he recalls setting up the new place to make life easier for them. "I remember that airport office was interesting because we tried to establish a network. This was before you could just go out and buy a network card, an ethernet [cord] and router and all that stuff. It was really highly technical and esoteric back then.

"Carlos and I found a program that would allow us to copy things from one computer to another via a parallel port, so we bought all these DB25 parallel printer cables and we plugged them into a printer switch box.

"We would copy files at the end of the day. We'd say to each other, 'What did you work on today? Did you change this? Did you change that? Well, shoot those over to me.' Then I would shoot them back and somebody actually had to turn the knob that said 'connect this wire to that wire' and copy these. Isn't that weird when you think about it? That's so primitive." Still, Al says, "We were happy, because before that we would have to copy it to a floppy [disk] and pass it around."

One of the joys of working in Fresno was Carlos's keen sense of wit. Always known to have a quip or droll remark for any situation, he would keep spirits up with comments like, "As long as your code has lots of white space and comments, who cares if it works," "When I say 'we' I'm really talking about you," and "That's *an* idea!"

Fellow programmer Robert Lindsley created a program called "Carlos Says" later on that a lot of people in the company would run at start-up on their computer, something that Al remembers fondly.

"Carlos made me laugh out loud at something he said, something clever and creative, all the time. He really contributed much of the silliness in the *Larry* games."

Programming on *Leisure Suit Larry III* was more difficult than its predecessor because of two design features Al included in the game. The first was the bamboo maze, a labyrinth that seemed massive but in fact was far less so. "It was one scene. We had the ability to reverse background scenes on the fly and we had the ability to reverse views, but they were actually cels of animations, or we could reverse a loop of animation," Al explains.

"I remember I was on an airplane flying someplace and I thought, 'How can I do a maze?' I hadn't done a maze in a game before; how can I do a maze and have it not take up sixty-four rooms/scenes on the disk? It would take ages to load and you had to worry about that stuff back then because that was seconds of time. People will put up with one room change for five seconds if you're in there for five minutes, but if you're in there for five seconds you don't want to be waiting for five seconds for the next one."

Art director Bill Skirvin and Al arranged for the scene to use differing cels of animation to block entrances and exits, depending on where the player was. "Bill and I designed a scene that had an asymmetrical pathway, lower left to upper right. We realized we could block that with various cels of overlay on top of it. We could have two, three or four exits," Al explains.

It was the programming on that scene that Al was most proud of, eager to share the technicalities of how he accomplished it: "Picture an array of bits. The scene number of the maze, if it was a chess board the upper left square would be 1 and the lower right would be 64. You would move over one bit into that array of bits and that would tell you if it was on, [to] use the reversed image. If it was off, that would tell you to use the normal image. Then there was an array of 64 bits for the left wall and an array of 64 bits for the right wall and so forth for the north and south. So the whole thing fit into 40 bytes of storage."

It was an impressive piece of programming, as disk space was crucial at the time.

Another idea Al had was easier to program but much more noticeable to the player. Knowing that Larry and Patti would get together after a hot night together, Al threw in a twist. As Patti is drifting off to sleep, she murmurs the name 'Arnold.' Larry is devastated – so much so that he decides to swear off women forever, gets dressed and walks out of the room. Instead of following Larry, the game instead stays with Patti, who wakes up and sees him missing. From this point on the player controls Patti, who makes it her mission to find Larry!

"I was kind of proud of that. It's a weird scene when you stop and think about it, because in the middle of the game the character you've been controlling gets up and walks off the screen and you're left in the scene without the guy you've been driving for two and a half games. I thought it was a real attention grabber," Al boasts. "Players have told me they thought, 'What the hell happened?' That was exactly what I was going for!"

Larry III's ending was also unique in that it didn't just break the fourth wall, it completely destroyed it. Clearly thinking this was definitely the final *Larry* game, Al finished by bringing Larry and Patti to Oakhurst, California and giving them jobs at a very familiar company.

With the two of them happily ensconced at Sierra, Larry works as a programmer and is tasked with writing a game based on his exploits. One of the final things Larry says in the game is that the story would best start outside a bar called Lefty's, a clear allusion to the beginning of *Leisure Suit Larry I*. Al even added a subtle joke in a nice nod to wrapping up the trilogy, revealing, "The graphics that are on the screen that's he's typing are a screen grab of the original source code for *Larry I*. How's that for esoteric!"

Chapter 7: A New Creative Direction

*Ken said, 'I want you to turn us into the Disney
of computer games.'*

Bill Davis, Creative Director

The early nineties were a golden period for Sierra. The company had gone public by then and raised much-needed capital. It was also a time when the creative juices of the artists were really flowing, and with the help of some key people, they turned creativity into a production line of successful games.

In Sierra's earliest days, the industry was so new that only a programmer could effectively head up a team. Bill Davis, the company's first creative director, explains that a lot of the creativity in those days came from programmers because every part of a computer game was scripted.

"The programmers were kind of the head of the projects, but you've got to understand back then everything was graphics-driven and there weren't any drawing programs at all. Nothing off-the-shelf and very few proprietary programs."

Bill says he had firsthand experience with that: "I actually started that way myself on a Commodore 64. I wanted to animate some sprites [characters] and I had to learn BASIC to make that happen. You had to actually write code to draw. Back then they didn't really have much choice except for the programmers to be everything. So the programmers would basically work out whatever they wanted the graphics to be on a piece of grid paper. Pixels on, pixels off. Then they would program that in. The graphics weren't done outside and brought in; the graphics were actually part of the code. You had to do it that way."

While it was logical at the time for the programmer to control the entire design process, it was Roberta Williams's vision as a writer and storyteller that helped to eventually push the game designer to the forefront of the process.

"Roberta really held the creative vision for the company," Bill says. "She was really the creative thrust from the get-go, back when they were in Simi Valley when they worked out of their home. She's the one who said, 'Ken, if I write this game, would you program it?' 'Is there a way to attach images to this text adventure?' or, 'Ken, is there a way to give it sound and music?'"

Further reflecting on Ken and Roberta, Bill claims that although they were often a joy to be around, Roberta wasn't somebody to be taken lightly or disregarded. "They were a lot of fun. My wife and I used to vacation with Ken and Roberta while I was with the company. We had a great relationship. It was important to know that Roberta wasn't going to hit you over the head, but when she made a request, you listened. Especially on the executive level. I saw a bunch of things like, 'I don't have to listen to Roberta; she's just a game designer here.' [People] wouldn't bring it up, it was just the conversation they had in their head. Then you'd find out they weren't there very long. You didn't want to dismiss her."

While Roberta was the creative force driving the larger vision of the company, she also earned a lot of respect for her ability to design and deliver winning products, time after time.

Guruka Singh Khalsa, Sierra's first executive producer, calls her "the Disney princess of Sierra. When she came into the creative area, everybody – whatever she said – everybody said, 'Yes, Roberta.' I think because everyone was honoring the fact it was her creative ideas that started things."

Creatively Directing

As team sizes increased, management added the position of producer to the process, a role that served as somewhat of a bridge between the programmers, artists and game designers, helping to bring all the various disciplines together into one cohesive unit.

Robert Holmes served as producer on *Hoyle Classic Card Games* and remembers it being an enjoyable experience: "That team worked together for about a year and a half. We had sort of a little room that we were all in. I approached being a producer in sort of the same way I had learned from watching and being a producer in record production in Los Angeles and film postproduction. It was very similar in putting a team together, getting people inspired, keeping the finances handled and the scheduling and helping people to produce their best work. Trying to get obstacles out of their way."

It's not easy to point to a specific game or event that saw the transition of creative influence move away from programmers to the game designer. The designer role was originally filled solely by Roberta Williams, with others joining the company as time went on, but a lot of those designers such as Al Lowe and Scott Murphy also had programming experience.

Only a few short years after the producer role was introduced, another layer of management was brought into the company, this time the role of creative director in the person of Bill Davis. John Williams, Sierra's marketing manager, believes Bill was one of the major catalysts in bringing the game designer to primacy.

"I tend to think of it in terms of thought leadership. In the beginning, Ken was the exclusive thought leader in the company, and so it was all about the programmers. As Ken started to focus more on the business side, Roberta became more dominant and there was more focus on art, music, etc. to enhance her work. After some small flirtations with Hollywood (Disney, Henson and Associates, and Sesame Street), the decision to hire Bill Davis led to the designers taking the forefront," John explains.

"I think the hiring of Bill Davis probably was the most important shift. He just brought a different way of thinking to the company that changed it fundamentally. One that led to great creativity but also probably some anarchy that had some good and bad things associated with it."

While John believes Bill was instrumental in that change of focus to the creative side of the game design process, Bill says the paradigm was already shifting by the time he got there: "Roberta and Al Lowe were well established. Christy Marx had already been hired to work on *Conquests of Camelot* [as a designer], so they'd already done that."

Nevertheless, hiring Bill Davis was a major coup for Sierra, bringing his talents as an artist, graphic designer and painter, along with his Emmy award–winning experience working as a lead graphic designer with NBC, into the fold.

It was an advantage that very nearly ended soon after it began when he was headhunted to work for one of Sierra's biggest competitors.

"What people don't know is I almost jumped ship after my first year at Sierra On-Line," Bill reveals. "I was being courted by LucasArts. I really thought at the time that was a better fit. I'd been up there several times talking with George Lucas's attorney, who was running his six companies for him at the time."

One of the draws was the chance to be involved in some highly popular series, he admits: "I would have been working on some of my favorite titles – *Monkey Island*, that period." Bill was very tempted, to the point where a move seemed inevitable. "We'd stopped remodeling on our home up here [in Oakhurst] and it looked like it was going to happen." In the end, although he seriously considered the offer, Bill decided to stay where he was, as seeing through the changes he had begun at Sierra was much more attractive at the time.

Bill Davis had always had an interest in video games, from the very early days of the industry. "I was a pretty hardcore gamer from the time of coin-op. Starting from *Pong* and things like that. In fact, my dad had brought home a Fairchild system,* so we had it right in our house. Pretty simple games. So I had been in gaming from really early."

He began directing television commercials in Hollywood and had developed a passion for the home computer, something that put him in good stead when Ken Williams phoned looking to recruit for the Sierra team.

"I was working with this one firm, directing for them for about ten years. I was the only guy in the company that had a personal computer at that time," Bill recalls. "I had an Amiga because IBM color computers were very, very expensive, and so were Macs if you got them in color. The Amiga was something I could afford. I was actually using it to test what I could do and [doing] prototyping of some commercials, mostly motion graphic commercials. I would later finish working with an operator in an online system like Quantel Paintbox or da Vinci Systems software. But I was the only one in the company that had a computer.

"When Ken Williams called, he was actually looking for animators. Our producer put the call through to me, saying, 'You're the only one who knows anything about computers; maybe you can talk to him,'" Bill remembers. "He was disappointed [by] how much animators made, because they made a lot more money than his industry could pay. But I kind of pointed him in the direction of the different art schools that were in LA and advised him he could hire someone right out of art school for what he was willing [to], or could, pay. It would be great for them as they were just starting out.

---

* The Fairchild Channel F was a cartridge-based video game console available in the late seventies.

"I thought that was the end of it. I told him to give me a call anytime he needed it. If he ran into any roadblocks, I would be glad to help him out because I was into computer games.

"Six months later he called me up and asked me if I could meet him and Roberta for breakfast in LA, because they were coming down and he wanted to talk to me about something. Basically, they made me this wonderful offer to become one of the first creative directors in the business. Being a chief creative officer. I was the vice president of development and creative director. They offered me double what I was making as a director in Hollywood, and stock options and a beautiful place to live in the Sierra mountains."

Bill Davis believes Roberta Williams deserves credit for his being offered the role and supporting him both at an executive and creative level. "She had a lot to do with the direction of the company. My assumption is she's the one who decided they needed me, and I assume she was my biggest supporter on the board. She was a board member on a high level. She was at all the board meetings; she was an executive there. I'm sure she's the one who decided they needed someone like me and she's the one who decided we should be the Disney of games. At least, I always assumed that all the time I was there."

But in Bill's mind, Ken was equally important in a complementary way: "They were a great team. He was a programmer, essentially, and he was running the executive side of it, and she was running the creative side of it, or inspiring the creative side."

Bill's role was quite comprehensive. He was in charge of the entirety of the creative process, including the artists, animators, game designers, and sound designers. After only six months, Ken Williams added the programming department to Bill's responsibilities as well. Bill was in charge of everything.

It was something Ken said during their initial meeting that really intrigued Bill about the possibilities of the job: "'Don't judge us by what you see right now.' When I joined, [Sierra was] doing EGA [Enhanced Graphics Adapter] games with 16 colors, and Ken said, 'VGA [Video Graphics Array] cards are supposed to come out next year and that's really going to blow open what we can do. If you come up, I want you to turn us into the Disney of computer games.' That intrigued me, and I took him at his word."

When Bill Davis first joined Sierra, the studio had a fairly simple executive structure, as he details: "Rick Cavin was the general manager when I started. At that time, he was also managing the artists and designers and things like that, so when I took that stuff over he was able to focus on sales and manufacturing. Ken at the top, then I was head of development. Then we had Rick, and John Williams in charge of marketing and advertising. And we had a chief financial officer too, Ed Heinbockel, when I first started. That was the executive structure. Then we had producers under that.

"When I came up there, they had a handful of artists – about five artists, I think. Most of them there were self-trained. I realized they had no production system; no one in the business did. In other words, they would just put some artists together with some programmers and they would start making a game. In many cases they would design as they went along; they would try different things and go from there.

"The first thing I realized we needed to do, because we were looking at really growing the company, I had to hire a lot of people for what we wanted to do because we knew VGA was coming down the pipe and my plans for that were a lot different from what we'd been doing."

The new production model caused a great deal of stress and anxiety in the company, although Guruka Singh Khalsa, producer of the first three *Quest for Glory* games, says it was a necessary step.

"Don't forget we had some disasters before that," Guruka says, such as the issues they encountered with *Codename: ICEMAN*. "It made us go back and redesign things tremendously. So at this point we said everything has to be storied out, every game has to be mapped out. So we did. We actually completely changed our production methods at that point. A lot of this was because it was early days; it was [learning] by making mistakes," he explains.

Corey Cole recalls that "there were major changes in the development process every time we did a game. For *Quest for Glory II*, they were in the process of changing over to VGA and had brought in animation cameras for scanning scenes and stuff like that."

Bill Davis had a plan to implement based on his knowledge of the animation industry. "The first thing I knew I needed to do was come up with a production system," he remembers. "One of the big flaws with all computer game companies at the time was you would do finished art and you would program it. With all games you would find out certain sections didn't work, and you would throw them away and you'd spend all this money making all this art and animation. 'Why are you guys doing this? I come from an industry, the animation industry, where we don't do anything until we make sure everything works. So let's find a way to do that here.'

"I started having the teams, first of all, build a design script, then we beat that to death until we thought it worked, then we would storyboard any sequence that actually made sense to storyboard, even some of the interface sequences – 'What happens if you click on this screen and it goes to this screen?' So we'd storyboard all that stuff out.

"Then we would do layouts in pencil; we'd lay everything out and design all the characters, then we would actually scan those layouts in as assets the size of the final game assets, and give those to programmers to start programming with them. We would get a working game in black and white, just from the pencil sketch layouts that people did, without putting all that time into the artwork. Then if we had a scene that we knew was going to work and stay in the game, only then would we start to actually turn it into color and spend a lot of time doing it."

This process created extra work for the programmers, as Corey Cole recalls when he was programming a simple desert scene in his *Quest for Glory* game using a pencil sketch.

"I had a scene where the Hero rides off into the plains in the distance. When the artist colored it in, I discovered that the plain he rode off into wasn't a plain, it was the side of a mountain. I had to completely recode that. Guessing what the pencil sketch was, nothing registered the same. The artist always improved the art when they went from the sketch to the colored [version], so all the programming had to change."

Part of the issue for Corey was the need to utilize artists of varying degrees of ability. "They only had a certain number of talented artists and they were trying to come up with a system that would allow people without much talent to still be helpful. A lot of the art staff there were former receptionists and secretaries and such at the company. Otherwise, some were straight out of high school."

The Graphics of Sierra

From the black-and-white stick figures and line drawings of *Mystery House* to the full-color 3D presentation of *Gabriel Knight 3*, Sierra always tried to stay at the forefront of computer graphics technology, innovating and moving the art form forward as they went.

For their earliest games, hand-drawn art would need to be plotted into the computer using coordinates, as if on a piece of graph paper. The game engine would generate the graphics based on these coordinates: a line would be drawn between two points, and a color would fill the spaces between lines. It wasn't an easy procedure, but it worked well and conserved disk space, which was always at a premium.

When graphics technology progressed to support 256 colors, the process became even more difficult, as creative director Bill Davis recalls: "If you worked in a digital paint program like Deluxe Paint, everything looked very, very pixelated. It was very difficult to make anything look smooth or to imply colors."

It was at this point that Bill decided they should draw backgrounds and animations with traditional media and then scan that work into the game, creating a much more realistic and less pixelated look than that of their competitors.

"We started painting with traditional media and then had our programming team develop some amazing codecs to scan the artwork in. That also allowed us to [draft] scenes for other people and send them overseas to places like Korea and have them paint them. So we could really up the production, because otherwise we never would have been able to raise the quality of production that we wanted to raise them to," Bill recalls.

Something else Bill looked at changing was the ever-evolving art styles of the games. As Josh Mandel explains, "[Bill Davis] had previously worked at NBC and had an Emmy and he was high up there. And he felt that Sierra games should have a definite graphic flavor through the series. He looks at *King's Quest* and every *King's Quest* looks different, and every *Space Quest* looks different. He really wanted to unify that and stop the chaos."

According to Bill, "I'm a big believer in suiting the art style to the genre. There was a lot of thinking in the beginning about picking what style was really going to have the most wow factor for these games when they came out. I don't think others were doing that in the industry; they were just doing art."

This was an extension of the approach he'd taken with the animated commercials he had been producing for a decade. "Whenever I would get a new commercial, I would try to pick a style that was best suited for the message we were delivering. It also made us a moving target with other companies, so they never knew where we were going to come out next," Bill says.

"So I would do things like, with *Leisure Suit Larry*, 'Why don't we do cubism? We could do it; it would be great and it would suit the kind of wacky world that Larry lived in.' When we started doing the edutainment titles, games like *Twisty History* [the working title for *Pepper's Adventures in Time*], we had a game that was going back in time to be with

Ben Franklin. I thought about Grant Wood, a great American artist who painted a lot of revolutionary scenes in America, so we styled it that way. So it was that kind of stuff."

Bill claims that "I really get bored with ... this kind of game realism that goes on now, that everybody copies. It's in most of the shooters. Each game does it a little better, but they all look the same. You don't have to do that; they can all look completely different, so that's what I always seek out. I'd be trying to apply the best look for each game."

Rotoscoping was another process Bill Davis introduced to Sierra as VGA games started to be produced, because any shortcuts the animators had previously used would be more noticeable with more colors available. "The animation was pretty crude and I realized once again [that] with 256 colors [the animation] could look better, but we needed to animate better so I started hiring real animators – we didn't have any – to do squash and stretch."

Bill elaborates: "You've got two different kinds of animation, even in features. You've got the way Snow White moves in *Snow White and the Seven Dwarves*, and you've got the way the dwarves move. So Snow White is rotoscoped, but the dwarves are done with what they call squash and stretch animation. So they're very exaggerated. The reason they call it squash and stretch is [because] when [the character's] weight comes down on a step, they squash down like a rubber ball, and when they jump up, they're very elastic and they stretch – so it gives a varied look to the way a character moves. They're much more bouncy and animated and the rotoscoping is much subtler.

"I wanted our characters like King Graham to be rotoscoped, so he moved in a very real way, but then I wanted any dwarves or trolls or other characters in the game to be squash and stretch. So I needed traditionally trained animators to do those," he concludes.

Creating a setup for rotoscoping was left in the hands of a talented programmer who came up with a unique way of dealing with the issue. Bill says, "We had this wonderful guy – a hero of mine at Sierra – a programmer named Dan Foy who would make these art tools for me. He was fast. He would say, 'What do you need this week?' and we'd have a meeting and I'd say what I need.

"One of the first ones was, I needed to find a way we could rotoscope walkers, so we set up a very dangerous treadmill without rails on it and he set up a system that could capture it. We'd take it into the tools and touch it up a little bit and that's how we rotoscoped. It sped up animation, I tell you. Now it's motion capture, but same kind of principle."

Art director Marc Hudgins recalls using rotoscoping in *Quest for Glory IV*, one of Sierra's last games to use pixel art and a 320x200 resolution: "A lot of the human actions, we would rotoscope. We would do full animation loops and then edit them down and paint over them with pixels. It might have been a little more naturalistic [than animating by hand]. And because [of the] lower resolution, I think it was a little more forgiving."

A clear indication that the changes made to the internal design process for 256-color games were successful was the recognition Sierra received from their competitors, as Bill Davis recalls.

"When we came out with *King's Quest V*, the first VGA version of the game, we heard through the pipeline that LucasArts was furious, saying they'll never be able to sustain that; they're going to go bankrupt trying to build games of that kind of quality. So we were doing what we wanted to do; we were hitting nerves with the other companies and trying to surprise them. It was pretty competitive, so you had to do that."

Technology was progressing at an ultrafast speed and Sierra was at the forefront of the evolution in gaming. In fact, they drove those changes in some cases. As the company left the EGA era behind and focused on the new technologies available, they went back to their major franchises like *King's Quest* to bring fans with them into a new and exciting age.

The Conflicts of Change

Another change Bill Davis made was to the structure of the teams. Previously, everyone who worked on a game sat together, but Bill saw this as detrimental to the growth of the company and quickly changed things. Teams no longer sat together based on the game they were working on, but in their own departments: artists with artists, programmers with programmers, musicians with musicians.

"We had a tremendous number of groups; we were growing and growing and growing. What made the most sense, and what made it easiest for all of us managers as well as the teams, was basically to have them all together," Bill says. "In those days we were located in a couple of different buildings, so even to see all the teams you would have to travel across town to another building. So imagine what it would have been like to have some of the artists in one location and some of the others in another location and the same thing with the programmers."

It was during the production of *Quest for Glory II* that the change to the team setup was made, and Corey Cole remembers how difficult it was.

"When we did *Hero's Quest*, everybody was in one little cubicle all sitting next to each other in one particular area and we could just turn to the person next to us and say, 'Okay, I need a flying animation for this creature because it actually flies,' and the artist would say, 'Oh, I didn't realize that,' and the artist would whip out some flying animation and the programmer would drop it into the game. Or they'd say, 'I'm looking at this animation you gave me and I don't really understand what these things are supposed to do,' and the artist would go frame by frame and say, 'This is for that' and 'This is for this setting' and it would get in very easily."

Despite the problems it caused, Corey understood the reasoning behind the change in seating arrangements. "The theory was, let's do this Hollywood studio animation–style, and we'll have some junior artists who are tweeners who'll do the in-between stages of the animations, and the senior artists will set up the key frames and so on," Corey says. "We don't want the designers bothering the artists, so you go off and work in your corner, and programmers will work in theirs, and the artists will work in theirs, and then all communication [will] only [go] through the team leader."

Lori Cole was disappointed by this major reorganization: "When they isolated the artists off into their own little corner of the universe and never the twain should meet with the programming staff, we had this kind of isolation and divide-and-conquer thing. You had no communication between people, so therefore all the synergy we had created and developed with the first [*Quest for Glory*] game was totally gone for the second one."

Corey was so frustrated with the new team structure and production techniques, he calculated all the production times. "I kept track of how much time we spent on each scene on *Hero's Quest* and then on *Quest for Glory II*. I benchmarked that it took literally three times the manpower to make a scene on the same technology. I complained to management about that and they said just to deal with it."

Only later did he come to see the value in it, saying, "in hindsight, that was necessary because they were training people on the process so they could do the other games that required those things. It had the advantage of allowing the artist to change back and forth between two projects and stuff like that. Pluses and minuses, but at the time we were extremely stressed and it was very hard for us. But we loved the game we ended up with."

Bill Davis was also responsible for starting an internal game design department within the company, which Josh Mandel was eventually assigned to oversee. According to Josh, "We had some great designers – Roberta Williams, Al Lowe – but what I wanted to do, I had some ideas of areas I would like to take games. You weren't going to convince Lori or Roberta or Al to do things; they had their own plans."

After working as a producer, Josh Mandel was given the new role of director of product design, in which he and the game designers would meet with Ken Williams and Bill Davis weekly to discuss proposals. "We would kick around ideas of directions we would like to go. They'd kick around their own ideas, I'd kick around mine. We'd actually prototype them up in scripts. It was hitting it from all areas."

Josh further recalls that "every week we would submit two game proposals. We learned to make these proposals very short because Ken didn't have the patience. He would read a couple of paragraphs and if you hadn't grabbed his interest by then, you probably weren't going to. Bill Davis wasn't this way; he was thoughtful and would read through the proposals and work to understand them."

It was from one of these meetings that Josh developed the initial idea for *Laura Bow: The Dagger of Amon Ra*, a game that Bruce Balfour would go on to design and develop. "My proposal was about a museum. I didn't have a name for it, but it was a museum with a display of a ceremonial Egyptian dagger that gets lost. Basically, the game, but summed up in a couple of paragraphs," Josh explains.

Even more significantly, Bill Davis recalls that Sierra's final major series came out of those game design meetings.

"*Gabriel Knight* was a really early design that Jane Jensen submitted. And it took us years to actually get Ken to finally sign off on it. *Gabriel Knight* was one of her first proposals. Jane had been writing some gothic vampire novels and short stories, so it was a real love of hers. When she first came in she was kind of assigned to work with Roberta and help Roberta with her designs and flesh things out. I fell in love with *Gabriel Knight*, but it took years and years for the world to catch up and the supernatural to become popular."

Even with such promising new ideas emerging, all the changes Bill instituted caused major conflict within Sierra, and Bill felt resented by a lot of people.

"I would walk around feeling like the most hated guy in the company. I never took it personally because I knew whoever came in and had to make these changes – and the industry was going to have to make them soon – [but] they were not going to be a popular person to people who had already been there."

Before Bill got to Sierra, "in the smaller industry that it was, you could take liberties; it must have been a wonderful time. If something didn't work out you could trash it and do something else. The costs involved weren't that much and the deadlines could be more flexible. Oh yes, [the changes] caused tremendous conflicts," he confirms.

The development of their own in-house graphic tools was another area Bill believed was wasting money and resources. "They had art tools for the artists that were designed by Bob Heitman and his team, an internal programming team. They were using those and they would update them whenever they needed to because a new card was available, and the breaking point was when we got to VGA and that was another battle, making myself enemies again."

Bill insisted that it didn't make sense to pour more money and effort into developing their own tools, saying, "It's crazy, you guys taking on this effort of refitting this tool so we can do 256-color when we can now buy software like Deluxe Paint right off the shelf. Then they're responsible for updating it and keeping it going. It doesn't have to all be built here; we can just buy it off the shelf."

Bill's rationale prevailed. "So that's what we did. When we went from EGA to VGA, we left the art tools behind to a great extent. We still used them for our walkers [character walking animations] and things like that, but to a great extent we started more and more using off-the-shelf tools."

Getting his controversial plans implemented were not the only battles that Bill had to fight, as he was also responsible for taking the case of artists' wages to Ken Williams and the board.

"Not only did I have a tough sell with my teams with the changes I was making, I also had a tough sell on the executive level because I was fighting so hard to get cash for my groups and trying to convince them we needed a bigger slice of the budget than everybody else. That was not popular. Even Ken said to me one time, 'Can't you just fire everybody and hire some of those starving artists I've heard about?' I told him, 'Ken, that's a fallacy. Those starving artists never really existed.' And they would not turn out the kind of games we were turning out," Bill remembers.

"So yeah, I had to fight hard to give them incremental raises but it was never anything [close to] what they would make in another industry in a big city. It was disappointing, but we did the best we could to get them more money."

Another change instituted under Bill Davis's tenure as creative director was to develop new game designers by teaming them up with an established mentor. The intent was to help the newer designers develop their skills, doing much of the design and writing on a title but having an experienced hand oversee their work.

"They started this star system thing where a junior designer would work with a senior designer," Josh Mandel explains, having worked as the junior partner to Al Lowe on *Freddy Pharkas: Frontier Pharmacist*. "The junior designer would do most of the work but the game would be released under the major designer's name to ensure sales."

It was a system that made sense to the company but brought about some displeasure within the teams. Some senior designers, like Al Lowe, were thoroughly engaged in the process. "Al was intimately involved on a daily basis on the entire design. He did the first [*Freddy Pharkas*] design completely himself based on his idea of a frontier pharmacist," Josh says. But others remained in more of a producer role, merely overseeing production and giving broad directives as to the direction of the game.

By then Roberta Williams was usually involved in a number of projects at a time, spreading her talents more thinly than she had in earlier years. For *King's Quest VI*, Roberta came up with the basic story and then worked with Jane Jensen to develop it into a cohesive game design. Jane would then go on to do the bulk of the writing, contributing over six thousand lines of written text and dialogue.

That was not the full extent of Roberta's contributions to the project, however. Robin Bradley worked at Sierra for over a decade and was responsible for quality assurance on a number of games, including *King's Quest VI*. He remembers working closely with Roberta through the process of testing, calling it one of the highlights of his time with the company.

"Though Jane Jensen was responsible for a great deal of story – and very good story – Roberta's genius was in the game playability and puzzle logic. She hammered out ream after ream of possible testing scenarios."

Two years later, *King's Quest VII* was similarly shipped and promoted as a Roberta Williams game, but while she designed the structure and story, a lot of the game was written by Lorelei Shannon.

Al Eufrasio, an animator on *Space Quest 6* at the time, could see both the benefits and drawbacks of the new system: "Try to bring a few other people up in the ranks; that's kind of what they did. That's one way to look at it, but another way is, people trying to take credit for other people's work! There was certainly some disgruntlement over that. . . . From a business perspective it made sense, because those were the names which sold. The next game, or possibly two games later, you could possibly go ahead and credit that other person fully."

Josh Mandel agrees, particularly with Roberta Williams having such a high profile in the gaming world. "I never examined the numbers to see if it was technically true, but I fully believed it and I believe it now. So much of the advertising was spent talking about her and she was present throughout so much of the company's history. [What] I did see was the fan mail. I got a chance to read the fan mail and there is no doubt that Roberta had an enormous share of the love."

Robert Holmes, music director on *Gabriel Knight*, says he believes the intention behind the policy was a good one, even if it ruffled some feathers with its implementation: "I think one of the unusual things about Ken and Roberta, they could be so brilliant and smart themselves, but they also were totally willing to share the spotlight. They were totally willing to create other stars within Sierra. That was really generous of them to do that."

Further conflict in this era was caused not by management so much as the different teams themselves, as Bill Davis recalls: "When I started in 1989, most of our programmers came from places like the aerospace industry, [while] the artists were coming straight out of art schools and most of them had never touched a computer before. All of a sudden we were throwing these two groups together.

"I come from a family where my father is a completely left-brain person and my mother is a completely right-brain person, so I learned to speak both languages. I learned to speak to both groups but they could not talk well or play well with each other. There were tears all the time, and arguments and people grabbing each other by the throat. It was very difficult to get the engineers and the creative people to play nicely together in those days."

Al Eufrasio started at Sierra in 1994, around the time that Bill Davis left, and recalls that the tensions between different groups at the company still lingered at that stage: "The thing I found odd – I sensed, actually, because it was just kind of *there* – was a disconnect between the programmers and the artists in terms of personality differences. Not that I remember any big conflict or anything like that between people, but in terms of people keeping to themselves or among their own kind. [Artists] and programmers seemed especially prone to that, and I never understood that."

He attempted to change this attitude with the people he worked with. "I would try to pick people's brains, [asking] what's the best way to do this, what would work, what wouldn't work, and even when I moved up to Seattle it was kind of like that. Here and there were little incidents of politics between people, but that dynamic was in play for quite a while and I never really quite got why it would be like that, or why anybody thought it was okay. Eventually we started doing more team outings to address that.

"In every consecutive company I worked at after that, it got better and better. Because you had engineers going to school wanting to program games and they had actually done projects while they were in school with artists and may have artist friends. So it became easier and easier. It was a very terrible time for a guy like me to be in there. You weren't a popular guy. You had to make decisions that were very unpopular."

In those days at Sierra, it was common for the game design teams to add references to real people in their games, and Bill Davis was "honored" in this fashion by being made the main villain in *Quest for Glory II* by its co-designer Lori Cole.

It's a relationship Bill and Lori both admit is a lot better now than in 1990. "Lori and I, I think we're good friends now," Bill says. "It was a tough time. I kind of understood their point of view. Here's this guy who comes in and makes all these changes and this isn't what they signed up for."

He also points out that not all his cameos in games were bad – his likeness was also used as Wolfgang Ritter in *Gabriel Knight: The Beast Within*: "There's a photograph of [Gabriel's] uncle who was also a vampire hunter, and that's me!"

By 1992, Ken Williams had started to see an overlap of responsibilities between Bill Davis's and Guruka Singh Khalsa's roles, and the decision was made to let Guruka go. "I had Guruka as an executive producer for a while. For a long while," Bill says. "Then Ken felt we had too much duplication of effort and one of my horrible tasks was asking Guruka, who I really, really enjoyed working with, to leave, which was really difficult.

"I think Guruka said that he kind of thought his role was mine before I started. For a while he was unsure where he was supposed to be. When he was performing in my role, he would do what I ended up doing, which was working with the designers, kind of as an editor to work with them on their designs, and also just a catalyst to help them get the most out of their designs. Offer them inspiration in areas or things they might not have thought about.

"I think that's why Ken felt it was a duplication of effort, because now I was doing it and Guruka was doing it, and Guruka was trying to figure out where things sat. He didn't really design games specifically himself, he did what I ended up doing, working with the designers to make the games the best they could. [We] kind of became a facilitator for them. It was unfortunate because he's such a wonderful guy."

Guruka says that he felt forced into leaving for a different reason: "They pressured me out in '92 because they realized that the way I created stuff was taking too long and was too meticulous and they wanted to get product out faster. Bill was one of the people who leaned on me to leave. Finally, in '92, I did leave."

Bill admits that one of the major changes he made at Sierra was to insist on stricter deadlines and controls over the game development process, and he acknowledges that a lot of people who were there before he arrived didn't appreciate it. "There seemed to be a philosophy among the game designers – Guruka supported it, too – that a game is only ready if the game says it's ready. When I came in and said, 'No, no, no, I've seen that in too many other industries where they have deadlines and they have budgets and they go belly-up if you continue with that.' But a lot of people held that philosophy."

Guruka agrees, saying, "That was at the point, 1992, when the company had just gone public. Ken was very focused on stock price. He decided to bring in a bunch of middle [managers] to manage all us unruly creative types. I tended to lean more towards the creative teams and defending them than towards the marketing people. Standing up for the fact the game wasn't ready to release yet. Standing up for the fact we wanted extra budget to put in what we wanted to put in. Then it became all about how we can streamline production. How can we get more games on the shelf? How can we get our stock prices up? He hired a couple of VPs. And he hired Bill Davis."

Bill defends the moves, claiming, "Everyone always thinks you're shoving these decisions on them, making all these decisions arbitrarily. They just don't understand until they're in that. Then you find out the hard way there's reasons why you have to hold people's feet to the fire and you have to make those decisions. If you didn't get this solved by now, we have to look at what we can shave out to keep things on track.

"It was a tough place. A very tough place to work. The most difficult place to work in the games industry. The most difficult. The most tension."

The reality was that both sides of the equation – the creativity that flowed at its own pace with the attitude that a game would be finished when it was finished, and the systematic processes like those that Bill introduced – were both needed to create the games Sierra wanted to make in the VGA era. Costs were higher now, both for production and in terms of a delayed or failed product.

Fortunately, even though he introduced a more streamlined and process-driven production where everything operated within a solid business model, Bill Davis was a creative at heart and understood that without creative people, the industry would fail. In fact, the creative director role is something Bill still believes was vital to the growth of Sierra, and he regrets that the video game industry still doesn't seem to respect the position like it should.

"This is the sad part," he says. "The majority of the industry still thinks it's a tech industry and they don't realize they're a commercial creative industry and that their competition is feature animation. So they need to think like feature animation companies and they still don't. Obviously I'm prejudiced about this, but the top people in these [game] companies need to be somebody like John Lasseter at Pixar and Disney. The top decisions need to be made on a creative level because that's what you are. You're a creative industry."

This was something he feels that Ken and Roberta got right early on, from Roberta's creative genius driving the company to Bill's own employment as creative director. "Back when I was at Sierra, there was a creative VP position right up there at the top. I think it's been pushed down [in the industry today]; creative is way down," Bill laments.

The processes that Bill Davis implemented were hard to take for some of the established employees within Sierra, causing a lot of anguish and frustration. The feeling was that it all came down to the mighty dollar instead of the creative vision of the designer and team. But without these processes in place, and with an increase in the cost of production, the business would have eventually suffered. It was a hard transition, but it set Sierra up for a golden era of computer gaming.

Interlude: Buying Power

Diversification was the key to continued growth. That's what Ken Williams strongly believed as Sierra entered the nineties. The company was in a strong position. They had come out the other side of the video game crash a few years earlier and built a successful business by mainly focusing on adventure games.

But Ken always knew there was more to the market than just adventures, and was looking to expand. Sierra's own internal teams had a lot of expertise, but why reinvent the wheel? Instead, over the course of the next few years, Sierra pursued and bought up a number of developers who made different types of games than they did.

Bill Davis, as head of production at the studio, had a big hand in assessing potential acquisitions Ken had found.

"Ken would find them himself first, and then he'd send us out there to do the forensics and say, 'I think this might be a good fit. You take a look at the development organization and design and see whether you think it's a good idea.' A lot of them fell through; they didn't work," Bill explains.

It wasn't only game developers that Ken was interested in, either. Anything that could increase Sierra's market share while complementing their existing business was fair game. Bill continues, "I think we actually looked at the accounting software company that does QuickBooks when they just had their checkbook-balancing program. We looked at a lot of companies; a lot of them worked out. We acquired a lot of educational companies."

One of Bill's scouting trips was with Ed Heinbockel, Sierra's chief financial officer, and they visited the first studio Ken purchased. "He and I often would make trips together to look at these companies for acquisitions. We did that for Dynamix," Bill says.

"The two of us would fly up there, so we spent a lot of one-on-one time together. He'd look at the company's books to see if they were viable financially and then I would look at the development organization and we would report back to Ken whether we thought they were a good property for acquisition."

Dynamix was founded in 1984 by Jeff Tunnell and Damon Slye, and over the first six years of the studio's existence they became best known for their simulators. *Stellar 7* was already a massive hit for the pair before they founded the company, and subsequent games such as *Project Firestart*, *Arcticfox*, and *A-10 Tank Killer* were also good sellers. Early distribution was handled by a variety of companies, Electronic Arts and Activision being two of the more notable ones. Sierra acquired Dynamix in 1990.

Jeff Tunnell was a different sort of manager than Ken Williams, and working at Dynamix was a much different experience as a result, something Mark Crowe discovered when he moved there prior to starting on *Space Quest V*.

"It was a very different atmosphere. Dynamix was set up in downtown Eugene [Oregon], which is a beautiful place, beautiful building; they had a really nice open office space environment. Everybody had offices and people had their own spaces and everything. It was quite a contrast coming from Sierra, which had kind of turned into a cubicle hell – one big open room with cubicles. Good or bad, I definitely see the merits of both. It was a very different kind of culture at Dynamix; it was a nice change," Mark says.

Mark credits that culture largely to co-founder Jeff Tunnell. "Jeff was really focused and driven. So was Ken, but maybe Jeff more so. Jeff's a creative as well; he has a creative vision and I think that's what drove him. He was the odd guy who could wear two hats: he was the entrepreneur and definitely wanted to make money, but very talented and knew how to pull talented people together and get the best from them."

Josh Mandel was someone else who worked with Dynamix after they were acquired by Sierra, and he had a memorable first encounter with Jeff Tunnell.

"Before I got to Sierra I was a game reviewer, and when I got to Dynamix to work on *Heart of China*, Jeff Tunnell was quite happy to see me. I didn't really know Jeff but I had reviewed one of his games. I was about the only person who had given that game a good review. It was called *David Wolf: Secret Agent*. It was an ambitious game because it combined simulator and arcade and adventure in three segments. So there might be a segment where you're piloting a plane and another where you're skydiving and another segment where you're beating up a guy and a segment of adventure. And I really liked it. It was far from perfect, but I could really see a wonderful idea in there. And Jeff, when I finally got to Dynamix ... he was overjoyed to meet the only person who'd given his game a good review," Josh laughs.

"It was a very cool place. Unlike Sierra, where people ranged in age from grandparents to kids who were so young they probably shouldn't even be working there, Dynamix was like all twentysomething guys and they had tons of energy and everyone was cool and casual, even more casual than Sierra.

"There seemed to be greater emphasis on coordination," Josh continues. "At Sierra, a designer would get a game and then they would go off and do their own thing. Dynamix was, I think, more methodical about their work. They wanted to make a great impression. Adventure games were a new thing for them. I got the impression they were a lot more tuned in to design theory and so on. You would never find a dead end in a Dynamix adventure."

Under Sierra's leadership, Dynamix continued to flourish. Ken had a hands-off approach to the company: as long as they kept building profitable, quality products, Dynamix could basically run itself.

Between 1990 and 2001, when Sierra's parent company at the time closed them down, Dynamix was responsible for the creation of a large number of best-selling games spanning multiple genres. Among them, three adventure games – *Rise of the Dragon*, *The Adventures of Willy Beamish* and *Heart of China* – were all critical and commercial successes.

Josh Mandel is credited as a co-designer on *Heart of China*, although he believes this is an exaggeration of his actual role. "[Sierra] had purchased Dynamix and I was assigned to be the creative liaison between Sierra and Dynamix and make sure their adventure game designs were kept not too far from what Sierra players would expect from a Sierra game," he explains.

"I went to Oregon where Dynamix was and I sat down with the designers and every puzzle in the game was 'find this, use it on that.' I said to them – and this was really the only direction I had for them – 'You need to think about layering these puzzles somewhat; they're too elementary in structure.' For instance, I designed one puzzle, that is the puzzle where the boy creates the cart like a little truck out of Chinese coins, some chopsticks and a box. This was using things in inventory on other things in inventory to create new things. They said, 'We get it!' They finished the design with that in mind and I stayed behind and wrote some text and dialogue since I was there."

Dynamix had great success with other games during Sierra's ownership as well. The *Front Page Sports* simulators, *Aces* flight simulators, *Incredible Machine* puzzle series, and *Earthsiege* and *Starsiege* games all went on to be major hits for the company.

One of Dynamix's eventual biggest sellers arrived in 1993 when *Betrayal at Krondor*, an RPG based on Raymond Feist's *Riftwar* novels, hit the shelves. Although sales started off slowly – so slowly that Dynamix and Sierra sold the *Riftwar* rights back to Feist – once it was released on CD-ROM the following year, the game became a huge smash.

Coktel Vision was another savvy business move by Ken Williams. Wanting to increase Sierra's footprint in Europe and believing that Europeans were more skeptical about American games than their own, Ken bought Coktel from its founder Roland Oskian. This not only gave Sierra a foothold in Europe, it also allowed Coktel products to be brought overseas and published by Sierra. Best known in the United States for their *Goblins* series of offbeat puzzle/adventure games, the company stayed with Sierra until being acquired by Mindscape SA in 2005.

By 1995, Sierra had a nice nest egg of cash and went hard after companies that would fit their plans. Impressions Games was high on the shopping list. With games like *Caesar*, *Lords of the Realm* and the *Civil War Generals* series, Sierra strongly established itself in the strategy market. Papyrus Design Group was picked up around the same time, their output focusing on the *NASCAR Racing* games. Flight simulator developer subLOGIC was also purchased in 1995. subLOGIC had been the developer of *Microsoft Flight Simulator*, but they had parted ways with Microsoft prior to Sierra's purchase of the company and had started development on their own flying game. The result, *Pro Pilot*, was eventually finished by Sierra and released under the Dynamix label.

All of these groups operated independently at first, although as the corporate structure changed they were eventually absorbed into Sierra itself.

Chapter 8: Old Favorites, New Tech

The market was changing to where most people didn't want to take the time to learn to type, spell, or figure out just how you talk to a computer via an adventure game.

Roberta Williams, Designer, King's Quest V

By 1990 VGA had arrived, and the graphic adventure genre would never be the same. *Quest for Glory II*, along with *King's Quest V* and *Space Quest IV*, went into production as Sierra was planning for the move from EGA (16 color) to VGA (256 color) graphics.

The End of EGA

Sitting at his desk in the middle of the night, working overtime, Corey Cole was more than a little frustrated. He knew that game production would always have its problems, that it was never a smooth process, but with his and his wife Lori's new game, *Quest for Glory II: Trial by Fire*, the challenges seemed to keep coming.

After production had already started, newly hired creative director Bill Davis turned things upside down, completely revamping the entire game creation process to better cater to the upcoming VGA games planned. Gone were the days of everyone sitting together and working on portions of the game as they were needed. Everything now had to be completely designed and penciled out. Sketches were required of all artwork, and these were to be submitted through team leaders to the producer, who then handed them off to the programmers. The game was to be built using those placeholder sketches, which would later be replaced by final artwork, forcing the programmers to go over their work multiple times.

It was hell.

Tempers were short, and everybody was tense. The stress of the situation became so bad that the anger even made it into the game itself. In a subtle dig at the changes being made at Sierra, the second city the Hero would visit was named Raseir, a brutal dictatorship and anagram of Sierra. The leader of that oppressive regime, Khaveen, was named after Rick Cavin, Sierra's general manager, while the major antagonist Ad Avis was named after Bill Davis.

It was the success of the first game that inspired the decision to put a sequel into production straight away. "We had originally planned the series to come out in bang, bang, bang, four consecutive years. For people to play all the way through from beginning to end. Ken had other ideas; he was going to have us do one game, then switch off to other stuff. But the success of *Hero's Quest* took them by surprise. It sold a lot of copies," Corey recalls.

Quest for Glory II followed a path similar to the first game by supplying the player with a number of quests to complete, along with two new cities and a vast wilderness to explore. This time, however, events demanded a more restrictive time frame, with certain essential puzzle elements occurring only on set days. This allowed for a more focused story, keeping to a slightly more linear path than the original, although players could still undertake secondary tasks and challenges at their own pace.

The Coles set to work to create a new adventure for the Hero in the desert land of Shapeir with a large portion of the team they had worked with on the first game still in place, including composer Mark Seibert.

Trial by Fire, although already planned as the subtitle for the game, would become a very apt description for the production.

After the game was designed and storyboarded, management called a meeting with the Coles and other designers to let them know that the new *King's Quest* game, the fifth entry in Sierra's flagship series, was running late and looked like it wouldn't be ready for a Christmas 1990 release unless people working on other projects joined the team. Sierra made most of its sales during the holiday period so they needed a new *King's Quest* product on store shelves.

Space Quest IV, by Scott Murphy and Mark Crowe, was also at the start of production and an offer was made to both teams. Corey remembers being told, "Either *Quest for Glory II* or *Space Quest IV*, we need to do in 16-color EGA [instead of 256-color VGA]." This meant that one of the two groups could continue working on their game as an EGA title to finish in time for Christmas, while the other would be reassigned to *King's Quest V* to speed up production, delaying their own game but allowing it to be released later with the new 256-color technology. "Mark and Scott said, 'We'll take the extra time.' We became the one that chose to be the 16-color game."

Even with all the animosity and structural changes, *Trial by Fire* was finally completed and released. But sales this time weren't up to the higher expectations created by the first game. There were a number of factors cited, with a major one being the name change from *Hero's Quest* to *Quest for Glory*.

Soon after the initial release of *Hero's Quest* in 1989, Sierra had received a cease and desist from Milton Bradley. The British board game company owned a similar trademark for HeroQuest, a fantasy board game they also had plans to license as a computer game.

"It was pretty clear that they owned the trademark, and so we changed it," says John Williams, who was in charge of marketing at the time. "Copyrights were harder to verify then. We didn't have the internet and there were no central online repositories to search, so things like this did happen. In general, it wasn't a big deal as long as we complied with the lawyer's instructions to stop selling the product under a name they owned, and we did."

One problem for Sierra was they didn't just design their games. They also printed the boxes, duplicated the disks and created the packaging. They even shrink-wrapped the finished product. Every aspect of the game and packaging had to be reprinted as a result of the name change and sent to retailers as a second shipment, at a major cost to Sierra.

The original name was another in the line of Sierra's well-known *Quest* titles. "We were basically playing off *King's Quest* and we figured if we had a game called *Hero's Quest* everybody would know, more or less, what kind of game it was," Corey explains. "[In 1989] the film *Glory* came out about the Civil War and a lot of people said, '*Quest for Glory*, this must be about the Civil War.' It's not a bad title, but it's got a different feel to it. It's actually, in a sense, all about making yourself important and making yourself famous and so on. Whereas the original title is about helping other people and being a hero."

One of the greatest advantages for the original *Hero's Quest* when it came out in 1989 had been that no *King's Quest* game was released that year. According to Corey, the plan was to alternate between *Hero's Quest* and *King's Quest* every year, allowing each series to have the Sierra fantasy market to itself. But *King's Quest V* did end up coming out in time for Christmas 1990, which surely cut into *Quest for Glory II*'s sales as well.

"What we didn't know is *King's Quest V* would make it out with all the extra staff put on it and shipped about two weeks after us. We basically shipped simultaneously. Here we had two games both in the fantasy space, one of them state-of-the-art 256-color and with all of the marketing muscle of Sierra behind it," Corey remembers. "Overnight, all the 16-color games died when the 256-color games came out. That meant we delivered an obsolete game from the minute it came out. That really hurt."

It's with hindsight that Corey looks back and reconsiders his opinion of the three men he blamed for making his life miserable during the production of *Quest for Glory II*: "At the time, we were totally stressed and we had our three archnemeses, Ken Williams, Rick Cavin and Bill Davis. [After leaving Sierra], Lori was president for several years of the Yosemite Western Artists group, and a few years ago Bill Davis joined the group and we discovered a few things. For one thing, we discovered that he is an enormously talented artist, which we didn't get to see at Sierra because he was managing and spending much more time with spreadsheets than drawing anything.

"Second is that he's a really good guy, and he really cared about making conditions better for his artists. Because if we thought the designers had problems, the artists were all massively underpaid. Some of them were making what they made in the late seventies and they were still being paid that in the early nineties. So it had not kept up with inflation. Generally, Bill made life better for the artists and he really cared about making the art quality of the games as good as possible and he succeeded in that. So, Bill Davis, archvillain, is actually a really good guy.

"Now we have Rick Cavin, who was the general manager, who we felt was a tyrant and expected everyone to adhere to his hours, which [meant] starting work at 7:00 a.m. In retrospect, Rick managed to keep the place operating through a lot of different dramas and changes. So we had our troubles with him, but he was actually a pretty good guy, too."

Finally, Corey reflects back on Ken Williams himself: "Talking to him years later, we discovered that he really intensely cared about the games he was making. It wasn't just about making money; he loved the games. . . . He thought it was really neat he could make a living making games and that this was just awesome, and when he merged [Sierra] into CUC International and later became Cendant Corporation, he did that to save the company. He said, 'These games are important and I want them to keep going, and if we have more money, we'll be able to make better games and keep the adventure games going.' So, all three of them [were] actually good guys, just working in impossible circumstances. All these processes that we hated at the time, all had a reason. They all made sense, we just kind of felt like we were the guinea pigs on it.

"Working for Sierra was really a roller coaster ride. When it was good, it was really good. When you got into the creativity, you got into working with great people, it was just amazing," Corey reflects. "Then when you had just these massive amounts of soul-numbing overtime and not getting enough sleep and coming in and trying to write code when you couldn't remember what you did last night and stuff like that, those were the bad parts.

"I got stopped by a local sheriff at one point at one or two in the morning, telling me I had turned a corner without stopping for a stop sign. He was convinced I had to be a drunk driver out at that time of night, and I said, 'Actually I'm just coming home from work,' and he eventually let me go with just a warning. But I was constantly coming home between midnight and two in the morning.

"Good times, bad times."

Return of the King

Innovation was again at the fore of every decision as Roberta Williams turned to designing the latest *King's Quest* game for Sierra. Bill Davis may have been the catalyst for bringing the company into the 256-color era, but he was also responsible for hiring talented artists like Andy Hoyos, who served as art designer on *King's Quest V: Absence Makes the Heart Go Yonder!*

"When I joined Sierra, I called in the chips on everyone I knew," Bill recalls. "It was so hard to get artists to come up, because you had no life up there. It's completely isolated. Look at it this way: if you've got a significant other, are they going to want to leave their career and come up there with you and be stuck up in the mountains? And if you don't have a significant other, there's no dating scene, so it was really tough to get people up here. Andy Hoyos was a friend from back in my days at NBC, so I got him to come up."

Together, Bill and Andy were determined to set a tone and feel for the game that was unique.

"I could work really closely with Andy because we'd done it for years," Bill explains. "So we'd sit down and talk about, 'What do we want this game to be?' Funny enough, my big inspiration for *King's Quest V* was the films of Terry Gilliam. What I told Andy was, 'Let's look at these things like through Terry Gilliam's eyes. Terry Gilliam never comes at things straight on. If a ship sails through the ocean in one of Terry Gilliam's films, when it gets to shore you realize it's on the head of a giant who's been walking on the bottom of the ocean. So that's how we want to approach *King's Quest* from now on.'

"That's how we came up with the hermit living in a boat on the shore. Not living in a shack as it was written, living in a lean-to, but a boat that was shipwrecked. He turns it on end and turns it into a home," Bill says. "That's how we ended up with a witch who conjured up her own dwelling out of the elements in the forest and not a gingerbread cottage anymore. That's how we came up with Mordack conjuring up his whole island, with a living castle with eyes that are watching you and walls that are breathing. We wanted his castle to feel like it was a living entity. That all came out of the films of Terry Gilliam."

These sorts of refinements to Roberta's design were Bill's responsibility as creative director, although the final decisions were always left for Roberta. "That was kind of my job to say, 'Have you thought about this?'" Bill explains. "Of course, Roberta was Roberta — I'd leave it up to her as to whether she wanted to follow my suggestion or not. But it was written as a gingerbread cottage; that's where she was coming from."

One of the major suggestions Bill made about the plot involved the ultimate battle between the evil wizard Mordack and King Graham. "The same thing, when we got to the end, the big battle scene. It's basically a magic battle. [Roberta] had them just pointing magic wands at each other and [seeing] whose wand was bigger and knocking them down. I said, 'No, why don't we have them shapeshift?'

"The whole [puzzle] here is, who is the smartest in what they shapeshift [into]? If you turn into a cobra, the other one turns into a mongoose, and you keep upping the ante. When he turns into a mongoose, you turn into a tiger. Finally, when somebody makes a mistake and they play their hand and make the wrong choice when they shapeshift, then the other one gets the upper hand by making the right choice. So it is magic, but it's more intriguing for the viewer. So that's the kind of input I would have in basically all the games. I tried to look at it from outside the box a little bit from what would be traditional."

With the improvements to plot and dialogue that each game brought, Roberta became increasingly frustrated with Sierra's traditional command-based interface. *King's Quest V* finally saw the removal of the traditional type-in parser interface, which was replaced with a mouse-driven point-and-click system.

"The market was changing to where most people didn't want to take the time to learn to type, spell, or figure out just how you talk to a computer via an adventure game," Roberta wrote in the 1994 *King's*

Quest Collection Series game manual. "I had to design an icon interface with that future in mind; something that's about as easy to use as it's going to get. On a design note, I preferred working with the no-typing interface because I had more time to think about the plot and puzzles instead of writing all those error messages for people typing things that alternated from the story."[17]

Bill Davis also worked on that new icon interface and remembers getting pushback from fans. "We'd [had] a text interface for years and years and years, and we realized all these new people that were coming to computers were coming to them with mice and they weren't going to be happy . . . having to type on a keyboard, so we made that decision to bite the bullet and use graphic interfaces on *King's Quest V* on up and take the heat for it, knowing that some people would be pissed but eventually they'd get over it. It was the right way to go. That was a hard decision."

One of the other changes, although minor, was the decision to standardize the Sierra logo that played at the start of every game they produced, with the famous Half Dome fading in. Composer Ken Allen was also tasked with creating a theme that would eventually be used in most Sierra games from *King's Quest V* until *Space Quest 6*.

King's Quest V: Absence Makes the Heart Go Yonder! was rereleased as a CD-ROM version a year after its initial launch. "It just seemed like the logical thing to do, especially where I came from," Bill recalls. "It was thrilling to know we had the capabilities. It was challenging. Doing our first CD-ROM, you've got to remember we were looking at all the different systems that were out there and trying to figure out, before CD-ROM players came out in America, what was it going to be. We looked at the Philips system, CD-i . . . we looked at all the different systems. It was a learning curve for all of us."

Bill explains that, "In the beginning you really had to lay out your blueprint for where everything was located on your disc because the readers were so slow, so the things that had to be accessed right away had to be wherever the needle drop was. You had to kind of plan out, 'How often is it going to go out to get this? If it's not going to be very frequently, can we stick it way on the outer edge?'

"We wanted to get into it so badly, the very first ones we did for a machine in Japan [were] *King's Quest V* and *Mixed-Up Mother Goose*. It just seemed like a natural progression as soon as we could do it. I'd been working with all those things in animation, so it was just natural."

Taking advantage of the extra room available on a CD-ROM, *King's Quest V* featured full voice acting recorded in Sierra's own custom-built studio within the Oakhurst building. Josh Mandel, who voiced King Graham, recalls, "It was tiny; it was like a six-foot-by-six-foot booth with the soundproofing around it and another room to record. I'm not sure when that was set up because we weren't doing voices up until then. It wasn't big, but it was decent."

Unsure whether a voiced game was worth the expense, Roberta decided against hiring Hollywood voice actors, instead utilizing the voice talents of the staff at Oakhurst. "We talked about [hiring voice actors] but it seemed like it was going to be way out of our budget," Josh says. "I wasn't involved with the *King's Quest V* budget or production, really, except as an onlooker. But I think they decided that using real actors would involve going to Los Angeles or something which they didn't want to do. They had made this little studio; they thought that would be good enough."

Cedric the Owl was the last major character cast, as programmer Richard Aronson recalls. "I had been at Sierra a couple of weeks and Roberta Williams comes up to me and says, 'I understand you have a theater and acting background.' I said yes and she said, 'We have one role we haven't been able to cast in *King's Quest V*, Cedric. I'd like you to read for it. We've auditioned everyone in Oakhurst and everyone in Fresno and I really don't want to have to go down to Los Angeles and hire a professional actor to do it.'"

Richard inquired about the character and says that Roberta had a very clear idea of what she was looking for: "She said, 'Cedric is a very, very smart five-year-old boy. He will make mistakes because he's so smart, so when he's not really sure about something he'll say it's the absolute truth, but he'll sound a little uncertain. And he's an owl.'"

Richard wasn't sure about the role at first, responding, "'I don't think that's something I'd really like to read for.' The BBC had just come out with [*The Chronicles of*] *Narnia* and they had all the owls in *Narnia* with the BBC radiophonic labs behind them. I didn't think I could do much with me and my voice compared to that. She said, 'We'd really like you to read for it, please?' She asked politely and she's like . . . Roberta Williams. So I read for it and obviously she loved it," Richard laughs.

The role was one of the largest in the game, and with such a distinctive voice, Richard worked hard to get it right. "Cedric is a big part and it's all falsetto and my throat got hurt. I sing bass. I've sung bass at Carnegie Hall. I've sung operas and opera choruses. Cedric was very hard. If you listen through the game you can tell near the end of the recording my falsetto was a good two to three notes lower than at the beginning just because I got so tired. But they always played Cedric for the tours because the kids always loved Cedric. Roberta's voice direction was very, very good. . . . She was the best voice director I've ever had."

It certainly didn't pay very well. "I got $100 for doing Cedric. My daughter got $100 for doing Scout in *Hoyle Classic* [*Card Games*]. And you were expected to fulfill your other daily obligations as well. I spent the better part of three weeks in the recording studio for Cedric. I'm just starting a new job and I want to be known as a lead programmer and not a voice actor, yet all my time is being eaten up." Despite its challenges, however, Richard believes that "it worked out well. In hindsight, if I'd done more of that then I could probably be doing that today. A much more lucrative career!"

The development of CD-ROM technology was also a boon for another game Sierra was working on at the time, a VGA remake of Roberta Williams's *Mixed-Up Mother Goose*. Ken Allen was involved in composing the score for the game and says that the music team took full advantage of the extra space offered by the technology.

"Ken [Williams] invited me and Mark [Seibert] and a couple of others in the music department to come down to the first floor and look at the new CD-burning module he had just acquired. It either had serial number one or something in the single digits. It was the very first Sony CD-ROM burner."

Knowing that Sierra was going to start releasing games on CD-ROM, Ken Allen did some research and discovered that CD-ROMs could be created in a mixed mode, where the first track was data and the subsequent tracks were Red Book audio, the standard for CD audio.

"Roberta said to us, 'We're going to take *Mixed-Up Mother Goose* and record all the songs with a children's choir.' I had done the music for the earlier SCI remake, and we took those and orchestrated them for live players.

"We recorded them down at Fresno in a recording studio. Mark belonged to a church that had a really good music program and his wife was the choir director for the kids' choir. They taught the kids to sing those songs during the normal weekly choir sessions, then brought them into the recording studio to record them.

"That game actually pushed the limits on what you could put on a CD-ROM. We filled the CD up with Red Book audio and Ken [Williams] was going, 'I give you a new technology that gives you more space and you filled it up on our first game!'"

A Real Pantload

Production on *Space Quest IV: Roger Wilco and the Time Rippers* began almost immediately after *Space Quest III* was finished in 1989. This had been standard for the entire series, which had begun to feel draining for Scott Murphy in particular, who was becoming burnt out from the furious production pace at Sierra. Scott's frame of mind began to come across in the direction the game would take, setting a darker tone than had previously been seen.

Mark Crowe remembers that another reason for the change in atmosphere was due to the upgrade in graphical ability from 16 to 256 colors. "I think we were trying to be heavier; at least I was, because I influenced everything with the visuals and was definitely going for an edgier look. That was influenced by the sci-fi films of the day, *Terminator* and all these other dark apocalyptic and futuristic kind of things. We injected that into the game. Not that we were trying to make the game serious, but give some of the scenes a weight."

As creative director of the company's entire line, Bill Davis was instrumental in implementing a number of graphical changes to Sierra's series during his tenure, but never felt the need to change the style Mark Crowe had created for *Space Quest*.

"Those were my favorite properties while I was at Sierra, the *Space Quest* series," Bill says. "And I told Scott and Mark that; I just absolutely loved that series. I thought they were intelligent; I thought the humor was as sophisticated as you wanted it to be. I thought it competed head-to-head with the wonderful humorous LucasArts titles.

"You have to realize, too, that Mark Crowe was the chief art director at Sierra when I started, as well as one of the co-designers on *Space Quest*, so you have to give him respect. That's just the right thing to do. So I tried to keep my hands off of *Space Quest* except for where they would accept approaches like where they would do the titles differently. Because I have a lot of respect for Mark Crowe. He did some amazing effects even before I got there."

An edgier side to their humor was also apparent in *Space Quest IV*, this time due to the voice acting that hadn't been available before. "There was more of that attitude, sardonic type of humor of it coming through," Mark remembers. "It was definitely one of the highlights of my time at Sierra, getting to go down and record [the narrator] Gary Owens. That was pretty amazing."

The shift from a type-in parser interface to a point-and-click mouse system made production on *Space Quest IV* a much different experience from earlier games. As Roberta Williams was developing the new icon-driven system for *King's Quest V*, Ken had approached Mark and Scott with a choice: would they consider using that for their next *Space Quest* instead of the text parser they had been using to that point?

Scott and Mark discussed the issue over the next few days. "I think we bucked at the idea initially, because there was definitely gameplay and humor to be mined from the parser aspect of the game," Mark recalls. "At the same time, we were of two minds because – at least speaking for myself – it was a lot of work writing all that parser stuff. So there was certainly the appeal of modernizing and going with the mouse input and everything. That was attractive."

Eventually the Two Guys decided against adopting the new system. Upgrading the graphics to 256 colors was a big enough change for one game and they both enjoyed the way the parser could deliver a wide range of options to the player, something they saw as being curtailed with point-and-click. Having made their choice, they returned to Ken and informed him.

A couple of months later, the opposite decision was made by Ken Williams and Bill Davis that *Space Quest IV* would use the new interface after all. While not recalling that particular encounter, Ken did believe it was the way they needed to go. "I do remember thinking that it was the right answer at that particular point in time," he says.

Scott and Mark weren't happy. "We were told that was pretty much the way it was going. 'Get used to it, get on board,'" Mark explains. The two adapted quickly to the new system, but unfortunately a lot of work had already been done, which was now looking like wasted effort. Mark Hood was a senior programmer at the time and was tasked with converting the Two Guys' existing work to the new system.

"Ken gave them the choice and they decided parser. They went along that way for months, then Ken told them they had to change it. The team said it would be impossible and they figured they'd have to rewrite everything," Hood explains. "I came up with a way where they could keep all their code for the parser, and the icon bar class would translate the point-and-click into the code as if someone had typed it. An eyeball on a door generated 'look at door' as if someone typed it. This was part of one of two patents I got named on, the other being the avoider [the ability to walk around obstacles automatically]."

It was because of this new system, and the previously created responses for a parser interface, that the decision was made to add two new icons to the mix: taste and smell. "We did have discussions about the extra icons. They wanted them for humor, some already coded, but also just for fun," Mark Hood recalls. "All this object-orientated stuff [of the SCI engine] did however allow me to port *Space Quest IV* from full parser-driven text input to point-and-click in a matter of a week. If it would have been procedurally coded, we would have had to recode the whole thing pretty much."

While the two additional icons were added ostensibly to accommodate existing content, they also served comedic purposes in lampooning the unwanted change. "We resisted and tried to find ways to poke fun at it," Mark Crowe recalls. "In fact, that was why we put the smell and taste icons on there, because we were basically making fun of the whole interface idea. We had fun with it."

Space Quest IV: Roger Wilco and the Time Rippers was future *Space Quest* designer Josh Mandel's first chance to write for the series. With a larger and more complicated game, some of the writing duties were assigned to Josh – the first time a script had been shared outside the Two Guys.

Josh remembers the first task he was given: "I went to Mark, and first I introduced myself and I had to wipe the fan drool from my chin. I said, 'I'm available if you need any writing done on any parts of the game or anything at all. I'm anxious to help because I don't want to be a producer all my life,' which he understood.

"He said, 'Here's the artwork for these boxes that are going to be in the bargain bin in the game; we need descriptions for all of these games. Oh, and by the way, you're Jewish right?' And I'm like, 'Yeah' – I was the only Jew in the company at the time, and maybe I'm the only Jew who was [ever] at the company! He took a picture of me, which he turned into the box art for [*Carmen Sandiego* spoof] *Hymie Lipschitz*. He said, 'You're Jewish; give me a Jewish name. I need a Jewish name for this box art.' And I said, 'Well, you can't get too much more Jewish than Hymie Lipschitz.' And he said, 'I like that, we'll go with that.'"

Along with forever immortalizing him as Hymie, Josh says Mark "gave me the box descriptions, the click messages for what might have been Xenon and the [Galaxy] Galleria – just things that were off the critical path. And also the interaction with the monochrome boys. So I wrote those parts of *Space Quest IV* and a lot of the manual."

Mark Seibert had been assigned to compose the soundtrack for *Space Quest IV*, but late in production he took his family for a short holiday. It was during this vacation that Bill Davis approached Ken Allen about creating some music for the game.

"Bill Davis came to me and said, 'The Two Guys are having a product review next week and we need to have music for the opening scenes. Would you mind spending your weekend producing some music for the opening of the game?'" Ken recalls.

Ken felt he had proven his ability to Sierra by this stage and had been wanting to work on one of the company's tentpole series, so he jumped at the opportunity to work on *Space Quest IV*.

"We put a video camera in front of the computer screen and taped the whole thing. I took home the video and scored the first few opening moments of the game over the weekend. I pushed the MT-32 [Roland MIDI device] just as hard as I could. They definitely wanted something epic. On Sunday I came back with the MIDI files and we put them in, and Scott [Murphy] and I reviewed and looked at what we could do differently. Scott had some suggestions, so I went home that Sunday night and implemented all the changes he wanted," Ken remembers.

On Monday morning, Ken took his changes to Scott, who added the MIDI files to the game.

"He played it, and as we watched the opening scenes to that game, Mark Crowe came over and he had a big grin on his face, saying 'Yeah, that's what we want!' After the music had finished, there was some applause from the office and I heard someone say, 'Play it again!'"

The work Ken Allen did on *Space Quest IV* is still the highlight of his career.

Sales for *Space Quest IV* were very good, with reviews calling it the best in the series to date. But well after its release, when Sierra was deep into working on the CD-ROM version of the game, they received a legal notice from Eveready, the company behind the popular Energizer Bunny battery commercials of the time.

According to Scott Murphy in an interview from the late nineties: "Our legal counsel at the time did contact [Eveready's competitor] Duracell asking permission to use a likeness of the bunny in our game. I'm sure they thought this as amusing as the rest of us did. I don't think [the lawyer will] ever forget this nor live it down. He eventually contacted someone by phone at Eveready and got a verbal agreement with a token fee in exchange and all looked fine. Hey, free advertising or 'product placement' as they call it now. After the disk version had been out for a full year and we had been working away on the CD speech version of [*Space Quest IV*], we did get one of those letters from a different member of the Eveready company. Ken's thought and rationalization for continuing to use it on the CD version was that we had already sold most of the number of units we expected to sell, we had the verbal agreement, it was a legal parody blah blah blah. Anyway, the back of the rabbit has a black and copper looking battery in it, it was ignored and finally went away."[18]

Aside from legal issues, the CD-ROM edition of the game was a real coup for the *Space Quest* series. Having another year of production time, Sierra upgraded some of the graphics and added voice acting. Unlike the amateur voice work in *King's Quest V*, this game seemed poised to get the very best.

"[Comedian] Robin Williams sends Sierra a letter saying he loved Sierra games and he played them all the time," Richard Aronson remembers. "If we were doing voice work, he'd love to work with us. They were going to do *Space Quest IV* on CD and so they sent Robin Williams a letter and his agent said his lowest fee was 20% of the entire game's budget."

With that dream casting no longer possible, they faced the daunting task of finding an alternative. "Gary Owens was a radio announcer and a TV guy on *Rowan & Martin's Laugh-In*. Very famous radio announcer in the US and did some TV work. He was the original voice of [animated characters] Roger Ramjet and Space Ghost. He's got real chops. Gary Owens was willing to work for scale. He had a recognizable and great voice and was a hilarious man. Very, very glib. So they brought him in and paid him scale, which still ended up being quite a bit of money, but a lot less than Robin Williams was asking," Richard says.

"He was incredible. He read every line as written. He said about half the lines, 'That's a pretty good line but I think I've got a better take on that. Can I give it a try?' And they always took his line as being funnier than what they'd written in the first place. Just a real genius and really made that CD game pop."

Mark Crowe supervised the recording sessions for Gary Owens and has nothing but fond memories of the experience: "He had the script, but I don't know how much reading he did beforehand. It was so fun because he was such a professional and it was amazing the stuff we gave him on that script. I don't think in the day[s] before people were doing video game voice-over, they were used to such long recording sessions and having to do so much text. Man, he just barreled through it and got it done. It was funny, because he appreciated the humor, and some of the lines he would just crack up. We had to do several takes just to get it done. He knew exactly what we wanted and just sort of rifled it off and we knew he was the right guy for it.

"Back then you were describing the scene and the narrator was telling you what you were looking at. Describing it in more detail than we were able to show graphically. He had nothing to go on when he was reading the lines. He really seemed to get it, the humor aspect of it."

Between the floppy disk and CD-ROM releases, *Space Quest IV* was a big hit, but it was also the last time the Two Guys would work together at Sierra.

Exit: Sonny Bonds

With the success of *King's Quest V* and *Space Quest IV*, it was *Police Quest*'s turn to get a VGA makeover.

Jim Walls developed the script for *Police Quest 3: The Kindred* the same way he had done with his two previous games in the series, taking elements of his own experiences on the police force combined with those of friends and colleagues, and putting them into a storyline that worked within the framework of an adventure game. But this time, the technology had improved to the point where they could aim for a higher level of realism.

"This is a much more complex game than the first two," Jim said in a 1991 interview. "Because the technology keeps advancing, each game you do is better, more involved. The limitations on space and memory are changing, so you can put more in each game. It makes the storytelling great."[19]

The story, however, felt too similar to the first two games to Josh Mandel, who was working on a VGA *Police Quest 1* remake at the same time: "I was always really frustrated with the *Police Quest* series because the plot was always exactly the same. Sweet Cheeks changes from old high school friend to girlfriend to wife. And the name of the villain changes but it's basically Sonny's loved one is imperiled by either Bains or a member of his family. And he must rescue her."

Graphically the third game was a big improvement over the previous two installments, with a much more realistic look. Mark Crowe was the project coordinator on *Police Quest 3* and says it had a much bigger team than they had previously worked with, which meant that his role involved less drawing and more coordination.

"I was the director, basically," Mark recalls. "Directing the artists and the development of the art and design. Set the look and basically art directing with a team of illustrators to draw and paint the backgrounds. I was really happy when that came out; we had some really talented illustrators with that one. Jim Larsen was one of the artists. I really loved working with him on that one; a really talented artist. I learned a lot from him, actually, as a painter."

The new mouse-driven interface was also a design challenge for Jim Walls and his team, requiring a major adjustment from their previous games. "The new parser-less interface is one of the big differences. It means you have to find a different way of telling the story, rethink everything you used to know about designing a game. But this kind of interface puts you into the game the way a typed-in interface can't. It gives you a more real feeling if you don't have to worry about what you have to type. It's more intense," said Jim in the same 1991 interview.[20]

Another major focus of the game was the soundtrack. For *The Kindred*, Jim Walls and Mark Seibert wanted something unique, so they signed world-renowned musician and composer Jan Hammer for the main theme. Mark and fellow Sierra composer Rob Atesalp then created further themes as well as realistic sound effects, all adding to the authentic tone they were looking for.

When the game launched, Jim Walls wasn't around to enjoy the fruits of his labor. Near the end of production, he was approached to work for Tsunami Media by Ed Heinbockel, formerly Sierra's chief financial officer and now running his own game studio in Oakhurst.

Jim wasn't the only person to leave Sierra around this time. Mark Crowe, who had created the *Space Quest* series with Scott Murphy and worked on all three *Police Quest* games to date, decided *Police Quest 3* would be his last project for the company. "When we were finishing that up and getting it out the door, that was about the time I was making my exit to Dynamix. That was the last project I did for Sierra specifically," Mark shares.

Police Quest 3 was another hit. VGA games were a huge success, and there were more to come.

They Really Did Skip *Larry 4*

Al Lowe had worked long hours to get his third *Leisure Suit Larry* game finished. After three adventures that wrapped up the story quite nicely, he had had enough. Anyone who asked about the next game was told that there would never be a *Leisure Suit Larry 4*. It was a promise Al kept.

Al's next project was nevertheless related. *The Laffer Utilities*, advertised as "America's leading non-productivity tool," was a spoof of popular productivity software such as Norton Utilities. Mostly containing programs that were simply time-wasters and jokes, *The Laffer Utilities* did have a few useful programs such as a memo pad and a sign creation package.

Josh Mandel briefly worked as a writer on *The Laffer Utilities* and remembers it as a fun little project: "All those desktop utilities and those kinds of suites were very popular around that time. I don't know whose idea it was to do comical ones with Larry. A quick kind of thing. I only wrote one portion of it that I specifically remember and that was the horoscopes."

After finishing with *The Laffer Utilities*, Al Lowe turned his attention to a new project he and Ken Williams had brainstormed: a *Leisure Suit Larry* multiplayer game. Al had a rough plan for the plot of the game, but most of the efforts were put into programming. Jeff Stephenson was assigned to the project as the lead programmer with an impressive pedigree, having written both the AGI and SCI engines for Sierra. Another programmer, Matthew George, would create the code required for players to communicate while Al would work on the design and game programming. In January 1991, they found an office and started working together.

It wasn't an easy process, made harder by the fact that most players didn't have modems and the majority of those who did still used slow 1,200-baud versions. It was decided to only send player data between players, with the main program files installed on each person's own computer, but even that wasn't enough. After a few months of frustrating work, the project ground to a halt with no progress made on the essential speed issues.

Al Lowe was eventually commissioned to design the next adventure game in the *Leisure Suit Larry* series instead, but knowing that he'd promised never to design *Leisure Suit Larry 4*, he simply skipped the number.

The question Al wanted people to ask was: where was *Larry 4*?

"*Leisure Suit Larry 4* was always just a joke. And it worked. People are still talking about it!" Al laughs.

Having fulfilled his promise – at least technically – Al started working on *Leisure Suit Larry 5: Passionate Patti Does a Little Undercover Work*.

Resuming the way he had created the first two *Leisure Suit Larry* games, Al worked from his home in Fresno, writing and designing his new adventure. This time, though, there were a few changes to the process, with Al relinquishing his programming duties. As Al amusedly remembers it, "I got thrown out of the code in *Larry 5*. The lead programmer said, 'You stay away from the code from now on.'"

Prior to *Leisure Suit Larry 5*, Al had been in charge of administration, but this time Guruka Singh Khalsa had been assigned to take over these duties. "Guruka was producer in that he was directly responsible for the team, tracking their hours, tracking their production of the game, the individual views and scenes and backgrounds and animations and all the stuff that had to be done," Al explains.

"That game was done remotely. I was working in Fresno writing and designing, and the team was based up in Oakhurst, so [Guruka] maintained day-to-day overseeing of that and left me free to write. We did a lot by phone and by modem. I would also come up once a week and see how things were going."

During these weekly visits, Al would sometimes show Ken Williams parts of the game he had been working on, although the reaction wasn't always what he was expecting. "What used to piss me off is I would work really hard and be really proud of something, and I would show it to Ken, and he would immediately have three ideas that would make it better that I hadn't thought of. Goddamn it, he's good! That part of it was frustrating but also admirable."

Another major change was the introduction of the point-and-click interface. Unlike the *Space Quest* team, Al embraced the change, feeling it would expand his audience: "I thought of it as a challenge. I thought it was a good idea. I realized a lot of people had trouble with vocabulary and spelling. I thought this would make the games more accessible to more people."

The change to a mouse-driven interface would also make the gameplay a lot simpler, something nobody predicted at the time. "What I didn't understand was how much easier it made the games," Al admits. "All of us were shocked when people finished them easily. Everyone was shocked because the games were as complicated and as difficult as they had been; it was just without the typing, it was a lot easier."

The ease of *Leisure Suit Larry 5* wasn't entirely unintentional, however, as the game was being used as a test case for an experiment, as Josh Mandel explains: "This experiment was by Ken's design. He'd noticed something in our warranty cards, which were used by the marketing department as surveys. We'd ask the customer what interest they had in various genres of games, basic demographic information, and so on. The cards indicated that a hefty percentage of respondents never finished the games they bought. Ken felt that this was an opportunity lost for a satisfactory customer experience. So making *Leisure Suit Larry 5* easier was sort of a trial run."

While the experiment seemed like a reasonable idea, Al Lowe remembers it being a lot of work. "We also tried a different technique where we gave alternative solutions to puzzles," he explains. "What it did was it made twice as much work for the team and it made the game solvable more easily, because if you didn't think of one thing you might have thought of the other one because there were two solutions to most every puzzle.

"Mostly people ended up at the end of the game, instead of 1,000 points I think you could actually finish with 250 or something. A lot of people ended up with 300 or 350, and the idea was, 'Oh, I'll go back and play it again and try and find the more difficult answer.' But nobody ever did that. That was a foolish thought on our part because that didn't happen.

"What we did was give ourselves twice the work, make the games go twice as fast and have people complain because the game is too easy. Well, it's only too easy because you only found the easy answers. If you found the difficult answers it'd have been a lot harder game. 'Yeah, but I'm not going to play it again.'"

A lot of customers complained, and so did critics for the same reason. The experiment was successful from the standpoint of gaining useful information, but it also showed that the market didn't want such easy games. Al concludes, "That was a dead end we tried and [it] didn't work so we didn't do it again."

Leisure Suit Larry 5 also introduced a new art style to the franchise, championed by creative director Bill Davis. "I wanted to use what we call [a] multiple viewpoint perspective approach to the graphics, which is kind of Cubist. It's something I always thought would look great in games," Bill says.

Ken Williams instead wanted a more realistic look for the series, along with the move to 256 colors, but Bill's plan eventually won the day, the argument being that Ken's vision would change the whole feel of the games.

"I came in and said, 'What you've got now is kind of an innocent politically incorrect game, but it's fairly innocent because it's a cartoon,'" Bill remembers. "As a cartoon, it gives it a particular feeling that you don't take it as seriously because it's a cartoon. But if you start using real actors and real action, you've got real naked women in hot tubs and stuff, it's going to be a completely different animal and I don't think you really want to do it.'"

Al wasn't completely sold on the Cubist style, but was willing to try it. "I noticed immediately that it was Bill's favorite style, as he had many examples in his office of other art done the same way," Al says. "I thought it odd that that one style would be 'perfect' for Larry. After consideration, though, I thought it would make Larry look different from any other game out there. To me, that was good. So I went along."

Al goes on to say about Bill's influence, "He also really helped the animation aspect of the games. He really convinced Ken that we should go to hand-drawn cel animation and hand-drawn backgrounds and all that stuff. We had been working with primitive tools and suddenly we started scanning real images. It made a difference; those games look different."

One complaint Al has about *Leisure Suit Larry 5* was the use of in-game advertising by the phone company Sprint: "I didn't like that. I don't like advertising anyway, and I thought it didn't have any place in a game. Obviously, I was wrong in that one. [In-game advertising is] everywhere, I guess, now!"

Regardless of the criticisms leveled against it, the fourth *Leisure Suit Larry* (with the wrong number in the title) won numerous awards and ended up selling over 250,000 copies,[21] similar to the earlier games in the series.

The new art style of *Larry 5* was also well received, and would go on to be used in the remake of Al's original classic as part of an attempt by Sierra to relaunch all their old titles in the amazing world of 256 colors.

Interlude: Edutainment

Sierra had been developing educational titles since their earliest days. Al Lowe's early games like *Bop-A-Bet* and his Disney work all had educational elements to them. Roberta Williams herself had designed *Mixed-Up Mother Goose*, a huge seller for the company that would go on to have multiple remakes as technology advanced. But the major shift toward educational games came in the 1990s from Bill Davis, who saw "a lot of potential there."

"I've always been into children's books and children's literature. I've worked on children's textbook series. I really love kids," Bill explains. "I saw that the graphic adventure was a perfect vehicle to actually teach, and teach in a different way. Kids would still really have fun while they were learning and be exposed to things that they would have no interest in otherwise, like *Twisty History* [the working title for *Pepper's Adventures in Time*] and *EcoQuest*. I proposed that to Ken, brought up a few treatments of potential games we could do, and he greenlit them. I think I was actually using the term 'edutainment' back then. We might have coined that phrase at Sierra!"

Ken Williams brought together everyone needed to flesh out what would become Sierra's lineup of educational titles. "Ken called all his designers, all the writers and management into a meeting," Corey Cole remembers. "He had each person prepare for that by writing up five to ten game proposals. Everybody then went over their proposals and he'd given a couple of sample ideas for what a proposal would look like, and one of his was *Mathematical Mansion*. I took that one and said, 'Well, let's turn it into this castle. We'll have this character Dr. Brain who'll be looking for a new lab assistant and he gives you a series of puzzles and tests to see if you are the right person to be his lab assistant. And that became *Castle of Dr. Brain*. I think largely because it was based on Ken's original idea, he loved it."

As Corey recalls, his wife Lori's idea was to "rip off *Mixed-Up Mother Goose* and do a thing called *Mixed-Up Fairy Tales*. And of course, being based off one of Roberta's games, Roberta loved it. So out of the hundred or so proposals, they picked three games which were those two and *EcoQuest*."

EcoQuest: The Search for Cetus, an adventure game with an environmental message that was relatable to children, was one of the earliest edutainment titles that Bill Davis conceptualized and designers Gano Haine and Jane Jensen would eventually design. It was a hit adventure game for Sierra in a new demographic, and it met all the goals Bill had discussed with Ken: it informed and educated children using cutting-edge game design and it was fun to play. A sequel called *Lost Secret of the Rainforest* was produced a few years later, this time designed by Gano alone as Jane had been given her own series by then, *Gabriel Knight*.

Castle of Dr. Brain was Corey's first solo design and one that Bill Davis loved from the beginning. "That was something that Corey proposed. We always tried to have an open-door policy so if somebody had an idea, bring it up and if it's something that sounds like it's doable and would be well received, let's do it. And that was Corey with *Dr. Brain*."

For Corey, "*Castle of Dr. Brain* was probably the most enjoyable thing I've done because Lori was off in San Francisco at the beginning of that, so I started sketching out the puzzles and the basic design of the game. First of all, I got to do it myself, then I got totally stuck and depressed and called up Lori and said, 'You've got to come home' and she said, 'No, I've got another week in this class I'm taking.' Finally, when she did get home, she helped me through some of the rough spots and helped me with some of the puzzles. So it was a collaboration, but [for] this one I got to feel I was the writer, I was the main designer. I just really had a lot of fun.

"My original thought on it was to take brainteaser books that I enjoyed as a child and do a whole series of brainteasers. A couple dozen of these books, it turns out that with all those books combined there's about five puzzle types in there. There is really hardly any variety. And most of them aren't suitable for a computer game. So I actually had to invent what's in there. We took a couple of things like an acrostic [a poem where the first letter of each line spells out a message]; I was very proud of that."

As with all of Sierra's games, though, the end result was a team effort. "I had the basic idea and I had it all in a very abstract form," Corey recalls. "I worked with Jon Bock, a Sierra artist. He owns an art gallery now; he's still in Oakhurst. He helped me put together a prototype of what the code room could look like and what the puzzles could look like and so on. We built that as a prototype and presented it to Ken and the rest of Sierra management, but [Ken] pulled Jon off and gave us Andy Hoyos as the lead artist then.

"I told Andy I wanted it to be a little wacky, a little mad scientist-ish. He came up with that amazing design for the exterior of the castle, which is just this weird mishmash, flamingos and everything else. Then, for the inside of the castle, he came up with the idea that instead of having regular rectangular corridors, everything was curved and organic. That just really made the game; it was really important to it."

The game's rock ballad–style musical score also makes it stand out, although Corey can't remember if that was his idea or composer Mark Seibert's.

A unique in-game hint system was introduced as well. "I thought I came up with an interesting mechanism and that was the hint coins," Corey says. "You earn coins for solving the puzzles, and that's your score at the end of the game, but if you want you can spend some of your coins in order to get hints. So you could lower your score in order to get help. I thought that worked pretty well."

Castle of Dr. Brain was successful enough that Sierra wanted another, something Corey had already signposted. "I named the sequel *Island of Dr. Brain*, and I foreshadowed it at the end of our game and was intending to write the sequel," he recalls. "The problem is, Sierra was on an economy kick, and [even though] I was paid a small royalty for *Castle of Dr. Brain* . . . they did not want to pay royalties to employees anymore. They were going to pay me a fixed amount and what they said, basically, was they would pay me $5,000 for designing the second game. They also didn't want me to work on it [during] work hours, they wanted me to work on it on evenings and weekends.

"So I said, 'You want me to give up all my evenings and weekends for six months to a year, in return for $5,000? No, I'm not going to do that.' I am the reason the first game sold so well for them. It made Sierra a ton of money and they should [have been] willing to pay me for that. They basically were not willing to compromise, and they said, 'We've got this writing department and we'll just get one of the writers from that to do it.'" Still, Corey doesn't regret the decision: "It would've killed me to work seventy-hour weeks for a year. I couldn't have done it. For $100,000, it still would've killed me."

Lori Cole designed another of Sierra's early edutainment titles, *Mixed-Up Fairy Tales*, one that she is extremely proud of.

"*Fairy Tales* was really good. We had a good team again; we had interesting people that were willing to work, and of course we had Stuart Moulder as producer. It was Stuart's idea to use classical music, which I thought was great, and we did a fine job of translating that to the limitations of our instruments. I thought it turned out really well. I thought it worked. At this point it didn't have voice, which it did need. It would have added that extra layer of interaction. [But] we wanted to teach reading, and you don't learn reading if everybody tells you everything.

Just as importantly, of the development experience itself, Lori says, "It was very easy, after everything we'd gone through [with *Quest for Glory II*], so it was a pleasure."

Sierra would go on to continue producing educational games under their Sierra Discovery Series label. *Pepper's Adventures in Time* was the only one developed internally, though, with other titles like *Quarky & Quaysoo's Turbo Science* and *Spelling Jungle* coming from their subsidiary companies Dynamix and Bright Star.

Bright Star Technology, founded in the early 1980s by Elon Gasper and Nedra Goedert, was purchased by Sierra in 1992, becoming one of the foundation stones of Sierra's move into the educational software industry.

Bright Star had developed a technology that appealed to Ken. Called HyperAnimation, it was lip-sync software that allowed a computer to synchronize a character's exact mouth movements with the sound that the player would hear. This new technology was quickly applied to a range of educational titles such as *Alphabet Blocks*, allowing children to learn not only what letters looked like, but also how they sounded and the shape a mouth would make when speaking that word. Partnering with Sierra was the catalyst for Elon's vision.

"Our dream at Bright Star is to use new technology to create talking personal tutors that interact with children, coaching them to read and write and do it well," Elon said in *InterAction* magazine in 1992. "Since these language arts and literacy skills form the foundation for further learning, I believe Bright Star's products will play a special role in realizing Ken Williams's vision of our coming educational revolution."[22]

Bright Star quickly became known for their best-selling language software for children such as *Yobi's Magic Spelling Tricks* (rereleased as *Spelling Jungle*) and *Spelling Blizzard*. They also formed a partnership with Golden Books publisher Western Publishing Company and released the highly acclaimed *Math and Spelling with Monker* educational game.

Marcia Bales started with Bright Star shortly after their acquisition by Sierra and has nothing but fond memories of Bright Star and its founder. "I was working for Elon Gasper, [a] really, really super brilliant man. Visionary man," Marcia recalls.

Within six weeks of her hiring, Elon approached Marcia about taking over as project manager on *Berlitz Live! Spanish*, the software she was working on.

"He was the one who came to me and said, 'It's not working.' When he asked me if I thought I could do this, I couldn't believe I said yes. Seriously, I had a little tiny Mac at home, a little all-in-one piece, before they were Macs – an Apple II or something. I sorta knew how to use it. It had a mouse and that was the one good thing: I knew how to use a mouse. So I get there and not knowing any software, just knowing how to draw on paper, I just faked my way into it," Marcia confesses.

"I remember him coming to me. I said, 'I'm not really experienced.' He said 'I don't care. I'll help you.' He did. That's the point I remember thinking, 'This is better than going to college. This is better than your first job. This is better than anything.' To have someone who really, really knows what they're doing help you out and help you become successful. Having the faith that you could do it. It was the coolest," Marcia gushes. "That's why I loved Sierra. I still can't believe I got to do the things I did. Who does that? Who lets people do things they don't have a history doing?"

Edutainment was yet another success story for Sierra.

Chapter 9: Colorizing Old Movies

On the whole, I think the [remake] is beautiful. I think they did a great job of making the environments way better. It kept true to the feeling of the original.

Corey Cole, Designer, Quest for Glory I

While Sierra was moving full steam ahead with the latest installments in their major adventure game series, they were also looking back to their earlier AGI games with a view to updating them in the SCI engine to be more appealing to a modern audience.

The first to get a makeover was *King's Quest I: Quest for the Crown* in 1990. Of all the games that received a makeover, only *King's Quest I* was done in 16-color EGA.

Josh Mandel had recently been employed as a junior producer, and one of the first tasks he was assigned was making sure the updated version was finished and released. "*King's Quest I* was a full-time job for several months at least. When I came in, what they said to me was that *King's Quest I* SCI had been in production for ages and they couldn't seem to get it out. Someone had already come and produced it and worked on it with Roberta, and I don't know what happened, but she was gone," Josh recalls.

"There were two programmers on it. I think the art was mostly done; I don't remember a lot of art being needed. But the whole game was not ready or made up and I played through the original *King's Quest I* and then through what they had for *King's Quest I* SCI."

After playing both versions, Josh had some changes to suggest: "I went to Guruka and asked if he thought Roberta would mind if I changed the text, because the text is still the text from the original *King's Quest* and it's very, very sparse. It doesn't really serve the purpose of text that I had come to feel after being a game player for so many years. If you couldn't actually do anything in a given room or with a given item, at the very least the response should make it interesting so the player hasn't wasted a click. I want every click, if it doesn't result in something that is actually germane to solving the game or moving the story along, at the very least it should be entertaining. I expressed this to Guruka and he said, 'I dunno, ask Roberta.'"

This was nerve-wracking for Josh. "I had a lump in my throat and Roberta didn't know me at all. I hadn't met her previously, and I finally met her and she was charming. I said to her, 'I have a request; do you mind if I rewrite the text?' and she said, 'No! Rewrite anything you want. Rewrite the whole game if you want. Make sure I see all your changes to approve them before they go in.' And I was delighted. I could not have possibly asked for a more receptive answer."

Another unique feature introduced in the remake changed the transitions between screens. "I did work with the programmers on stuff and actually we – I shouldn't say 'we' because I actually had nothing to do with it except requesting it – the programmers invented on *King's Quest I* a sliding room change where it looks like you're scrolling from one room to the next. You're not really; it's not scrolling. It's just a fancy way of loading the new room, but they came up with it vertically and they came up with it horizontally. Neither of which the company had ever had before, the sliding room changes. They took them for *King's Quest V*. So, although the *King's Quest I* project created them, we weren't the first to market with them."

Josh and his team wrapped up production on the remake, proud of their accomplishments. Unfortunately, it shipped within weeks of *King's Quest V*. With the latter boasting cutting-edge, 256-color graphics, hand-drawn backgrounds, and the new mouse-driven interface, *King's Quest I* paled in comparison, with its antiquated 16-color EGA graphics and type-in interface. The remake seemed obsolete and old-fashioned from the day of its release, and its sales reflected this.

Space Quest I: The Sarien Encounter was another of the major adventure games that received a makeover, although without a great deal of input from either Mark Crowe or Scott Murphy. "I was just so busy on other games and working on [*Space Quest IV*]," Mark says. "It was kind of nice somebody else was creating the remake. I didn't have to get too involved. For good or bad, been there, done that. I was ready to move on to something else."

A certain amount of consideration was given to making the parser puzzles from the original game work in a mouse-driven environment. Josh Mandel was responsible for some of the writing on the *Space Quest* remake, too, and remembers the process well. "That was the first time we were really going crazy trying to retrofit a game's puzzles to a point-and-click environment," he says. "There was a lot of feeling around that we had sort of gutted the gameplay, made it too easy and made it too straightforward."

The majority of effort, however, went into overhauling the aesthetic, as Josh recollects. "It was a chance for Doug Herring to redo the art with a real theme behind it instead of just the utilitarian art the original had. So I think a lot more effort went into the artwork of that game than went into any other part of it."

Doug Herring had been brought on board as art designer and was given the task of redoing *The Sarien Encounter*'s art while staying relatively true to the original designs. Taking inspiration from acclaimed comic artist Wally Wood, Doug settled on a retro 1950s sci-fi look. One of the major changes involved the nine screens on the planet Kerona, which Doug reimagined as the skeleton of a large prehistoric-looking creature, instead of brown and yellow mountains. *Space Quest I* VGA wasn't easy for Doug, as a lot of the actual art was outsourced to Korea and came back to him in varying states of quality, which he and his team then had to touch up as best they could.

While Bill Davies didn't influence the art style for the remake, he did have a suggestion for the title screen. "There's this style of coffee shops that happened in America in the 1950s where they used a lot of these artist palette shapes and have all these Sputnik-looking spheres with little points sticking out and lightbulbs on the ends of them. So we kind of did that with the titles for *Space Quest*. The style is called Googie. I don't know why they call it that but that's what it's called."

The largest and most expensive remake Sierra commissioned was *Quest for Glory I*, which Lori Cole worked on at the same time she was designing *Quest for Glory III*. "For the remake of *Quest for Glory*, while I wrote the script they [artists and programmers] were off doing their own thing, and they had all these crazy ideas," Lori says.

One of those ideas was the addition of talkers, or dialogue portraits: a close-up picture of a character's face that appears during conversation. While most of Sierra's games of the era used more traditional hand-drawn pictures, *Quest for Glory* used a process similar but not identical to Claymation.

"They used clay models for everything and then in the computer they then modeled the mouth and things. They animated in the computer. Which is not Claymation, but it was an interesting idea," Lori says.

Her husband Corey has a few "quibbles," as he puts it, with the remake. "We could not convince the programmer these were not arcade games. So he put in a couple of timing sequences that are so tight, you basically have to do them perfectly or you die. That was never the intention of the game. The graveyard we designed so that if you went in there without the undead unguent, or something like that, a ghost would slowly drift towards you, and if you just stood there it would capture and kill you. But you could just walk off-screen. He reprogrammed it so if you walk in there without the undead unguent it takes away player control and just kills you. So that was contrary to the design.

"Another one was the whole brigand area, the brigand cafeteria, got really tight arcade game timing and you had to do everything perfectly to get through there. Yorick the jester was part of that also. That was designed as a slapstick comedy, where you kept falling through holes and trapdoors and such and you'd end up back where you were. But in the remake the timing was too tight on it. Once again, you had to hit it absolutely perfectly in order to get through it. So it lost the flavor of the original."

Richard Aronson worked as a programmer on the *Quest for Glory I* remake and explains what caused these issues.

"There's a thing at Sierra we called Fred. Fred was a little invisible guy that would walk across the screen immediately after install and we would time how long it took for Fred to reach from here to here. That gave us a ratio that determined how much we were supposed to speed up or slow down the game, because we knew that people were playing the game on different qualities of CPUs.

"For about one year, Fred was broken and we didn't know. It took a while for them to figure out and fix it. The *Quest for Glory* [remake] came out and it was one of the games with the broken Fred and now machines were many, many times faster. So the whole thief sequence at the end of the game, that was mine. Where you had to lock the door, then kick the chair across the room to lock the other door, then jump on the chandelier and swing across the room to knock those last guys through the door. Then go back and fight the two guys and take a bow. It was way too fast because Fred was broken. Not because the room was broken."

Another critical SCI bug was discovered and fixed during the production of *Quest for Glory I* VGA, as Richard explains: "We used polygons as borders to limit where the avatar [player character] could move. If the polygon was a multiple of 30 degrees and you were coming in exactly splitting the polygon, you could walk through the polygon. There were random [fatal errors] where people were wandering around where they shouldn't, and they couldn't figure out how to get back, then they had to go back to a saved game to start up again.

"That shipped in every Sierra game for like fifteen months. There were a bunch of reports on every single game about that bug. Every single game. I see this bug and I make it happen again. Then I call up Larry Scott, who was head of our systems programming. I say, 'Larry I've got this bug where you're walking through polygons.' He said, 'We've had that bug for more than a year. If you can get to where you can reproduce it and I can see it, we can fix it. But if we can't reproduce it we can't fix it.'"

Richard was determined, responding that he needed an hour. "Half an hour later, with a saved game, I could do it about two times out of five. I called him over and the third time I was able to do it and he said, 'Okay, stop it. Run our debugger, look at a few variables,' and then thanked me. So I fixed the bug we had for fifteen months. Or at least, I led to it. It was something that had to be greater than 30 but less than 31, but they were both greater and less than 30 so it was exactly 30. One of those weird things."

Technical quibbles aside, Corey Cole is of the opinion that, "On the whole, I think the game is beautiful. I think they did a great job of making the environments way better. It kept true to the feeling of the original even though we went from typing in [questions] to [dialogue] menus, which spoiled some of the surprises because the menus tell you what you can ask. But I think they really worked."

While Sierra went on to produce VGA remakes of *Leisure Suit Larry I*, *Police Quest 1*, *Mixed-Up Mother Goose* and *Oil's Well* (a cartridge-based arcade game from 1983), none of them were big enough hits to warrant pursuing more. What had originally started out as a plan to reskin old games for a modern audience had turned into overly expensive productions that nearly equaled the cost of producing a new game. And the sales numbers weren't great, with only the *Quest for Glory* and *Mixed-Up Mother Goose* remakes being reasonably successful.

Josh Mandel, who oversaw production on three of the remakes, says that it just wasn't worth it to Sierra. "I think they were not selling well enough to justify their unanticipated cost."

Fans to the Rescue

Although Sierra stopped remaking games, some later titles eventually did get the remake treatment – just not by Sierra.

In the early 2000s, Sierra games weren't easily available to purchase. By then the company was a subsidiary of Vivendi Universal and had moved past the classics that made it so successful. But the fans hadn't forgotten the beloved adventures they had grown up with, and some of the more devoted formed into groups whose purpose was to bring back those old titles.

One of the earliest and most successful fan groups was a team who dedicated themselves to remaking what were then unavailable games from Sierra's catalog, ultimately releasing updated free versions of the first three *King's Quest* games, as well as a remake of *Quest for Glory II*, in the style of Sierra's VGA remakes. Calling themselves Tierra Entertainment at first, they changed their name to Anonymous Game Developers Interactive (AGDI) as part of the contract they signed when they negotiated an official fan license with Vivendi.

Their initial *King's Quest* remake, based on Sierra's EGA remaster of *King's Quest I*, marked the first time a fan team had recreated a full Sierra title. One of the highlights was the inclusion of fully voiced speech with Josh Mandel, the original voice of King Graham, reprising his role. Released in August 2001, the game was a mammoth success and as of 2020 has been downloaded over 1.7 million times. It was so popular, in fact, that a common belief held by the AGDI team is that in the early months of its release, the sales for Sierra's *King's Quest: Mask of Eternity* received a large boost, pushing that two-year-old title back into Sierra's top-selling list.

Following this success, AGDI branched out and in 2002 released their reimagining of *King's Quest II* with a new subtitle, *Romancing the Stones*. AGDI's version included an expanded storyline that changed some aspects of the original game while giving the world and characters much more life and vibrancy.

It was after the release of these two titles that another fan group, Infamous Adventures, was formed and created two Sierra remakes of their own. Like AGDI's games, their version of *King's Quest III* was fully voiced and starred Josh Mandel as King Graham. They also had Sierra art director Andy Hoyos, the original voice actor for the evil wizard Mordack, return to that role, along with performing Mordack's brother Manannan, the villain in *King's Quest III*.

One of the highlights of the game, as related by Infamous Adventures co-founder Shawn Mills,[*] was the addition of certain cutscenes that for all intents appeared to be created to flesh out the

---

[*] Yep, that's me. Talking about myself in the third person. I co-founded Infamous Adventures with Steven Alexander in 2001 for the purpose of remaking old Sierra games.

story. "Truthfully, we always said that the extra scenes were for story purposes, but the reality is we just wanted to write more stuff for Josh and Andy to say. You'll notice those cutscenes are mostly King Graham, Mordack and Manannan talking!"

King's Quest III was a success for Infamous Adventures, although not on the same level as AGDI's remakes. A greater achievement was their *Space Quest II* remake, released in 2011, which went on to be downloaded over 2.1 million times.

"I love *Space Quest II*, especially the irreverent sense of humor," says Steven Alexander, the other co-founder of Infamous Adventures. "I think our remake works so well because [Shawn and I] both get the humor of *Space Quest* more than we ever did *King's Quest*. We had a lot of fun working on that game and redesigning the entire asteroid section was a blast. I wanted to keep the cold, empty feel in places, but also make it feel like a legit space fortress for a villain like Vohaul. It also showed us we had the ability to make our own games, so that's what we ended up doing."

The biggest and most professional Sierra adventure game remake, however, belongs to AGDI, who in 2008 released an updated version of *Quest for Glory II*, bringing it up to a level of graphic quality similar to Sierra's own third and fourth games in the series.

While they were not involved in the making of it, Corey and Lori Cole were happy that a particular detail removed from their own game finally made it into a release. "The Saurus repair shop was an Easter egg put in the original game by Brian Hughes, one of the programmers," Corey explains. "We had to cut it out at the last second because we couldn't fit it on the disk. [AGDI] got back in touch with him and he gave them his notes and stuff and they brought back the Saurus repair shop, which was kind of fun."

Overall, the Coles were pleased with what they experienced of AGDI's remake. "It looked really good, and the little bit I did play had a nice feel and was really true to the flavor of what we were doing with the game, so I thought they did a great job of it," Corey says.

One amusing anecdote that emerged from playing the game highlights the only "flaw" Corey found with it. "I was so entranced with the beauty of the scenes and Lori's dialogue and stuff brought to life, it was really nice. I wandered outside of town and got attacked by something and tried to defend myself and it slaughtered me in about ten seconds. I realized I had just been playing the game for an hour and hadn't saved it. There was no autosaving. I said, 'forget this' and stopped playing," he laughs.

Chapter 10: A Bandit, a Detective, and a Detour

Every single beta tester is going to want a copy of the game.
They're going to show off. They're going to feel proud and
invested for working here.

Richard Aronson, Lead Programmer,
Conquests of the Longbow

L ike *Conquests of Camelot* before it, the broad concept for *Conquests of the Longbow: The Legend of Robin Hood* came from Roberta Williams. "I was in the earliest stages of thinking about a game based on Greek mythology using goddesses," Christy Marx says. "I was aware that a number of Robin Hood movie projects had been announced, but when Roberta mentioned them to me I didn't pay attention. It didn't relate to what I was thinking about.

"A day or so later after the first mention, Roberta said to me, 'I had this dream last night that you were doing a Robin Hood game.' I suddenly realized that what she was really doing was dropping hints that they wanted me to do a Robin Hood game."

What exactly is the Robin Hood story? This was the question Christy had to grapple with when she started working on her second game for Sierra. As is common with legends hundreds of years old, the telling of the tale has changed over time, so the first thing Christy did was to follow the story as far back as she could.

Researching the earliest accounts of Robin Hood and the ballads of King Richard helped Christy form the main premise in her mind. The story of *Conquests of the Longbow* would be one of Robin trying to raise the ransom to free King Richard, who had been betrayed and captured by King Leopold of Austria on his way home from the Third Crusade in 1192. While this was to be the main plot, extensive work also went into developing the character of Maid Marian and the love story that would unfold.

While the person of Robin Hood may actually be a myth (even scholars can't be certain), the locations involved in his folktales are all real, and that was an area that Christy could research and portray accurately in the game.

"I went so far as to purchase a huge book that reprinted land maps from medieval England so that I could make Watling Street, originally an ancient Roman road, as accurate as possible (traces of it remain as a major highway in England today). I contacted the museum at Nottingham and purchased useful reference materials from them, including a large poster of what the castle originally looked like," Christy says.

Richard Aronson had recently been installed as a lead programmer at Sierra. His first game was *Conquests of the Longbow* and he recalls the collaborative way in which Christy worked.

"It's my first week there. [SCI systems developer] Bob Heitman comes up to me and says, 'I'm concerned about the amount of art called for in this game. I asked the lead artist for an art list, I asked the producer for an art list, and neither of them had one,'" Richard remembers. "'I want you to work out the storyboards and build a list of all the animations and backgrounds required for this game so we have an idea of just how much it's going to cost.'

"So my first three weeks at Sierra, I was not doing any programming at all. The net result was that the design was about 50% larger than the game was budgeted for. The way we resolved it was by reusing rooms. You would go into the same room on a different day; that lightened up the art load, but programmers had to code the rooms in two different days. So it was still a problem. That's part of why it was such a big game, because we worked really, really hard to get it right."

Another issue occurred during the climax of the game, where Christy had designed a sequence that Richard didn't believe would be possible to produce in the SCI engine: "Originally the combat was supposed to be one of the first real-time strategy games in Christy's design, but I looked at the process of moving two hundred man-sized things on a screen in the VGA world and how much processing power that would take and said, 'No, we can't possibly implement that in this system. We don't have the processing power.'

"So eventually she just handed combat over to me and I wrote five plans and she edited them and rewrote several. Each of Robin's men would present a plan and I would resolve that with the number of men you had alive. Little John would always have terrible ideas except for the last one, which is the best one. Part of your score is based upon how many men you had; politically King Richard is much more likely to reward Robin of Loxley if he has a band of fifty behind him than if he has a band of six behind him. That indicated loyalty and leadership and that he's a strong guy and so forth. It fit within the game sequence."

Richard wound up doing a lot of the design of the Nottingham Fair himself. "Part of why Sierra hired me was I had ten years' experience working and eventually leading workshops at the Los Angeles and San Francisco Renaissance Faire, so I had a very strong background in medieval history. My degree is in English history. When [Christy] got around to that section, she said I could design all the interactions, which I did and then she just edited them. Christy was very collaborative in that way, and so were Corey and Lori [Cole]. Others were less so. It varied."

An important area in which Richard Aronson left his mark was insisting on a way to help people with disabilities play Sierra's games. "My brother-in-law was a quadriplegic. He used to play Sierra games with a wooden stick strapped to his forehead to hit the keys. Then he hit one of our minigames or arcade sequence and he'd have to wait until the nurse beat the minigame for him to continue," he says.

"There were dozens of people in just his convalescent hospital playing these games and they all had the same problem. So when I started at Sierra, I said, 'You know what? A lot of people play our games that have these other issues. We should have a bypass [where] you beat the [minigame] with a score of zero, but you can progress, for people who are physically challenged. We should make sure we have a text display option on all our games for people who are deaf. That should be important.' These are now somewhat standard in the industry but I'm proud of that because I think it helped a lot of lives."

It was during the quality assurance rounds that Richard introduced another new idea to Sierra: crediting all the testers. "Back then, the lead programmer got to write the About screen," he explains. "I wrote the About screen and I sent an email over to the lead QA [tester] and said, 'I want the names of all the testers' and they said, 'Why?' I said, 'I want to put them in the About screen' and they said, 'We don't do that' and I said, 'Why not?'

"About a week later I got called into Ken Williams's office for a meeting on that. He said, 'Why are you doing this?' and I said, 'First of all, it's free. It's not going to add any extra disk space. Second of all, it's going to tell the world we test our games. Third of all, I've written a couple of really good jokes [to include in the credits]. And finally, every single beta tester is going to want a copy of the game. They're going to show off. They're going to feel proud and invested for working here. You motivate your employees, it doesn't cost you anything. You get to improve your PR with the world. Why don't we do it already?' Ken says, 'Okay!' So, we did it and it was well received."

The testing was done in shifts, with a team of testers focused on compatibility issues during the day and another team looking for game bugs at night.

"Most of our testers worked in the daytime and then there was another team that only worked at night because, when you're in crunch mode, you'd do a build before you go home at the end of the day. They'd work on them all night on machines that were very standard, so therefore there's not compatibility issues; it's going to be game bugs that are found. Then you show up first thing in the morning and you'd have your list of bugs. It's a very efficient way to work," Richard describes.

"So I'd list everyone. Executive producer Ken Williams always comes first. Then I'd say QA team one. Long list. QA team two. Long list. Then these people, long list, fixed the bugs that were found in the night. So that worked out really well and became part of the standard."

Conquests of the Longbow: The Legend of Robin Hood was released in December 1991 and went on to become another bestseller for Sierra. It was Christy Marx's last game released with Sierra.[*]

"It was a Christmas release," Richard says. "We made it with a few days to spare, but not many. Actually, I think there [were] like eleven games that Sierra shipped that Christmas, and *Longbow* was the second cleanest. There were no documented [fatal bugs] and only fourteen unresolved bugs that we couldn't fix before we shipped. I'm very proud of that."

"Let's Get *Laura Bow 2* Done"

As product design director, Josh Mandel recalls his first task in the role. "The first thing they said to me was, 'How about *Laura Bow 2*? Let's get *Laura Bow 2* done.'"

Bruce Balfour was a published science fiction writer and game designer who had been working in Southern California for one of Sierra's biggest competitors of the era, Interplay Entertainment. He had been heavily involved in the design process of a number of their big hits including *Neuromancer* and *Battle Chess*, and had prototyped a couple of adventure games such as an adaptation of Robert Heinlein's novel *The Moon Is a Harsh Mistress* and a horror game called *Blood Feast*. In 1990,

---

[*] It was not the last time she worked with Sierra, however, as she came back a few years later to help design the unreleased *Babylon 5* game.

while working on *Battle Chess*, Bruce heard Sierra was looking for writers and designers with game credits, so he placed a call.

"They offered to pay for my visit to see them in the little mountain town of Oakhurst, in the Sierra foothills. Ken and Roberta liked to lure people up there so they could see what a beautiful environment they'd be living in, with easy access to Yosemite, if they chose to work there," Bruce remembers. "When I arrived at the giant metal shed where they were all housed, I wasn't too impressed, but it looked like regular office space inside and there weren't too many rats visible in the hallways, so it turned out okay.

"When I visited, my future manager was to be a new guy hired from Infocom, Michael. I met the head producer, Guruka Singh Khalsa, creative director Bill Davis, the Coles, Christy Marx, Scott Murphy, Josh Mandel, and they all seemed like they'd be fun to work with. I think Josh was supposed to design a game called *Little Larry* at the time. My last interview was with Ken, who thought I was overdressed because I was wearing a button-down shirt instead of a T-shirt. Michael called me a couple of days later and offered me a job, so I figured I'd start several months later in January 1991. However, things changed while I was gone."

Josh Mandel was well aware of how those changes came about, being right in the middle of the whole situation. "Before I became head of the product design department, this guy Michael had been in charge of the department and he seemed like a really nice and level-headed guy. People like Jane Jensen came in under his auspices," Josh recalls.

"Roberta had taken a liking to me by then and said, 'I want you to do the *Laura Bow* sequel. We also want to do this thing called *Little Larry's Guide to Life*,' which was to be a *Leisure Suit Larry* game for teenagers that discussed real modern issues that teens have to deal with, like parental divorce and birth control. It was a horrible idea. She said, 'Josh, I want you to do this sequel to *Laura Bow* and we have this new guy coming on, Bruce Balfour. Let's have him do *Little Larry's Guide to Life*,' which I'd already specced out a rough design document for."

But Josh claims Michael had other ideas. "This guy Michael said, 'It makes no sense at all. Josh has a background in comedy and Bruce has a background in murder mysteries. He should be doing *Laura Bow 2* and Josh should be doing *Little Larry*.' They said to Michael, 'No, this is the way we want it. Definitely.' Then they all went off to a conference: Ken, Roberta and Bill Davis.

"While they were away, Michael said, 'All right, what they want doesn't make any sense, so we're going to switch it. Bruce, you take

Josh's idea for *Laura Bow 2* and do a rough design spec. Josh, you do your description of *Little Larry's Guide to Life* and you do a design spec.' So while everyone was at GDC, Bruce and I worked on our individual designs and then when [Ken, Roberta, and Bill] got back, Michael handed these two documents to them and said, 'Read them over.' They read them and he said, 'How do you like them?' They said, 'These are great; let's move ahead with these.'"

When Michael told the Williamses of having changed the two designers against their wishes, however, they weren't happy. "They said, 'You're fired. Josh, you're the new director of product design.' So that's how I got into that position."

Aware that the previous person in his job had been fired for his decisions about the game, Josh was apprehensive, but still said to Roberta, "'You know, I hate to say this, but Bruce really is a better choice to finish *Laura Bow 2*,' and Roberta said, 'Okay!' So they really fired this guy because they were angry with him, not because they disagreed with his decision."

Bruce was unaware of this drama. "A programming team was due to become available and needed something to work on for the last quarter of 1990, so Sierra called and asked if they could put me up in a hotel room there for a few days to draft an initial design for a sequel to *The Colonel's Bequest*," he recalls. "I remember watching the Gulf War on the TV in my hotel room while I worked on it. When Josh Mandel had originally talked to Roberta Williams about it, he had suggested a story about a lost Egyptian dagger in a museum. The lead character was to be Laura Bow from *Colonel's Bequest*.

"I've always been a fan of mysteries, museums, and ancient Egyptian history, so I had a good time blasting out the concept and storyline for *Laura Bow 2: The Dagger of Amon Ra*. After I left town, my design then went to Bill Davis, who came up with an art deco style for the game that would be suggestive of Leyendecker, a popular artist of that period. Roberta and Josh reviewed it as well. By the time I returned to start my job as a designer / director / senior producer, Andy Hoyos was working on the production design and Bob Gleason was about to do the detailed art design. Brian Hughes was our lead programmer. Really a great team and fun to work with overall."

Josh, too, remembers it being a great game to work on, saying, "Bruce went ahead and designed it and I did a lot of the click events for it and I think Lorelei Shannon did too. And the three of us generally sat in one room and worked on the game. We worked on all those documents that came in the box. It was just a great time and we all just did everything."

While it was a positive experience for Josh, Bruce had an even better time, meeting his future wife Leslie on the project. "In the early 1990s, Sierra had developed their technology and production teams to the point where running *Dagger of Amon Ra* was much like writing and directing a film with a large crew, except that this film had a 600-page script, as opposed to the typical 90-page film script," Bruce remembers.

"Having had two years of film school, the process of making a Sierra adventure looked familiar, particularly when I was directing voice talent at the Maximus recording studio in Fresno or directing the action we were rotoscoping from Sierra's new motion capture studio in Oakhurst. We used in-house bodies for the motion capture, and several in-house voices, but opened up the voice casting because there were some complicated accents and more advanced acting skills required for some parts. We went as far as the Defense Language Institute in Monterey, California to find a good modern Egyptian accent.

"We'd had the most trouble casting Laura Bow with her southern accent, Yvette Delacroix who was French, and the upper-class British narrator. When Leslie Wilson showed up for the audition, she was able to do all three of those accents and had a lot of acting experience, so we put her under contract. Since she was playing two of the biggest parts in the script, as well as Yvette, we spent a lot of time together at the recording studio in Fresno. So, naturally, we got married four years later.

"During that time, she was hired as the editor-in-chief for the new Sierra magazine and also worked on special projects like the promotional humorous documentary *Current Inside Copy: Space Quest – Behind Closed Doors* (1994), which she directed and co-wrote with Barry Smith, a hilarious animator who worked on a couple of my projects."

Sierra was continually expanding the boundaries of what was possible in games, something Bruce Balfour saw firsthand when he was developing *The Dagger of Amon Ra*: "Sierra was always pushing the envelope of what was technically possible to do on a PC at that time. They had developed Sierra's Creative Interpreter (SCI) as their in-house coding platform, and there was a back room with a bunch of systems programmers crammed into it whom we rarely saw. They had just developed a tool for the designers so we could link the dialogue lines from our scripts directly to characters in particular scenes, thereby reducing the chance of getting the wrong words coming out of a character's mouth. This meant we had to go through line by line and tag everything with special codes. While this was tedious, it was faster than writing the short chunks of code I'd had to do at Interplay.

"We also pushed the limits to get good sound, rotoscoped animation on top of the painted backgrounds, and the *Dagger of Amon Ra* magnifying glass tool that worked like a real magnifying glass when the player passed it over parts of a room. Very high-tech for the time."

A Detour Into War

Unlike the back-to-back schedule of the first two *Quest for Glory* games, there was a two-year gap between the second and third games in the series, during which time the Coles worked on *Castle of Dr. Brain* and *Mixed-Up Fairy Tales*.

Production began on the third *Quest for Glory* game soon after Lori finished *Mixed-Up Fairy Tales*. Early on in the development process, the decision was made to ignore the end credits of *Quest for Glory II*, which had touted the next game as *Quest for Glory III: Shadows of Darkness*. The Coles had plotted out a four-game series during the earliest days of the original *Hero's Quest*, but *Wages of War* was never part of that story.

"When we came back to *Quest for Glory III* we said, 'Okay, it's two years since the previous game; players are going to have forgotten the plot points and such," Corey says. "We had intended for [*Shadows of Darkness*] to be a really advanced, very tense, high-pressure game. We said, 'We're going to get a lot of new players because of the two-year gap, so we'd better bring in a transition somewhere in between.'"

"Part of the theory was that *Shadows of Darkness* was going to be such a change of pace; it was going to be the darker one, it was going to be more story-driven," Lori adds. "We thought we would be bringing in more people, and the new people would never understand what was going on. It was changing so many things; it was going to point-and-click and everything else. We felt like, 'If we want to catch our audience back in and get people introduced, we should go with [*Wages of War*] and experience that before going with [*Shadows of Darkness*] being so much more dramatic."

Once the Coles opted to make the third game a reintroduction to the series, they had to come up with a story. Setting the game in an African environment was decided on, as they felt it was a change from the previous environments they had used and there weren't many games that featured an African setting.

It was a chance conversation with fellow Sierra designer Ellen Guon that gave them the basic plot. "Ellen made a casual remark: 'I know what you're doing with *Quest for Glory III*' – because we hadn't revealed any secrets at that point – and she said, 'You're going to tell the story of Rakeesh [a Paladin introduced in *Quest for Glory II*] going back to his homeland and his fight with the demon prince,'" Corey reveals.

The Coles agreed this would make for an excellent premise. With the pieces now in place, development on *Quest for Glory III* could begin. Corey was unavailable to assist Lori until he finished his work on *Dr. Brain*, so he came in at the tail end of the project and did some proofreading and text writing – and extensive playtesting.

"I loved the game," Corey raves. "I mean, obviously I knew the basic storyline and so on, but I had not been in on any of the development, so I got to play it beginning to end and said, 'This is fun!'"

Since *Quest for Glory II* had been made at the end of the EGA era, *Quest for Glory III* was the first game in the series to be in 256 colors. Another first for a *Quest for Glory* game was that some of the artwork was outsourced. This created some problems for the team as they couldn't easily consult with the Korean artists and no iterative changes could be made after the designs were sent. The decision was also made to use overhead maps of the land instead of seeing the Hero travel screen by screen over vast distances, as had occurred in the first two games.

The music for *Quest for Glory III*, this time composed by Rudy Helm with the help of Mark Seibert, was added toward the end of development. Corey admits that while players have only seen the final, polished version of the game, mere months earlier it was terribly incomplete. "Three months before the release, there was no sound," he says. "I can tell you those games are no fun to play as silent games. So we finally got the music and sound effects in and suddenly, life! All of a sudden the game took on an entirely new dimension. Let there be sound!"

One issue that arose during production was related to the continually evolving nature of the player's statistics. The skill development system the Coles had created for the first game was beginning to show its age. Says Corey, "We had played a trick on players from the beginning, where we gave players skills from 0 to 100 in the first game and that made it feel like it was percentile. But we knew all along we were going to raise the limit to 200 in the second game and 300 in the third and so on."

This increase created some unforeseen consequences, however. Corey explains that if you were in the 200 to 300 range for a particular skill, the game was pretty balanced, but if you added a new skill that started out as 100 or lower, it took a long time to get that skill up into the range the game expected. "So we had a hard time getting the skills to balance; it was very repetitious. People would sit there and pick up rock, throw rock, pick up rock, throw rock to get their throwing skill up. We didn't want the gameplay to be tedious."

Another result of Corey's minimal involvement in the design process was a lack of puzzles and roleplaying elements in the game compared with previous entries. "Lori is much more story-focused and I'm much more puzzle-oriented. So we ended up with a game that was pretty much story-driven."

The thief character was the least developed, with only a single hut to break into and nothing to do in the city at all. Corey felt this lack of roleplaying with the thief was the only major negative to the game. "But as a story game, I think it's really fun and it's a really good story and great morality play. There's a lot to it. I'm glad we did it."

Production was easier, and *Quest for Glory III: Wages of War* enjoyed sales comparable to the original game. Corey calculates, "It sold in the 100,000 to 200,000 range. Which was adequate under the budget and certainly enough to have Sierra get us to make *Quest for Glory IV*."

Interlude: The *Hoyle* Connection

When the chance to pick up the rights to the *Hoyle* games became available in late 1988, Ken Williams pounced on the opportunity to further diversity the company's product line.

Sierra produced a number of titles in the *Hoyle* card game series over the next fifteen years, with the original run of four games finishing in 1993. The franchise was relaunched by Sierra in 1995 and continued to receive new product releases until 2004, when the series was taken over by Encore Software.

Bill Davis was the creative director during the days of the original *Hoyle* games and remembers they were always a profitable property for Sierra, although not always a big focus: "They generated revenue. I think Ken saw the opportunity to pick up the property and he looked at it and said, 'We could do these.' They didn't involve the kind of coding that a graphic adventure game engine would require; they were straightforward. Warren [Schwader] liked to work alone, and it was kind of a one-programmer project, so it was ideal to keep this really talented designer/programmer happy and at Sierra On-Line. Warren is an amazing guy."

Warren Schwader had started at the company in 1980 – the first outside programmer hired – and developed *Hi-Res Cribbage*, a reasonably big seller for what was still On-Line Systems at the time. Warren was not only the designer and programmer on the first installment of *Hoyle* but worked on some of the graphics as well.

An early decision was made to utilize the extensive Sierra roster of characters as opponents. Gamers could play against King Graham, Princess Rosella, *Police Quest*'s Sonny Bonds, or any number of other characters.

Hoyle's Official Book of Games: Volume 1 was released in 1989 and contained six different games – cribbage, crazy eights, gin rummy, hearts, Klondike solitaire, and old maid – all played according to the official Hoyle rules.

The first *Hoyle* collection was a hit, and its production costs were much lower than adventure games, so Warren was commissioned to design the sequel. This time he concentrated on a single game, solitaire, allowing players to try twenty-eight different variants of the classic card game. Released in 1990, *Hoyle's Official Book of Games: Volume 2* was another success, so of course a third game was quickly greenlit.

Following in 1991, *Hoyle's Official Book of Games: Volume 3* was a collection of board games that included snakes and ladders, backgammon, checkers, parchisi, yacht, and dominoes. It was unique in that it was the only *Hoyle* collection released without Warren's involvement. It was also the first of the series to use VGA graphics.

The first project for artist Marc Hudgins at Sierra was animating on *Hoyle 3*. "I was taking 16-color talkers and making them into 256-color talkers. You know, the little head portraits. That was my first day – terrible work – to get used to the tools," Marc recalls.

The fourth and final game in Sierra's original *Hoyle* series was released as *Hoyle Classic Card Games*, although in reality it was simply a VGA upgrade of the original *Volume 1* with the addition of two games, bridge and euchre.

Richard Aronson consulted on the artificial intelligence (AI) for several of Sierra's *Hoyle* card games, including making some of the AI decisions in euchre. "I'd never played euchre before but Warren taught it to me; it's a great game," Richard recalls. "We decided which version of euchre we were going to implement, and Warren used a variant that is really popular in Wisconsin and nowhere else."

Richard was also assigned as programmer on the bridge portion of *Hoyle Classic Card Games*, and as a ranked bridge player himself he wanted to make the best reproduction he could. He told Ken he could program it but that it would take three years to do.

"When Ken approached me about *Hoyle*, before he told me I had to do it, I was in a meeting with the producer and Ken in his office. Ken said, 'Why do you need three years? I could program bridge in three months on my summer vacation.' I said, 'That's going to be a much more economical version than anything I could turn out. I recommend you accept that offer' – which he didn't like at all," Richard admits.

"Ken just had no idea how good the bridge market already was. *Bridge Baron*, which was probably the best bridge product at the time, had something like thirty-five developer years involved in it, and we were starting from scratch basically. All right, we had an animation engine, but it's not an animation game, it's an AI game. Everything had to be from scratch. It was just going to be one of eight games."

What Ken and others didn't understand at first was that bridge was not only an immensely popular game but an extremely complicated one as well. "Bridge is right up there with chess and to a lesser extent poker as the most studied games of all time," Richard explains. "If you go to Amazon and [look up] 'how to play games,' those books will have by far the most results. Included in those titles are a lot of very complex mathematical work, the most dense of which is by a PhD candidate in France who wrote his entire thesis on the mathematics of bridge, which wound up being published as an almost 200-page book which almost every serious bridge player has.

"When you deal out all the cards, you have to know where the missing cards are. It really has strong impacts to AI. I have all those books. . . . I did put in insane overtime on *Hoyle Classic* because I didn't want my name to be reviled in the bridge world. I didn't want the bridge community to think, 'Look at this crap that Richard Aronson did.' My dad died during *Hoyle Classic*. I drove down, spent one day at my mom's, attended the funeral and drove back home. That was it. Three days' bereavement because the game was late."

Despite Richard's efforts, *Hoyle Classic Card Games* was the first of the *Hoyle* games to ship late. "The game still shipped about three months late, but it was not primarily my fault. There were art issues that caused delays," Richard claims, though he admits, "I caused delays to improve the bidding; bidding was really a problem. But the game shipped and did extremely well. Sold like half a million copies, which back then was over twice what Sierra hoped for. At a time when over 100,000 is a bestseller, Sierra hoped that over its lifespan *Hoyle* might get 250,000 but it reached over half a million."

Chapter 11: The Golden Era

*For me personally, King's Quest VI was the crowning
achievement of my decade with the family.*

Robin Bradley, QA Lead, King's Quest VI

Production of *King's Quest VI: Heir Today, Gone Tomorrow* started in
May 1991 and was to be yet another groundbreaking and
ambitious project for Sierra. But it was one that Roberta Williams
was very nearly not involved with at all.

Roberta had been designing *King's Quest* games for eight years and
she wanted to hand over the series to other designers and try something
new. As she recalled in an interview from 1992, "I felt I was getting
stale, that I'd used most of my good ideas on *King's Quest* already. I
wanted to do other things I was excited about. I really felt I was being
underutilized doing only *King's Quest*. . . . It's such an established series
with a strong look and feel. I find it hard to believe that other strong
people can't carry through with it."[23]

Her original plan was to move into a more consultative role,
overseeing the designer instead of her usual hands-on approach, but it
wasn't long before she realized that she did still want to work on *King's
Quest*, just not to the extent that she had in the past.

Roberta's first change to the team was to bring on board another
designer, Jane Jensen, who would help out with getting the majority of
the details of the game designed.

According to Bill Davis, creative director at the time, *King's Quest
VI* was a game that worked because of the two talented designers
working together. "For me, that was still Roberta's game," Bill says, but
"in the past, where Roberta would have written every line herself in the
game design, now she became more of a director."

He claims that a more collaborative approach was necessary
because "the games became much more vast; every game had many
more rooms in them. Jane's a super creative person too. I look at it like
it's becoming more like the animation industry is. As an animation
director and designer, I worked with some fabulous animators and every

one of those animators brought an amazing amount of talent to the table and their scenes would not have been their scenes without them. The same thing was becoming the case with games. You had a team of very talented people and those teams were getting larger and larger but each one of them was bringing their voice to the conversation. I think *King's Quest VI* would never have been what it was without Jane there. . . . But it also still wouldn't have been what it was without Roberta."

In June 1991, Roberta Williams began working on *King's Quest VI*, laying out the basic story and making the big decisions such as who the main character was going to be and where the game would be set. After that she brought in co-designer Jane Jensen, and for the next five months both women worked on the game, usually at Ken and Roberta's house at Bass Lake. "We went through the game from beginning to end. We wrote every puzzle, every object, every action you could do in the game," Roberta was quoted as saying the next year in Sierra's *InterAction* magazine.[24]

As well as having a script and design collaborator in Jane, Roberta also shared the director's job with Bill Skirvin, who had been brought in to assist with production. Previously, tasks such as working out the look and feel of the game and overseeing the artwork would have fallen to her alone, but now she was able to delegate some of those responsibilities, easing her burden and allowing her to begin working on her next project, *Scary Tales* (the working title for *Phantasmagoria*).

Robin Bradley served as the QA lead on *King's Quest VI* and remembers the experience as one of the best of his career.

"For me personally, *King's Quest VI* was the crowning achievement of my decade with the [Sierra] family. I worked closely with Roberta Williams as lead QA, and later on *Phantasmagoria*. She made the job of testing easy and enabled me to focus on simply disseminating her directives. Therefore, I was the luckiest [tester] in the world," Robin says.

"We developed in stages. When a portion was complete enough, according to the programmers, I would begin testing that portion. We developed in successive builds. Each time a build was tested it would be developed further, causing more issues that compounded the difficulty of testing. Often a build was barely playable as we developed particular engines and the underlying system code that the entire game would depend upon.

"Once the system code was stable enough, we could start serious design testing where continuity issues are addressed. Then, after the entire project is near to completion, it is submitted to the QA department to begin full-fledged bug testing. Ultimately, the bug buck stopped with me. I took a great deal of pride in making the games I led in the QA aspect to be as fun and free from problems as possible. It was my own personal mission statement: The Bug Stops Here!"

When *King's Quest VI* released in 1992, it is estimated to have sold over 400,000 copies in its first week, making it Sierra's biggest and fastest seller to date. The following year a CD-ROM version was launched with full voice acting that included Hollywood actor Robby Benson, who had recently voiced the Beast in Disney's animated movie *Beauty and the Beast*, along with a greatly expanded introductory cinematic.

King's Quest VI refined the adventure game formula into a highly polished example of the genre, one that has consistently topped best-of lists in the decades since its release.

A Dynamix Space Quest

After the 1991 release of *Space Quest IV*, Mark Crowe and his wife made the decision to move to Oregon. Sierra had recently acquired Dynamix and Mark was intrigued by the prospect of working with the team there after many years at Sierra.

"It's just that the timing was right. We were wanting to move out of where we were, there in California. It was kind of drought-ridden with wildfires and that sort of thing. We were just really scared. We had always spent our summers traveling around in Oregon and always thought that would be a beautiful place to live," Mark recalls.

"When [Sierra] acquired Dynamix and I got the chance to meet that bunch up there, got to talking to Jeff Tunnell, they were doing some really cool innovative stuff as far as adventure games went. Stuff that I was hoping Sierra was going to adopt. They had their own adventure game engine and it was really attractive to me to maybe get to do some stuff on that. One thing led to another on that and we got to talking and basically talked myself into moving up there."

Ken Williams knew Dynamix was interested in Mark, but he believes there were other factors involved in the move as well. "There was also occasional friction between Scott [Murphy] and Mark. My guess is that it was a combination of Mark wanting to live in Oregon, Dynamix wanting Mark, and various personal issues," Ken suggests.

After moving to Dynamix, Mark was asked to prototype a number of new games, with no restrictions. But he couldn't escape *Space Quest*.

"That was kind of the ironic thing," he says. "I spent several months working on game concepts when I got up there; I was given carte blanche to come up with game ideas. While I was doing that, the powers that be decided we needed to get going on another *Space Quest* game, and I don't know all the details about what was going on down at Sierra, but they approached me about doing it up at Dynamix. I thought, 'Well, I don't have anything else going yet; I don't have a project and I like to eat! I guess I'll take this on and do it up here.' I thought we were going to do it with [the] Dynamix engine; that was the attractive thing for me. Later we were told we were going to use SCI. I thought, 'Oh great. This puts me in a real awkward position.'"

Things were changing back at Sierra and there was a belief that Scott Murphy was too busy working on other projects to be able to devote time to *Space Quest V*. Josh Mandel had been asked to create a design outline for a possible fifth game but eventually the decision was made to move the project to Dynamix and use it as a platform for teaching that studio Sierra's SCI engine.

As Mark Crowe describes it, "I've got a team up here that doesn't know how to use SCI, that does know how to use the Dynamix engine. What to do? We hired one of the programmers from Sierra to come up and train all the programmers and . . . be the lead programmer on the project. That's how *Space Quest V* got started."

Space Quest V: Roger Wilco – The Next Mutation marked a change from the previous formula in that it focused its parody on one television franchise: *Star Trek*. Up to that point, all the games had spoofed a wide variety of sources, from *Star Wars* to *The Terminator* to *RoboCop*, among all manner of pop culture icons.

A major influence on the new game was co-designer Dave Selle, who "was a big part of that game design because he was such a big *Star Trek* nerd," according to Mark. "I knew I wanted to poke fun at *Star Trek* because we hadn't really done that a lot in the previous games. *Star Trek* was so big and had such a big fan base that it made sense. Everybody had heard of *Star Trek*."

And yet Mark's relative unfamiliarity with the franchise brought some challenges. "Dave was just totally immersed in that, so I relied pretty heavily on him to assist me in coming up with gags and parodying *Star Trek*. The overarching storyline about StarCon was me, and then I had him fill in with all the *Star Trek* gags."

Along with its distinctly *Trek* flavor, the use of cartoon speech boxes and other enhancements were introduced by the new team, all made possible by the engineers behind SCI. "That's the thing about

Sierra's toolset," Mark says. "Every team that was using it contributed ideas to making it evolve. It was great. We had such an awesome team of engineers and programmers that would listen and they wanted the thing to shine as well. They were always willing to do what they could to get those features in there for us."

Space Quest V was released in 1993 on floppy disks. It was popular upon launch and early production on an enhanced CD-ROM version was started, but Dynamix was in some financial difficulty at the time and needed another big seller on the shelves. They couldn't afford to spend another year working on an updated version of an existing game, so production ended – and with it, so did Dynamix and Mark Crowe's involvement with the *Space Quest* series.

A Pharmacist for a Hero . . .

While *Space Quest* was being developed at Dynamix, other design ideas were being thrown around at Sierra's Oakhurst office and a lucky accident led to the development of *Freddy Pharkas: Frontier Pharmacist*, as Josh Mandel remembers.

"We were all in a meeting together where they were talking about what Al [Lowe]'s next game would be. They didn't want to go to a *Leisure Suit Larry 6* straight away. Al was saying we could do one about a frontier, and I think what he trying to say was 'farmer.' But the words got tangled up and he ended up saying 'pharmacist,' laughing and then saying, 'Wait a minute! Frontier Pharmacist!' It was purely a slip of the tongue that led to that game. Bruce Balfour had already proposed a comedy western that they had rejected. It was one of those back when we were developing two concepts a week."

Al Lowe and Josh Mandel were given the go-ahead to design the game, another example of Sierra's star system of teaming an established designer with a less experienced designer.

While some felt that the more established designers took a lot of the credit for little work, Josh didn't feel that was ever the case working with Al. Josh had a plan for *Freddy Pharkas* that was different than what Al was used to. "They said I was going to be junior designer on *Freddy Pharkas* but going to be doing most of the work. I thought, well, this is a chance to give Al a reputation for doing things other than fart jokes. Wouldn't it be nice if *Freddy Pharkas* was clean? Clean enough that nobody had any compunction about playing it with their seven-year-old or eight-year-old? But Al wasn't to be deterred. That's how the fart sequence ended up in the game. I didn't like that it was on a timer, but I think Al thought that with the rewind button, that would take care of any objection by people of the timer."

The whole process turned out to be a great experience for Josh. "Al is so easy to work with. I've worked with a lot of people over the years but Al is very easy. He's open to new ideas; he's also quick to dismiss new ideas! But he'll hear it and he'll consider it, and if you can convince him that the idea he doesn't like is the way to go anyway, he's open to that. He's very collaborative. In fact, that's the reason that when it came time for me to assemble a team for *Freddy Pharkas*, some people said no."

According to Josh, "Some people said no because they wouldn't work on an Al [Lowe] game, period. Because they were very religious, perhaps they just objected to the content. But a couple of people wouldn't have worked on the game because they felt Al had taken too many of their ideas for previous *Larry* [games] and not credited them for their contributions."

Whether that was true or not, Josh never found that to be the case when working with Al.

Al Lowe worked off-site at his home most of the time and developed the story and design for the game while Josh Mandel assembled a team. "I did the original design for that game," Al says. "I think almost all the puzzles and stuff were in the game before [Josh] came around on the project. He ended up being the project manager, and because I was off-campus and he was in Oakhurst with the team, he ended up doing lots and lots of additional filler material. And he's a writing fool; he just loves to write lines. So a lot of those things that I would have never bothered doing, he loved doing. Lots of that humor is Josh's."

After assembling the team, Al and Josh got together and worked through the design, as the latter recalls. "Al and I went over his design; we took out some big portions of it and added a big portion that I had designed. And then we started going. Every day, whenever anything came in, whether it was artwork or a room being programmed or a bunch of texts I had written, I sent it off to Al for him to give his stamp of approval to or change what he wanted to change. I made a lot of suggestions that he thought were too far-out or unworkable offhand, like the ballad," he laughs.

The ballad was conceived as a way to tell the game's backstory without having to animate an entire complicated introduction, but Al didn't think the idea would work. "He didn't want to do the ballad," Josh claims. "I said, 'It's a great way; there's a lot of exposition here, and it's keeping with the time.' He said, 'All right, you try it and if it sucks we won't use it.' I said okay. He wrote the music and I wrote the lyrics. He was like that with just about everything I suggested. 'We'll try it but be prepared.' But it all came together beautifully."

Josh is still pleased with *Freddy Pharkas*, saying, "I don't think I've ever worked so hard on anything except maybe *Callahan's Crosstime Saloon.** We were really proud of the way it came out."

As was now common when a game shipped, the team got together to celebrate. In the case of *Freddy Pharkas*, they went skydiving, although Josh recalls that not everyone participated.

"Al didn't go, and a couple of members of the team didn't go," he says. "But [I] went. I think what might have made the difference was the people who went were the people without kids. Al had two youngsters at home at the time; maybe that was part of his decision.

"It was an idea I had kind of carried over from the *Quest for Glory II* team. They were planning on going skydiving and then one of their team members unexpectedly [died]. Suddenly they decided they couldn't go skydiving anymore." But for the *Freddy* team, it was, "'Let's go skydiving.' And no one got hurt."

Released on floppy disks in 1993, *Freddy Pharkas* was a success, but not successful enough to convince Ken Williams to commission a sequel. However, sales were good enough that the decision was made to do a CD-ROM version of the game, as Al explains. "Because the CD-ROM games with the voice-overs were selling . . . I convinced Ken for a few measly grand we could add voices and do a version of *Freddy* that was CD-ROM with the voice-overs. We knocked that out really fast."

Although the CD-ROM releases of Sierra's games were generally enhanced versions, a lot of Josh's lines from *Freddy Pharkas* weren't recorded, something Al says was unavoidable: "The only lines we cut were, you click this weird inventory object on that weird inventory object and you got a text message that Josh wrote particularly for that. It was something like 1,400 or 1,800 lines that nobody would do normally. He wrote them for completeness. God bless him for that."

"When we started recording them, we realized this is going to take days of studio time and it's going to be very expensive and I don't think anybody is going to do it. I called Josh up and said, 'I know you're going to hate me for this but I want to put up just the text message instead of having the audio recording as well for these weird text messages.'

---

* A 1997 adventure Josh Mandel designed for Legend Entertainment.

"I think he hates me for it still," Al jokes. "He did a lot of work for the design. The typical response there would have been 'those two don't go together,' then you let it go at that; it's just an error message. But he wrote a message for every combination of every ingredient. It was like, 'OH MY GOD!' In fact, I'm not sure it would all fit on one CD!"

A Fresno Experience

In between the initial *Freddy Pharkas* release and the CD-ROM version, Al Lowe worked on the next installment of *Leisure Suit Larry*. With Al still living in Fresno, Ken Williams once again set up a Fresno office to accommodate the *Leisure Suit Larry 6: Shape Up or Slip Out!* team.

"People were living in Fresno and working in Oakhurst and there's a two-lane road that's very crooked, mountainous and deadly. There were a lot of car crashes on that road. It was very dangerous, and people hated that commute," says Al Lowe.

Knowing that a lot of his staff lived in Fresno, Ken made the offer to Al to open a new office there and let him build his team from local residents so people wouldn't have to face that drive. Al accepted the offer. It would be more convenient for him and his team, and he'd be able to increase efficiency without the need to commute each day.

"A lot of the good people who lived in Fresno, when Ken said, 'Why don't you open an office in Fresno because I bet a lot of people would love not to commute,' suddenly I had a great choice of people who were local and didn't have to drive all day. What I said was, if you were going to leave for work at 7:00 a.m. and get home at 7:00 p.m., why don't you just come to the [Fresno] office and spend twelve hours instead of driving. For many of them, it worked!"

While Al built his team, renovations to the office building were also required, which meant that instead of starting production in December or January as usual, the group wasn't able to settle in until early February 1993.

"We rented a small space that was kind of centrally located in the north end of Fresno, so it was easy to get up the road to Oakhurst," Al remembers. "We had just enough room for an art bullpen – kind of a bunch of tables where the artists could work and talk and play their music and make noise and stuff together. And we had private offices for the programmer, musician and the QA guys. We had a small conference room we could all fit in. It was a lovely work environment and I really liked it as much as any place I've ever worked."

With the office fully renovated and his new team assembled, Al and his group quickly got to work. "When we moved in there on February 1, the first time we had the whole team there, we got together and I passed out copies of the design document and we spent hours going through the entire document talking about what was in there. The game [design] was pretty much done," Al says.

That same level of efficiency largely continued throughout the remainder of the development process. "We were organized and pretty much got going. Everyone was experienced; we had almost no new people to train so it was enjoyable working with everybody. We got a lot done quickly."

Although the production team was based in Fresno, the game's producer was initially based in the Oakhurst studio. Al quickly realized this wasn't an ideal situation. "We had a producer in name but he was off-campus and pretty well detached and didn't have much contact with the team on a day-to-day basis. So I kind of went back to producing that one. With *Larry 6*, I thought it would be better if I got my hands back in the team, back where it was my team instead of his."

Though the team was working well together, they encountered a problem in the game design that threatened to take production off course. Al admits, "I had too many women in the game. I kind of overreacted and I said, 'We'll go for a calendar.' We had twelve women and suddenly, as the summer wore on and it looked like if we did all twelve women we'd miss shipping in time for Christmas, we sliced out two of the less important ones. But we still did the calendar. We just added a picture of Patti and someone else, but that design was pretty much done before the team was even assembled."

During production, Al realized he needed a piece of music written specifically for a particular scene, so he approached Josh Mandel to write the lyrics. "The song was called 'Cell Block Love,'" Josh remembers. "Al had come to me and said, 'I need a song. It needs to be a country song; that's my only requirement.' I said sure. Again, I didn't write any of the music, just the lyrics.

"It's actually the story of *Police Quest* told from Marie's point of view. How she used to be on the streets and her husband was a cop and she never knew if he was going to come back every night and everything. So I got a huge kick out of that song."

Using Sierra's SCI engine was par for the course for the *Larry* games by this stage, but during the creation of *Leisure Suit Larry 6* a major issue arose. The internal programming team in Oakhurst was developing a new version of SCI to run on more modern 32-bit computers and support higher resolution artwork, which meant *Leisure Suit Larry 6* would soon be outdated. The *Larry 6* team had started programming the game in the older 16-bit version but were expected to update when the new version was available.

According to Al, "In the middle of the summer we realized SCI32 was in trouble and it wasn't going to make Christmas. I didn't get paid unless the game shipped, and I didn't want to take the chance on missing. I'm thinking maybe June or July we locked down the interpreter and said, 'We're not going to accept any more changes from Oakhurst. We don't want any more new versions; we're not going to mess with SCI32.'"

Knowing that Sierra required a hi-res version of the game, the team created all the assets in higher resolutions but persisted with the older, stable engine. "We created all the images in hi-res because we knew it was coming. We created the backgrounds in hi-res, but we chose to ship the game first on floppy disk in standard res with no sound and no voice-over, just text. As soon as that game shipped, Halloween [1993] or something, we turned around and started working on the hi-res version and figured out a different interface for that. Because the interface is entirely different.... We turned that around, I think we ended up shipping that game in March [1994] or so."

Leisure Suit Larry 6 was yet another success for Al Lowe and Sierra, going on to sell over 250,000 copies,[25] similar to the other *Larry* games.

After a Detour, Darkness Arrives

Soon after *Quest for Glory III* released in 1992, Corey and Lori Cole turned their attention to *Quest for Glory: Shadows of Darkness*, set in the Transylvania-like land of Mordavia. Few changes were needed to the original story idea the Coles had developed before their detour in *Wages of War*.

"We had the whole story," Corey explains. "Before we did the first *Hero's Quest* we had the four games loosely plotted out. So we knew that was going to be in Transylvania and it was going to be the whole paranoia thing, trying to get the trust of strangers, vampires and all the rest of it. We knew we were going to bring back Baba Yaga; she was essential to that. We had the basic story plotted out very early on."

Because *Shadows of Darkness* was coming out three years later than they originally expected, the quality of the art was much better and allowed for much greater detail. Counting themselves fortunate to have had one of Sierra's best art directors, Andy Hoyos, for *Wages of War*, the

Coles were equally happy to be assigned Marc Hudgins for the same role in *Quest for Glory IV*.

"We had Marc, who had just moved up into that position, so we had a very strong art team," Lori says. "*Shadows of Darkness* used full screen talkers drawn in an exaggerated cartoon style, moving away from the realistic talkers that had been used in the previous two VGA games in the series. Marc had very strong ideas, which is why we went with those cartoony talkers instead of the more realistic style."

Marc had plenty of talent to work with on the project. "We had a lot of good artists then," Lori continues. "Marc put Tim Loucks in as character artist, so we had this very unique style and team, and all the programmers we had just because of the right time and place."

The goal was to get the game out for the 1993 Christmas season, but according to the Coles that deadline was a problem from the beginning due to a series of questionable decisions by management.

Faced with the same SCI32 engine issues that the *Leisure Suit Larry 6* team had encountered, *Quest for Glory IV*'s programmers were already four months behind schedule by the time they finally got access to the new engine, and even when they did, the new engine contained a number of bugs. The programmers sat idle for those four months, and then had to work long hours to catch up.

Meanwhile, the quality assurance department was understaffed, unable to adequately test all the games Sierra had in production.

Lori claims that, "I couldn't be prouder of the team; it was crunch time the entire time. We had programmers shipped in from India to work on it. We were on crunch time for approximately six months of overtime. And towards the end, even more hours were mandatory. There was no time off."

Unfortunately, the deadline had to be met regardless of the condition of the product.

"We were killing the team," Lori contends. "So when it came to the release time we said, 'This is not ready; we need more time.' They said, 'We don't have it.' So the team refused to work on it. The head programmer said, 'No, we're burnt out. We can't handle it. We don't want to even look at it now.' So they killed the programming team effectively."

Lori accepts some of the responsibility for the complications, however, admitting that "the fault did not lie with the team. It was just terribly complex and that was the problem with the way I design things. There's always these interrelationships; there's all these character things and things result from behavior you've done early which really does screw things over later in the game if you can't keep track of them."

Mark Hood served as one of the producers on *Quest for Glory IV*, in addition to his newly appointed role as the head of the Oakhurst studio, and remembers the stress everybody was under. "It was a frigging nightmare. SCI32 bugs and game bugs everywhere. We worked our asses off and I myself tested a ton and worked with [QA] and Corey to try to get it acceptable. We'd have a good build, then a horrible build in a cycle for weeks. It was often hard to tell if it was game code or SCI32 code failing, and QA was getting really frustrated."

Even with all its problems, Ken Williams was constantly saying that the game had to ship, and ship on time, further adding to the stress of the production. "Finally, we got two good builds in a row, and Corey and I talked about where it was," Mark recalls. "We often would patch small things after we mastered everything, so we both felt we could probably patch the small things left and get it to replication. We were wrong."

Quest for Glory IV shipped in time for Christmas, but it was notoriously buggy. "I took the blame and responsibility and still do. I should have said no and not shipped it yet, but it was really my first round of games where I was in charge of the studio, and Ken kept telling me it *had* to ship," Mark confesses. "The patches were a disaster, and the game had a lot of issues on some machines and not so many on others. It really was a shame, and I regret shipping that one that way to this day. Ken blamed me too, not for shipping it before it was finished, but for not getting the bugs out by the time he said it had to ship."

Regardless of the technical issues and stress they were under, Mark feels he worked well with the Coles and enthusiastically praises their professionalism. "Corey and Lori are both really smart, really dedicated designers and gamers, and in Corey's case programmer."

Corey also agrees that the game was released far too early. "It came out probably six months before it was finished. It was extremely buggy. Very unplayable. Because of that, we convinced Sierra they had to do a new build of it and they assigned one junior programmer to it. He managed to fix probably three-quarters of the bugs, and since they were taking extra time they also put in the voice acting, which was absolutely fabulous. The second version is, as far as we're concerned, the only one."

While the glitches were being worked out and some further additions such as a new introduction graphic were being included, Corey worked as the producer for the voice acting, an experience he says stood out as one of the highlights of his time at Sierra. "Those two weeks I spent recording the voices for [*Quest for Glory IV*] were probably about the most amazing time I ever had. Working with these immensely talented and wonderful voice actors. John Rhys-Davies was just a joy to work with. The whole thing, that was really nice."

Welsh actor John Rhys-Davies was cast as the narrator, the largest role in the game, and the sheer amount of work required was overwhelming. "Normally voice actors only work one four-hour session a day," Corey explains. "You tell them how many lines there are and the problem is a 'line' in a *Quest for Glory* game is a paragraph of text. A line in a Saturday morning cartoon is, 'Hey, look over there!' So when we told [John] he had twenty thousand lines to do, or whatever the number was, he was like, 'Oh, that's a lot, but I can do that.'"

The initial process began by giving Rhys-Davies a cue where he would read the line and then rerecord it another three or four times with different intonation and emotion. With five days of recording scheduled, it soon became clear they would run out of time. "We got through four or five pages of the script like this and he looked at the rest of the two hundred more pages he had and said, 'We're never going to finish this! I've got a planned vacation next week and I don't want to miss that,'" Corey says.

"At first he offered to double the booking, two four-hour sessions in a day. Then he said, 'Forget these cues, I'm going to go through line by line and read them through and you can sort them out afterwards.' He then proceeded to one-take practically the entire script. I had to stop him maybe five times to go back and redo lines, but the other thousands of lines he just went right through one line after another. Every line with perfect intonation, perfect emotion for the line. Unbelievable to work with. He jokingly said, 'Well, this is the CD-ROM from hell' because it was far, far more work than he had expected."

Pleased with John Rhys-Davies's performance and happy that his agent had renegotiated higher compensation for him, Corey and Lori presented the actor with a huge bottle of champagne. "I think he loved working on it, but it was hard work. He did bring it up in later years; he was very proud of the work he did on it. As of course are we," Corey says.

Quest for Glory IV's 1994 CD-ROM, professionally voice acted with most of the major bugs resolved, pleased both Coles. "Despite all the screw-ups and all the bugs, *Shadows of Darkness* was actually the one I was very proud of," Lori claims. "I worked with all members of the team, and they all worked for the whole."

Chapter 12: Continuing Success

The great thing about Sierra is you'd work for months and months and months and then when it was time to ship you could walk over to the warehouse and watch them package the games and put them on the trucks.

Robert Holmes, Producer and Composer,
Gabriel Knight

Sierra was still growing in 1993, and Ken Williams realized he needed to make Sierra more attractive to potential top-tier management and talent. It was around this time that the company moved its headquarters out of Oakhurst to Seattle.

Originally the plan was for Ken and Roberta to move to Seattle along with the business departments, leaving the Oakhurst location as a game production studio only. But game development soon followed the Williamses to Bellevue anyway when core members of the creative teams moved to the new location as well, essentially duplicating the Oakhurst studio.

Al Lowe, creator of *Leisure Suit Larry* and employee number twenty at Sierra, says that "when Ken went away, suddenly we all realized, 'Oh, shit! This was not an accident. This did not become a successful company with a market capitalization of over a billion dollars just because there were a bunch of us guys who liked to make games. A lot of it was to do with Ken's management and the skills he had.' So when he was gone, suddenly all that area was vacated."

Marc Hudgins worked in Oakhurst from 1991 until 1999, working his way up from an animator to art director and animation director on some of Sierra's biggest titles. He understands the reasons for the company moving some of its operations, but also remembers Oakhurst being a great place to live, having spent the majority of his twenties in the area while working for Sierra.

"The games were fun but the community is what kept me there," Marc recalls. "You had to kind of put yourself there. It's this very small rural community nestled up against the Sierra Nevada mountains. The town is comprised of people who work for the phone company, or the local hotels and restaurants, sheep farmers and the occasional guy who's still panning for gold down at the creek. At the same time, there's also a lot of misfit people who washed up against the Sierras because it's where the mountains stop and it's where the roads end."

Add to that mix "a bunch of game developers. A bunch of artists and programmers and writers. We were all shoved up against the mountains there, living in this small town or nearby. You couldn't avoid them, so we embraced each other as a community. You'd run into people all the time. You always knew what was going on; you knew everyone's business. I haven't seen that in any other job I've worked at. We're just by nature more diffuse. There you could leave work at work, but you couldn't leave the people you worked with at work.

"The advantage Sierra had [when the company started] was there were much fewer opportunities if you wanted to really do that sort of thing. They didn't necessarily have trouble attracting people to a remote area like that initially," Marc notes. "One of the reasons they moved to Seattle is the company was growing and they couldn't attract the level of senior talent they needed to go live in the woods. A bunch of us scrubby artists were happy to be out there."

The logistics of running a large company from such a remote location also tipped the balance towards relocating to Seattle.

Craig Alexander, general manager of the Oakhurst studios from 1994 until 1999, is of the belief that the Williamses just couldn't see a way to operate Sierra from Oakhurst much longer. "It's an hour southeast of Yosemite National Park up in the mountains, about an hour and a half from Fresno, which is not a top-tier city in the US. From the airport it's a struggle to get anywhere except San Francisco or Los Angeles and maybe a handful of other places. You can't run a sales force out of there; you can't do a lot of things.

"So they ultimately decided to move it to the Seattle area. By moving it there they felt they could scale it. That was the strategic reason they moved. There were tax reasons as well. They had built up quite a bit of value by that stage and the state income taxes in California are pretty high but in Washington they're much more favorable."

Marcia Bales explains that the offices of subsidiary Bright Star Technology, where she worked, became the Seattle headquarters for Sierra, and slowly Bright Star was absorbed into the Sierra fold.

"We stayed Bright Star for a very long time. Sierra did that a lot. They bought the studio, but they didn't change the name. The owners of

Sierra were brilliant, just brilliant. They also gave people a lot of leeway to run their businesses," Marcia says.

"It just seemed smooth and seamless. Eventually they were rebranded but it was just kind of slow. When a new product came it got rebranded Sierra. We were working on both [Sierra products and Bright Star products] and it was fine. It felt [organic] to me. I'm sure there was a lot more thought to it than I ever saw. I wasn't in marketing or anything like that. I was having so much fun creating products that I didn't really pay attention to how that materialized, but from my perspective it just seemed right."

The move was also at least partly motivated by the fact that Ken and Roberta enjoyed the Bright Star environment, according to Marcia. "They moved their headquarters there because they liked the offices. Everyone got along and it just seemed natural and normal. Ken and Roberta moved to Seattle; their home wasn't very far away. They all kind of moved into that area and moved in and we slowly just renamed it Sierra. We were just absorbed as new products came in."

A Knight to Remember

Gabriel Knight was the last of the major adventure game series developed by Sierra but is widely considered to be its most critically acclaimed, thanks primarily to its designer, Jane Jensen.

Growing up, Jane had always been interested in writing, but when deciding on her college major she came to the conclusion that she would be better served studying programming. It made sense. Jane had a logical mind, she loved logic puzzles and games, and her father was a mathematician. Plus, she would be paid as a programmer, with writing jobs far from a sure thing.

After graduating from Anderson University in Indiana with a BA in computer science, she went to work for Hewlett-Packard, but her drive to be a writer came to the fore and she resigned and moved to Europe to start her first mystery novel.

In her downtime, Jane played two Sierra games, *Manhunter: San Francisco* and *King's Quest IV*. She was hooked. Quickly working her way through Sierra's catalog, she realized that writing adventure games would help satisfy all her interests.

After moving back to the US, she wrote to Sierra and tried to get a position with them. She was qualified to help with quality assurance, programming and writing, but what she really wanted to do was design games. Eventually Jane landed an interview and a job writing game manuals and dialogue. She moved to Oakhurst and worked as a writer on *Police Quest 3* before co-designing *EcoQuest: The Search for Cetus* and *King's Quest VI*.

Jane first pitched *Gabriel Knight: Sins of the Fathers* through the new internal design department meetings implemented by creative director Bill Davis. According to Bill, by this time Jane had shown she was capable of designing her own game. "Jane proved herself and that helped her get *Gabriel Knight* through, so whether she knew it or not, doing that work and seeing what a talented designer she was and talented writer made Ken more receptive to *Gabriel Knight*. Everyone realized . . . not just me because I interviewed these people and I worked closely with the in-house design team, but everybody else was seeing how talented this group was."

While Bill Davis was a supporter of Jane's idea from the start, there were still a number of doubters in the company. Sierra had, up to that point, mainly concentrated on comedy or family games. In fact, this seemed to be the industry standard for PC games as their major adventure game competitor LucasArts had also been quite successful with their comedic games. Although Sierra had released the *Laura Bow*, *Police Quest* and *Manhunter* series, they had rarely touched on darker content and barely ever on occult themes like those in *Gabriel Knight*.

Another major difference in *Gabriel Knight* was the main character himself. While previous protagonists had been heroic kings or loveable losers, Gabriel was different. He was a womanizing lout, only out for himself. But beneath that facade was a deeper layer of complexity. Gabriel would learn through the course of the game that he had descended from a family of Schattenjägers, or Shadow Hunters, who hunt down evil and destroy it. This new level of depth to a lead character was a distinct change from what Sierra had done before.

Robert Holmes served as both producer and composer on the first *Gabriel Knight* game. Balancing these dual roles was difficult, but he ended up working out a system to handle it. "I had two desks. I had my normal desk and I had my keyboard setup. I would spend the first part of the day being [a] producer, and the second half of the day on the keyboard writing. Basically I worked a simple piano theme. The main theme was one of the first ones; I'd sit Jane down and play her pieces of it. Or we'd have maybe [artist] Michael Hutchison bring up a sketch of one of the rooms. I would sit that sketch up in front of my keyboard, do the music that was appropriate for that sketch," he explains.

Production on *Gabriel Knight: Sins of the Fathers* ran fairly smoothly, with the exception of the continual changes to SCI that caused delays.

But the team worked through them and delivered their final product, a game they were all proud of, in time for Christmas 1993.

"The great thing about Sierra is you'd work for months and months and months and then when it was time to ship you could walk over to the warehouse and watch them package the games and put them on the trucks," Robert Holmes recalls. "It was a really fulfilling experience to see that. I think that sort of first flush when *Gabriel Knight* first came out and we were getting Game of the Year [awards] and we were getting a lot of the attention and it was for all the right reasons, it was for exactly the way we wanted to be perceived. That was a really fun period."

Rodney King's Quest

Meanwhile, the latest *Police Quest* was also in production for a 1993 launch, and this time even more realism was sought. Gone was the series creator, retired California Highway Patrol officer Jim Walls, along with the entire established continuity of the first three *Police Quest* games. Instead, *Police Quest: Open Season* served as a franchise reboot, introducing detective John Carey as he solves the homicide of his best friend, officer Robert Hickman, and a seemingly random string of gang-related murders.

Ken Williams had been looking for someone to replace Walls, who had left Sierra for a rival company after *Police Quest 3*. Ken wanted someone with experience for the role and struck on the idea to contact former Los Angeles police chief Daryl F. Gates to fill that void.

Gates had been in charge of the LA police for decades and was well known for working on the Hillside Strangler case and the Manson Family murders, as well as heading up field operations during the Watts riots in 1965. Here was a veteran with a wealth of experience from forty-three years on the police force.

But Gates was much less favorably remembered for the 1992 Los Angeles riots, which began after a trial jury acquitted four officers of the Los Angeles Police Department for using excessive force in the arrest and beating of Rodney King – a horrific display of unprovoked violence that was videotaped and played on television to a shocked worldwide audience. Gates himself was a divisive figure who was personally blamed for supporting a culture of discrimination and abuse of the African American community as police chief.

Ken, however, saw Gates's high profile as an asset and actively pursued him after his resignation from the LAPD. John Williams had a firsthand view of the decision to employ Gates and recalled how it came about in a 1993 interview: "Ken continued to talk to Gates and a handful of other notable law enforcement professionals over the next few months, but despite conversations with less controversial men, the decision kept coming back to the Chief. When you figure that Gates was with the LA Police Force for 43 years, and you think about the way that LA has changed in that time, you get a real feel for what he brings to the table."[26]

Daryl Gates himself saw the opportunity to help people gain a much better understanding of the police and detective work. It wasn't at all like the movies or television, and he wanted to inform the public about how dangerous yet thrilling the job could be.

"It's a job that's really fun, it really is," Gates claimed in 1993. "It's a rewarding job. It's exciting. It has all the ingredients that make you want to go to work every day – but it has its downside, too. Stress is one of the downsides. There's hardly a day that doesn't go by without your guts tightening up and the adrenaline flowing because of the unknown. You have to make split-second, life-and-death decisions on your own and be responsible for them. It's a tremendous burden. Some officers can't handle it. They become ill. Sometimes they have to retire. It's a very, very difficult thing."[27]

A lot of the staff at Sierra were from the Los Angeles area and didn't approve of Ken's decision to employ Gates. Josh Mandel, at the time director of product design, wasn't happy with the choice and encouraged Ken to instead try Joseph Wambaugh, an LA detective who had become a best-selling crime writer, but Ken had set his mind on working with Gates. On the day Gates came into the office to meet Ken and the teams for the first time, some people were inexplicably away sick, while others simply shook his hand and returned to work. There was little enthusiasm for the man, with the staff even nicknaming the game "Rodney King's Quest."

Gates, though, ended up being used more as a consultant than as a designer; former *America's Most Wanted* producer Tammy Dargan wrote the story and designed the game, with notes from Gates incorporated into the final product. The story was a lot grittier than the previous installments in the series and created controversy for its use of swearing and clichéd portrayal of African Americans.

The game's graphic style was also designed to show Los Angeles in a more realistic light. To achieve this realism, photographs of actual locations were taken by cinematographer and director of photography

Rod Fung on a state-of-the-art Kodak digital camera capable of holding a massive fifty photos.

Unfortunately, it wasn't long before they realized that photographs by their very nature have an extremely limited field of vision, even using an 18 mm wide-angle lens, and weren't going to be suitable for the game. But a solution was found by stitching photos together, as producer/designer Tammy Dargan explained in a 1993 interview:

"Rod uses a video graphics program to merge ten different photos together. When he's finished, we have one rich, clean, atmospheric background. Then he repeats the process for the next background. And so on. If the team is unhappy with the results, he goes back for another photo shoot."[28]

All the controversy surrounding Gates's appointment to the *Police Quest* series didn't help the game sell any better than previous releases, but it did well enough that Daryl Gates and Tammy Dargan would go on to team up once again on *Police Quest: SWAT*, the fifth installment in the series and a much greater commercial success for Sierra.

Princeless

The popularity of *King's Quest VI* had shown that the games were still a surefire hit with consumers, so another new sequel was required.
Roberta Williams had always been inspired by Disney and this time she wanted to make a game that showcased that style. *King's Quest VII: The Princeless Bride* was going to be the most cinematic, Disney-style game that Sierra could produce.

The first major concern was that Roberta was overseeing two massive projects. Along with *King's Quest VII*, she was also in the midst of creating Sierra's first full motion video (FMV) game, *Phantasmagoria*. To help her with the new *King's Quest*, Lorelei Shannon was asked to co-design the game. Lorelei was an experienced writer who had co-designed *Pepper's Adventures in Time* with Jane Jensen. *King's Quest VII* would be an opportunity to establish herself as a top-tier designer at Sierra.

Although the artists were still located in Oakhurst for production, Lorelei and Roberta worked together out of the company's new offices in Seattle, as well as over the kitchen table in Roberta's house, creating a story and characters for the game.

In 1994, Lorelei said of working with Roberta, "Sometimes when we were jamming on ideas, coming up with every possible solution we could think of for a puzzle, we'd get really silly and just crack each other up. We'd be there with our heads on the table giggling wildly, and Ken would come in and roll his eyes at us and say 'Don't you have WORK to do?' That would only make us giggle harder. Let me tell you a secret. That's where great ideas come from – fun. The more you laugh and open your eyes and enjoy the world, the more your mind will open and ideas will flow. Don't get me wrong. Designing *King's Quest VII* was hard work. Sometimes it was stay-up-all-night-and-drink-coffee-til-your-eyes-bug hard work. But it was always fun, because Roberta made it fun."[29]

Marc Hudgins, the animation director on *King's Quest VII*, recalls the partnership between the two women. "I know [Lorelei] worked closely with Roberta. Lorelei, as far as I know, was doing the bulk of the writing at least, and the designing. When it came down to actually getting the game going, Roberta came down from Seattle the whole summer and into the fall. She directed it at that point. Making sure that things were getting hooked up," he remembers.

Early decisions were made based on the fact that by 1993 computers were becoming more widely owned but not everyone was an expert in operating them. Simplicity became the keyword, and the mouse-driven interface was overhauled.

"I would say the toughest things to deal with are the interface and the technical aspects of how you want the game to work," Roberta reflected in 1994. "I'm not a technical person by any means, but I have enough of an understanding to know what I can and can't do on the machine. I put lot of thought into that before I start working on a game. There's a certain visionary aspect to that. If you're thinking about a game to be released two years from now, you have to take into account what the technological advances will be."[30]

The new interface was revolutionary. No longer requiring the player to select a verb icon, the "smart" cursor would simply highlight options the player could click on as it was dragged over the screen. Other improvements included an autosaving feature, as well as an increase to the higher Super VGA (SVGA) resolution for the artwork.[*]

The background visuals were overseen by experienced art director Andy Hoyos and were another step up from anything Sierra had previously produced. The game had nearly one hundred scenes, all hand-painted at the higher SVGA resolution, and these were drawn wider than the screen so the background would scroll as the player character moved, creating a more cinematic feel.

---

[*] VGA's maximum resolution is 640x480; SVGA supports up to 800x600.

The change in resolution was something that brought greater clarity for the player but caused problems for the production team. "We were getting to a point where there was enough resolution where the warts would begin to show. You couldn't cover them up; you're still making weird choices about what you could do to clean up a drawing. It wasn't high enough resolution to do really clean animation, and it wasn't low enough you could kind of make it fudged."

King's Quest VII turned out to be a massive job for Marc, who took on additional responsibilities when the game's art director, Andy Hoyos, moved to Sierra's new Seattle studio.

"That was a rough one," Marc remembers. "It was probably the most ambitious hand-animated thing we'd attempted there. Roberta's idea for this thing – this was going to be full-blown hand animation like a Disney film. It was a big game. I looked at the scope of it, and I looked at the time we had to get this thing done. I came on board in February, maybe January at the earliest, and it was going to ship by Thanksgiving. Less than a year to make the most ambitious game we'd ever tried in terms of hand-drawn animation."

One of Marc's main tasks was to reduce the production to a reasonable size. "The first thing we had to do was cut at least two chapters out to at least get the scope down to something that was possible. Which of course introduced problems when I started going through and trying to break down the animation into things that make sense. Because when you're dealing with animation, you're dealing with story. 'Oh wait, there's this part in this chapter that refers to something we cut.'

"So a lot of what I had to do was alert Roberta and Lorelei to sort out these breaks that occurred because of it. You can say [to] take out these two chapters, but there were a lot of stems that led into existing chapters. So it was really a big job untangling it. And that was on top of everything else I had to do."

Marc says his most enjoyable part of working on *King's Quest VII* was filling it with characters. "I designed all the characters. Between eighty and one hundred. That was fun; I love character design."

Another issue the team encountered due to the increase in visual fidelity was that animations required more frames than had previously been necessary, which meant a lot more work was needed from the artists. This was a major area of concern for the game, with Sierra not having the in-house ability to produce the amount of higher resolution artwork required.

Eventually, the extra work was outsourced to four different animation studios: Animation Magic in Russia, Dungeon Ink & Paint in South Carolina, LA West Film Production in Croatia, and Animotion in New York.

Marc Hudgins says there was great difficulty in getting the studios to understand the requirements for computer games as opposed to the cartoon animation they were used to: "We didn't really talk about frame rate in those days. It was more about optimizing data. You didn't want things to get too big. I think we were probably timing the stuff to something closer to half of TV; I think we were working at about fifteen [frames per second].

"We didn't have enough in-house staff to do the animation so . . . the first thing we did was, we got this company in Saint Petersburg, Russia and they said, 'Yes, we can take it on.' So we went over to Saint Petersburg and set them up with our tools and explained the process to them. We started getting stuff back, but after less than a month, they said, 'You know what, we can't do all of this,'" Marc remembers.

Taking some of the work away from the Russian studio, they contracted the rest of the animation to the other three studios, which caused different problems. "We had no time for revisions, so my job was to try to make sure that it looked, as best I could, like it was all drawn by one person. Which I don't think I really succeeded at. Some were really tight, some were a lot looser than others. It was a real challenge.

"That was the first time I had really encountered that level of management. I spent my life on fax machines because we didn't have the internet yet, not in any meaningful way. I would fax drawings off to these studios and I would make phone calls at weird hours because I'd be calling Saint Petersburg, Russia. It was nuts.

"Everything would come into the studio raw from these places, and we basically took people off every single project in the studio and had them cleaning up the animation for the game. So I probably had about thirty people in the studio actually working on it. Just taking this raw stuff in and cleaning it up and making it appropriate to use in the game. There were no retakes. Everything went in; we fixed what we could. I think those studios did the best they could, but we were all under enormous pressure to get that thing out on time."

King's Quest VII was scheduled for release in November 1994, and according to Marc there was no opportunity to delay the game. "Back then games got done in like a year or less. I don't know if there's any truth to it or not, but I heard a story how basically Ken made a deal with the board of directors that there was going to be a *King's Quest* for Christmas and by God, there was going to be a *King's Quest* for Christmas. We went onto mandatory overtime. I was on mandatory overtime for about six months. It was pretty rough," he remembers.

Al Eufrasio had recently started with Sierra as an animator and was put on to the project near the end of production. "It was the last couple of months and they were entering crunch mode. I just remember catching the flu or pneumonia or something; it was right around November when we had to ship it. The day before Thanksgiving [in the US].

"If I remember correctly, what they did was they thought [they] weren't going to have it out on time, so they shipped boxes with vouchers. It kind of became a pre-buy. Buy this box and here's this voucher so when the game comes out you can go get it. So that people can actually put it in a Christmas card or something like that in case it didn't ship on time. It was available by Christmas, but they were trying to account for the key time in November when everybody did their shopping."

Al recalls one particularly humorous story involving the quality assurance team: "When I first started working there, I was working on my very first project *Capital Punishment*,* and our office space was right next to the QA room. We'd hear a lot of the scuttlebutt of what was happening in QA. At some point they'd hired a QA manager who was so full of himself he thought he was the second most powerful person in the company.

"They were testing *King's Quest VII*, and towards the end of the project Jerry Bowerman or somebody important in management had gone on vacation and this guy started telling people that, 'I'm technically the most powerful person in the company now because I can approve or reject whether something is released based on how it's performing bug-wise.' Whoever this guy was, he was only there two weeks tops because of this.

"I just remember the whole QA department being up in arms about this person. He'd made some comment, 'If it was up to me I'd fire Mark Seibert because he's not making sure these bugs are taken care of!' Everybody was like, 'Wow!' It lasted a couple of weeks, then whoever it was got fired, I suppose, and you never heard about it again. Very strange thing."

---

* An unreleased Al Lowe game.

As usual for Sierra, there was a lot of stress and plenty of challenges, but in the end the game was completed and people loved it. *King's Quest VII* was another major seller for the franchise, proving that Roberta hadn't lost her drive to successfully innovate and that her series was still the golden-haired star of Sierra's gaming empire.

Chapter 13: The Sierra Network

*We hate arguing with fourteen-year-old boys who we've caught
dead to rights about how they're not really cheating.*

*Richard Aronson, Designer and Programmer,
The Sierra Network*

Being online was a crucial part of Sierra On-Line's vision. It was, after all, right there in the name. From the early days of low-speed modems for the personal computer, the company had maintained a presence online.

CompuServe was the biggest online player in the eighties and Sierra had an established bulletin board where players would answer each other's questions and discuss the games. Some staff, like Guruka Singh Khalsa, frequented the chat room. Sierra enlisted CompuServe users for beta testing and even connected there with people they ended up hiring, like Josh Mandel.

Sierra also started their own BBS (Bulletin Board System), which they promoted as a way to get official hints, patches and demos. With thirty-two lines available, they boasted thirty-two thousand monthly visitors by the end of 1989 according to John Williams, who as marketing manager was responsible for advertising the BBS.

The future of gaming was believed to be online, and Sierra was poised to get into the business in a big way with The Sierra Network. By 1989, Sierra was investing heavily in designing their own network. Initially dubbed Constant Companion, it was eventually renamed The Sierra Network (TSN) and launched in 1991.

Creative director Bill Davis was there at the time and remembers the origins of The Sierra Network. "Originally Ken was going to market it to senior citizens. He thought it was an opportunity for people who had retired in Florida to play with their kids who were in California or New York. And he thought the best name for it was Constant Companion. I told him it sounded like adult diapers, so luckily it migrated to The Sierra Network," Bill says.

"I was involved with the foundation of it, with what kind of interface we were going to use, building avatars, all that kind of stuff. Coming up with the village. Originally we had a village concept where that was our interface; that was mine."

The village was the central location players saw when they logged into The Sierra Network, and it was a far cry from what players were used to on services such as Prodigy and CompuServe. Instead of plain text or a basic graphical interface, it looked like a Sierra game. The village even changed to match the seasons in Oakhurst.

The locations on the map denoted different lands the player could visit. The Clubhouse hosted traditional games like chess and checkers, while SierraLand featured games like *Boogers*, a humorous take on the classic board game Othello. LarryLand, later renamed CasinoLand, was where gambling and card games took place, and MedievaLand housed the network's RPGs. Ever evolving, new games were constantly added, including online versions of titles such as Dynamix's flight sim *Red Baron*, as well as trivia, card and board game adaptations. Content also included an electronic post office, multiple bulletin boards, chat rooms, and regular special events hosted by the developers.

In 1991 the service was promoted solely in California, although users in other states could get a discounted membership fee, an attempt by TSN to account for customers in other states paying for long-distance phone calls. But TSN needed to expand to be successful, and after a massive advertising campaign in early 1992, the network officially launched across the entire continental United States. Once nationwide, the cost for access to the network was a maximum of thirty hours per month for a flat fee of thirteen dollars.

With the number of users jumping to nearly twenty-five thousand by the end of the first year, and due to the continued need for updates and additions to the network's games, Sierra moved the now spun-off company into its own building in Oakhurst, a former steakhouse known as The Old Barn.

John Williams headed up the marketing for TSN from the very beginning and says that, while it was a visionary idea, it also had a lot of problems: "[TSN] was an idea well ahead of its time and had several fatal flaws that kept it from ever being a very viable business. At first we didn't know that, but I think by the end, Ken and most of middle management knew it, and we really dodged a bullet by being able to offload it to AT&T when we did."

One of those serious flaws was placing the servers in Oakhurst. "It was a horrible, horrible idea to have [TSN] servers operating in

Oakhurst," John says. "They were fragile, so we had to have them close to us, but Oakhurst was not a place that one should have been running an online business."

He goes on to explain that "we had T1 [high-speed internet] service, but we had no redundancy as T1 service was hugely expensive then, and doubly so as Oakhurst was several hundred miles away from a main internet trunk. If the line went down, there was no work-around and it went down often. We were in the mountains with snowstorms and windstorms and the lines were mostly unprotected and went down often. To make matters worse, some yahoos were fond of blowing out the telephone relays with a shotgun."

TSN never turned a profit for Sierra. Pressure within the company was immense, and Ken negotiated a deal with communications conglomerate AT&T to purchase a 20% stake. A further 20% was purchased by General Atlantic Partners, a venture capital group who had helped finance Sierra in the past.

One of the first things to change after the sale was the name: The Sierra Network became The ImagiNation Network (INN).

From its earliest incarnation to the newer INN version, one consistent challenge was letting the general public know about the service, something John Williams worked hard to achieve.

"For a product like INN, there were two key focuses: acquisition and retention. Acquisition was getting new customers to try it and hopefully become paying customers. Retention was getting them to stay with us for multiple months," John says. "Our model was 'try it free,' which worked to a point, but each time the system went down, cancelations rose and satisfaction levels decreased. I'd be running a free trial that was doing well and suddenly we would go down [for] three days out of seven due to winter storms, destroying our sign-up rates.

"Free trials then included sending out thousands of kits at a time via mail with CDs. It cost about four dollars a kit, so we could be talking twenty thousand dollars per test, and results were dismal due to technical issues. It was impossible to put together a viable testing plan for the business, and as losses mounted, there was more and more focus on measuring new customer acquisition, so being a marketer on the project was actually a minor slice of hell.

"We did ads in *InterAction* and in Sierra game boxes. I remember printing the inserts for those game boxes in 100,000 quantities. We sent out game CDs and offered free CDs in mailing pieces we sent to key customer lists. We did a lot of PR work and got a few really good hits with major news and TV programs."

In addition to targeting traditional advertising channels, fledgling online options were also used. "We hit the Sierra audience pretty hard," John remembers. "We had the mailing lists and even some email addresses. This was a long time ago and mass email programs were not yet viable, but we did do some email programs where we could and there was a lot of promotion on our stores and forums on CompuServe and AOL [America Online], until both services decided that INN was a competitor and made us take the info down." Sierra also sold a boxed version on store shelves alongside their other games in an attempt to expand the market.

Marketing ImagiNation to Sierra's existing customers seemed like a logical strategy to John, but others within the company weren't so convinced. "There was a contingent inside of INN that really wanted to break away from marketing towards Sierra customers, which I considered downright stupid, but sometimes you test things to see if there's any success," John reasons.

"We paid a fortune to have [child actors Jonathan Taylor Thomas and Zachery Ty Bryan] from *Home Improvement* do some PR work for us, which was money we might as well have flushed down the toilet, and we did some promotion in some magazines that were outside of the computer gaming industry, which was money that was also poorly spent."

According to John, "Marketing towards Sierra users wasn't sexy, though, and the guy we had put in charge of INN liked the stuff that didn't depend on Sierra audiences. I think he knew that INN was going to need to be sold to someone with deep pockets well before any of us was willing to admit it. We poured a lot of money into alternate channels, placing ads in places like the *Atlantic* magazine, and got dismal results. This was at a time before anyone even knew what the internet was and people would read about online games and not know what the hell we were even talking about.

"We understood early that the people were the product in INN. The games were fun, but what made INN different was the people. So we gave away free trials by the thousands and would often let people who had not actually switched to a paying service continue to access the system well after their thirty days. It was a small universe, and we actually identified a number of people that were great fun to be around and encouraged them to interact and gave them free memberships. We were incredibly lax about anyone who lived in Oakhurst or Coarsegold switching to a paid account and managed to develop quite a cult of local game players."

Card Games and RPGs

Richard Aronson, originally employed by Sierra as a producer and programmer, moved across to what was then still TSN in 1993. "My wife worked on it two years longer than I did," he says. "When Sierra hired us, I had always been a PC programmer and she was more of a server programmer, so she went to work for TSN which needed server programmers and I made games for Sierra On-Line.

"In December of 1991, *Conquests of the Longbow* had just shipped and I wasn't on another project yet and Ken Williams came up to me and said, 'I hear you run roleplaying games,'" Richard recalls. "I ran Los Angeles Mensa's RPG group for more than a decade. . . . I had all this RPG experience and I was probably more famous for writing this story called 'Eric and the Gazebo' than for anything I did at Sierra. 'Eric and the Gazebo' was one of the first major humor memes on the internet back when it was still called ARPANET. I said, 'Yeah, I love roleplaying games.' Ken said, 'Would you like to run one for The Sierra Network?' I said I'd need a week or two to build a game system because I was concerned using an existing game system would have copyright issues. It turned out I shouldn't have been concerned, but I was concerned. So I threw a game together in a week and had a game for the testers; this was when [TSN] hadn't really gone live.

"It was the first time ever the conference room [a virtual room on the network] got completely full," Richard boasts. "The systems programmers were thrilled because they found out all kinds of functionality that didn't work right and I immediately designed a shared dice roller, a mute feature to shut someone up who was bothering you, a whisper feature to send a private message – the first of all of these on the internet anywhere."

Having run a lot of RPGs over many years, Richard knew that players liked detail – and lots of it – from the person running the game. So he also implemented a feature that allowed the game master to upload prewritten text files to the players. It meant thousands of words of description could be written before a gaming session, which was important for maintaining the immersion of a roleplaying game.

"One of the people in the conference room was Chris Williams, Ken and Roberta's son. Ken asked him how he liked that game and Chris said it was cool. So he thought, 'Richard can design a roleplaying game,' and stuck that in the back of his mind. I had no idea. Basically, all my career as a game designer comes back to a fourteen-year-old boy liking my roleplaying game I'd hastily thrown together online," Richard laughs.

"[In 1993] there was a company reorganization, one of many while I was there. The way they determined the layoffs, Sierra had a drafting system for who worked on which games. When they were planning their games for the year, the project managers would sit down in a room and say, 'I want this person to be my lead designer.' Roberta Williams always got first pick, of course. They'd go around and pick all the people, and sometimes you'd be a lead and sometimes you wouldn't, depending on the timing of the games. They did a final draft in March of '93, and anyone who wasn't drafted for the teams they had [was] laid off. I was finishing *Hoyle Classic* and nobody at Sierra had drafted me. I thought, 'Okay, I am in crunch mode. Do I get my resume out there now and find a job before everybody else hits the market? What do I do?'"

It turned out Richard's talents were in demand after all. "What really happened is I had been drafted by The Sierra Network. Stuart Moulder was up in Seattle in negotiations with Microsoft to try and buy us, and I wish they had. It took him a couple of days to get back to me, but he said, 'No, no, you were the first one I drafted!' They had roleplaying games they wanted me to work on, as well as bridge and my wealth of card game experience. That's how Sierra was."

While the people were what made TSN/INN unique, it was the games that drove customers to the network. Richard Aronson, who ended up staying with INN until it was closed by eventual owners AOL, says, "bridge, spades, hearts, and the three MedievaLand [roleplaying] games were the only ones that made money for INN."

Bridge was the first online project Richard worked on, using the knowledge he had gained working on *Hoyle Classic Card Games* to good advantage. "They called me Mr. Hoyle because I had three big volumes I had inherited from my father. The oldest one was from the thirties, so I could show the evolution of the newer card games like euchre and spades as people tweaked the rules to make them a better game overall. We did some of that for euchre and we did a lot of that for which game rules we would use on TSN for all the card games there."

Most of Richard's time was spent building the first team bridge game on the internet. "Team bridge was a really big thing," he explains. "It involves eight players on two different teams, and they're playing the same cards. It's the way almost all the major bridge tournaments evolved, certainly the bridge world championships, where two of us would sit north–south at one table and the other two would sit east–

west at the other table, and you would compare the score against the other team. It's a game of complete skill, but it's also eight players instead of four players or fewer.

"There had to be synchronization in the communication methods and comparisons of the scoring and making sure they got the deals at exactly the same time. You can't have someone on the phone saying, 'Watch out for this 5–0 split,' that kind of thing. [Bridge] on TSN was the most popular bridge game. I got to play with many world championship bridge players there. It's a great way to practice."

Card games were a good investment for The Sierra Network because of the low amount of data that needed to be sent and received over the network, something the company had to pay for. In comparison, flight simulators and RPGs required a lot of information to be sent, which cost the network more.

According to Richard, "Bridge is a very easy game to send. The hardest one we ever did was *Red Baron*. It requires a constant synchronization of location and vector control of the plane you're in compared with the other planes you're shooting at. That one was a real stressor. We had to basically pay a nickel for every packet we sent, so it was also a big money loser. That's why we designed the *Red Baron* waiting room along the lines of the way some of the longer lines at Disneyland are: in a way that's so engrossing that you don't notice it's taken you an hour to get on to the Indiana Jones ride. Anything we could do to reduce packets."

MedievaLand was another popular and profitable destination that hosted three games: *The Shadow of Yserbius, The Fates of Twinion,* and *The Ruins of Cawdor.* The first, designed and programmed by Joe Ybarra, was a major hit and its sequel, *The Fates of Twinion,* was quickly commissioned.

Richard Aronson was asked to test the games and wasn't impressed. "Ken had signed up Joe Ybarra, who had made *The Bard's Tale.* He hired him on a contract to make an RPG for TSN. They insisted that I test [*The Shadow of Yserbius*] and there were some things I didn't like about it. There were a couple of problems that in order to solve them required prior knowledge of the solution. To me they were just unsolvable. I said, 'How can you figure this out?' The one where you have to stand on this square and bounce off this wall, and someone else in a different room had to stand on a different square and bounce off a different wall, which unlocked both doors in order to move safely forward one step each and repeat that in different directions and so forth.

"That's the only way through; that's not something that can be solved by trial and error, not something that can be solved within the game. They said, 'Now you know so you'll tell other people.' To me, that's not game design, that's punishing the players. Having to depend upon an in-game communication method that was outside the game breaks the suspension of disbelief."

Despite these objections, Richard says "the game shipped and they made sure the information was disseminated widely. There were a lot of bugs with it, but on the other hand it had a lot of nice PvP [player versus player] for its time. Ybarra had solid RPG systems going from his other games. That was good."

The Fates of Twinion had similar problems. "It shipped when QA said, 'We're not going to test this anymore. We've reported all these fatals that haven't been fixed. It's a waste of our time to test this game if all these fatals haven't been fixed.' So the game shipped over QA's objection and the management of TSN said at the time, 'Okay, this is what we'll do. We'll give you $50,000 and you'll give us the source code and you'll give us three days of support. Otherwise we'll just write our own [game] from scratch because otherwise all these bugs are too much for us.' So Ybarra said, 'Well, $50,000 in the hand is better than a bird in the bush.' So they bought the source code, then hired me to work on *The Ruins of Cawdor*."

The Ruins of Cawdor was the third and final RPG commissioned, which Richard Aronson worked hard to make both unique and authentic. He even traveled to England to research Cawdor Castle and the history surrounding *Macbeth*, the Shakespeare play he based the game on.

"There were a lot of goals in it," Richard says. "One of them was to make a more social roleplaying game. A lot of the roleplaying games out there are played by single players not working in groups. The goal of INN was, 'We're a social network. We want people to work with other people.'

"In order to unlock any level, you had to form a group to get into that next room. In the early levels, the key to who you needed in your party was in the name of the room. So you knew the next room you were going into, and all of the rooms had names that had one of the eight character classes in them; one or more. You had to have a party that had an initial that matched up to all of those initials that were in that room. So the conservatory had a C for Cleric, and an R for Ranger and a T for Thief. So you needed those three to get through the door. Once you were through the door, you could go through yourself and you could serve [as] an opener for other people to go through the door. It wasn't onerous, but you had to do that. Forge relationships," Richard explains.

"One of the other things I thought was important was to give players a sense of familiarity. I based it on *Macbeth* because every sixth grader in California – I foolishly thought the whole nation – had to review *Macbeth* and *Romeo and Juliet*. I knew there would be broad familiarity with the play on which it was based, and then I set it about one hundred years in the future and all the major characters are ghosts and your quest is to slay the ghosts. So, sense of familiarity, setting in Cawdor castle."

One of the first things Richard did was take a vacation in Great Britain. "We got to visit Cawdor, which gave me a lot of background. I also did a lot of research into the English-Scottish border wars so most of the clan names were original. The crimes were obsolete crimes that were still on the books or crimes that we called by different names or slang names for certain crimes," he says. "In medieval times you'd go to a big fair where there's lots of strangers and you'd spot someone who had had three or four drinks and they were feeling pretty good and you'd go, 'Cousin!' like you're a long-lost cousin. 'Cousining' is the act of impersonating someone else for purposes of fraud."

One major problem Richard Aronson needed to fix before he could work on *The Ruins of Cawdor* was a technical one relating to a player attempting to run away from a turn-based combat encounter. "There was a synchronization issue. As long as we could keep certain indexes synchronized, it worked fine. [But] there was one way in PvP where they could desynchronize the indices that all the testing never found," he admits.

The only way Richard was able to resolve this issue was to have four PCs in his work area, something management wasn't willing to do, insisting he could do it with only two. So he worked from 5:00 p.m. until midnight to access the computers he needed to track down the bug.

Designing and programming *The Ruins of Cawdor* was an arduous task, with Richard putting in more than twelve hours a day, every day for thirty-five days straight. But when he presented the game to the INN systems programmers – the team that connected the game into the network itself – he discovered he had been working that hard for little reason, because the INN code wasn't at a point where it could run *Cawdor* online.

"My boss who had brought me over to INN, Stuart Moulder, had left for Microsoft and they hadn't replaced him and no one had told me that the systems programmers were late," Richard says, explaining that he was then asked to polish and refine the game, sending it through multiple rounds of QA for the next five months, which meant the game shipped virtually bug free.

"One of the things I insisted when I started, because I had read bug reports on *Twinion* and *Yserbius*, was this game is going to be based on Shakespeare; I'm going to be borrowing a lot of Shakespearean language. If I use a word you've never heard of and it's in the Oxford English Dictionary, I'm going to cite the dictionary and return the bug as fixed. Someone in the company then bought me an OED [Oxford English Dictionary], which I still have. I didn't want to have all these bug reports back and forth and back and forth about language. I said, 'If you're going to do a game that is Shakespearean, Shakespeare's language and Shakespeare's own words have to be acceptable.'"

Richard recalls that during the testing phase, he was approached with a special request. "About halfway through testing, the lead QA came up to me and said there was a beloved tester on [INN] who had just been diagnosed with pancreatic cancer and she was very ill. Was there some way I could put her into the game? I said, 'Okay, give me her name and details' and I immortalized her in a portrait in the rogues' gallery and changed the text and said she was the most beloved thief and nobody knew that she had been the one that had always been picking their pockets, or something like that."

The Ruins of Cawdor was a major success for INN, and Sierra published a standalone version for retail as they had with the two previous installments.

"*Cawdor* made more money in its first week then *Front Page Sports Football* made in its entire lifetime. We had to pay a whole lot of money to license *Front Page Sports Football* because they thought there's all these football fans out there, but it didn't translate well," Richard says.

The game Richard worked on that he feels most proud of is *Cawdor*, not only because of the quality of the game but the effect it had on at least one of its players.

"I got a letter from a player who was entering tenth grade. He wrote me that he had never done anything good in school but he liked playing games, and because of *Cawdor* he decided he would read *Macbeth*. Then he was given a book report in ninth grade and he asked the teacher if he could do it on *Macbeth* and the teacher said, 'That's a much more difficult work than I was planning, but if you want to, then yes.' It was the first A he had ever gotten and he started to enjoy his English classes and he got As in English and turns out he could write. Now he's getting much better grades and he actually thinks he can go to college. Because I motivated him with enough references to the play in the game, and that's the moment that sticks with me.

"That's what games at their best can do. They educate and inspire and they entertain. I don't know if he's the only one in the world that ever felt so motivated, but probably not. So I think I helped some people learn some things. All the remedies I stuck in *Cawdor* were based on medieval herb lore at the time. Bark tea and all those things. The crimes were historically accurate, the clan wars, the border wars. They were all historically accurate. The names I was using – why not use a real historical setting in a game which is in a historical setting?

"Throw in a bit of education and some of it might stick and be useful someday," Richard concludes.

Bad Behavior

Richard Aronson also worked to fix the major issues that had plagued the two previous Sierra Network RPGs, player cheating and bugs being the biggest. "I met with the user groups a whole bunch before I got started. I also met with the sysops [systems operators]. The number one complaint of the user groups was people were using macros – the most popular one was called Vitamin F – to cheat. That's because the packets are sent in the clear [not encrypted]; a little bit of hardware and software and you could intercept the outbound packet and change your health numbers to something much, much bigger. It really made the player versus player impossible if you were cheating against people who weren't cheating, and vice versa."

To fix the cheating, Richard encrypted all the health information but left a fake health number in the code to show the network's administrators who had been cheating. "We could detect it and automatically send you a letter saying, 'It appears you have violated our terms of service by hacking. We're going to give you a one-week suspension.' And that took sysops out of the equation altogether, because the number one thing sysops complained about was, 'We hate arguing with fourteen-year-old boys who we've caught dead to rights about how they're not really cheating.'"

The way people interacted on the network was a constant issue for both sysops and management, according to John Williams. "In these days of Xbox Live, a time when we've grown used to the idea that someone will describe the ways they fornicated with your mother and how much she liked it each time you do battle, it's going to sound extra naïve that we had no idea what we were going to be in for when we created this online gaming service. Oh, the horrors of seeing the worst of humanity online looking to suck the joy out of others," John remembers. "Foul language was the least of our problems, one that we solved by having a filter that turned dirty words into nonsense, but it was a Band-Aid on a hatchet wound."

One of the more disturbing incidents that occurred was the harassment of a female character within *The Shadows of Yserbius*, something John says sticks with him to this day. "Multiple male characters ganging up on a female one and providing abusive, sexual and frankly ugly messages, and the 'in character' young lady just stayed online and took it all. I hoped it was an isolated incident, but it wasn't. Some of the stuff I read in transcripts turned my stomach.

"We also had a call from a mom who wanted to let us know that a 'boy' her daughter had met on our service had asked to meet up in real life and in doing so was discovered to be a sexual predator. So what happened in *Yserbius* jumped to real life. That one turned my stomach as well, and that feeling of queasiness got worse when I was tasked with rewriting our terms of use in such a way that we could make sure we could fight it in court should someone try to sue us for having something to do with it," John reveals.

"What do you do when someone in your chat room tells everyone that they have taken an overdose of drugs on purpose and that they are committing suicide while they chat? Do you attempt to engage them? If you do you can make yourself liable for the results, we found out the hard way."

Fortunately, not all the online interactions were bad. Loving relationships developed out of online encounters, and friendships were born that grew over the years.

"There were some good things," John says. "Multiple marriages. Lots of people had fun and I think we created some of the rules for how online games should work that were adopted elsewhere. I met some incredibly good people and actually ran into some friends that I hadn't seen in years who happened upon the service and recognized me from my work in the ImagiNation newsletter and my regular work with the moderators."

It also turned out that a lot of online encounters became sexual, something that hadn't even been considered when starting the network. It wasn't a well-known fact, but moderators had the ability to join any private chat room without the other participants being aware, which brought these sorts of issues to light.

"I think a lot of very horny people found out about cybersex for the first time on INN," John claims. "They seemed to enjoy it and lord there was a lot of that, especially after around eight at night!"

Selling ImagiNation

In November 1994, AT&T completed a total purchase of INN for $40 million. What had started out as a venture into the online world had ended for Sierra with a buyout from one of the biggest players in the communications industry. Sierra's involvement was reduced to being a contractor to supply updates to INN and new content in the form of additional games.

AT&T itself struggled to make a profit from INN and eventually sold the network to AOL in August 1996. Richard Aronson was there until the end and says that AOL bought the network for the server code, a far cry from Ken Williams's vision for The Sierra Network.

"History shows AOL made a terrible mistake," Richard says. "We were at least eighteen months ahead of them in a necessary server rewrite that allowed better spreading across multiple servers. And AOL at the time was at five million users and couldn't handle any more because people were complaining they couldn't find their friends. It just depended on where you logged in and there was no way they could stop that without a complete rewrite."

Richard believes buying INN gave AOL a cheap way to save two years of server development, "and that enabled them to grow up to 25 million users, which enabled them to get so large that they eventually bought Time Warner instead of the other way around. They became AOL-Time Warner and eventually AOL got spun away and they fired us because they didn't like gamers. They still thought of themselves as an ISP [internet service provider] as opposed to an internet company, and gamers cost them money.

"As I recall, the average gamer session was about forty-five minutes and the average other AOL user was about ten minutes. The same as with health clubs; they make their money when you sign up and don't use it. They didn't like the gamers . . . it was going to free them from that side of things. They were the biggest content provider in the world. Six months after they fired everybody, they were looking for more game developers because they were falling behind because they weren't providing games, and games were one of the biggest reasons to be an AOL member. It was a horrible decision."

Interlude: The Buyout

One of the results of going public in 1989 was that Sierra now had a board of directors that Ken Williams answered to, and it was one of his board members who would eventually change the course of the company permanently.

In February 1996, Walter Forbes approached Ken after a meeting and made him an offer. His company, CUC International, wanted to expand into the software development industry and Forbes had decided to buy Sierra, whether Ken liked it or not.

Ken and Roberta were still majority shareholders, but since the company was public they couldn't make the decision on their own. As president, Ken was forced to take Forbes's offer to the other shareholders. Sierra at the time was trading at close to $25 a share, and the offer from Forbes and CUC was $48 a share. It seemed too good an opportunity for the shareholders to pass up.

In July of that year, CUC acquired both Sierra and another software company, Davidson & Associates, for $1.858 billion, the majority of which was paid out in CUC shares.[31] These were the first two software company acquisitions of what CUC envisioned would lead to many more.

CUC was a massive and, at the time, unique company. It wasn't a computer game developer, publisher, or even retailer. It wasn't a traditional retail business at all. The principal business of CUC was selling memberships in its buying clubs.

In today's world we call it direct marketing, but in the early 1980s, when Walter Forbes developed the idea, it was new and unknown. In traditional retail, a company builds a product. The product is sold to a middleman or wholesaler, who might purchase goods from a number of manufacturers and then sell them on to different retailers. The retailer then goes through the process of selling the product to a customer.

Walter Forbes, as CEO of CUC International, set out to change this time-honored dynamic. He inserted his company into the middle of the process, cutting out both the wholesaler and the retailer – in essence, bringing the manufacturer and customer together.

CUC didn't make its money from the transactions but from memberships. The company's main asset was its membership lists. Regular consumers would pay a monthly fee to join one of CUC's many lists, and in return would gain access to catalogs of products from manufacturers. A customer would browse the catalog and buy an item, and CUC would then pass that purchase order on to the manufacturer, who would post the item directly to the customer. By the mid-nineties, CUC had 50 million members across their different clubs, with more than 250,000 products on offer. As an average annual membership cost around $49, it's fair to say that CUC was doing well.

Getting into the software business opened up a new avenue of advertising for CUC's primary business, enabling ads to be included in the software boxes and even in the games themselves.

After a successful public offering in the early eighties, CUC had purchased more than twenty-five other companies, usually in the same manner as they would later go on to do with Sierra: by paying down the purchase price with a large percentage in CUC stock. By the time Walter Forbes made his offer to purchase Sierra, CUC was worth in excess of two billion dollars and was an industry leader in direct marketing.

Ken Williams had no reason not to trust Walter Forbes. He was a respected businessman and had been a valuable board member at Sierra for a few years, regularly offering good business insights and progressive ideas that helped move the company forward. While Ken felt blindsided by the offer, he could see the potential advantages in Forbes's idea of creating one large software company. The purchase of both Sierra and Davidson & Associates, who owned new rising star Blizzard Entertainment, was intended as the first step in creating this new empire.

The major advantage for Ken Williams and Sierra was the merger of manufacturing and distribution departments within the companies, creating a giant division that would drive sales growth and compete with their major opponent in the games industry, Electronic Arts.

It turned out to be a deal that was too good to be true.

Chapter 14: Changing Adventures

Computers still hadn't really caught up to doing 3D animation. But Sierra was working on it.

Marcia Bales, Designer, Shivers

A cultural change occurred in the early nineties that saw computers become a staple in most homes. They were no longer just for the tech-savvy, and as more and more people began using them throughout the decade, games and software were simplified to reach a broader audience.

More importantly, the technological advancement to 3D would become one of the major downfalls of the point-and-click adventure. While fast-paced, action-oriented games increased in popularity, the more cerebral adventure genre no longer dominated the market.

Another aspect of adventure games that became an issue for a more mainstream demographic was their limited replayability; once you've finished a story-driven game, there's little need to go back and play it again.

Bill Davis was creative director at Sierra from 1989 until 1993 and saw the change in direction the industry was beginning to take: "We did have *Wolfenstein* [*3D*]. We were playing it at the studio. We just didn't realize things were going to go that way and shooters were going to be so popular. Sierra was far from being a shooter company."

Bill still saw the major *Quest* series as essential to Sierra's continued growth and sustainability. "I always thought the power was in their brands and I think I'm being proven correct," he insists. "They were really good properties and they could still be going strong."

Corey Cole, designer of the *Quest for Glory* series, saw the writing on the wall for adventure games. "The nineties was when *Wolfenstein 3D* came out and people at Sierra were blown away by it. People were playing it when they were supposed to be working. Just as they had done previously with *SimCity*, *Civilization* and *Lemmings*. They were the three previous ones that everybody stopped to play."

That was only the beginning, Corey says: "When [id software] came out with *DOOM*, that kind of shifted the entire industry. Adventure games were at that point . . . costing a million dollars to make. And these first-person shooters, as they were being done then, were costing a couple of hundred thousand. They were really cheap to make compared to adventure games. They sold as well or better. So from a company bottom-line viewpoint, it didn't make any sense at all to make an adventure game. They're too expensive."

If Sierra was going to survive the decade's evolving gaming market as an adventure game producer, they were going to have to adapt instead of relying solely on their existing franchises.

A *DOOM*ed Sale[*]

Ken also saw the changes to the industry and realized early on that one big reason for that change was a company called id Software. Co-founders John Romero, John Carmack, Adrian Carmack and Tom Hall had released the incredibly popular *Commander Keen* games through publisher Apogee. These smooth-scrolling platformers showed that the PC could handle fast-paced arcade-style games. Their next title was to completely redefine the computer game market: *Wolfenstein 3D*.

John Romero was a huge fan of Sierra. As an Apple II programmer in the eighties, John had followed and admired the games Sierra produced for that system. He was also an adventure game fan.

"We had just finished making our second trilogy of *Commander Keen* games," John recalls. "*King's Quest V* had just come out and it was really fun. It was VGA and 256 colors! We had just got a next-generation computer and John Carmack needed some 256-color graphics to do what's called vector quantization – basically separating the color values of every pixel and see[ing] if he could compress it smaller than JPEG. This was back in the day when JPEG was not really used.

---

[*] John Romero's quotes in this section are shamelessly appropriated from the *Back Seat Designers* podcast, season 4, episode 6 (http://www.backseatdesigners.com/2017/02/19/s4e6-ive-made-a-lot-of-mistakes-and-youre-not-my-first-one). Thanks to Gareth Millward, Fred Olsen, and Troels Pleimert for letting me use it. As Troels said when I asked, "Honestly, just the idea of having our crap show in print is enough justification for this to be funny." Special thanks to John Romero for clarifying some of the details with me, too! Plus, *DOOM*. Thanks for *DOOM*.

"I got a screen from *King's Quest V* that [John] could play around with. I got thinking, you know, Roberta likes educational stuff because they'd been doing *EcoQuest* and some other games like that at that time. So I sent her copies of our latest *Commander Keen* games. She got back to me and basically said, 'Oh my God, we've got to have you guys out here to California.'"

John Romero, Tom Hall, John and Adrian Carmack, and Mark Rein from id flew out to meet with Ken and Roberta Williams in January 1992. It was to be a memorable trip for a number of reasons, but one sticks out in particular for John Romero. "We got a tour of the offices and we got to meet an Apple II programmer from ten years before; his name is Warren Schwader. He did *Threshold* and *Hi-Res Cribbage* and other stuff we admired. We actually got on our hands and knees and bowed to Warren Schwader, saying, 'We're not worthy!'" John laughs.

After their tour, the visit moved to Ken and Roberta's home. "We went to the house and while I was talking to Ken, Tom Hall was talking to Roberta and she was showing him her big design book of *King's Quest VI*," John remembers. "I'm talking to Ken and he's showing me *Red Baron Online* they had been making for The ImagiNation Network and I showed him *Wolfenstein* [*3D*]. Ken comes from the Apple II world and he remembered *Castle Wolfenstein*, but when he saw it he didn't really do anything; he didn't act like he was blown away or anything. He was like, 'That's pretty neat. Let me show you *Red Baron*.'"

The day finished with a long evening for the five visitors and the Williamses in a private room at a local restaurant called Erna's Elderberry House. Before the id team left the following morning, they returned to the office for a final talk with Ken.

"We went back to Sierra the next day, just before we left, and they offered to buy us for $2.5 million," says John. "We were very excited about it and we came back to Madison, Wisconsin, which is where we were at the time, and we talked about it and went, 'This is amazing!' We looked at how much income we were making at that time and basically saying, 'Do you know how long it would take to make $2.5 million on what we're making right now? This is awesome. We should totally do it.'"

As it turned out, however, the sale was not to be. As John describes it, "I told Ken we would do it if we did a letter of intent and got $100,000 down on it and then finish all the paperwork and sell the company. Then Ken basically said, 'Ah, never mind.'"

Although disappointed, the id team moved on and continued working on their follow-up to *Wolfenstein 3D*. A short time after the Sierra visit, *Wolfenstein 3D* won a highly coveted Software Publishers Association award.

John says, "Tom Hall and I went up on stage to get the award and before we left we said, 'We'll be back next year; we're making a game called *DOOM*.' After the show was over, we were walking down the hall and there's Ken. We went over and even before we said anything he said, 'I know, I know. I admit I've made a lot of mistakes and you're not the first one.' He was a really nice guy."[32]

While Sierra did make a number of other wise purchases in those years, id Software would forever remain the one that got away.

Adventures in the First Person

Released in 1993, *Myst* was a runaway success for its developer Cyan and went on to become the best-selling PC game of all time (*The Sims* later took the crown in 2002).[33] *Myst*, by the sheer fact of being the first game to break the million-copies-sold barrier, had set a new standard for sales, one which most Sierra games couldn't hope to reach.

Most of the *Quest* series Sierra had relied upon for so many years were still only moving 250,000 copies in total – good numbers by 1980s standards, but way too small compared to the benchmark set by *Myst*. The games hadn't decreased in quality, or even popularity, they simply weren't selling as well as a publicly listed company now required of them, especially with cost consistently rising.

Ken Williams saw what a phenomenon *Myst* was and wanted a piece of the first-person adventure pie. So finally he turned to Marcia Bales, a designer with subsidiary company Bright Star Technology, to deliver Sierra's first game in the new style.

With a background in comics and Saturday morning television production, Marcia had started with Bright Star in 1993, applying for an animator's position. "I answered an advert where they were looking for artists," she says. "I had previously worked for a studio that did Marvel comics layout animation, and of course that company was extremely regimented; everything was organized and that's kind of what I thought I was going to when I answered the ad. They wanted animators. I wasn't an animator, but I knew the concepts and I figured I could do it. I was pretty presumptuous."

After only six weeks at the company, Marcia saw there were already major problems. "Back then, when I got hired, they were still counting pixels in a floppy disk, so there wasn't much animation going on, as you can imagine," Marcia explains. "They got a contract from Berlitz to do a language learning program. Coincidently, that program was the very first CD-ROM that Sierra ever did. They were going to try it out on Bright Star.

"A lot of people don't know this. They wanted us to make all the mistakes. Because everybody was so used to counting pixels, they knew there would be limitations. Didn't know what those were, so they didn't want to screw up a really big game like *King's Quest* or something like that. We were the first one to go to market. That doesn't mean they weren't working on a new game in tandem, but they were waiting for us to go through the packaging and all that kind of stuff. I got hired for that.

"There was no project manager. There was no designer. It was the engineers designing everything. They could design things when you're doing floppies because there wasn't much art to it. But there's too much stuff, too much gameplay, too much everything that would go into a CD-ROM and it was really, really disorganized. So I just started organizing things, because I was used to that. I'd only been working six weeks and they made me a designer. I had no idea what I was doing!

"I had bluffed my way in. I didn't even know how to use Photoshop at the time," Marcia laughs. "I bluffed my way completely through everything. I remember going home to my husband and saying, 'This is the funnest job anyone could ever have. I can't believe they're paying me to do this.' Because it was super fun. That's how I got to be a designer. I bluffed my way into it."

After a few years of working on Bright Star's educational titles, Marcia was asked to design what would turn out to be *Shivers*. Marcia was experienced in product development but had never produced a game, although Ken and Roberta had faith that she could deliver a great-selling adventure.

"I was working basically in the educational division. We had a few kids' education products, but they liked the look of the products that I was working on. I was at that time designing gameplay and stories and things like that. They asked me if I could do a *Myst* game and of course once again, I said, 'Sure, I can do that!' In fact, it was pretty exciting."

Not having experience with a narrative-driven adventure game before, Marcia was given the rare opportunity to learn from Roberta Williams herself, being sent to Oakhurst during the production of *Phantasmagoria*. "I went to California because up in Seattle they didn't have any designers other than me. I had never worked on anything that wasn't educational. This was my first time," Marcia says. "I was sort of just shadowing Roberta; she was mentoring me.

"I didn't design gameplay or anything like that, but we did talk through storylines and talk through the design because I was doing a game with puzzles and stuff in it like she did. She would talk to me through these things. Then when I did [*Shivers*], I would send her a lot of things and she mostly gave me lots of encouragement and lots of really good thoughtful comments like, 'Have you thought about this, have you thought about this? Maybe this needs to be brought out in the story a little bit more.' That's the sort of thing she did. It gave me the confidence to do it."

Marcia has nothing but positive things to say about her time working with Roberta. "I was in California only two or three weeks. While I was there I was writing the story and working on the gameplay, and between her working on *Phantasmagoria* and us talking about the gameplay for that, I would go to her and she'd give me feedback. After that it was phone calls and emails. I appreciated it so much. What a marvelous opportunity. I love her. She's a wonderful, wonderful woman."

As for *Shivers*, she continues: "I wrote the text, I wrote the gameplay. I pretty much did all the writing. We hired a wonderful, wonderful art director for the game, and here's the other thing: prior to this, nobody had done anything in 3D. We were kind of just starting that. But we didn't have to do too much 3D, just the backgrounds. We weren't animating in 3D at that point, although they were starting it. But everything was so slow still. Computers still hadn't really caught up to doing 3D animation. But Sierra was working on it.

"We hired artists, I did up the gameplay and the story and it was again a lot of fun. It came out [for] Windows and [Macintosh]; it was kind of the last [Mac] game they did because Apple was dying at that time. When *Shivers Two* came out we didn't do it [for Mac]. It had dropped below 3% of the market; it's hard to believe that now. And it was sad for a lot of artists especially, thinking 'Oh no, am I going to lose my Mac? Are they going to quit making software for it?' When it dropped below 3%, you had to stop and think, 'Can I afford to do this?' It's like translating into a foreign language that's less than 3% of the market. You just don't do it."

Shivers was a first-person horror-themed adventure set in a museum haunted by South American ghosts, designed with a unique inventory system that only allowed two items to be held by the player at any one time. *Shivers* rewarded Ken and Roberta's faith in Marcia, as it was indeed a great-selling game for Sierra, moving well over half a million copies, according to Marcia.

Although she is happy with the final product, she believes now that the game is simply too demanding. "I didn't realize that until I played it through. I thought, you really have to be a game lover to get through this. It takes too long to do things. They need to be faster. They can be hard, they just need to be faster to get through them. There were too many parts of the game."

Shivers came out in 1995 and a sequel was put into production quickly after. Marcia was again commissioned to design and write the script, but this time she wanted to try something different.

Instead of a direct sequel, Marcia designed a game that was set in the same universe but wasn't related in any way to the story of the first game. Another first-person adventure in the style of its predecessor, *Shivers Two: Harvest of Souls* sees players assume the role of a friend of the rock group Trip Cyclone, who must solve the mystery of where the band disappeared to and why their music videos are turning people into zombies.

Sierra showed they hadn't lost their innovative edge, as *Shivers Two* showcased two new ideas that would soon become industry standards. Vision 360 was a technology that offered the ability to pan the camera around the current area with the mouse, allowing for full immersion in the 3D world, while full use was also made of audio advances to have sounds come from the appropriate direction relative to where the player was facing.

The second *Shivers* game garnered favorable reviews and sold reasonably well for an adventure of the time, but a further sequel was never placed into production.

Another attempt at carving out a slice of the *Myst*-dominated first-person adventure pie was *Lighthouse: The Dark Being*. Jon Bock had been with Sierra since the early nineties, working as an animator on *Space Quest IV*, *Police Quest 3* and *Castle of Dr. Brain*. Well-respected by his peers and management, he moved into art designer roles on *The Island of Dr. Brain* and the strategy game *Outpost* before being asked to design *Lighthouse*.

Called into the office of Ken Williams and shown a copy of *Myst*, Bock was asked if he could make a similar game. When Jon expressed his willingness to do it, *Lighthouse* was greenlit and went into development.

Lighthouse differed from Sierra's usual inventory- and dialogue-heavy adventure games due to its focus on logic-based puzzles that required the player to observe what was happening and manipulate the environments, which were made up of static prerendered backgrounds. While widely praised for its immersive graphics, it was criticized for its difficulty. Sales, while reasonable, just weren't up to that new *Myst* benchmark so no sequel was ever commissioned.

"*Lighthouse*, a *Myst* and *Riven* clone, is a beautiful game. I think it suffered from the adventure game problem," says Sierra's general manager at the time, Craig Alexander, referring to the fact that the genre was no longer selling in the numbers that a modern developer required.

Other first-person adventure games were developed at this time as well, *Rama* being a notable example produced at Dynamix and released under the Sierra label. Unfortunately, Sierra's attempt at entering the first-person adventure market wasn't overly successful, although the games they did release were largely well regarded by fans and critics alike.

Adventures in Full Motion Video

The use of full motion video (FMV) was another way Sierra attempted to push the adventure genre in new directions and gain more customers in the nineties. FMV games had taken off with the overwhelming success of Trilobyte's *The 7th Guest* and *The 11th Hour*, and Sierra decided to follow suit with three live-action games of their own: *Phantasmagoria*, *Gabriel Knight: The Beast Within* and *Police Quest: SWAT*.

Roberta Williams had become known for her fantasy games, with Sierra cultivating her reputation around the family-friendly *King's Quest* series, but she had a lot of ideas and not all of them were about King Graham and his family. In 1992, Roberta approached designer Josh Mandel about collaborating on her next project. This was to be something completely different for her: a horror game.

As Josh remembers it, "We got together and at that time it was called *Scary Tales*. It was sort of related to the fact that Roberta had been known for fairy tales and now Roberta was going to be known for *Scary Tales*. We worked together really well until we had a huge falling out, then she didn't speak to me for between six months and a year."

Why the rift? Roberta had given a long-form interview to a popular computer magazine and when it was released, Josh discovered a notable omission. "I had been putting in a lot of work and I had contributed a significant percentage of the design elements of the game, and I was very upset when the interview came out that she hadn't even mentioned she was doing it with someone else. Or me in particular. I was kind of hurt by that," he shares.

"I mentioned it to Steve Joseph, who was VP of development at that point, and Ken and Roberta had gone on vacation and they were out of the country. Steve said, 'I think you should write her a letter about it and here's what you should say.' I wrote a letter about it to her, very respectful, and I think he made a couple of changes to it before he sent it on to her on vacation. She sent a message back to me saying she absolutely did talk about me in the interview and that's the end of that. She didn't talk to me for a long, long time after, and after she did it was like nothing had happened. She had apparently forgiven me."

After Roberta returned from holiday, production of the game resumed without Josh, but in a different direction. This time the design was purely Roberta's, although she did get some assistance from Andy Hoyos, the art director on the project and an avid horror fan. The story they ended up with was nothing like the original *Scary Tales* concept, and the game was renamed.

Phantasmagoria was Sierra's most ambitious project and, at a cost of over $4 million,[34] certainly the most expensive to create. Although the game was made using the SCI engine, the process was completely different from anything before it. The entire game was filmed and recorded on video – similar to a movie, although twice as long – and the live actors had to record in front of a blue screen, with high-resolution backgrounds added during postproduction.

With no facility in Oakhurst capable of facilitating the team's needs, Sierra built a new studio with Sierra technical director Bill Crow put in place as studio director and head of all studio production. The studio was outfitted with what was dubbed the "blue cave" (a large room painted entirely blue). The studio also had cameras, recording equipment, and a control room with computer systems running Ultimatte, video compositing software used to merge the backgrounds created by Sierra's artists with the video footage being recorded.

Using 3D tools, wireframe models were made of the backgrounds Andy Hoyos had created. High-resolution skins and textures were then placed on the frames, producing a final environment that could be composited with the actors' recordings.

Filming took place over the summer of 1994, with the crew and actors working six days a week for over three months. Each shot was meticulously set up, with blue boxes and other objects arranged in the blue cave to portray different objects and items in the scene. The actors would then perform the scene using their imaginations to work out how it would look in its final form, with each scene recorded multiple times to get the best take.

In the control room, Bill Crow, producer Mark Seibert, Roberta and the crew were able to observe the scenes with the backgrounds overlaid, and to offer suggestions or request retakes if required.

Putting all the assets together was a monumental task for the programming team at Sierra. They had never done anything like this before and had to rewrite significant portions of the SCI engine to accommodate Roberta's vision. Decisions such as frame rate – something they hadn't given much thought to for previous adventure games – were now vital and demanded serious consideration.

Eventually the game was put together and extensive testing performed. Cast members were called back in early 1995 to record additional footage, and *Phantasmagoria* was finally released to the public in August of that year.

It wasn't an easy sell. Reminiscent of earlier times and the controversy surrounding the release of *Softporn Adventure*, *Phantasmagoria* was met with harsh criticism from some quarters. Leading computer retailer CompUSA refused to stock the game due to its violence and sexual content, in particular a scene that depicted the rape of the main character. The Australian government denied the game a release classification, effectively banning the game in that country; the *New York Post* even called the game "sick." Yet despite the controversy, Sierra under Ken Williams didn't waver. The game was simply marketed as an adult product and voluntarily labeled with a mature rating.

Even with its massive seven CD-ROMs, *Phantasmagoria* was Sierra's biggest hit of the year and went on to sell over a million copies.[35] Gaming had finally grown up.

Another of Sierra's FMV games was the second *Gabriel Knight* adventure, *The Beast Within*. Eighteen months of production were fraught with a massive overrun in budget so bad that the threat of cancelation was held over the team's head the entire time. Perhaps the one saving grace is that the project was made easier by the systems established during the production of *Phantasmagoria*.

Jane Jensen again wrote the game, crafting a story that took the player right back into Gabriel's world. However, since this was to be an FMV production, cuts were made to the number of dialogue interactions allowed. The first *Gabriel Knight* game had featured extensive conversation options between characters. This time Jane had to limit the number of possibilities to keep filming costs down.

Another change from the first *Gabriel Knight* was that the perspective alternated between that of Gabriel and his assistant Grace, with the player controlling both characters at different times as the game progressed.

The most obvious difference between the first two games in the series was the recasting of the title character. Acclaimed Hollywood actor Tim Curry had been cast as the voice of Gabriel in *Sins of the Fathers*, but Jane felt that while he sounded like Gabriel, his look was nothing like she imagined the character. An extensive audition process was undertaken, and Dean Erickson eventually won the job.

"I got the role of Gabriel through a fairly typical casting process," Dean recalls. "Dan Parada was the casting director and put out a breakdown, which is a description of the role that goes to all the agents. My agent thought I fit the physical description perfectly and submitted me for the role. It was clear that Sierra's producers were looking for a 'type' that captured the physical essence of Gabriel as depicted in the first game.

"I went in to audition for Dan, read a scene or two, and then went home to wait. Fortunately for me, the producers were in a bit of a hurry. As I recall, the first Gabriel was let go or backed out, so they were replacing him."

Dean received a callback a day or two later. "During the next audition, Will Binder, the director, was there. Will is a smart, calm guy and someone I trusted easily in the audition. He remains a friend to this day. As director, he knew what he was looking for and was simply trying to find it in an actor. I was in my ponytail stage then, so he asked if I would consider cutting my hair. I said something to the effect of, 'You can do whatever you want with it.' That might have been an exaggeration, but did I mention that actors just want the part?" Dean laughs.

It was only a couple of days later that Dean received the call he wanted, but he still hadn't landed the role. Will Binder liked him for it but told him that Jane wasn't convinced he was right for the part. Even though he looked like Gabriel, Will revealed to Dean later that he believed Jane wasn't convinced he had the fire or strength as an actor to perform the role. So Sierra flew Dean to Oakhurst, where he met with the production team over lunch and Jane asked him to read a scene for her.

"I read the scene, I believe, right there at the restaurant," Dean says. "As I was reading the scene – acting, as it were – I knew exactly by the look on Jane's face the moment she understood I would be a good choice for the role. She looked scared. There was some fire in the scene, some anger, some strength, and I think Jane just had to see that I wasn't simply a nice, easygoing guy. Once I scared the you-name-it out of her, she knew I had what it took. Anyway, that scene reading at the restaurant sealed the deal for Jane, and I became the living embodiment of Gabriel Knight."

Through discussions with Jane about exactly what she wanted from the character, Dean prepared for the role to make it distinctive from Tim Curry's performance in the first game.

"I read the script many times, over and over," Dean says. "That's where most of your clues are as to your character, especially when you have a great writer like Jane doing the writing. I don't recall ever playing the first game, though I likely saw snippets, nor do I believe playing it through would have helped me. How could I begin to emulate a great actor like Tim Curry? No, I had to make the character my own. Besides, a live character is very different than a voice-over in animation. I had to ground my character in his truth, and personally believe in the importance of what I was trying to accomplish."

Dean remembers the filming experience being an enjoyable one, although also a lot of work. "Due to time and budget constraints, we got very little rehearsal time on set. When I performed on *Frasier*, we had most of the week to prepare for a live shoot in front of a studio audience. Believe me, each process held its own thrill. Most of the low-budget movies I've done were similar to working [on *Gabriel Knight*]. Work fast, get what you need for the shot, and move on to the next scene to save time and money.

"Will did a great job in preparing the *GK* shooting schedule and keeping us on track, along with the crew. I would know the next day's shooting schedule the night before so I could avoid surprises and make final preparations. Because we shot on a stage in a blue screen environment, I usually asked Will what physical things would be around me once the background was installed. That way, I could refer to things specifically rather than play the scene without any physical variation or reference points."

According to Dean, "Normally, we'd get the shot in one, two, or three takes and we'd move on to the next scene. Will was specific in his direction and the other actors were very professional, so we got what we needed pretty quickly. Besides, we didn't have a big enough budget to waste time."

Much of the technology being used on *Gabriel Knight 2* was familiar to crew, as the game used Sierra's by-then-standard SCI engine with the enhancements made during the production of *Phantasmagoria*. Compositing the scenes from the live-action footage and photographic backgrounds was an almost identical process, while the recording process for the actors was also very similar.

This time, however, the decision was made to build their own video player to play the movie scenes. It was a cost-saving measure, as they wouldn't have to pay for a proprietary system like they had previously, but it caused a lot of issues since the technology was new to the engineers and consistently crashed or gave errors. While most of these problems were solved during production, some did make it into the public release of the game.

Another major change was the use of real photographs instead of artwork for the backgrounds. Nathan Gams, who served as creative director on *The Beast Within*, was responsible for all the backgrounds. Like a movie scout, Nathan found locations and took extensive photos of them. It took three trips to Germany to get all the pictures required, with producer Sabine Duvall (who happened to be German) assisting Nathan to identify locations in her country of origin. To minimize the number of people in any particular image, Nathan did most of his work in the early morning hours, and any people or unwanted objects in the shots were removed back at Sierra using the latest in computer graphic software.

Released in 1995, *Gabriel Knight: The Beast Within* was another successful FMV game for Sierra, although its sales numbers were nothing like those of the first *Phantasmagoria*, which had shipped the same year. This game, though, was a major critical success, with fans loving the level of attention to detail and immersive storyline that Jane Jensen had so carefully crafted.

More FMV Sequels

With *The Beast Within* and *Phantasmagoria* both proving successful, it made perfect sense that Sierra would order another *Phantasmagoria*. This time, however, Roberta wasn't interested in pursuing the sequel, so production was handed over to one of Sierra's new generation of designers.

Lorelei Shannon had been with Sierra for a long time and had worked her way from writing for *InterAction* magazine and hint books to writing on games like *The Dagger of Amon Ra*, before finally co-designing and writing *King's Quest VII*. It was after working closely with Roberta

Williams on *King's Quest VII* that Lorelei was finally given her own project, *Phantasmagoria: A Puzzle of Flesh*.

With a healthy budget, Shannon set about redesigning the series. While the original game had taken a campy, jump-scares horror approach, Lorelei wanted something more psychological. Instead of a proper sequel, Lorelei turned the game into the next installment of a horror anthology, designing *A Puzzle of Flesh* as a psychological thriller with science fiction elements – a far cry from its predecessor.

The story she developed threw away the established characters of the first game and instead focused on Curtis Craig, an employee of a pharmaceutical company who had recently been released from a psychiatric asylum. The production again used full motion video, but instead of recording in front of a blue screen, Lorelei decided to record on location and use actual sets, as if it were a Hollywood movie.

The game was filmed using Digital Betacam from February to September 1996, mainly in the Bellevue, Washington area where Sierra was producing the game. While the majority of scenes were recorded on location or sets, blue screen was still used for a couple of places, with the actors superimposed on the computer-generated footage later.

The video was processed back at the studio and eventually formatted using Duck TrueMotion compression to make it ready for use. The biggest challenge was that SCI wasn't capable of playing this particular format and the system programmers were constantly rewriting the engine in order to make it function. Every few weeks the game programmers would receive a new engine update and have to rewrite portions of their code that no longer worked.

When *Phantasmagoria: A Puzzle of Flesh* was released, like its predecessor it met with controversy. The game was too violent, according to critics. Some countries banned it entirely while others, like Australia, only released it after edits were made to the content. The controversy was expected, but the lower-than-projected sales were not. Discussions about a third game began but quickly faded.

Before it was quietly canceled, Marcia Bales, designer of the two *Shivers* games, was approached to design the next game in the *Phantasmagoria* series but declined the opportunity.

"They wanted me to do an adult game and I was not interested in that. I just didn't see why we needed to do another *Phantasmagoria*," Marcia says.

Another series to get the FMV treatment was *Police Quest*, which found new life in tactical SWAT (special weapons and tactics) simulations instead of the adventure games they had been up to that point. Moving the traditional procedure-based gameplay to a SWAT environment allowed the franchise to reach a much larger audience, making it, as Craig Alexander describes it, "a little more mass market–friendly."

With Daryl F. Gates consulting once again, designer Tammy Dargan crafted an experience that put the player in the first-person role of a SWAT team member running through training scenarios and tactical missions.

In the same way that both *Phantasmagoria* and *Gabriel Knight: The Beast Within* were developed, actors would perform their scenes on film, which was then composited with digital photographs taken of the Los Angeles area, although some cutscenes were recorded on location in training facilities and the city streets of LA using real SWAT members.

With its expanded demographic reach, when *Police Quest: SWAT* released in 1995 it became the best-selling title in the *Police Quest* series to date. "It sold very well," Craig Alexander recalls. "It sold over a million units if I remember correctly, which back in the day was a lot." Despite these impressive numbers, however, *SWAT* would be the only *Police Quest* game to rely on full motion video, and subsequent sequels would go on to distance themselves even further from the franchise's adventure game origins.

Overall, Sierra's FMV experiments met with more success than failure. *Phantasmagoria* was the first Sierra game to top one million sales, though its sequel never came close to those numbers. *Gabriel Knight: The Beast Within* also sold extremely well and won multiple Game of the Year awards while, according to studio manager Craig Alexander, *SWAT* was 1995's second biggest earner for Sierra, behind only *Phantasmagoria*.

With the advent of FMV, the future seemed bright, but it was a false dawn. As Craig portends, "The 3D revolution hadn't hit. [We thought FMV] was going to be the next big thing. It turned out to be rather a fad."

Sierra's Return to Online Gaming

In 1996, Sierra again attempted to enter the online market, this time with what would now be considered an MMORPG (massively multiplayer online roleplaying game), although that term hadn't been coined at the time. Developed internally, *The Realm Online* combined online chat, turn-based combat, and roleplaying elements into a game played over the still relatively new internet.

The Realm Online can be credited with establishing a number of protocols still used in MMORPGs to this day, as Marc Hudgins, who was an early art director on the game, recalls.

"The idea of an MMO didn't exist, except Ken had said, 'Let's make multiplayer *King's Quest*.' A lot of the fun of that was sitting around with the team coming up with ideas for things that this sort of game should have. We should have mail where you can send things to people. Weird things that are really standard now. The obvious things that are just standard in multiplayer games now were all new to us at the time and we were just making it up. I had some fun doing design work on that."

Animator Al Eufrasio remembers it being such a difficult project to work on that he requested to be reassigned. "[*The Realm Online*] just kind of felt orphaned from the beginning. It was so ahead of its time Sierra didn't really know what to do with it. I was young. I was in my early twenties at the time, so I would never consider doing something like this today, asking to be taken off a project. But it felt like the wheels were spinning a little bit too much on this. People weren't sure what they were going to do. People didn't want the project to get canceled; suddenly they were trying to scramble and figure out a place to put me or figure out whether to let me go instead. In hindsight it was kind of unprofessional but there was so much indecision.

"It was like a decade ahead of its time, even more. An MMORPG. They were kind of trying to make this super ambitious thing, kind of adapting Sierra's traditional approach to things but not quite. So it was hard to figure out how to do that. Okay, we're going to animate characters, then we have to animate costumes for them. How exactly is that going to work? Are we going to have overlays? Nowadays it's really obvious, but back then we were blazing a new trail. It was really frustrating because we'd end up having to do certain things over so many times, it was ridiculous."

According to John Williams, *The Realm Online* was relatively successful and had a lot of devoted fans, but he also admits that the company's internal issues at the time caused more problems for the project than its design or development.

"That was a game that had a lot of followers. A lot of people really loved that game, but we could all see *EverQuest*, *Ultima Online*, *World of Warcraft* and other game developments coming, and so we never really invested much into it," John says.

"The designer [Jordan Neville] was a young and brash guy, and while he did a great job with the initial design, he just didn't have the support within Sierra or the expertise that would convince us to finance to redevelop the game so that it could compete, and we pretty much all knew the game's days were numbered from practically the beginning. It's terrible to say, but everyone understood there was a great game there, but pretty much everyone in management knew that it wasn't going to win and kind of treated it like a red-headed stepchild.

"The *Realm* gaming audience was militant about it and nothing seemed to please them. I can't blame them; they really loved the game and couldn't understand why no one would take it seriously. So it was a game with no future and an absolutely caustic audience. People who did join [the team] pretty much all quit because they started talking to people and found that the audience was bitter. It was just an all-around bad situation," John recalls. "I probably made matters worse, as I very early on held a kind of gamers' summit where I told people the number one priority had to be to bring more people into the game if we wanted to survive. Boy, that didn't go over well."

John still believes *The Realm Online* was good, but it came at the wrong time for the company. "If it had come a year or so earlier we might have spent more time with it, but by the time it was really playable we had heard all about the big Sony effort [*EverQuest*] and the big EA effort [*Ultima Online*]."

With a view to revitalizing the game's base and attaching it to an existing property, general manager Craig Alexander reached out to Lori Cole, designer of *Quest for Glory*, with the intent of rebranding *The Realm Online* as *World of Quest for Glory*. When this idea didn't end up working out, *King's Quest Online* was also considered, but ultimately decided against as well.

Unlike The ImagiNation Network, *The Realm Online* did make money for Sierra, but it wasn't a huge hit, which to Craig was understandable for the time. "*Ultima Online* I guess was technically the first successful [MMORPG], but even it had challenges. *Ultima Online* was the one that scaled, then *EverQuest*, then *Asheron's Call*."

Even so, *The Realm Online* continued to exist, eventually being sold to Codemasters and then to Norseman Games, who still operate it today.

Interlude: A Larry Platform Game

Stephen Nichols, who got his start with the company working on The Sierra Network, developed a side-scrolling engine for platforming and pitched the idea of making a game with it in 1997. The engine was unique because it could perform parallax scrolling, a technique in which the background images move slower than foreground images, creating an illusion of depth in a 2D scene — something considered near-impossible on the PC at that point.

The initial plan for Stephen's engine was to develop a typical fantasy game where the hero went around with a sword killing enemies. Marc Hudgins was assigned as art director on the project. While management was happy to see the game proceed, they decided that it should be tied to an existing franchise, as Marc recalls.

"There's a risk aversion to all new gameplay and all new [intellectual property]. 'Let's at least tie it to something we know people like.' The idea — and this is crazy — [was] 'let's try *Leisure Suit Larry.*' Well, what can I do with *Leisure Suit Larry* as a platform game?"

Marc goes on to explain how he came up with the original story for the *Leisure Suit Larry* platformer: "I just sort of went with my own proclivities at the time and I said, 'I'm going to make him the accidental spy.' He gets mistaken for this James Bond type of guy and gets caught up in this very cartoony version of a James Bond story.

"The bad guy looked a lot like Larry, but imagine really ugly Larry; a bald mad scientist named Doctor Formaldehyde. Dr. Formaldehyde could not get laid because he was hideous and a mad scientist. So he was developing this thing called a babe magnet which was literally this giant magnet that was going to bring every beautiful woman on the planet to his secret lair. And he would turn them into these robotic zombies.

"Larry somehow ended up on this island. So the whole platformer game was he was going through these levels trying to defeat [Dr. Formaldehyde] and free the zombie babes. It was super fun. I have all these drawings still. It was really great."

Al Eufrasio was hired by Sierra to work on this untitled project and recalls the early days: "When I interviewed for the job, the way it was explained to me was they were working on a platform game and this one group of people really wanted to do it. They were trying to figure out how we could make a cool game that would see the best potentially out of everything in the company. They came up with *Leisure Suit Larry*. Al [Lowe] was peripherally involved at this stage. Oliver Brelsford was the producer; I assume it was him that made the final decision on hiring me."

It wasn't until much later that Marc Hudgins realized he had conceived a game that was very similar to the first *Austin Powers* movie, because the game was designed a number of years before the movie came out.

"We were completely on the same wavelength. I think it was because we were spoofing the same things, because Dr. Formaldehyde and Dr. Evil were not that far apart because they were basically still [James Bond villain] Blofeld. They had the fembots, I had the zombie babes who were being mind-controlled. I had these bad guys that were like sumo wrestler girls who would beat him up. It was a lot of fun," he recalls.

Marc remembers working hard on the design of the game, but at some point it was taken away from him and given to Al Lowe, who changed the direction completely and named it *Capital Punishment*.

According to Marc, "It was no longer going to be this game I had come up with and turned into the political game. A lot of it was based on the Clinton Whitewater scandal. One of the levels was literally white water rafting with Bill and Hillary Clinton. Al is a very funny guy. It was this politically motivated game using this side-scrolling engine."

Al Eufrasio remembers the new political version well, having designed some of the art assets for it. "It was kind of a political satire. At the time – and the same still holds true now – political punditry was getting very big. Talk radio and things like that were really expanding. A lot of new political magazines were coming out. I started three weeks [after his job interview] and by the time I got there it had switched to this political thing. Same engine, almost the same basic concept in that it was platformy and you're guiding something on a side-scrolling world, but that was about it. We were kind of trying to design it on the fly as well. The cracks started to show and they canceled it."

As the turn of the millennium drew closer, Sierra had already begun setting its sights on a future beyond adventure games, to varying degrees of success. But the beloved franchises the company had built its astounding success on for so many years were not ready to go down without a fight, even if they had to change radically to survive. More sequels were still to come – though unfortunately in many cases it would be their last.

Chapter 15: All Good Things . . .

*These games are really all collaborative efforts. If we came up
with the same design but a different team, you'd come out with
a completely different game.*

Corey Cole, Designer, Quest for Glory V

Even as Sierra continued producing games in their major tentpole series, they were determined to experiment with different technologies and styles throughout the mid-nineties. General manager Craig Alexander was a big proponent of these changes, trying to marry the company's existing properties with new ideas and advancements. Some were successful, like *Police Quest: SWAT*, while others weren't so lucky. By 1999, each of the major series had run their course at Sierra, some ending on a higher note than others.

One Last Mess to Clean Up

Space Quest 6: Roger Wilco in the Spinal Frontier was released in 1995. Credited as being written by Scott Murphy, it was in fact primarily designed by Josh Mandel, who had risen through Sierra's ranks from a beta tester to a producer, head of the writers, and eventually a designer. Josh had written some treatments for a possible *Space Quest* sequel after Mark Crowe left for Dynamix, but these had been put on hold while Mark and Dynamix developed Roger Wilco's fifth adventure. Now management wanted to revisit one of them and Josh was asked to design it.

"I don't think that they were all that thrilled with what Dynamix were doing with the adventure games," Josh says. "They weren't doing anything that was breakthrough, certainly from a sales standpoint. I don't know how well *Willy Beamish* did and that was the last adventure that [Dynamix] did under the Sierra label. So I don't think they wanted to give *Space Quest* to Dynamix again."

Josh wasn't sure if management had already asked Scott Murphy to design the game, but he was very firm about wanting Scott involved.

"I had made several proposals for *Space Quest V* before the decision to give it to Dynamix, and it was one of those proposals that they said, 'We would like you to turn this into *Space Quest 6*.' And I think they envisioned my taking over the series alone. I'm the one who pushed for Scott to be part of the project," Josh recalls.

Scott agreed to serve as a creative consultant along with performing his programming duties on *Police Quest: Open Season*, which was running months behind schedule.

Josh remembers how he and Scott worked together, saying, "We would get together and talk about various concepts and he would always seem very agreeable. I don't know if he really agreed in his heart or if he just said yes because he didn't care, which is probably more likely. But every single day I would work up one or two rooms descriptions and I would put them on Scott's desk. I would not give them to the programmers, the artists, the sound people; they didn't go to anyone until Scott checked off on them. Certainly, if he wanted to change anything, I was always saying to him, 'Feel free!' He'd look at everything, or at least he told me he'd looked at everything, and approved all of it."

Josh continues, "I felt pretty good about a lot of areas of the game, but there were others that I knew were going to need to be altered at a later state when we had people to playtest and we could fine-tune things and change things around."

Production was complicated by the introduction of Super VGA graphics and a 640x480 screen resolution, more than double that of the previous games. Though cartoon graphics were still used for the characters, many of the backgrounds were rendered in 3D, which was a new technique for Sierra and served to give the game its distinctive look.

Leslie Balfour was much more heavily involved in the planning for the never-released *Space Quest VII*,[*] but she also contributed to *Space Quest 6*, according to Josh. "She was the voice of Sharpei, at least in the demo. She had also come up with this absolutely brilliant marketing line that I love to this day: 'In space, nobody can hear you clean.' I would have loved to see that played up in some great way. I think they used it but I don't think it got quite the airtime it deserved."

Sierra's original intention was to move Josh to the Seattle studio to work on *Space Quest 6* when his current project was finished, but with

---

[*] Note the shift from *Space Quest V* to *Space Quest 6* to *Space Quest VII*. The seventh game was internally dubbed "Return to Roman Numerals" at one point during its preproduction stage.

his contract under negotiation, a change in management ended up making him feel like he had no choice but to quit the company.

"They were planning to have me promoted in terms of having my name featured more on articles and boxes and so on. In fact, they were going to have someone design the sequel to *Betrayal at Krondor* and put my name on it, which I wasn't interested in. I told them I wasn't interested in having my name on anything that I wasn't directly involved in heavily," Josh explains.

"I looked at a contract where they would pay for my move to Seattle and I would have this game to work on and that game to work on, and they asked, 'Who do you want to be your project manager there, on the next game you work on?' There was only one name on that list that I wanted and that was Mark Hood. 'Okay, you've got Mark.' They scheduled this and that and said they'd write up the contract and everything.

"Then a couple of weeks later I'm walking down the hall and I see Mark [Hood] and I said something to him about the next *Space Quest* we'd be working on in Seattle together, and he said, 'Oh, that's not what I'm going to be working on.' [I said,] 'Well, yeah, I just finished my contract and having you as my manager is in my contract,' and he said, 'Oh, well they took me off that and put me on something else.'"

Going to see the manager who had written his contract, Josh asked what had happened. "'Wait a minute, you just changed the terms of our contract without even telling me.' [He said,] 'Yeah, well, that's the way I do business.' What I saw was that handwriting on the wall and I said, 'Well, that's not the way I do business.' I went upstairs and wrote out my resignation."

Josh had already completed a large portion of the *Space Quest 6* game design by then, including the office of Doctor Beleauxs, the Ascend-O-Pad and the entire DeepShip section, but the team was left to finish the rest without him.

With Josh gone from the project, Scott Murphy was asked by management to step into a more active role and finish development of the game, but his previous hands-off role left him unclear on the details of some of the more intricate puzzles Josh had designed, with the worst oversight affecting a puzzle involving a Datacorder. The original design had included a comic strip, which would reveal the solution to the puzzle, to be hidden in a room. Unfortunately, with the change of designers the new team hadn't completed the comic and it wasn't in the game. Only a phone call from Josh weeks before the game shipped highlighted the problem.

"I called Scott and was talking about the game and I asked him how the comic was going," Josh says. "He told me they hadn't done it; time issues as usual. When I asked how they had players solve the Datacorder puzzle, he said, 'Oh, shit! Is that what it was for?' They hurriedly got it into the documentation, as that hadn't been printed yet, but now it looked like copy protection instead of a puzzle."

One of the changes that occurred after Josh's departure was to the game's original subtitle, *Where in Corpsman Santiago is Roger Wilco?* Josh claims, "The way I heard it, a lot of the decisions about marketing and the title got made after I left. I didn't hear it was called *The Spinal Frontier* until I was living in Virginia and I got a copy of *InterAction* magazine and I read about it. Ken had always said to me, even back when I pitched the original proposal of the plot for *Space Quest V*, 'I don't know how Doug would feel about this; you're probably going to need to change the name.' Doug being Doug Carlston from Brøderbund [publisher of *Where in the World Is Carmen Sandiego?*], who was a friend of Ken's."

Josh says he still has mixed feelings about *Space Quest 6*. "I remember there were moments that made me think, 'Oh my God! They totally didn't get it!' They really didn't get what I was after and I wish they'd asked me. And there were other times I laughed out loud. Which is rare for me. Either I was really delighted with the way they had implemented something I had put in the design, or it was something they had added which I hadn't expected. So I have very mixed feelings about it."

The Guy from Andromeda not involved in *Space Quest 6* was Mark Crowe, who only got to play it later on. "When it came out I really didn't have time to play it, I was so busy working on other projects at Dynamix," Mark admits. "Art style–wise and everything, it wasn't really my cup of tea. But looking back at it now, it's really a great-looking game and has a style of its own. I think it stands on its own two feet that way. I played bits and pieces of it but I never took the time to grunt through the whole thing. There's some great writing in there and Josh definitely did an awesome job on his parts of it."

Upon its 1995 release, *Space Quest 6* was only moderately successful, as were most of Sierra's adventure games of the time. Due to its disappointing sales figures, Sierra quietly stopped production of the *Space Quest* series. Fans weren't happy and instigated a letter-writing campaign to Craig Alexander, the studio head at the time. "I used to get bombarded with thousands of emails trying to get the next *Space Quest*," he recalls. "Scott did work on it at our Oakhurst office. We did try to get that going, but it never worked out."

Out with a Bang!

When Sierra opened its new Seattle headquarters in 1993, a large portion of the administrative staff moved to Seattle, but initially the only members of the game development staff to make the move were Al Lowe, Roberta Williams and Mark Seibert. With Roberta not working in the office a great deal, Al and Mark had the opportunity to bond, explore the city, and start assembling the team that would go on to produce 1995's *Torin's Passage* and 1996's *Leisure Suit Larry: Love for Sail!*

"I had not worked with Al before," Mark says, "so it was great fun getting to know him and discovering Seattle. *Torin's Passage* and *Larry 7* are two of my best memories of working in the industry."

After *Torin's Passage* was finished, the bulk of that team moved on to *Leisure Suit Larry*, and according to Al it was the first time he felt in full control of the entire process. "It wasn't until *Love for Sail!* that I really felt I knew what I was doing," he says. "I remember vividly sitting down and saying, 'Now I know how to do this thing! Now I can write a game,' and it came really easily. Until then it was always, 'I hope nobody finds out we're totally lost; nobody knows what they're doing. We're making this up as we go along.'"

Mark Seibert served as the producer on both titles. "Without a doubt, [*Love for Sail!*] was probably one of the best team experiences I had working in the gaming industry. That team was largely the same team from *Torin's Passage*, and we had worked together for a couple years at that point. I think everyone felt empowered to contribute creatively and had a sense of responsibility to the team and the product."

One of the animators in that group was Al Eufrasio, who also regards *Love for Sail!* as a high point of his time at Sierra. "It was kind of a funny, obnoxious project so we all got caught up in the humor of it all and kind of acted inappropriately," he admits. "We'd bring in *Playboy* magazines for reference; that was when sexual harassment in the workplace had become a big issue. I recall there being a general understanding around the building that if you're easily offended, don't go in this team's area because they're working on *Larry* and you're liable to see something you don't like."

He continues, "We had our cubicles in the middle, and along the wall were the offices, and the offices in the back of the room were like the general manager's office, Mark Hood. Then you had executive assistants and secretaries sitting there in the last cubicle before [the general manager's] office. So we had a rapport with them, but we had to bite our tongues every once in a while in how we joked. I just remember mainly we got very immature in our humor, between myself, [animation director] Jason Zayas and [animator] Bill O'Brien."

One particular example of that immature humor stands out to him: "Management ordered a sound booth for Dave, our sound guy, and it got delivered in several pieces and we had to assemble it. It was this big cubicle wall sort of material, but heavier and covered in foam, as they were soundproof. We spent a whole morning and part of an afternoon hauling this stuff up the elevator and into the building and into the sound room and setting it up as we were going along. Each piece came in these big cardboard pieces that were fastened together with some kind of connector. Bill O'Brien took one and the way he had his desk set up in his cubicle, he was able to put it between his desk and cubicle wall and make this little sliding cardboard door for himself.

"On the back, on his side, he had these *Playboy* magazines and he hung up these couple of centerfolds and they would kind of disappear behind his desk if it was open, so whoever was in there wouldn't necessarily see them. We would catch him off guard every so often and flip it around on him. He would reach his cubicle and reach around and close the thing and the centerfold would be facing out now. So Mark Seibert or somebody would be, 'Oh, Bill . . .' and he would turn around and be, 'Oh, shit!' It was hysterical. Stuff like that went on almost every day."

While the team certainly had a lot of fun, they didn't feel their antics were out of control. Indeed, although general manager Mark Hood's office faced the animators' work area, he says the animators kept their joking low-key enough that he never heard about it.

Although Al Eufrasio believes that *Love for Sail!* was "not pornographic; it's more bawdy than anything," he recalls some concerns raised about game itself. "There was another guy on the team whose wife started going, 'Hey, how far are you going to go in your career if you're working on this game?'" Toward the end of production some of the artists came up with the idea of putting in Easter eggs that showed some of the ladies of the game completely undressed. "You could type in 'push' and something as simple as that would supply an Easter egg. Al [Lowe] was a little, 'Uhhhh . . .' 'But Al, you don't cut funny!' Somehow we convinced him. But it also prevented the game from being rereleased," he says.

One change to the team's development process was the addition of a Friday afternoon meeting to discuss what had happened during the week and what should be produced during the next week. "That became a standard business thing that caught on at the time, which was, 'What did you do, what are you doing, and what do you have planned to have done next week?' It's kind of the big three-part thing," Al Lowe says.

"We kind of followed that formula. It's a pretty effective way to try and coordinate people. In the process you find out if, say, a programmer working on a scene is going to need something specific that is going to [require] somebody to work on [it], that needs finishing. It's a great way to coordinate."

Al Lowe was someone who worked extra hard on Thursdays to make sure he had met all his targets from the week before, not wanting to be embarrassed in front of the entire team.

"Mark Seibert was the producer on [*Leisure Suit Larry 7*], and he's a professional musician so he and I got along famously. He had this wonderful management technique [of meeting] at 4:00 p.m. on Friday. And boy did it make you want to get done. Nobody wanted to sit around and talk. Everything was very businesslike. Everybody wanted to get things done and move on," Al admits.

"Part of this technique was having everyone at the table, everyone on the project, announce to everyone else in the room what you were going to get done in the following week and then when you came back the next Friday, you had to explain what you did or didn't get done from that. Oh my God, I would stay and work until three in the morning on Wednesday and Thursday night because I didn't want to sit in front of those guys and say, 'Ahhhh, I didn't get my stuff done. I said I would but I didn't.' So it was a great motivating technique. Peer pressure for getting things done."

Mark Seibert agrees, but also explains that one of the reasons for those meetings was to give everyone a chance to change the direction of the game if something wasn't working. "Our end-of-the-week meetings gave everyone a chance to know where we were and where we were going. As Al said, it gave everyone a lot of self-motivation, but also gave us a chance to make group design course corrections to help keep us on target. This group was a very talented bunch of guys that went on to work on many other top projects in the industry."

Al Lowe is equally effusive in his praise for the *Leisure Suit Larry 7* crew: "I think that was the best team overall of any team we ever had. And all those guys have gone on to great things in the business. All those guys are successful – with other companies, of course!"

Like its predecessors, *Love for Sail!* sold around 250,000 copies[36] and most people on the team regard it as the best game they worked on.

"You had a lot of very funny people contributing humor," Al Eufrasio remembers. "It was a very open design process. Everybody was free to submit ideas or make suggestions and jokes and things like that. It all worked out because you had so many people's stuff being included that, no matter what, you're bound to find something funny. I love it; you're playing through and it's rapid-fire. If something funny is not being said, you have something funny to look at."

Mark Seibert wholeheartedly agrees, declaring that "*Leisure Suit Larry 7* was a blast. It kind of evolved into the funnest project that everyone on that team worked on."

Although 250,000 copies had once been considered a good number for Sierra, *Leisure Suit Larry: Love for Sail!* didn't perform well enough to meet the sales figures that Sierra now demanded. With references teased in *Love for Sail!* and an outline already worked out, Al Lowe looked to management to approve *Leisure Suit Larry 8*, but for the first time he found a lack of interest in adventure games, once the main staple of Sierra's catalog.

"Sierra had started its downward spiral," Al laments. "The manager was a big fan of first-person shooters and not of adventure games. What he thought was, what the company should do is put out [first-person shooters]; he was big on *Half-Life* and not big on anything else. In spite of the fact all my games had come in on budget and on time and had made profits, which is what I thought the company was supposed to do, he didn't think we should keep doing that. He said, 'No, adventure games are dead. It's old-style and we're not going to do those anymore. But go ahead and do the game and we'll negotiate a contract later.'"

Mark Seibert finished working at Sierra around this time, after watching the development team he and Al had helped assemble gradually disappear.

"Sierra had a very inglorious ending. As the company got bought and sold, with each new year came the loss of technology that was written off, talent that left, and projects that were started and canceled. After a few years of that, the development part of Sierra slowly crumbled away as marketing focused more and more on the third-party developers. So, after *Larry 7*, we watched the development staff slowly dwindle down to about fifty people. I was let go about six months before in-house development finally ended," Mark shares.

Seeing the layoff as a new start, Mark broadened his career. "That opened new opportunities for me. I got to work on some simulations for the International Space Station, and then for an [Electronic Arts] developer doing *Lord of the Rings* and *Command & Conquer*. But by this time, development had turned into *big* development. So I started looking for ways to get out of the industry. I went back to school and got my master's in education, and now I teach math, music, and computer science at the high school level."

Al Lowe spent a little while longer working with his ever-shrinking team, coming up with prototypes for a new *Leisure Suit Larry* game in 3D, but was eventually let go as well.

"We kind of fooled around a couple of weeks. I think Jason Zayas created a loop of animation, and we animated it on the fly so people could see what it might look like. The whole idea was, 'Here's what's possible; this would sell. Give me a contract and I'll design it.' The manager played me for a long time. Finally I said, 'I'm not going to come in if you're not going to give me a contract,' and then in February 1999 they called and said, 'Come clean up your office.' Turned it into a conference room, I think," Al recalls.

While Larry would not headline another adventure game for Sierra, he did get a brief reprieve in 1998 in *Leisure Suit Larry's Casino*, an online gambling game based on the company's high-selling *Hoyle* titles. But that wasn't the end of the franchise. An action-adventure game, *Leisure Suit Larry: Magna Cum Laude*, was developed by High Voltage Software and published by Sierra in 2004. Following this, Codemasters acquired the rights and authorized 2009's *Leisure Suit Larry: Box Office Bust*, another action-adventure designed by Team 17 and published by Funsta (part of the Codemasters company). These games were widely criticized both in their own right and as inadequate continuations of a once-beloved series. Neither game had any input from series creator Al Lowe.

Josh Mandel, who worked closely with Al Lowe on a number of projects at Sierra and later on a post-Sierra crowdfunded remake of *Leisure Suit Larry in the Land of the Lounge Lizards* released in 2013, believes that one of the major challenges the franchise faces today is that times have changed too much for the character to resonate as he once did.

"It's funny. In some ways you look at what Larry did and you could never get away with that today, so we haven't progressed, we've regressed in some ways in what's permissible. You could do another *Larry*, but I think the nature of the game would have to change for the current times. There has to be a different approach taken, a different twist to his character that makes him contemporary because he's aged out."

Craig Alexander agrees, saying that he saw this as an issue even in *Leisure Suit Larry's* heyday, though he enjoyed the series. "The problem with that franchise even by the mid-nineties was the leisure suit joke was getting old. It's sort of a seventies thing. Maybe it was funny in the eighties. Maybe it's one of those things whose time had gone."

Al Lowe acknowledges the arguments but disagrees. "The concept of a fish out of water remains valid. The problem was he couldn't be forty years out of water. You can't believe that; that's too far. We decided early on he would remain in the eighties and he would be a guy from the seventies who was six years or eight years out of date, not somebody who's thirty years out of date. I don't think that would have been funny. I think it would have been mentally ill or something instead!"

Al goes on to say that as much as he loves the series and the world he created, he doesn't believe it would be picked up by a publisher if it was pitched today. "And rightfully so. I think also that's one of the reasons, among many, that the [2013 remake by Replay Games] didn't sell very well. It had the nostalgia going for it but it didn't have a lot of other currency."

And yet there may still be life in the venerable franchise after all. In a welcome return to a more traditional point-and-click adventure game format, a soft reboot of the series was released in 2018 to much better critical and fan reception than the other post-Sierra games. With no input from Al Lowe but with Jan Rabson returning to reprise his role as the voice of Larry, *Leisure Suit Larry: Wet Dreams Don't Dry*, from German developer CrazyBunch, addressed some of the inherent issues by abruptly dropping Larry into the twenty-first century and having him embrace social media and online dating. Only time will tell if this was just a final swan song or the start of an ongoing revival for the original forty-year-old virgin.

Chapter 16: . . . Must Come to an End

We were like, "We can devise cool things to put in the world,"
but it was kind of design by committee and it could go either
way. Obviously, it went in the not-so-good way.

Al Eufrasio, Animator,
King's Quest: Mask of Eternity

Along with introducing a wider variety of games in an attempt to increase mass appeal in the latter half of the nineties, Sierra tried to invigorate two of their older series using 3D technology. These endeavors were met with limited success, ultimately sounding the death knell for the rest of the company's popular adventure game franchises.

Heavy Is the King's Crown

After finishing the CD-ROM version of *Quest for Glory: Shadows of Darkness* in 1994, the Coles turned their attention to the fifth and final entry in the series. Tentatively subtitled *King's Crown*, the game would complete the Hero's story arc and use technology similar to the recently released fourth game.

Two months after starting work on the basic design, they were called into a meeting with the head of the studio, who delivered bad news. As Corey recalls it, "At that point we had a meeting with Mark Hood where he said basically the mandate had come down from top management that all games had to have budget cuts by 20%."

Corey wasn't happy. He explained to Mark that *Quest for Glory IV* had shipped as possibly the buggiest game in Sierra's history, and the main reason was not having enough time. "You're going to end up with a mess on your hands if you try to do this for 20% less budget; it's not enough. The budget has to go up, not down," he insisted.

In retrospect, Corey believes he could have simply agreed to the budget cut and Sierra would have finished the game regardless of the cost overruns.

"My problem is I've always hated lying. The right thing to do with 20/20 hindsight at that point would have been to tell Mark, 'Absolutely, we'll do that. We'll keep this budget as tight as we can,' and then gone on to do whatever we had to do, because the fact is that management didn't actually know what the budgets were; [they didn't] know what [the games] cost. If we had done the game for the $900,000 or $1 million that it needed, it would have gotten done and it would have been a great game and finished up the series. Sierra, if they put that much money into a game, they wanted to finish it."

Mark had no choice in the budgets set by higher management, however, and the game was canceled. Leaving the company, both Lori and Corey Cole went on to work on other projects for other companies, the most notable being *Shannara* for Legend Entertainment, a game based on the eponymous series of novels by Terry Brooks.

A couple of years later, following changes in management at Sierra, general manager Craig Alexander believed the company needed a new fantasy game in the catalog and reached out to the Coles.

"Originally he brought Lori back to look at *The Realm*, which was Sierra's MMORPG," Corey explains. "They said they wanted to rebrand it as *World of Quest for Glory*, and they wanted Lori and possibly me to write quests for it. We discovered that it was almost finished but they had no mechanisms for quests. Nobody had put any thought into making quests for it. We didn't see how we could shoehorn that in and call it *Quest for Glory* at that point.

"But that got us talking to them again, and they came back and met with us and said, 'Do you want to do *Quest for Glory V*? Because we've gotten thousands of fan letters demanding it; how would you feel about that?' [We said,] 'Sure.' [They said,] 'Well, we can't commit to it, Corey. We can bring you back into the systems team to write systems code and you might or might not get a chance to work on the game and we might or might not do it.'"

Rejecting this offer, Corey went to work for another company, but Lori got started on game design, using the same story she had intended for *King's Crown*. Eventually Sierra agreed to make *Quest for Glory V: Dragon Fire* and Lori started development, with Corey joining her a year later when his other job was finished.

When Corey rejoined Sierra as a contractor, he was assured by management that *Quest for Glory V* was almost ready to ship, but that proved not to be the case. "It turned out that they had an engine. They had characters walking around and so on because they redid it all from scratch in C++ instead of SCI. Nobody had looked at the 500-page game bible. Again, we were in a situation with no quests, no mechanism for doing scripting."

Corey worked with the lead programmer to introduce the scripting system for conversations, stats, combat, and all the other elements the game required. "I built prototypes of scenes of the game just like Bob Fischbach had done for me back on *Hero's Quest*. I showed the new programmers how to code in C++ and make scenes. None of the programmers on our team knew how to do C++; they were all SCI programmers."

Mark Hood was working in management at the time, and although he didn't have any involvement in the production of the game, he was certainly perplexed by some of the choices management had made.

"There were some strange decisions made on that game for the sake of innovation, like [using] voxels [volumetric pixels] right as video cards were making polygon-based games rock, as well as side-scrolling and a lot of other things that to me missed the point of the game," he says. "I know the pressure that was being put on all of us to create games that were new and different. Which was a great concept, but sadly there was no acknowledgement from upper management that doing things new from scratch, with new stuff every time, would take longer and cost more than simply using the SCI engine to do another adventure."

Again, management issues at Sierra caused no end of troubles for the development team. Ken Williams's approach had been to oversee production and make large resourcing decisions but leave the designer and producer to write the game. "Every other game we did for Sierra, management took the total laissez-faire approach," Lori explains. "They never looked at my designs; they didn't even look at what we were doing. They just set us in motion and went. Then for this game, we had the president of the company actually read the script.

"For instance, I had come up with a very simple form of gambling that was taken directly from the Hoyle book of gambling. He thought it wasn't complex enough, so he had somebody else rewrite the entire gambling system to make it more like Vegas. There were no checks and balances in that sense, because I would have said, 'This is a minor aspect of the game. Just throw it away; it's not that big a deal.' But no, we had to go back in and redo that."

The aspect of *Quest for Glory V* that Lori is most proud of is the combat system. With a new programming team that wanted to focus on the combat, they ended up with what she regards as a very enjoyable system.

"We had a team of programmers that wanted to turn this into an RPG with artificial intelligence [AI] that was very sophisticated for the time, using fuzzy logic systems for things like that. We had used some fuzzy logic on *Quest for Glory IV*, but when the fifth game came we had independent systems; each monster had their own little AI that was making them self-sufficient and independent. We weren't plotting their moves anymore. We were plotting their paths. So we could make a combat system that was really robust, which was something I really wanted because I am very much into the action part of the game in that sense.

"I was very fond of it because that meant to me [that] you could go into the brigand's lair and play it [again] as another character and suddenly [the brigands] aren't behaving the same way. You can't predict; you had to stop and watch. You had to learn the game all over again if you played a different character, because it wasn't predictable. In that sense, it gave the player so much more of an experience with replay than we had in the past."

Another feature the Coles both consider a highlight of *Dragon Fire* is the soundtrack composed by Chance Thomas, who has since gone on to score other hit games such as *Dota 2*, *The Lord of the Rings Online* and *Marvel Ultimate Alliance*.

The game took three and a half years to complete instead of the standard eighteen months, which Corey believes gave Chance an opportunity to write and refine his music, ending up with a soundtrack that the team was particularly impressed with. "They brought him in at the beginning, so he was there for the entire development," Corey says. "He was constantly writing new themes and improving them. Chance was instrumental in helping to get the motion picture academy to consider digital to be on a par with the awards with movie scores and such. Our game music at that point is indistinguishable from a movie score."

When first assigned to the project, Chance spent time gathering information from the team and fans of the series regarding what they thought would work best musically. "Mark Seibert's name came up several times, and so I dug into his work and learned all I could," he explains. "But my first instinct was to take that knowledge and then go my own way. Especially with the main theme – that proved to be a big mistake!"

When Chance Thomas sent his first version of the main theme around to the fans via an email mailing list, they ripped it to shreds. "'Where is Mark Seibert's classic *Quest for Glory* theme?' they all seemed to echo in unison. Lesson learned. I went back and completely reworked the main theme, creating an overture which began with a new and exciting motif leading directly into a deliberate tip of the hat to the old theme," he recalls. "Finally, near the end of the new *Quest for Glory V* overture, I offered a beautiful treatment of Seibert's classic theme with flute and orchestra. The fans of the game loved it, and I finally found my footing."

Voice recording was completed early in the process, with the game not even half-finished. While Lori was happy with most of the voice-overs, the extra time required to finish the game allowed her to go back and rerecord two voices she wasn't entirely satisfied with. One was the original voice for Gnome Ann, which she found appalling: "It was this squeaky little voice that was so annoying that nobody would ever listen to her."

Craig Alexander also requested a new recording of Elsa Von Spielburg, which Lori agreed with. "We had this German voice director. He picked out the voice for Elsa, an actress who had a very Germanic voice. She was German; she had the right accent and everything. Except to the ear of an American she sounded French; she didn't sound German," Lori explains. "She didn't have the stereotypical German voice and you could not understand her. We got a much better actress for Elsa. At least we could understand her voice and she had the stereotypical things. It was not overblown, it was realistic."

For Lori, "Voice acting is awesome. It's my favorite part of doing games in a lot of ways. When you get the right actor, they're in character immediately. They're going with a cold script that they have never seen before and they just go with it. When I found the person to do Gnome Ann, she could read those lines cold and really catch the character. Gnome Ann wasn't over-the-line cartoony. So because the process strung out for [so] long, we could do things like get those voices fixed and we weren't stuck with voices that nobody would want."

Quest for Glory V: Dragon Fire was released in 1998 and an expansion disc was planned to follow with new quests and additions to the storyline. Set after the Hero has become the King of Silmaria (or not, depending on the player's choice), these quests would have further explored the Hero's marriage and other threads left open in the main game. The biggest addition to the expansion would have been the inclusion of a multiplayer mode, something that was originally conceived for the main game but had been set aside for budget and time reasons.

Unfortunately, *Quest for Glory V*'s market performance didn't meet the expectations of Sierra management. Due to the lower-than-expected sales – a few hundred thousand copies, according to Corey Cole – the expansion was never produced and the programming team was disbanded shortly after release.

For Lori, *Quest for Glory V* is a game she still likes, unlike others she has created. "I never enjoyed playing our games. I hated them. Because you saw every flaw; you think, 'That's not what I envisioned.' You're constantly criticizing and critiquing what's going on, what works and what doesn't. And you can't do anything about it. You're stuck at this point."

She sees the flaws in *Dragon Fire* as well, including certain aspects of the art. "We had these beautiful plans drawn for Science Island by an artist who came out of the book illustration industry. It was really complex and awesome and then when it gets textured and put down it's so dull and boring. I really can't stand looking at it."

What allows Lori to look past the problems with this game, she says, is that "I really did enjoy playing *Quest for Glory V* for the combat and things like that. Gameplay-wise, I think it's awesome in a lot of respects. So I'm really proud of that part of it."

Corey is also proud of the game, though not content with the technology used at the time. "It came out very well, but I think the 3D was primitive. It wasn't as pretty as the previous games and it had a lot of problems. But story-wise, it's the equal of any of the others, perhaps even more complex because Lori had three years to work on the story."

Overall, Corey describes developing the *Quest for Glory* series with terminology from today's popular MMORPGs like *World of Warcraft*.

"Developing *Hero's Quest* was a dungeon run. We had our team of three programmers and three artists, a writer/designer, and I was one of the programmers as well as co-designer, and one musician. We had a very small team all working together in a limited environment making a game. By the time we got to *Quest for Glory V*, we were a full-blown raid. I think there's a hundred names in the credits. So it's a bit like making an animated film, almost.

"It's a very different experience doing a raid than a dungeon [run]. In every case, you've got a group of people working toward a common goal with some direction from the leader, but really everybody is making use of their own skills and doing the best job they can toward finishing it. It works best when you get this synergy between the team, when an artist gets bored and sketches something and a programmer looks over and says, 'Oh, that's hilarious; I know how we can put that in the game.' They might or might not even tell the designer. I think Brian [Hughes] had his entire Saurus repair shop done for *Quest for Glory II* before he showed us. We said, 'Oh yeah, that's hilarious; that's cool.'

"These games are really all collaborative efforts," Corey concludes. "If we came up with the same design but a different team, you'd come out with a completely different game."

A Final Visit to Daventry

Three million dollars to develop. Three years in production. Three different game designs. A corporate buyout. Changes in management. It's fair to say that *King's Quest: Mask of Eternity* wasn't an easy production for Roberta Williams and her team.

Roberta had been thinking about the next *King's Quest* game since 1994. Finally, when production was wrapping up on her epic horror game *Phantasmagoria*, she knew it was time to return to the series that had made her the most renowned game designer of her era.

With the story Roberta had in mind, she wanted to move away from the familiar royal family. Although she considered using Prince Alexander as the hero, she decided instead to concentrate on a new character, originally conceived as a statue that turned human when a magic spell petrified everyone else. He was eventually made into a simple tanner who happened to be in the right place at the right time – or, rather, holding the right artifact – when the curse hit. As a preview in *InterAction* magazine described in 1996:

"You enter the Kingdom of Daventry as Connor mac Lyrr (the son of a fisherman), who alone has been passed over by an evil spell that turned every mortal inhabitant to stone. Connor must find a way to restore them to flesh and blood. At the heart of the dilemma is *The Mask of Eternity*, which was broken into seven pieces and scattered by the Cosmic Winds to seven different lands at the moment of Connor's birth. A piece of the Mask touched Connor as he was born, leaving a vivid scar on his cheek. He carries this scar as an adult – a sign that he has been marked for greatness. The quest to find the seven pieces of the Mask and restore them to the Island Temple is his destiny. Only by accomplishing this can he end the chaos that now rules the land."[37]

One of the first moves Roberta made was to bring in Mark Seibert. Mark understood *King's Quest*, having been the producer on *King's Quest VII* and worked as a musician on others. This time, as well as producing *Mask of Eternity*, he would also be co-designing the game.

"Roberta asked me if I would be interested in helping with the design of the game," Mark recalls. "We were being asked to break the 'adventure game' mold, and I think she was looking for some ideas that were outside the conventional thinking. I had become a big fan of RPG games and started showing her some of those. RPGs at the time tended to be big story games. We started playing with the idea of making something RPG-ish, but less tedious on the RPG elements; keep the action but simplify the gaming system."

Roberta knew that 3D was the next major innovation for adventure games. *DOOM* and *Tomb Raider* had taken the PC marketplace by storm in the mid-nineties, and the faster, fluid action of those games appealed to a wider audience.

Mask of Eternity was originally designed as one massive open world. Additions such as an underwater world, a more fully formed Daventry with all the locations from previous games, and a new seaport town were considered and planned in the initial stages of development. Roberta and Mark also discussed adding multiplayer capabilities, which would have allowed players to swap items within the game, but the change to 3D was complicated enough and that idea was shelved.

These early designs were plagued with problems. The reality of the situation was clear: Roberta's initial ideas simply weren't possible with the technology available. Her husband Ken had been able to create new techniques and technologies for her earlier games, but this time there wasn't a viable way forward.

Complicating the matter was the fact that Sierra had moved away from their long-used SCI engine and were instead using 3Space, a 3D level editor that Dynamix had developed. While it was perfect for the games it was designed for – the likes of *Stellar 7*, the *Earthsiege* series and *Aces of the Pacific* – it proved to be unsuitable for what Roberta envisioned for her latest adventure. As a result, the team that had been brought together for the game's initial development was disbanded, with only a few people left to begin the process anew.

The second attempt focused on overcoming these problems. The first major change was overhauling the open world plan. In its place would be a linear set of worlds, each unique within the code. This freed up memory – a major issue in the failed first design – and allowed for a smoother transition between worlds. Another issue in the original design was that each zone had a unique color scheme, and passing from one to another was jarring. This was less of an issue in the new iteration.

Changes to the story were also made, with both puzzles and characters redesigned and major differences in the plot introduced. The biggest shift, however, was the inclusion of combat, a roleplaying element suggested by Mark Seibert. Combat not only brought the game more into line with current market expectations, it also helped fill in the vast empty areas between puzzles that existed in the large 3D world. But it was this addition that would cause many of the problems with the second attempt as well, along with the story's dark themes and religious overtones.

In July 1996, CUC International acquired Sierra On-Line. Shortly after, Sierra and other software developers owned by CUC were merged under one corporate banner, CUC Software. The CEO was Bob Davidson, who with his wife Jan had founded Davidson & Associates, a development studio famous for their educational *Math Blaster* series of games. The Davidsons were not fans of Roberta's previous work, *Phantasmagoria*, or another major Sierra series, *Leisure Suit Larry*, and were concerned about what they perceived as occultism in *King's Quest: Mask of Eternity*.

Roberta quickly noticed that the best-selling *Phantasmagoria* stopped being promoted, and the Davidsons began to exert their influence on *Mask of Eternity*. "I was assigned several 'managers' to work above me and those managers were told to not really listen to me and do things [the Davidsons'] way," Roberta disclosed in 2011.[38]

Working in this environment was hard for Roberta, with her vision for her own game being subverted and ignored by people who wanted a censored and family-friendly version. The team suffered, and many people asked to be reassigned or left Sierra completely. John Shroades, the lead artist, became disillusioned with the experience, feeling they were trying to make something with an engine that couldn't handle the design. Adam Szofran, one of the user interface programmers, and Layne Gifford, responsible for 3D textures, were both transferred to other projects before leaving the company entirely.

Animator Al Eufrasio was another member of the team who left the project, then Sierra, during this troubled production period.

"*Mask of Eternity*, that was a little bit of a struggle because everyone was learning 3D at Sierra at the same time. That had its ups and downs, mostly downs," Al recalls. "That's a project where people were like, 'I don't want to work on this anymore.' The economy was doing really well at the time and a lot of companies were popping up around the area, so people were actually taking advantage of that to quit Sierra so they wouldn't have to go back and work on *Mask of Eternity*. It was kind of a sad situation but that's what was going on at the time."

With producers being assigned to oversee Roberta, Al saw Roberta around the office less and less. He believes that the buyout by CUC and the management situation was very hard for her.

"I'm sure there were so many things happening in the background that I wasn't aware of. I kind of got to know her a little because she was always there talking to Al [Lowe]. We were just randomly talking one day and we found out we had the same birthday, so we connected on that level. She'd come down and I'd always make sure I'd say 'hi' to her and 'how you doing,' that kind of stuff. I could totally see her being the kind of person that would sincerely get hurt by some of those underhanded things that happened.

"There was definitely something up," Al continues. "She was not there at seemingly critical times. She was just letting us design around her general idea. We were like, 'We can devise cool things to put in the world' but it was kind of design by committee and it could go either way. Obviously it went in the not-so-good way. I just remember Roberta not being around for a lot of the development. Mark Seibert started taking more and more of it over."

Although he was taken off the team at the end of the first attempt at production, Al Eufrasio was again offered a position for the subsequent effort. He couldn't see himself working on the game again. "That was in the air, with me going, 'Ahhhh, I'd rather not.' We still heard how it was going. And we were using the first release of 3D Studio Max on that. Not a pleasant piece of software to use; it would just crash. It had a lot of shortcomings; nobody was really all that happy with it," he remembers.

In 1996, screenshots were released to the public, drawing much criticism from fans. Was this even going to be a *King's Quest* game? What was Roberta Williams thinking? Was this an adventure game? The backlash clearly added to the other pressures the team was going through. Roberta responded to these criticisms herself, posting on Sierra's forums that she wasn't to be told by either management or fans what constituted a *King's Quest* game.

"First of all, I have to say that *King's Quest* comes from ME and each one is different and has its own flavor. Some have a darker tone, and others have a lighter tone. Some touch upon violence, and some don't. *King's Quest* reflects the mood that I am in when I go to tackle another one. *King's Quest* really is a reflection of me and how I'm feeling about the subject and upon the reference material I am using and how I approach the subject. Basically, *King's Quest* comes from me and my heart and it always isn't going to be exactly the same, because I'm not always exactly the same, and I, like most people, feel a need for a change of pace and a sense of moving forward and of trying and experiencing something new," Williams wrote at the time.[39]

Roberta's post went on to explain her design choices for *Mask of Eternity*, defending the game from accusations that there was no story and it was simply a violent RPG.

"*King's Quest 8* indeed has a story; actually, a much more profound story than prior *King's Quests*. It is a new telling of the ultimate 'quest' – the quest for the most powerful, spiritual, benevolent item of all: the Mask of Eternity. This story takes its cue from two sources: the Quest for the Grail, and the Christian story of the struggle between God and Lucifer. When we say that the story is very dark that's really not true; it's just that the story is more profound and seriously looks at the struggle between good and evil. Rather than taking a bubbly, Disney view of good and evil, I chose to look at the struggle between good and evil from a more serious, traditional, almost spiritual, viewpoint. If you look at the traditional stories of the Grail and even in past Christian legend, you find that it is not light-hearted, gooey, and bubbly. Those stories are filled with conflict, peril, finding one's own morality, proving oneself a hero by overcoming evil creatures of Chaos, but yet proving oneself virtuous and good with all things good. That is the theme with this game.

"I feel very proud of this game and the story which goes with it. Do NOT gain any preconceived ideas which may be wrong about this game from some preliminary screenshots which you will see at this early date. As time goes on we will supply you with more screenshots which will show other aspects of this game which are not 'fighting' oriented.

"The reason it appears that this game is all about that is because we have not ever done a game which has that element so we're concentrating on that element right now. The other elements; the story elements, the character elements, the animation elements, the inventory object elements, the puzzle elements . . . are all stuff we've done before and will be much easier for us to put in place . . . we just haven't done those yet . . . therefore, you're getting a skewed view of this game which is WRONG."[40]

Roberta's frustration is visible in her response to the early public backlash, but luckily for the project, in early 1997 the Davidsons left CUC Software for family reasons and Roberta was placed firmly in control of her vision once more.

This third phase of production was a lot more efficient. Dynamix's 3Space engine just wasn't being upgraded fast enough to keep up with *Mask of Eternity*'s production demands, so the team instead opted to develop their own in-house engine. This pushed the release date back from Christmas 1997 into 1998, but it seemed like the only way they could get the game finished.

With the engine issues sorted out, the team's attention turned to creating the game itself. The story and puzzles from the second attempted design were left relatively intact, although two of the seven worlds, and their accompanying Mask pieces, were removed to speed up production.

Mask of Eternity shipped in November 1998, in time for the Christmas season. Sales were brisk and the game continued to sell well into the 2000s, with sales reported to be around 750,000 copies, another big-selling *King's Quest*.[41] And yet even those impressive numbers weren't enough to satisfy management.

General manager Craig Alexander recalls the challenges that *Mask of Eternity* faced when it was released. "We tried to make *King's Quest: Mask of Eternity* 3D but it just couldn't compete with *DOOM*, *Quake*, *Unreal* and all the other shooters."

Early production of a ninth game in the series was started, with Mark Seibert once again back as producer and designer, but it didn't get far. "The work on *King's Quest IX* at Sierra was very focused on console ideas and did not really progress very far before the Sierra collapse," he says.

Although it remained alive through fan projects in the early 2000s, the franchise that put Sierra on the map was finished – until 2015, at least, when developer The Odd Gentlemen released a reimagined *King's Quest* episodic adventure in cooperation with Activision, who now own the rights to most Sierra properties. This reboot was the first commercial *King's Quest* game without any involvement from Roberta Williams, though she did offer the game her personal endorsement.

Sierra's Final Damned Adventure

Gabriel Knight was the last of Sierra's major adventure game series to get a sequel with *Gabriel Knight 3: Blood of the Sacred, Blood of the Damned*.

It was anything but an easy production.

Jane Jensen had begun planning the game in December 1996, and the consensus of those who had read the design was that it was well thought out, well researched and, most of all, told a great story that people would want to play.

Set four years after the events of *The Beast Within*, the new *Gabriel Knight* game would see Gabriel and Grace investigating vampire-like creatures who seem to be attacking a French prince. While the overall plot revolves around the kidnapping of the prince's young son, Jane combined these vampiric beings with an eclectic mix of treasure hunting tourists, Freemasons and the Knights Templar to craft what would be the final *Gabriel Knight* mystery.

Jane created her design document early in production and continued to maintain it throughout the troubled development cycle. Her years of experience and the amount of work she had put into her design helped keep the process running despite the numerous issues that arose.

The challenges on *Gabriel Knight 3* were many, with the first major obstacle being the introduction of 3D. By the late nineties, Sierra had largely lost interest in developing adventure games, especially installments of what management saw as the tired major series, but they were willing to take a chance on *Gabriel Knight 3* as long as it was made in real-time 3D. It was, after all, the future of gaming. The team, unfortunately, had little understanding of the new 3D technology, and their lack of familiarity hindered production from the start as they worked to get themselves up to speed.

The artists also faced a steep learning curve with the move to 3D. *Gabriel Knight 3* ambitiously offered a free-roaming camera that players could move wherever they desired, rotate to view the scene from any perspective, and zoom in and out on demand. While this was a great innovation for players, the artists soon realized it required a lot more work on their part. Instead of developing a scene they knew would be seen from only a specific angle, such as the front of a building, they now needed to fully render the building to look good on all sides. This significantly increased the cost and time involved.

Sierra had by this time abandoned their proprietary SCI engine, meaning the team had to build an engine from scratch (the *King's Quest: Mask of Eternity* and *Quest for Glory V* engines were also custom-built for their respective games), along with the associated tools. While this did free up the engineers from the limitations of SCI, it created a whole range of other issues.

Jim Napier, an experienced and respected engineer with Sierra, was assigned to *Gabriel Knight 3* and created the G-Engine, which provided the 3D rendering, sound and animation foundations required. Having completed the base engine but without any of the tools needed for full production, Jim created a sample application to show the team. Happy with his work, they made the decision to use this new engine.

Around this time, management reassigned Jim to work on *SWAT 3*, so the team proceeded to build *Gabriel Knight 3* with Jim's initial sample application. Because this application was only a prototype to showcase the engine's intended capabilities, however, adding the *Gabriel Knight* code on top of it created a series of problems that became almost insurmountable.

New features were implemented haphazardly with little attention paid to how they would be maintained or changed, making the whole game unstable. Each time a new feature was added, the problems and instability grew. As more game content was added, the engine grew slower and slower with even the start-up time stretching to over a minute.

Pushing on with production, the team kept plugging more and more content into the broken engine. Most of the content was hard-coded in C++, with dialogue files no longer kept separate and easily accessible as was standard practice. Making any adjustments required an extensive amount of time, a programmer to make the changes, and a complete recompilation of the code base – a lengthy process in its own right. New artwork also had to be added by programmers, with new assets taking up to two weeks to make it into the game.

To help solve the technical crisis *Gabriel Knight 3* found itself in, Scott Bilas was brought aboard in mid-1998 to oversee programming of the project. He quickly discovered, despite assurances that the game was nearly ready to ship, that it was nowhere near being done.

Scott realized that the game would never get released if they kept going the way they had been. The engine needed to be rebuilt from the ground up if they had any hope at all of finishing. This decision, supported by management, was unpopular with the general team but the results spoke for themselves. Once redesigned, production increased exponentially and a lot of the earlier problems were no longer an issue.

Scott's first decision was to assemble a roundtable discussion with the *Gabriel Knight* engineers and other Sierra engineers like Jim Napier. Collectively they developed a structure for how the engine would work, what systems they needed to implement, and how the systems would interact with each other. Also discussed were the tools required to make production quicker and easier for the non-engineers. Another decision was to put as much of the dialogue as possible into text files so that the writers could input their text straight into the game.

The roundtable discussion was a major success, and the team went away and over the next month completely redesigned the engine and developed the new tools required. These included the Sheep toolset, a flexible scripting system that allowed non-engineers to script portions of the gameplay and see their results straight away. Production entered full swing with the redesigned engine and tools. Now the process of adding new artwork and seeing it in-game was reduced from what was as long as two weeks under the old system to a matter of only a few minutes.

Morale was another major issue during *Gabriel Knight 3*, due in no small part to Sierra laying off a large number of the team in mid-1999, six months before release. Management requested that those who were let go stay and finish the project, but the result was, understandably, a lot of angry people who were actively looking for new employment. It didn't help that LucasArts's *Grim Fandango*, a game many at Sierra felt represented the pinnacle of the modern adventure genre, had been released but even it was selling poorly.

Despite its many hurdles, the game was eventually released in November 1999 and met with acceptable sales figures. It wasn't a big enough hit, however, to assuage the feeling within Sierra that adventure games were dead. Sure enough, *Gabriel Knight 3: Blood of the Sacred, Blood of the Damned* was to be Sierra's final adventure game.

Interlude: Theme Songs and Academy Awards

Even amidst all the internal chaos that plagued the company's troubled adventure game productions in the late 1990s, the music department's contributions were as strong as ever, if not more so. Sierra's soundtracks had always been an invaluable if somewhat underappreciated part of the company's success, but as the years went on they continued to push industry boundaries in important and influential ways.

One area given more attention was the crafting of end credit songs, something that had already been standard in the motion picture industry for decades.

It was actually *King's Quest VI*'s "Girl in the Tower" that marked Sierra's first attempt at a closing song, composed by Mark Seibert with lyrics by Jane Jensen. A love ballad between Prince Alexander and Princess Cassima, the music expanded on a theme Mark had conceived for *King's Quest V*, when Alexander and Cassima first meet.

"I think we wanted the games to feel a bit movie-like. Many movies have the song that plays at the end. So there was the reasoning; besides, it was fun to do," Mark says.

Included in the game box was a note asking people to call their local radio stations and request "Girl in the Tower," which Mark admits was a marketing ploy. "The idea to have people call radio stations and request it was not my idea, and typically stations play their playlist and not random discs sent into the station. That being said, someone must have played it because I did see – albeit very small – royalty checks for airplay."

Even at Sierra, however, the practice of composing full songs for closing credits hadn't yet become common in 1998, when *Police Quest: Swat 2* finished with "Just Another Day in L.A."

Chance Thomas was early into his career as a game composer, working on the *Quest for Glory V* soundtrack at the time. Stationed close to each other in the Oakhurst studio, Chance was impressed with the soundtrack fellow composer Jason Hayes had created for *SWAT 2* and had an idea: "Jason created such a sweet vibe for the game with his original music score. I asked him if he thought a closing credits song would be cool, and he thought it might add a nice touch."

Explaining the process of writing the song, Chance says: "I got together with game designer Susan Frischer and we wrote some lyrics around this idea that Los Angeles's SWAT team members face all kinds of insane things on the job all the time – things that you and I would totally shrink from. But for them, it was 'Just Another Day in L.A.'

"After we finished the lyrics, I wrote the music and hired a great singer named Randy Porter, whose day job at the time was being a parole officer. There was some serendipity in that for sure! Rich Dixon played all the guitar parts, and Jason Ramirez snagged a recording of actual police chatter during a Hollywood bank robbery which we inserted into the bridge of the song. I recorded everything on ADAT [Alesis Digital Audio Tape] tapes and mixed the song in my music studio at Sierra."

At the same time, Chance's *Quest for Glory V* soundtrack was one of Sierra's most ambitious game scores to date. Chance recalls the experience and how much time he had to devote to it.

"It reminds me of how lucky I was to have so much time to work on my first big game soundtrack. Not only did that give me time to flesh out one of the world's first live orchestral video game scores, but it also gave me time to dig into the implementation with super intelligent guys like lead programmer Eric Lengyel, so that we were able to create one of the world's first truly adaptive music scores using digital audio streams rather than MIDI," Chance says.

As well as being one of the earliest game soundtracks ever to feature a live orchestra, it also deserves special mention for playing a critical role in Chance's bid to get video game music recognized for major awards. "The *Quest for Glory V* soundtrack was my Exhibit A, my opening salvo to the Recording Academy, in the campaign to open the Grammy Awards to video game music."

Chance's efforts started when he met one of the members of the academy and mentioned that he composed music for video games. The gentleman scoffed, until Chance told him that his latest project utilized a full orchestra and was in fact very similar to what musical scores delivered for movies. Pushing the opportunity further, Chance asked how they might institute Grammy categories for game scores and was, to his surprise, told to write up a proposal and send it in.

His pursuit was fully supported by the Oakhurst studio's general manager Craig Alexander, who helped finance trips to Los Angeles and allowed Chance company time to assemble and argue for the proposal. After two years, the campaign succeeded and video games were added for consideration to the Best Soundtrack Album, Best Song, and Best Instrumental Composition categories.

While affixing a box with a banner exclaiming that the game's musical score was composed by a Grammy Award winner would certainly have been a marketing masterstroke for Sierra, Chance's accomplishment more importantly placed game music rightfully at the same level as movie compositions. It marked a significant evolution from the beeps and boops of yesterday.

Chapter 17: Game Over

Let's imagine that a stranger had walked up to any of us, on the street, in 1979, and said: 'Would you like to move to one of the greatest cities on earth? While you are there, you can play a key role in creating a company that just about everyone will know and respect.' . . . Even knowing it wouldn't last forever I would have followed that stranger anywhere.

Ken Williams, Founder, Sierra On-Line

On February 22, 1999, Sierra was effectively shut down as a computer game developer.

From Ken and Roberta's suburban Los Angeles kitchen to a publicly funded company with a market capitalization of over a billion dollars, Sierra's development history ended with termination notices, tears and a lot of heartache.

What happened?

Why was a company that helped build the highly lucrative gaming industry and pioneer entire genres forced to close its doors? Where did it all go wrong? Did the products lose their edge? Did Sierra miss the latest changes in gaming? When did the financial decline start? Was the marketing misguided? Where and when did Sierra lose its way?

There is no one answer to such a complex issue. Certainly it's clear that the shift in the market away from adventure games and toward shooters and strategy titles hurt the company. Sierra never seemed to have a grasp on what sort of games they wanted to make when the adventure genre started to fade, which caused a scattershot approach to production. While this method produced some hits, it also resulted in a number of poorly performing products and a multitude of ideas that never saw release.

Marc Hudgins was there until the end of Sierra's development life and believes that after years of leading the industry in technological advances, the company just wasn't well situated to move forward in that respect anymore.

"I don't think it's because people weren't putting out good games. Adventure games were losing a lot of ground in the market. I would say first-person shooters were killing everything at that point. And because we were so based on building games using SCI, we had a template that every game fit. That made us very ill-positioned to switch to any new kind of game. We made adventure games and we made them very well," Marc says.

"We were not ready to make a *King's Quest* [one] year and the next big first-person shooter [the] next Christmas. We didn't have the people, we didn't have the tech to do that. I think we tried to limp along doing what we knew how to do. *King's Quest 8*, where they tried to do 3D, was a valiant try, but I think in hindsight it was probably an inappropriate mix. They just didn't have a good vision of how that worked. I think we just got caught. We didn't see where things were going. We made three or four projects at a time, but they were all based around the same technology and we weren't ready for a change."

Marketing manager John Williams believes the answer is even simpler than that. "Where did it all turn to shit? One man's opinion, obviously, but I think the core problem came from having too many irons in the fire. We simply had too much going on.

"There was so much competition for resources and so many good ideas and strong personalities that we just got too many games going in too many directions and all of our efforts got watered down. [Sierra acquisition] Papyrus was making great *NASCAR* games that sold in huge numbers, but suddenly felt the need to launch plane racing and other things rather than focusing on their franchise product. Dynamix felt the need to put out games like *Professional Bull Rider* and another *Incredible Machine* rather than focus on the simulations and mech games that were their forte.

"Sierra Entertainment seemed to get bored of *Quest for Glory*, *Leisure Suit Larry* and *King's Quest* games and launched huge development efforts in every direction imaginable," John explains. "While our competitors were putting together huge efforts around a single game, we were splitting up our creative teams to work on a cacophony of products that all seemed to make sense on their own but became absolutely unmanageable when you looked at them in aggregate."

John describes how Ken Williams spent a lot of his time visiting the various studios, looking at products in development and taking proposals for new games from "multiple designers and art directors who had worked on some game that had done well, all looking for their opportunity to bring their own game design to market. Say no to an idea and you might miss a big opportunity. Say yes and you just diluted the talent pool because a successful game team just lost a producer or art director that was off now building his own team.

"There was only so much budget, but how do you say no to a Jeff Tunnell and his passion project or deny a new game design project from an art director that had worked on six different successful games?" John asks.

"So our attention got pulled too many directions."

John sums up his feelings about the demise of Sierra by saying, "It would be easy to blame CUC for the loss of Sierra, or maybe even the advent of the new 3D universes like *Half-Life* or *World of Warcraft*, but in reality it was entropy. Not enough focus on the critical things that mattered."

From such a promising start in 1979, Sierra ended its days as a developer twenty years later playing catch-up in an industry it had helped establish, though the company would continue on as a publisher for third-party products until 2008.

A sad byproduct of the closure of Sierra's development studios was the loss of artwork and other assets that had been generated over the years, as Marc Hudgins explains.

"At one point I wanted to find some of the old background paintings we had done to use as reference. We used to keep them in this really nice climate-controlled container in the building. The idea was, I think, at some point Ken had thought maybe we'd do hi-res versions of the games and we'd not want to recreate that work. Or maybe it was for preservation, I don't know. . . . It was a very big box; it was the size of a freezer that you'd have in your garage or something.

"Somebody decided it was taking up space and they rented storage space at some self-storage unit in town and they just put cardboard boxes of this stuff up in the storage unit. So when I wanted to get reference for it, they gave me a key and they gave me a storage unit number and I drove over there. There was just a bunch of cardboard boxes sitting in this tin shack. I think the mice had gotten to some of them; there was evidence of that."

When Sierra shut down, the art was thrown away. "When they closed it down – I don't know who was in charge of that – there was stuff just going into dumpsters," Marc recalls. "They just emptied the building. I had a box of my own stuff, some drawings and things that weren't in the general stuff, and I walked home with that."

The Gradual Decline of Oakhurst

Though no one knew it at the time, perhaps the beginning of the end occurred in 1993 with the move of Sierra's headquarters from Oakhurst to Seattle.

Ken's brother John Williams had been with Sierra's marketing department from the very beginning and saw the move as a positive one that allowed the company to grow with exceptional speed in the space of a few years, but he also believes that when Ken moved, the game development team in Oakhurst suffered a loss that it never truly recovered from.

"With the move to Seattle, the thought leadership started coming from people like Mike Brochu,[*] who was a great businessman but didn't really have much interaction with the game development at all. To be fair, Sierra had gotten so big and diverse that someone needed to watch over the business and manage it as such, but focusing on the business at that time, we didn't respond fast enough to some of the fundamental shifts that happened in the marketplace," John says.

With Ken leaving Oakhurst, a series of managers were brought in to run the operations. Marc Hudgins remembers what it was like before Ken left and how the changes affected the staff: "We had Ken for a long time, and Ken was Dad. As Dad he could be the strict Dad or he could be the good Dad. It was really a Mom and Dad psychology there, Ken and Roberta. Then they went to Seattle. All of a sudden Mom and Dad left and they gave us this string of babysitters that some of us got along with and some of us didn't. Frankly, I think the perception was most of them were just puppets of Seattle; they were just proxies. Some of them handled it better than others."

Mark Hood had started at Sierra in 1989 as a programmer and had gradually moved into management roles with the company, serving as a producer and director on games as well as working with the technical teams that developed and maintained the core internal software. He recalls the first big change in management to occur.

"Steve Joseph was hired from Hewlett-Packard to bring some process and software engineering principles in. At first he left things as they were, but then decided [on] strict teams. So I had the choice of working on a game or 'game services,' which was everything to do with the teams," Mark says. That role included overseeing localization,

---

[*] Sierra's president and chief operating officer from 1994–1997.

alternate platforms, audio, training, hiring, and programming duties associated with the internal engine, SCI.

Mark was given the role of director of development jointly with another long-term Sierra employee, Bill Crow, working under Steve Joseph as president of the company. When Steve left in 1993, after only a year at Sierra, another manager was brought in. Jim Thomas had previously worked as executive vice president for fellow game company MicroProse and brought with him both industry knowledge and vast technical expertise.

Marc Hudgins remembers seeing Steve following his resignation. "Oakhurst was a small town; you saw everyone everywhere. I ran into him at the supermarket and said, 'Oh, what are you going on to?' He said that 'I'm at this new thing; we're going to make maps. We're going to help you find locations on the internet. It's called MapQuest.' He was really a good guy. He was really tech savvy – the guy who had been around for a while. He was a really good manager," Marc says.

In Seattle, Jerry Bowerman became the executive vice-president of the company in 1993. Jerry's role was to take charge of long-term planning, acquisitions, and recruitment for the company as a whole. After the series of changes in management at Oakhurst, Ken sent Jerry there to run the studio, and one of Jerry's early decisions was to hire Craig Alexander as his assistant general manager.

Craig remembers working with Jerry Bowerman in California for only a short time: "We overlapped in Oakhurst for nine months, maybe. He basically hired me to replace him. He got promoted to run all production and development for Sierra and went back to Bellevue, Washington where he was from."

There was a lot of discontent over the rapid changes in management. Between 1992 and 1995, the Oakhurst studio had three different vice presidents of development, each of whom brought a different style and organizational approach to the studio. As well as the new development heads, a series of middle managers also joined the studio, something that didn't help the creative process.

"There were a lot of suits around that time coming into Oakhurst. I don't know what the point was; maybe to try to make it as profitable as they wanted it to be," Josh Mandel says. "It was very chaotic."

Josh, who worked at Sierra between 1990 and 1994, recalls that "with multiple heads of development moving in and juggling things around and then juggling things around again, I really began to feel that when I went into the office each morning I had no idea what to expect – what large scale changes would have been handed down, or edicts delivered, or sweeping changes in structure would have occurred overnight. I was not functioning very well creatively under those kinds of circumstances. It was quite a lesson, not just in how to tear down a company, but also the limitations that I have in terms of needing a certain stability or calming environment to do my best work."

Freshly hired as an animator in 1994, Al Eufrasio remembers the downcast feeling in the Oakhurst studio clearly: "I got there and people struck me as being very cynical. Very pessimistic. Not everyone, but certain people. I felt bad because you had these very talented people whose work I immediately admired and the high level of talent I saw in that place, and then to realize they were worried about their jobs because the company headquarters had moved up to Seattle."

Al goes on to explain that "everybody was kind of downbeat about it and complaining. Very low morale. Probably not as low as it eventually got, I imagine, but low enough. To the point where I wasn't confident I would stay there or not. There were several years where there's all these rumors going around that this place is going to close down. They were right eventually, but they were very premature in predicting that."

Jerry Bowerman and Craig Alexander represented different management styles for Sierra, coming not from the gaming industry but from finance and business. Both brought different skills to the company and helped to grow it further than it had previously. They also, crucially, brought a sense of stability to the studio, something that had been lacking since Ken Williams left a few years earlier.

Craig remembers how he got started at Sierra: "A venture capitalist [VC] told me about the role and I was thinking of becoming a VC, [to] do investment funding. This VC suggested I do something operational and told me about this job."

As Craig recollects, "Jerry called me shortly thereafter and said, 'Hey, I need somebody to replace me.' At the time there weren't a lot of people with management experience who also understood computer games. I'm young enough that back then, anybody older than me didn't understand it at all because the industry was too new. I had a good mix of management experience, I'm an engineer by training so I knew software development, and I loved gaming. So they hired me. I moved out there and was there for six years; it was a long time. It obviously changed my career path. I ended up meeting my wife there and got married. I still have fond memories of Sierra."

Craig Alexander was to stay at the Oakhurst studio until it was closed in 1999, moving briefly to Bellevue, Washington before leaving

Sierra to join Electronic Arts, making him the longest serving president of the Oakhurst studio since Ken Williams.

Different Genres

Realizing that adventure games and the major series that had sustained Sierra for so many years were no longer selling in sustainable volume, before shutting down as a developer both the Seattle and Oakhurst studios started looking at other genres, trying to find a new style that would be a winning formula for the company.

"In the end, adventure games, they weren't going to make it," general manager Craig Alexander says. "There just wasn't the interactivity [in] puzzle-solving that you got with the first-person shooters, the strategy games, and the roleplaying games. The writing was on the wall. I started shifting genres. I was doing all sorts of games."

Al Eufrasio remembers when management called a meeting with all the staff at the Seattle studio and asked them to bring fresh ideas to the table.

"They did this big call for new games. 'We're going to have this big company meeting and we want you guys to use your imaginations and come up with some new game ideas, not necessarily franchise-based things, but new things.' So we did. People got into little mini-teams and wrote up proposals and presented them at this meeting, and you had some valid ideas, but they ended up not picking any of them."

Al continues, "I think the only one they went forward with was *Gabriel Knight 3*, which was a franchise. My thinking was, what do they want? They're asking for original ideas but they're too afraid to go forward on any of them. Also, marketing held a lot of power in that company. If marketing said, 'We don't quite know how to market this,' instead of hearing, 'You'd better learn, that's your job, figure it out!' managers would be like, 'We'll just cancel it and call a tax loss on it. At least that way we save some money and get a tax credit.'"

One unreleased game Al Eufrasio worked on was called *Vampire Wars*. "It was a strategy game and we were trying to get Blizzard's blessing on it. We were trying to convince them to let us call it *BloodCraft*.* We had it as far as an early prototype. I thought it was a pretty sound design at the time, but I'm not a big strategy gamer so I could be wrong. They had all kinds of critiques on what we were doing; they didn't necessarily want us to call it *BloodCraft*. In our defense, we

---

* Blizzard by this stage had released popular strategy titles called *Warcraft* and *StarCraft*.

didn't have it anywhere near finalized; we only had the most basic gameplay in."

During Sierra's quarterly reviews, the game was canceled. "They were having quarterly product reviews with some of the big managers upstairs and we had the misfortune of being the last project to be reviewed that day," Al remembers. "They had just got bad news from a couple of the projects that came before us and nobody was in a really good mood. There was no reason to be optimistic, really, from reports they'd gotten earlier in the day."

The current build of *Vampire Wars* was essentially the same as what the team had shown three months previously, and management wasn't impressed. "Visually there wasn't much change," Al says. "A lot of change under the hood; a lot of new programming and things were running smoother and more efficiently, but art-wise everything was pretty similar. We hadn't really gotten a chance to put [any new graphics or sound] in yet. They just thought we hadn't made any progress whatsoever because there was nothing there they could see.

"One thing that pissed them off was that certain people on our team had the whole presentation planned out, and they weren't aware management had just had a couple of situations that they weren't too happy about in earlier meetings that day. Our person came in all upbeat, 'Hi, welcome! This is our *Vampire Wars* update,' and he started tossing rubber toy bats across the table, or something like that. So the corporate manager-type people who weren't creative types didn't take kindly to that. Generally, in the game industry, that would have been perfectly fine.

"That was the Nintendo 64 era, where things were starting to switch over to 3D and platform games were becoming more predominant than adventure games. So people suggested a few things that were more along the lines of platform games and such. I did propose a cart racer; everybody started putting out cart racers so I thought 'I'll suggest one with the theme of farm animals racing around tracks on a farm or something.' Again, we'd have to create a whole new division to make that game because it's not like anything else being made."

A different proposal, which Craig Alexander thought was excellent, was to be a shooter in the mold of Tom Clancy's *Rainbow Six* and similar games. Sierra's Oakhurst studio was working on *Navy SEALs*, a game ahead of its time, before anybody else was making military shooters. Unfortunately, the 1999 closure of the studio forced the cancelation of this title.

Only two games made the transition from Oakhurst to Seattle when the axe fell in 1999, and even those were discontinued soon after.

The Lord of the Rings Online, previously called *Middle-earth Online*, was a project that Craig Alexander pursued vigorously in his time at Sierra. Along with his belief that a new style of game would work best with an existing property, he also felt that a multiplayer game set in J. R. R. Tolkien's world was sure to be a hit.

"Sierra is where I signed all the Tolkien licenses even before the movies [came out]. I got out in front of it. *Lord of the Rings Online* did eventually get built, but built by what became Warner Bros. [Interactive Entertainment]."

Craig recalls some resistance to his pursuing the exclusive rights to *The Lord of the Rings* during his time at Sierra. "I remember the naysayers saying, 'Why would you pursue a fifty-year-old book? Nobody cares about this.' Basically, being in on the ground floor of the greatest franchise of all time. It's probably not *Star Wars* but it's pretty darn close. I was there on day one. That was cool. That was probably the biggest accomplishment. And it was an accomplishment that I personally made; a lot of things I inherited but that one was mine. I worked on and off in that space for twenty years. I made a career out of it."

Although Sierra's version of *The Lord of the Rings Online* was canceled soon after the game's production was moved to Seattle, the rights moved to a different company before ending up with Turbine (now Warner Bros.), who eventually made the game.

One of the most famous games never to be made from this era was *Babylon 5*. Originally starting out as a different project called *Echoes*, it was something that Marc Hudgins put a lot of effort into over a long period of time.

One of Marc's jobs in the later years in Oakhurst was to develop multiplayer titles for the ImagiNation Network. As part of the contract when INN was sold, Sierra was to continue delivering new games on the platform for new owner AT&T, so Marc and his team came up with a number of designs.

"I got to do a lot of concept art, game ideas, and pitches for different ideas. There were some pretty cool ones. There was one where it was basically *World of Tanks* twenty years ago. There was a game where you were a caveman. 'Let's make multiplayer caveman games where you fight dinosaurs.' It was cartoony like *The Flintstones*. Weird stuff. It was a very fertile period, but nothing shipped," Marc says.

Far more promising was an adventure game in the style of *Myst*. "One of the ideas that came out of [this period] was one that I liked so much I actually went to management and said, 'This is too good for them; I want to pitch it to you guys. Let's see if you're interested before we throw it to AT&T.' This game was called *Echoes*."

In an era when traditional adventure games were starting to fade and *Myst* had transformed the whole genre, Marc and his team came up with a unique idea. "The idea behind this game was – and it sounds kind of clichéd to me now – an alien base gets dug up by an archeological team on the Earth's moon. It's like ten thousand years old and it's abandoned. It became this whole thing where you go through this ancient alien ruin on the moon discovering what they were about, where they came from. Solving puzzles basically to get through it."

Getting the green light from studio executives, the team started working on the game. A lot of work was put into the technology driving it. Moving away from Sierra's familiar SCI engine, the new game would use a combination of real-time 3D and the prerendered graphics in the style of *Myst*.

Once the game world and alien cultures were designed, *Echoes* went under review, a common practice at the time. What Marc Hudgins didn't expect was a question from Ken Williams. "Ken asked me if we could turn this into a first-person shooter, because he was really into those at the time. And I was, 'Man, it's really not a shooter.' This is my big career mistake, because I probably should have said, 'Sure!' I said, 'I don't know how to turn this into a shooter, sorry.' So it got canceled."

That decision didn't go over well with Marc. "I remember writing a very . . . I wouldn't say nasty, but bitter letter to him when he canceled *Echoes* because I couldn't turn it into a shooter. I had a team who had really bought into it and they really wanted to do it and I was sticking with the team. I think if I'd been more mature . . . I'd been in games for, what, five years. I had, like, zero experience and I'd gone from being a junior animator to being a game designer in a very short time. I think if I'd had a little more experience I probably would have managed it better."

With the benefit of hindsight, Marc continues: "I think, now, [that] Ken was actually a better person than I might have given him credit for at the time. He was the man, you know what I mean? I felt then that he was the guy who spent all day keeping us from making our dreams come true, but when I think about it, it was his money. Trusting us with his money was a pretty big thing right there. He probably gave me more opportunities than I deserved. I don't think I was the best employee."

As it turns out, that wasn't the end of the project, or Marc Hudgins's involvement with it, though it would go on to take a much different form than originally intended, as he explains: "They said, 'Hey, we really want to do a space combat game. Can you come up with something there?' The same team that was basically doing *Echoes* started doing a space combat game that had the same aliens in it. We'd written this really elaborate backstory for how they came into contact with the Earth. We thought, 'Let's forget about this game *Echoes*; what if the aliens are coming back? How would Earth deal with that and what do they want?'"

One of Craig Alexander's ideas was to try to tie new products into existing franchises as a way of ensuring the best opportunity for success. At first the decision was made to make the game part of Dynamix's *Earthsiege* universe, calling the new game *Starsiege*, but it's wasn't long before Dynamix decided they wanted to work on a different *Starsiege* on their own, so a new franchise was needed.

According to Marc, "It was decided, 'Let's tie this to a really big franchise! We can't do *Star Wars*; what else is out there?' *Babylon 5* was really big at the time and we had a couple of people in the building who were real advocates for it. So Craig Alexander, who was the studio president at the time, negotiated a deal with Warner Bros. and before you know it we were making the *Babylon 5* game."

Christy Marx, designer of the *Conquests* series at Sierra and a writer on the *Babylon 5* TV series, was brought in to write the new game. She recalls that "Craig Alexander contacted me because I'd written for *Babylon 5* and had a personal relationship with Joe Straczynski [creator of the *Babylon 5* TV show]. I knew how to bridge the two disparate worlds of games and Hollywood, which often don't mix well.

"They were well into designing the game before Craig brought me on officially. I was meant to be the 'speaker to Joe' to help bridge that gap. Peter Ledger [Christy's husband] had been killed in a car accident in 1994, but I had remained living in Oakhurst in a house that we'd bought, so it was convenient for me to go to the office and work on the project. That's how I met Randy Littlejohn, who was part of the core design team. We had Dan Foy for engineering, Marc Hudgins for art, and Randy for storytelling – what we now would call narrative design."

Christy goes on to reveal why production of the game didn't go smoothly from there: "Sierra was determined to make a space combat simulator for the first *Babylon 5* game, hoping it would do well and lead to more *Babylon 5* games. Joe was deeply unhappy about that and wanted a story-driven game, which I could certainly understand, but it didn't fit the market or the company's plans.

"We were able to shoot live-action cutscenes using many of the original cast, and the original sets and costumes before they were destroyed [after the TV show's cancelation in 1998]. There were rough spots around that process because the *Babylon 5* people didn't understand games and treated it with condescension, and the game people didn't understand the demands of TV production."

Despite these obstacles, Christy says that "we were developing what I feel would have been a fantastic game with huge potential."

Marc Hudgins also believes it would have been a great game. "We were getting near the end. The video was all shot, the missions were all designed, the AI was designed, the flight sim was designed. We just needed to sew it all together. It would've been fun. We had a good time working on it, mostly."

The public seemed receptive as well. "We had an alpha we debuted at E3 [the Electronic Entertainment Expo] that was pretty well received. It was just a combat system but people had a good time playing it. I did too," Marc says.

When the Oakhurst office was closed in 1999, only certain members of the team were given an offer to move to Seattle and continue working on the game. Randy Littlejohn, who by this point was in a relationship with Christy, was someone who did not, so both ended their association with the project.

It wasn't long after the move to Seattle that the project was dropped completely, as Marc explains: "We had a limited-window contract with Warner Bros. and we had to renew it before the game shipped. I don't know what the cost of that was but it wasn't insignificant, and as far as I can tell *Babylon 5* at that point was canceled. Management probably said, 'Why should we renew the license on a show that's dead for a project that's been in development for a very long time?' All the advocates for the project we'd had were gone. We had been moved up to Seattle with new management who didn't know anything about us. We knew some of the people, but they really couldn't advocate for us in any meaningful way. I think it was just a very cut-and-dried business decision."

Christy says that some time later she and Randy heard the project was dead and they were both devastated by the news. Something they had put years of work into had been canceled with little fanfare, the worst part being that the game was nearly complete and ready to release.

It All Came Crashing Down

Prior to the sale of the company, Ken Williams worked hard with CUC to develop a plan for the new software division. He wanted to make sure that the jobs of his Sierra employees were safe, his shareholders were happy, and the business would continue to grow and prosper. Central to this was the goal of maintaining Sierra's independence within the larger group.

Ken's own role with the new group was designed to take advantage of what he was good at: making games. He would retain control of Sierra's development studios in Seattle and Oakhurst as well as all the subsidiary companies Sierra owned, such as Dynamix, and he would oversee product development across the entire group. Structures were also put in place to resolve any conflicts between the different brands if they arose.

Some of Sierra's employees had reservations about the buyout. While a lot of these concerns were natural – the business was changing hands and things would be different in the future – there was also some unease at the prospect of CUC, in particular, purchasing the company. After all, they had no experience at creating software, or any other product.

Craig Alexander was one of those who had some doubts about the buyout. "They had no game experience. No media experience. They ran a bunch of consumer brands, real estate firms. It didn't make any sense."

It turned out those fears were well-founded. The post-sale future of Sierra and CUC Software didn't turn out as Ken Williams expected or had been assured it would. Davidson was put in charge of all sales for CUC's software division, which created many problems for Sierra.

Davidson & Associates was a market leader in educational software, releasing best-selling titles like *Math Blaster* and *Reading Blaster*, but Sierra had a large and diverse catalog. Selling educational titles was a far cry from producing more adult titles or horror-themed games.

"Sierra's sales force was consolidated with Davidson's, and there were problems with the Davidson sales force selling Sierra products," Ken said in 2010. "They had been selling educational software which had a very different sales profile than computer games. There were also issues with a cultural difference between selling preschool software and *Leisure Suit Larry*. Some of our biggest hits were offensive to some people at Davidson. It was an issue no one had expected."[42]

Just as unexpectedly, Bob Davidson, who had been running the combined sales department for CUC, left the company in 1996 and Ken anticipated that he or someone from Sierra would be asked to fill the role. "I felt that I, or someone from my senior management team, should have been installed to run the company, but CUC brought in a member of their senior management with no experience in software."[43]

By 1997, Ken had become so frustrated with the direction the company was taking that he quit CUC and Sierra, the company he had founded, and left the software business entirely.

In December of that year, CUC International and HFS (Hospitality Franchise Systems, a hotel franchise owner) merged to become Cendant, a business that oversaw CUC's vast direct marketing business and its newly formed software division, along with HFS's chain of hotel franchises and their own direct marketing business. It was during the merger of their accounting departments in April 1998 that Cendant uncovered fraud in the CUC books, which turned out to be the biggest financial scandal in United States history at that time.

Investigations by Cendant revealed several years of inflated earnings, increasing the recorded revenue of the company by $500 million prior to the merger with HFS. Walter Forbes was forced out of the company in March 2001 before he and a fellow executive were indicted and eventually convicted by a federal grand jury of massive accounting fraud.

When knowledge of the scandal became public, Cendant lost approximately $14 billion in value. Stock that had been trading at $42 a share tumbled down to $9 nearly overnight, causing serious financial damage to the employees at Sierra.

Al Eufrasio remembers the day they found out about the criminal accounting activity at their parent company: "Everybody was up in arms. It was a lot of standing around in the aisles talking that day and not much working. 'What the hell is happening? Are we going to lose our jobs? What's going on?'"

Craig Alexander recalls how it affected everyone in the company, especially his staff in Oakhurst: "A lot of our teams had ownership; they had a lot of shares in the company. The share price just collapsed. It was awful. There were people that for tax reasons were converting share options to shares, borrowing money basically to hold the stock; you get tax advantages for doing it. Then when the stock collapsed they lost everything. There were people losing their homes. It was terrible. It really wreaked havoc on the company."

Soon after the accounting fraud was revealed, Cendant sold their software group comprised of Sierra, Davidson & Associates, Knowledge Adventure, and Gryphon Software to French communication company Havas, with Havas in turn being bought by another French company, Vivendi.

In an effort to return their software division to profit, Vivendi closed the Oakhurst studio in February 1999, then closed all development at Sierra soon after.

Marc Hudgins was there when the studio shut down and has his own theories about why it happened. "They closed down the Oakhurst studio, I believe, to probably get rid of a studio that was struggling and fix up the balance sheet a little bit. But they moved two projects up to Seattle and [those were] *Lord of the Rings Online* and *Babylon 5*. Sierra Oakhurst was closed in February and we moved up there in May. We were working out of the old studio up to that point. It was a ghost town. By September they had canceled both projects and laid off both teams again."

Believing the fraud scandal was what eventually forced the closure of Sierra, Craig Alexander says: "With all the financial fraud going on at CUC, that ultimately destroyed every studio that was part of the Sierra family, and there were like six or seven of them. Except for Blizzard. They had some megahits that kept them alive: *Diablo*, *Warcraft II* and *StarCraft*. They were financially wealthy enough [that] they survived the storm and all the divestments."

Craig has one memory of the CUC fraud case that sticks out more than others, as he was in the courtroom the day Walter Forbes was convicted.

"I was at the criminal trial here in Connecticut on the East Coast. I saw them convict the CEO; I was there. I was just in the area for a totally unrelated reason – I was interviewing for another game job – and I decided, 'I'm going to stop by.' I saw the bailiff and when I told him who I was he asked, 'Are you a member of the family?' 'No . . . not quite,' I said, and he asked, 'What are you doing here?' I told him the story and he said, 'Oh, I'm going to get you a front row [seat].'

"It was the largest financial fraud case. This was long before Enron and Bernie Madoff; they dwarfed what this guy did," Craig continues. "But at the time, he was the first. Lucky me, I got to be in the middle of that mess. Yuck."

John Williams believes that Sierra was still producing good games when the company was sold to CUC. "I'd say a lot of the game development groups were operating on all cylinders right up until the time of the sale to CUC. Just about every major studio under Sierra was cranking out some great games, and even our productivity groups were producing some very strong moneymakers," he claims.

"Truthfully, the only group that was struggling at that point was Sierra, and a lot of that could be blamed on the move from Oakhurst to Seattle by the company. That whole move just destroyed the synergy of that whole group and it never got repaired."

Maybe the story of Sierra On-Line is best summed up by Ken Williams himself. In 1999, after the studio was closed in Oakhurst, Ken penned an open letter to the now-former Sierra employees in which he expressed his sorrow at the way their journey had ended.[44]

"I console myself in the following way, and perhaps it will help you to cope with what has occurred," his letter concluded. "Let's imagine that a stranger had walked up to any of us, on the street, in 1979, and said: 'Would you like to move to one of the greatest cities on earth? While you are there, you can play a key role in creating a company that just about everyone will know and respect. Your grandchildren will be amazed when they learn that you once worked there. You will be the envy of your peers, because they will know that your team created the largest collection of hits ever to come from one company. There will even be years when you will have played a role in over half the products on the industry's top ten lists! You will be surrounded by incredibly intelligent, hard working people, who will work 20+ hours per day when it takes it to get the job done. And, you will have more fun than you ever thought possible. There's only one catch though. This will only last for twenty years.'

"Even knowing it wouldn't last forever I would have followed that stranger anywhere. I'm disappointed that it didn't last forever, but, a 20 year ride on the greatest roller coaster on earth beats the heck out of life in the slow lane any day. Life may never be the same, but it also isn't over, and we all have some great memories we shall never forget.

"Good luck, and I miss you all."

Epilogue 1: The Shoulders of Giants

"With multiple highly successful franchises, Sierra was renowned for pushing the boundaries of writing, game design, animation, sound, music, and – with the advent of CD-ROM – even acting. Today's gaming storytellers stand on Sierra's shoulders."[45]

These words were used to introduce Ken and Roberta Williams at the Game Awards in 2014, where they were honored with the prestigious Industry Icon award. It's well-deserved recognition, as Sierra and its husband and wife founders have left a deep legacy on the computer game industry in general, and adventure games specifically.

But how is something as ethereal as a "legacy" defined?

Mystery House is an obvious point to start from when defining Sierra's enduring imprint. It represented, after all, a momentous evolution of an entire genre, which certainly qualifies as the start of a legacy.

Women in the game industry also owe a lot to Sierra. Consider for a moment that – in what is still a male-dominated industry thirty years later – three of the six flagship adventure series Sierra produced were designed or co-designed by women.

Roberta Williams, credited with creating the graphic adventure game, developed the *King's Quest* series and pushed the boundaries of acting in games with *Phantasmagoria*, as well as being responsible for launching the popular *Mixed-Up Mother Goose*. Jane Jensen conceived the *Gabriel Knight* series, bringing more mature themes and stories to adventures, and shared design and writing duties on *King's Quest VI* with Roberta. Lori Cole was the principal designer of the award-winning RPG/adventure series *Quest for Glory* and designed *Mixed-Up Fairy Tales*, a spinoff of the *Mother Goose* original.

Of the other three major *Quest* series (*Police Quest*, *Space Quest* and *Leisure Suit Larry*), Tammy Dargan was mainly responsible for the design of *Police Quest: Open Season* and the first *SWAT* game, while Leslie Balfour worked closely with Scott Murphy on *Space Quest 6* and was to be credited as co-designer on the unreleased *Space Quest 7*.

Sierra was never afraid to give prominent projects to women designers. Christy Marx, Lorelei Shannon and Gano Haine were also notable Sierra designers through the years. Christy spearheaded the *Conquests* series, while Lorelei took the reins on *Phantasmagoria 2: A Puzzle of Flesh* and co-designed *King's Quest VII* with Roberta Williams. Gano, responsible for both *EcoQuest* games, also shared design duties on *Pepper's Adventures in Time* with Lorelai and Jane Jensen.

Regardless of gender, it was the people employed by Sierra who made the company unique and successful, and while some, like Ken and Roberta, have retired from the industry, others have remained active and gone on to create new titles independently.

Jane Jensen designed a number of casual games for Oberon Media, a company she founded, as well as adventure games *Gray Matter*, *Moebius: Empire Rising*, and a *Gabriel Knight: Sins of the Fathers* remake before retiring from the industry to write romance novels under a pen name. Corey and Lori Cole developed the critically acclaimed *Shannara* for Legend Entertainment and self-published *Hero-U: Rogue to Redemption*, a spiritual successor to their *Quest for Glory* series. Mark Crowe was studio design director for Pipeworks Software before rejoining Scott Murphy to crowdfund *SpaceVenture*, a spiritual successor to their *Space Quest* series. Josh Mandel has lent his talents to numerous games, both as a writer/designer (*Callahan's Crosstime Saloon*, *Insecticide*) and actor (*Asylum* and four *King's Quest* fan remakes).

Not all alumni have stayed in adventure games, but many who got their start at Sierra have since moved into senior positions within the wider gaming industry. Marc Hudgins, whose artwork credits include the *Quest for Glory* series, has gone on to work on *Sid Meier's Civilization* and *The Elder Scrolls Online*, while Chance Thomas, who composed the soundtrack for *Quest for Glory V: Dragon Fire*, is now an Oscar- and Emmy-winning game musician known for his work on *The Lord of the Rings Online* and *Dota 2*.

When considering Sierra's legacy, the pioneering use of technology must never be overlooked.

Always seeking to make their products more immersive, the company became the first to commercially create a game that supported the AdLib sound card and external sound devices such as the Roland MT-32. For *King's Quest IV*, players were offered the choice of hearing the soundtrack composed for the cheaper AdLib card or the top-end Roland MT-32. Both versions were vast improvements over the single-sound-generating PC speaker that came with the IBM PC and its clones.

Sierra's early adoption and support of CD-ROM technology allowed far greater immersion in adventure games and helped popularize the new medium. The 1990 remake of *Mixed-Up Mother Goose* was one of the earliest games produced on CD-ROM and the first to use a mixed mode that allowed for normal audio tracks as well as data, which also left room to allow for voice-acted speech to replace (or complement) the in-game text. It should be noted that Sierra was not the originator of this trend. Although *Mother Goose* and *King's Quest V* are both regularly credited as the first CD-ROM games, Cyan's *The Manhole* was released on CD-ROM in 1989, a full year before both Sierra titles. Still, Sierra was far more prominent at the time than the fledgling pre-*Myst* Cyan, so the company's role in fostering acceptance of the new technology was highly instrumental.

This support for CD-ROM technology progressed to the point that it enabled the now-common use of Hollywood talent in games, featuring actors such as Robby Benson in *King's Quest VI* and John Rhys-Davies in *Quest for Glory IV*. The cast of the first *Gabriel Knight* game included big names such as Tim Curry, Leah Remini, Mark Hamill and Michael Dorn, showcasing Sierra as the early leader in computer game vocal talent.

Another measure of lasting legacy is to look at the legion of dedicated fans, those who not only bought the games but also became personally invested in the characters and worlds Sierra created.

One such fan is Rudy Marchant, who in 2008 began his own attempt at preserving the rich history of Sierra through his website The Sierra Chest. When asked if he believes today's gamers still benefit from Sierra's legacy, he says, "Yes, but they mostly don't know it. It's like asking a kid these days what the influence of the Lumière brothers was on movie making, and they answer 'Who?' completely unaware of the fact that they invented motion picture."

Rudy goes on to say, "Just because most current-generation gamers haven't heard about Sierra doesn't mean Sierra has lost its legacy. In many ways they pioneered new technologies in gaming and nothing can ever change that. Even in one hundred years, Sierra will still be the first developer to use a Roland sound module and the first studio to [let you] play games over a modem. As a lifelong Sierra fan, there's always some disappointment when a young gamer doesn't recognize the classic Sierra titles, but at the same time I always enjoy the opportunity to explain how things came to be – how the games they play these days would not exist if it weren't for the often groundbreaking developments of the old studios, many of which no longer exist."

In the early 2000s there was an upswing in interest for all things Sierra. Somewhat ironically, at a time when Sierra had closed their internal development studios and were no longer pursuing their landmark adventure game series, the internet gave rise to a field of fan-produced games. Some groups of avid adventure gamers harnessed the spirit of the genre's heyday and succeeded in making their own entries in the worlds Sierra created.

One such group was Phoenix Online Studios, a group of committed *King's Quest* fans who started working on their ultimate fan project *King's Quest IX: Every Cloak Has a Silver Lining*. Their game was an attempt to tie up the *King's Quest* stories after what they considered the lackluster official final installment, *Mask of Eternity*. Running afoul of Sierra's then-owner Vivendi Universal, they eventually negotiated a fan license to continue the game episodically as *The Silver Lining*.

Katie Hallahan, designer and PR director for Phoenix Online, believes that part of the enduring legacy of Sierra is that fans grew up and matured along with the games.

"These were some of the first games that came out when computers were becoming household items. So I think in a way a lot of people remember them so strongly because [Sierra's games] were their first exposure to [computers]. It's kind of the thing that's been with them the longest," she says. "And also, at the time, although they might have flaws looking back now, they were fun games. They were things that you could play with your kids; your whole family could get involved with playing. Since those series were successful, you just continued growing up with them, I think. They had characters you could become attached to."

Phoenix Online was hardly alone in keeping the spirit of Sierra alive. Frederik Gonzalez Olsen worked on two unofficial free *Space Quest* fan games, *Incinerations* and *Vohaul Strikes Back*, and he says that another reason for Sierra's endurance is that the games sparked people's imaginations with the potential of so many untold stories.

"Sierra crafted all these rich universes, always using cutting-edge technology to make them come alive, and they left us hungry for more. In comparison, most adventure game companies at the time had one flagship series. Depending on your disposition, Sierra had several. What happens to Sonny Bonds or John Carey when they've locked up the big baddie? Which supernatural phenomenon will Gabriel Knight brandish his Schattenjäger talisman against next time? Is Sludge Vohaul ever going to return to stain Roger Wilco's golden mop?

"There are stories left to tell. There are questions left to be answered. There's potential to be fulfilled. There are sequels to be made, commercial or otherwise. Ken and Roberta's vision is now pushing forty. I'm sure it'll continue to inspire fans the day it's pushing fifty as well."

Robert Holmes, composer and producer of *Gabriel Knight*, agrees that part of Sierra's enduring appeal is the variety of its catalog. "One of the things I think Sierra did really smartly was they didn't just make one kind of game. The people who liked *Gabriel Knight* were very different from the people who might like *Space Quest* or very different from the people who might like *Laura Bow*. There was a lot of great diversity. I come out of the film industry, so it was a lot like the early days of MGM; you would have entire film units doing certain genres and creating really good stuff in that genre."

Many people making adventure games today were also inspired by Sierra games they grew up playing, something former Sierra designer Josh Mandel says is a sure sign that the company left an enduring mark.

"Those games are proof of that, aren't they? So many people putting so much work into fan games and fan fictions and remakes and here it's twenty or twenty-five years later, longer I guess. You don't get that level of attention decades down the road unless you've done something tremendously right and struck a chord with so many people.

"I meet people who tell me they don't personally remember playing Sierra games but they remember sneaking into the living room and seeing their father play *Leisure Suit Larry* or something like that. It's going to be a long time before Sierra's legacy fades, and with the current uptick in the popularity of adventure games in general, I think you're going to see a renewed interest."

Nowhere is that renewed interest more apparent than in the relaunch of the Sierra brand label and the surprising return of *King's Quest* in 2016. Though designed by The Odd Gentlemen, the five-part episodic series was given a rousing endorsement from Ken and Roberta Williams and proved highly popular with longtime series fans who finally got an authentic final adventure with King Graham in Daventry. But will it really be the final one after all? The series itself left the door open for future games in the beloved franchise, and Sierra fans have proven themselves to be remarkably passionate about keeping the flame alive. What the future holds is anyone's guess.

John Romero – co-founder of id Software, designer of the original *DOOM* and an industry icon in his own right – has also acknowledged the pioneering work and legacy of Ken and Roberta Williams at Sierra.

"[They] built a great company we all admired for a long time. He and Roberta are legends, even back then. Graphical adventure games are still around! Starting with *Mystery House*, there have been thousands of graphical adventures and they are still being produced all over the world. Not a bad legacy!" John says.

Whatever your defining measure of that legacy, one thing is certain: Sierra produced a remarkable pool of talent and a prolific catalog of games that continue to inspire people and bring players joy, whether directly or through others who have stood on their shoulders to reach new heights.

Impressive legacy, indeed.

Epilogue 2: Why Sierra Matters

As I said in the introduction to this book, Sierra matters to me. I grew up on their games and they've been a constant in my life both through my formative years and now as a married man with three kids of my own. Through my research I've heard a lot about the company, the people who worked there, the stories, the disagreements, the fights (a couple of which I was sworn not to ever put into print!), and many reasons why Sierra no longer exists as a developer like it did when I was younger. But in the midst of all of that, one mainstay has been the fans.

Many people grew up on these games, as I did, buying (or pirating!) and cherishing them as they were released, while others came to Sierra later, perhaps discovering the games online or being introduced to them by a loved one. Either way, Sierra matters to the fans.

Sierra's designers helped foster a family feel by putting their names and faces on the boxes and in the games themselves – what other game besides *Space Quest III* tasks the player with rescuing its own designers? – as well as through their personal interactions by responding to fan mail. My friend Troels Pleimert (better known online as the Space Quest Historian), who described himself as "an overeager and annoying kid who wanted to know everything about *Space Quest*," was able to correspond directly with designer Scott Murphy and studio head Craig Alexander back in Sierra's heyday. What company does that?

I've seen that fan appreciation firsthand when it comes to this book. Asking for crowdfunding is a daunting thing, but Sierra fans backed this project lock, stock, and barrel. In return for their support, I am pleased to give some of these backers the opportunity to share their stories of why Sierra matters to them. Because if it weren't for the fans, this book wouldn't exist.

Serena Nelson

Graphic adventure games are important to Serena Nelson, and Sierra's games in particular have played a consistent role in her life. Having been exposed to computers at a very young age, Serena was enamored with Infocom's text adventures, playing through them on her Atari ST. But it was when her father arrived home with a bunch more adventure games for her to play, including some early Sierra titles, that her real love for Sierra began. "I instantly took to playing them. The rest, as they say, is history. I fell in love instantly with them and had to get more," Serena remembers.

To this day, Serena treasures that special connection with her father. "They were one of the few things I remember growing up that I really enjoyed doing with my father. While I played a lot by myself, he was the one that got me into the graphical adventure genre and I still thank him for giving me the opportunity to experience what would become my most beloved genre. These games were with me for the majority of my formative years and I guess I still enjoy them because of that."

The first Sierra games she recalls playing were *King's Quest* and *Leisure Suit Larry*, dating back to her middle school years "or maybe even a little bit before that," but it's another franchise that stands out to Serena the most.

"My favorite series has to be *Space Quest*, hands down. For the longest time, the original was my favorite for various reasons, but I've come to think the fourth one had the most interesting plot.

"I still remember that the very first computer game I ever bought with my own allowance was the original *Space Quest*," she says. "My family and I walked into Egghead Software and I saw the glorious box sitting on one of the shelves. I pulled it down, looked at it, and instantly knew this was a game for me. I bought it, brought it home, and couldn't stop playing it."

Serena's love of Sierra's games continued through the fan-made *Space Quest* games and AGDI's *King's Quest* remakes, and she became much more personally involved in 2012 when a number of former Sierra designers and prominent fan groups crowdfunded new adventure games. "I didn't realize just how big the fan community was until the Kickstarter craze," she laughs.

"I was a big proponent and supporter of every Sierra-related game from the return of the old alums to fan-created games like *Quest for Infamy* and *Mage's Initiation*. I've been on the testing team for *Leisure Suit Larry* (both a high and low for me), as well as a very vocal presence on several forums. I was even part of the social media team for Phoenix Online Studios (who did Jane Jensen's *Moebius* and the *Gabriel Knight* remake) for a while. I wrote extensively for *Kickstart Ventures* and *Cliqist*, focusing on adventure games, as well. I was busy for several years until the madness died down."

As much as she reveres the games, Serena cites the friendships she has made through her fan involvement as the highlight of her love for Sierra. "I've gotten to know other passionate fans, and even gotten to know a lot of the alumni a lot better than I ever thought would be possible. Writing, testing, and just having a good time on forums has been a blast, to the point where I'm glad to have found Kickstarter and the many others that have influenced who I am to this day."

One of the former Sierra employees that Serena has become acquainted with is Josh Mandel. "Josh was an active part of the testing team [on Replay Games' *Leisure Suit Larry Reloaded*] and I got to talk to him a bit through email. He also was a big supporter of mine. He's a great guy and I'm glad to have gotten to know a little bit more about him beyond the games he's worked on. It also means so much to me that he voiced the main character in the free-to-play Senscape game *Serena*.* I'd like to think we're good online friends. I hope he feels the same way."

He does. "Serena, as long as I've known her, has always been one of adventure games' biggest boosters," Josh says. "It's a pleasure to know her and a pleasure to call her my friend."

Luke Jensen

Richard Aronson, lead programmer on *Conquests of the Longbow*, told the story earlier in this book about one of the things he was most proud of: that he encouraged and developed ways to allow people with physical challenges to access Sierra's games. This not only affected a member of Richard's family, it also benefited a lot of other people, like Luke Jensen.

Luke was born with cerebral palsy, a neurological disorder that, in his case, causes stiff and uncoordinated muscles and makes walking impossible, requiring him to use a wheelchair. This meant that growing up he wasn't able to play outside, at least not without a lot of help, and even inside play was limited since a lot of toys were designed for physical manipulation, coordination, and fine motor skills.

The computer was a natural match for Luke, as it allowed him to play and have fun with a minimum of physical effort. Luke's family got

---

Serena is a collaborative 2014 game by multiple developers honoring Serena Nelson as a display of appreciation for her passionate support of the adventure game community and numerous Kickstarter campaigns.

their first PC when he was about five, and Luke remembers that it didn't come with any quality games, a situation that led his mother to drive many miles to the nearest software store to buy something the family could play together. She returned with *King's Quest III*. The Jensens were so new to computers and adventure games that they watched the introduction over and over before realizing that they needed to press a key to begin the game!

"Over the weeks and months that followed, my parents and I would have regular 'quest nights' where we'd play the game together after dinner one night a week," Luke reminisces. "We got through nearly the entire game on our own, until the time came to get rid of Manannan. We figured out that we had to hide the cat cookie in the porridge, but try as we might, we couldn't come up with a verb the game would understand. My parents bought the hint book. Of course!

"After my parents and I finished *King's Quest III* and we moved on to *King's Quest IV* the following year, from about then on we were an almost universally 'Sierra household.'"

Sierra turned out to be an important part of Luke's life, and that's best conveyed through the relationships he has built over the years. Luke was one of the founders of the fan project that became *The Silver Lining* from Phoenix Online Studios. During production, Luke realized that he didn't have the time or energy he felt the project deserved, and as a result he handed over his lead designer responsibilities to others who took the game in a different direction than Luke had envisioned. Luke eventually decided to move on and it wasn't a pleasant parting, but relationships have mended in the years since, and the break resulted in one of Luke's most personal Sierra-related memories.

"I wanted to have the freedom to produce the game I had originally sought to create. This meant asking [the *Silver Lining* team] to remove all material I had contributed to the game up to that point, something I couldn't do easily since relations between us were obviously a little strained.

"I opened up to an artist on the team, Michael Fortunato, who was the first person to truly lend a listening ear and validate my feelings. The next summer (2003), I visited family in New York, where Michael also lived at the time, and I had made plans to meet him in person while there. I was apprehensive at first, but once we caught sight of each other, he ran toward me screaming my name in pure joy. We hit it off big time, and Michael even took it upon himself to come to Texas a year later to attend my college graduation. We're still in touch and consider ourselves brothers. Accordingly, he's raising his son to consider me his uncle," Luke says.

Another relationship Luke developed as a result of his love of Sierra was with Anonymous Game Developers Interactive co-founder Britney Brimhall. Luke and Britney became friends while he tested *King's Quest II: Romancing the Stones* and *Al Emmo and the Lost Dutchman's Mine*,[*] and in 2007 Britney visited Luke in person.

"As Britney sat at my kitchen table, along with a mutual friend of ours who was also a Sierra fan, she showed us a huge binder full of concept sketches, design documents, maps, and full-color art from her team's projects. She allowed the two of us to choose one item each from within it. I immediately chose a color drawing designed as the unofficial 'box art' for *King's Quest I VGA* and Britney autographed it, writing a heartfelt personal message on the back. I still have it to this day, one of my most prized possessions."

During that conversation, Luke also mentioned that *King's Quest III* was his first Sierra game, which resulted in Britney asking if they could keep a secret. "Then she revealed that AGDI had remade *King's Quest III* behind the scenes, and that nobody outside her team knew except us. I remember her next words very clearly: 'If it gets out, we'll know where to look!' I can proudly say I did indeed not tell a single soul . . . well, except my parents when they got home that evening!"

For Luke, Sierra was and is all about family. "Since it was founded by a husband and wife team, and since they seemed to present a caring, folksy image, I felt like family. Sierra helped my parents and me to bond, to become a stronger family. Playing Sierra games was such a joy for us – and for me in particular – that it felt like spending time with close family friends. And being a member of the Sierra fan community has led to some of the most powerful family-building experiences of my life, both virtually and 'in real life.'"

Luke further explains that through Sierra games he was able to develop a sense of accomplishment for himself: "Sierra gave me the freedom to explore, to have some control over the environment and the destiny of a character. In hindsight, this was vitally important for someone like me. So much of my life, particularly as a young child, was dictated by things 'happening to me' or 'happening for me' since I

---

[*] *Al Emmo and the Lost Dutchman's Mine* is a 2006 game developed by the same core team that made AGDI's fan games, but was released commercially under the banner of Himalaya Studios. The same team also released *Mage's Initiation: Reign of the Elements*, a crowdfunded *Quest for Glory*–like adventure/RPG, in 2019.

needed help with almost every conceivable task, from getting up in the morning, to using the toilet, to even getting a book off a shelf. Other people, the world around me, and my disability directly or indirectly controlled what I did, when I did it, how I did it, and sometimes even *if* I did it in the first place. Computer games gave me a concrete sense of mastery over something, something *I* could take charge of and be responsible for. Prince Alexander finally found and married Princess Cassima thanks to *me*. *I* saved Tarna from the ravages of civil war. I don't think I consciously realized it very much at the time, but that feeling was incredibly powerful and liberating."

Christopher Brendel[*]

Lytton, California: the fictitious town in which I began my journey – not only as a Sierra fan but also as a game designer. The year was 1992. I was eight years old and already an avid fan of video games, thanks to my Nintendo, but nothing could have prepared me for what I was about to experience.

My parents owned a PC, which they used for simple word processing. To me, the computer was a mysterious box that, at the time, I wanted to stay as far away from as possible, preferring the simplicity of inputting cartridges into my Nintendo Entertainment System. Then, one day, my mom took me to an Electronics Boutique. I held in my hands the first money I had ever earned, a result of having done my first year of household chores, and I wanted to spend it. We walked inside, and I saw shelves lined with all kinds of games – not video games, but computer games! I decided to give them a try. It took me nearly an hour to make my choice. I finally decided on a game titled *Police Quest: In Pursuit of the Death Angel* by Sierra On-Line, released that same year.

Police Quest is a third-person adventure game. You play the role of Sonny Bonds, a police officer, as he attempts to track down a crime lord. The gameplay features many of the standard adventure elements that I would later come to love: exploration, character interaction, inventory management, and puzzle solving.

---

[*] My usual method is to frame these epilogue stories in a prose style interspersed with direct quotes similar to the rest of the book. In this case, Chris – the creator of such games as *The Filmmaker*, *Stonewall Penitentiary* and *Summit of the Wolf* – has written something so great, I don't want to change a thing! And so I present his answer to the three-part question: What was your first experience with a Sierra game? Has Sierra / Sierra games influenced your life now? Is your career [partly] a result of playing these games?

Although I could not wait to try the game, I remained skeptical. After all, I was not used to playing games on a computer. As soon as I first ran *Police Quest*, however, I knew that I had made the perfect choice. *Police Quest* featured quality graphics – superior to the Nintendo's. It also featured digitized sound effects and cinematic music. What drew me into the game, though, was its story. It felt like an interactive movie, in which I played the lead role. I was hooked, completely drawn into the game's world. I became attached to its story and characters in a way I had never before experienced. For the first time in my life, I was not playing the game to get a high score or beat the next boss; I was playing it because I wanted to see what would happen next. I wanted the main character, Sonny, to succeed in solving the case, and I wanted to see the story's resolution.

When I finally beat the game, I was ecstatic. At that moment, I knew what I wanted to do with the rest of my life. I wanted to make games that, like *Police Quest*, focused on story, characters, and drama. *Police Quest* had affected me in a way that no other games of the time had managed: it inspired me to create my own.

From that moment on, I began to learn everything I could about the process of game making. I taught myself how to program in QBasic that same year and started to invent my own gameplay mechanics. The interest became a hobby, and soon the hobby became an obsession. Since that early age of eight, my love of game design has only grown stronger, and I have never diverted from my aspiration, that childhood desire to make games.

Needless to say, I started collecting Sierra games as well. They were both my entertainment and my inspiration. At a garage sale, I picked up the *King's Quest V* guidebook, which also contained a short section at the end about Sierra's game-making process. This became my holy bible – a guide upon which I could design my own content.

Today, I run my own indie studio, Unimatrix Productions, through which I make adventure games. This would never have happened had my eight-year-old self never picked up that box that introduced me to Sierra's games.

Sierra still matters, because I fervently believe that without its influence, adventure games would not exist as they are today. Sierra pioneered many of the mechanics that we take for granted in today's games, and their titles remain timeless classics. Sierra's titles managed to accomplish a lot with very little. Their stories and characters are memorable, and I still get more excited at the thought of replaying a Sierra title for the umpteenth time than I do about playing most new games that come out. And, of course, Sierra still matters because without them, my life would be very different today.

Jason Mical

The *Quest for Glory* series, in particular the original EGA *Hero's Quest: So You Want to Be a Hero,* was a formative experience for Jason Mical on several levels. "I took the game's message of selfless heroism pretty seriously, and I think that really helped me make some good life choices in my teens and early twenties," he says.

His love of *Quest for Glory* led Jason to a personal highlight of his fandom: speaking with Lori and Corey Cole, the designers of his favorite series. "They always responded to my emails and gave great answers to my questions, and it was obvious from those exchanges how proud they were of what they'd created so many years before," he recalls. "From a personal point of view, I was glad I had the chance to tell *them* what *Hero's Quest / Quest for Glory* meant to me. It's always a little intimidating meeting your heroes (no pun intended) but the Coles were so cool about it, it just seemed natural."

As well as the heroism in the games Jason admired, it was their blending of writing, mythology, and the way the characters interacted with each other that would have a major impact on his professional life. "It was a major point of inspiration for me becoming a writer, which I've done professionally now for almost twenty years. It was something that buoyed me in my lonely middle school years and helped me connect with the friends I had then, and with friends I'd make later."

Majoring in writing and English literature in college, Jason's dream was to move to New York City and work in the magazine business, but two things stood in his way. "That was 2001; not a great time to get into magazine publishing because the internet was already actively destroying it by that point. After a summer [in New York] I decided to go back to Tulsa.

"Then September 11 happened and I opted not to go back to New York. I started doing little freelance jobs here and there for local newspapers and magazines; small articles, movie reviews, sometimes video game reviews, that kind of thing. Two years later I had a job offer from a [tabletop] game company called WizKids to come work for their marketing team for HeroClix [a collectible miniatures games based on superhero comics], so my wife and I moved up here to Seattle. I used my portfolio and the connections I made in the tabletop games industry to get more freelancing work, and slowly continued to build my portfolio.

"In 2012 I landed my first really big [tabletop] RPG writing job doing an adventure for *Deadlands Noir*, which led to me writing for *Star Wars: Edge of the Empire* and *Force and Destiny*, which led to me writing some fiction for *Delta Green*, plus a bunch of work on the *Eclipse Phase* RPG, including a few chapters in the new second edition that just came out. After having my first child in 2016, it put the brakes on most of my freelancing work but I did manage to write the missions text for the first *Kerbal Space Program* expansion (*Making History*), and used my knowledge of that game and orbital mechanics in general to write a chapter for the *Expanse* RPG, which then led me to more work for that game."

And so a career in writing was birthed when Jason first played *Hero's Quest* and fell in love with it. For him, it was seeing how the stories unfolded in Sierra's games, "and how they infused stories with myth and legend, and how they blended everything with stunning visuals, that inspired me to keep going and get into this field."

Michael Della Pia

Michael Della Pia loves Sierra adventures. His first experience with one was *King's Quest II* and his favorite is another Roberta Williams title, *Phantasmagoria*. What stood out then, and still does now, is the devotion that Michael felt went into the games from the design teams.

"For me, these games had *heart*. You can tell that whoever was creating them really loved what they were doing and wanted us to have the best experience possible. I own every Sierra game I can find on GOG,* and even now, all these years later, they take me away to that special place and make me feel like a kid all over again," he says.

Sierra was always at the forefront of technology, pioneering sound and visuals that set the standard for today's billion-dollar gaming industry. To hear the latest *Space Quest* the way the Two Guys had intended, Michael had to learn how to install new sound cards. Higher memory requirements on games like *Phantasmagoria* meant he learned how to upgrade the RAM. It was all a learning experience, and through playing with computer hardware as a kid he gained valuable knowledge and experience that would serve him well later in life.

---

* GOG (http://www.gog.com) is a popular website that sells a large selection of the Sierra catalog and other old games, updated to work on modern computers.

"Playing these games helped me get comfortable with a PC at a very young age," Michael says. "I was a super young kid and was opening up towers adding memory, graphics cards and sound cards. I knew all through school that my future was in computers, and in 2003 I opened my own IT company which I still own and operate today."

Craig Harman

Craig Harman grew up in Perth, Western Australia, and as for many of us Aussies in the eighties, the only way to get copies of Sierra's games was either through the major computer retailer Tandy Electronics, from one of the handful of "mum and dad" computer stores scattered across the city you lived in (which, if you were lucky, had a couple of Sierra titles for sale), or by "borrowing" disks from friends and making your own personal backup. Just in case something happened to your friend's original disks, of course!

As Craig explains, his first Sierra memories were more along the lines of the latter than purchases from a computer store. "My first few Sierra games simply appeared in a large disk box next to our family computer as copies provided by family friends. The first time I flicked through the box and put in a disk labelled 'KQ1' I wasn't even sure what I was looking at. Being five or six, I recall just being happy walking the character round the screen – and didn't even realize you could type commands until much later! And so it was that *King's Quest* helped me to learn to read and type."

One anecdote that still gets brought up at family gatherings involved Craig playing that first *King's Quest* game. "I'd get up early in the mornings before anyone else was awake and start playing while everyone slept," he says, "although my dad had to stick a sock in the PC speaker so he didn't hear the familiar 'bleep bleep bloops.' But even then he wasn't safe. A family favorite story was me walking into their bedroom early one morning and saying, 'Dad, don't wake up, but how do you spell *scepter*?'"

It was through Sierra's adventure games that Craig met his best friend Khrob, the son of one of his father's co-workers who also loved Sierra games and was a similar age.

"I believe we first chatted over a phone call where I provided the sentence 'kill Dracula with stake' to help him complete *Kings Quest II*. For a while my dad would answer the phone 'Sierra hint line' due to the number of calls from friends coming to our house to chat about the latest Sierra game. Khrob and I soon arranged a meeting at his uncle's house, where we immediately started designing our first Sierra-style adventure game. We have been the closest of friends ever since.

"About five years later, we sent a two-page synopsis and game map of *Underwater Adventure* to Sierra while I was holidaying in the US with my family. (Our tour bus drove past the Sierra building but we didn't get to stop!) A few weeks after returning we got a polite reply, 'We don't accept outside game proposals.'"

Still, the pair were excited, even having been turned down. Not only had someone at Sierra actually seen their proposal but they'd taken the time to reply and "seemed to take the scribbled drawings of two eleven-year-old boys at least semiseriously."

Twenty-odd years later, this mutual interest in Sierra, and computer games in general, has led both men into careers in software development. "Although I was interested in computers before playing *King's Quest*, it was Sierra games that got me hooked. I started learning programming and wrote a short text adventure in BASIC," Craig says. "Khrob and I tinkered with various programming languages over the years with the goal of making a Sierra game. We both ended up studying computer science and becoming developers."

Khrob and Craig are still the best of friends, with Craig recalling that they still share Sierra-related inside jokes like "save early, save often" at every opportunity. At his recent fortieth birthday, Khrob surprised Craig with an adventure game he had written, chronicling their thirty-five-year friendship. A friendship that started with two boys' love for *King's Quest*.

Reverend Paul Miller

Paul Miller's journey with Sierra games has been an interesting one. While the first Sierra title he played was *King's Quest VI*, which came with the CD-ROM drive in his family's first PC in 1993, it was *Quest for Glory* that really cemented his love for the company's games.

"I had played casually and did speedrunning of the *Quest for Glory* series," Paul explains. (Speedrunning is an attempt to play a particular game in the fastest possible time.)

"It started during elementary school as a hobby on Saturday mornings. There is a glitch that allows a character [to be] exported from *Quest for Glory IV* and then imported back into the same game to play through it again with the same character. I started using it as a way to familiarize myself with the routes, and eventually it became a game: 'I wonder how long it would take to win if I did this . . .' This was long before the days of the modern internet, so speedrunning communities weren't a thing even for popular games. It continued through high school, but after graduating, I stopped.

"Shortly after becoming a father for the first time, and two months after we bought our first home, I was laid off suddenly from what everyone thought was a fairly stable job in investment banking. I was stuck at home for a while waiting while my resume went out everywhere. And with nothing but time, I went back to my old hobby. And I haven't stopped since!"

After being let go from his job Paul took a life-changing career turn, becoming an ordained Christian minister, and he gives part of the credit for this change of calling to the *Quest for Glory* series.

Paul explains, "The lore that Sierra games pulled from was important for me, but it was more being able to interact with that lore in a way other games at the time did not allow. To make a long story much shorter, Sierra games encouraged me to read and think.

"Sierra games are partly responsible for my becoming a pastor as an adult. Critical thinking, problem solving, abstraction, logical reasoning, perseverance – all were necessary to beat the game, and all have become important as a theologian. And the lore embedded into the *Quest for Glory* series was certainly a help to push me farther, as my focus has tended to be in ancient and medieval studies, as well as the cultural studies that surround those time periods."

Through the internet, Paul has been able to meet with other fans and speedrunners, contributing to an active community of like-minded people and posting videos of those speedruns for others to enjoy. "When I started posting videos, *Quest for Glory I* [the original EGA version] was a twenty-minute speedrun. It's now under two minutes . . . *Quest for Glory III* was a thirty-minute run. It's now under ten minutes, even if things go wrong. *Quest for Glory V* was over an hour long but through some intended abracadabra, it's under six minutes now!

The highlight of Paul's speedrunning happened during the RPG Limit Break 2016, a charity event in Salt Lake City that raised funds for the National Alliance on Mental Illness, where Paul livestreamed a speedrun of the entire *Quest for Glory* series.

"Corey and Lori Cole, the creators of the *Quest for Glory* series, were on the phone for commentary [on the video stream] during the run. Talk about a fanboy moment for me! Having permission to break a game in front of its creators is something I'll never forget. That was also my literal first time streaming ever; the fact that they trusted me on camera at all is amazing.

"Something that stuck with me was one of Lori's comments during the event. I said something to the effect of, 'Sorry, this might not be the way you intended people to play the game.' She said, 'We intended the games to be fun, no matter how you play them.'

"Sierra games are just fun, no matter how you play them. I've never looked at the games the same since."

Chris McGee

When he received *King's Quest III* as a gift as a child, Chris McGee was immediately hooked. Playing it was a memorable experience, but it was a difficult one for someone who was only ten years old. In particular, Chris recalls walking up and down the mountain to the evil wizard Manannan's house, causing his character to fall to his death many times over. Overcoming such obstacles was a challenge, but it was one that he thoroughly enjoyed. Even if he did have to buy the hint book, as he explains.

"Once I got to the tavern and shop, I got stuck and ordered a hint book. This was back when the hint books used a highlighter-type marker to make the answers visible. I later discovered that the text fades again over time; I still have some hint books that are all 'highlighted,' but you cannot read the answers anymore. I think this was the first time I used any sort of help to get me through a video game."

Although he can't say with certainty that the Sierra games he played in his youth helped him through any difficulties or rough patches, Chris does believe that they were important. "I can say that they were a big part of my youth and formative years. Thus, I look back on them with fondness and warm memories."

It's those memories that have stayed with him all these years. "I remember being thrilled when the next game would be released in a series and it supported 256-color VGA graphics. Oh, how stunning they were! I just had to wow my friends with those color-cycling moments in the beginning of *Space Quest IV* or the lovely scenery in *King's Quest V*," Chris says.

Once the games made the transition to CD-ROM with fully voiced characters, he was even more eager to show them to his friends. "I, at least, didn't care how awful the voice acting was in *King's Quest V*. Just the simple fact that I could hear real people's voices coming through my computer speakers was magical."

Chris shared his love of Sierra games with others, in particular one friend whom he recalls playing with. "I think I must have converted at least one of my friends to the love of PC games with my admiration of Sierra's titles, because whenever a new one was released, we would play it together. And by 'together,' I mean that I would play the game while he watched and attempted to help out by making suggestions. We'd have a great time, laughing at the 'urinal cakes' line in *Leisure Suit Larry* and playfully mocking the narrator's pronunciation of 'the foyer' from *The Adventures of Willy Beamish*."

That love of Sierra games carried through to their adult years. "Once we were old enough (or close to it), we would even make a drinking game out of our gaming sessions," Chris laughs. "Every time I saved the game, we'd take a drink. Yeah, there were some nights I don't remember playing beyond a certain point in a game!"

Chris's fondest memory of Sierra, though, is the music. "Listening to a *King's Quest* or *Space Quest* soundtrack is bound to put a smile on my face, even when I'm at work. To this day, I still find myself singing 'Girl in the Tower' while I'm in the shower or humming along to 'The Bandits' from *King's Quest V*. This is helped by the fact that I made it my mission to find the soundtracks to these beloved games some number of years ago. I listen to these on an almost daily basis to spark those childhood memories."

Shawn Jones

For Shawn Jones, "the main reason I wanted to contribute to this project is as a tribute to the memories and family bonds that formed around games and were forever bound with Sierra."

Shawn's parents separated when he was almost five and he remembers the good times of traveling around New England with his father and younger brother. Each year, once the boys were old enough, their father would take them to visit his "wayward bookish sister and her jokey, computer nerd husband" in New Jersey, a six-hour drive from their home in Massachusetts. Shawn looked forward to that trip every year, but "not just because I was happy to see family, though that was certainly part of it."

The added bonus was that Shawn's uncle was a computer engineer and had a state-of-the-art computer system. "He had those racks full of massive tapes for running different programs," Shawn remembers. "He also frequently picked up all manner and variety of computer games available at the time."

It was on these trips that Shawn gained his great love of Sierra's adventure games. The *Space Quest* series evokes particularly special memories for him. "As long as I can remember, I've been fascinated with space and science fiction. The hapless Roger Wilco really struck a chord with me because he's just a regular guy simply trying to get through his day – at least when we first meet him. Sometimes he tries to do the right thing (he has a heart) and sometimes he's just trying to save his own hide, and somehow [he] always [manages] to get mixed up in some fantastic adventure, fumbling the whole way through. Can't say I've ever saved a planet from peril, or stopped a universal threat, but I can at least really relate [to] the bumbling part. Roger really shows us that, despite appearances or lot in life, even a simple janitor can manage to do great things."

Those hours spent playing *Space Quest* or any of the other adventure games Shawn's uncle owned really created a unique bond between Shawn, his father and brother, and his uncle and aunt.

"Sierra games were paramount in establishing a family connection with our distanced relatives. We'd regularly all sit together in the room, huddled around the computer screen, helping each other solve the puzzles – or, in the days of typed commands, just trying every possible combination of whatever came to our heads," Shawn remembers.

"As happens, as time wore on, the distance grew between [us and] our aunt and uncle. Although we did reconnect now and then throughout the years, it never had the same feeling or impact – we rarely, if ever, played games together and spent more time reminiscing than indulging in the games that we loved growing up.

"Sadly, just this past decade, both Aunt Rosemarie and Uncle Ralph have passed away. I look back on those times together fondly, wishing we had reconnected one last time to embark on an old favorite or a new adventure. Nevertheless, these memories I will cherish forever and reflect upon thoughtfully, with reverence and love. Whenever I partake of the many games that grace the digital sphere, I'll be transported back to that room, with my family huddled around the glowing screen, enjoying a simple pleasure of life, together. Always."

Michael Martin

Growing up in Melbourne, Australia, Michael Martin's first memory of playing Sierra games was through family friends who lived nearby. Only six years old at the time, Michael was intrigued by a game they were playing, the original *King's Quest*.

"I was fascinated. I was able to move this person around the screen, and when I changed screens I would watch the computer draw and then colour in the newly drawn screen," he remembers. "I got quite excited when I saw a rock get drawn over this hole in the ground, and on each screen I would make suggestions about what to do like 'move rock,' 'climb tree,' or 'knock on door.'

"Whenever we were over at their house after that, I would ask to play 'that game.'"

Two years later, at the age of eight, Michael and his family moved to a small country town and school changed for him. Instead of hundreds of students, there were now only a handful. It was a tough time for him; he was the new "city kid" in a rural town where everybody knew each other. But soon after he moved, the school received some computers as part of an education campaign and on them was *King's Quest*.

"It was the first time I'd felt happy at that school," Michael remembers. "We would be given time to play *King's Quest* during lunchtime. The game would be discussed and there was excitement when someone worked out something new."

Right before he started high school a few years later, Michael's parents purchased their own IBM-compatible PC, an Amstrad PC1640, and for Christmas gave him the first three *King's Quest* games and soon after *King's Quest IV*. Again, it was Sierra games that helped Michael make friends at his new school.

"I met friends over discussions about computer games, especially the Sierra games. Just like when I was in that small country school, my friends and I would talk about our progress in these games. In high school I discovered the library of games Sierra had made and every year for Xmas, my family would endeavour to get more. Even into my late teens I was still looking at what Sierra were doing and I made sure I purchased *Phantasmagoria* before it was withdrawn from sale."[*]

In 2008, when Michael and one of those high school friends he had made over their mutual love of Sierra games traveled to the United States, they decided to make a special visit.

"We agreed that we had to go to Yosemite National Park. It was a pleasure seeing the Half Dome and discussing the memories we had about the Sierra games we played."

---

[*] *Phantasmagoria* was removed from stores in Australia due to censorship issues. The government at the time had no classification above MA15+ for games.

Alastair Mclellan

Most of the fans in this epilogue came to love Sierra games through their own experiences playing them during the eighties and nineties. Alastair Mclellan is different. He didn't discover Sierra games until after the company had stopped all internal development, but he started young. The first title he remembers playing was *King's Quest I*, at only five years old with the help of his mother.

"She was into all of the Sierra games back when she was in college and happened to keep them around, so I can thank/blame her for my appreciation of retro games," Alastair says.

"It was right around the time when I was starting to read, and I guess that she thought it would be a fun way to get me to learn. I remember making most of the decisions, but she probably helped me out a lot as well. Overall, we were able to get through the game pretty easily, but I was incredibly frustrated by trying to find the condor. I must have wandered over the map dozens of times before finally getting a quick glimpse of it and having a lightbulb moment," he laughs.

Alastair knows that his younger age is something that sets him apart from a lot of Sierra fans.

"Sierra adventure games were pretty much the only computer/video games that I played from [the] age of five to twelve. What I think is most interesting about my situation is that this was the early 2000s, and Sierra as we know it was basically dead at that point in time. I was just experiencing my mom's old games that she enjoyed as a young adult.

"On one hand, this was great because whenever I finished a game the sequel was probably already out there, waiting for me to continue the quest. On the other hand, there was a sort of persistent bleakness in knowing that these series that I was enjoying had already ended with no real hope of a future. The library of Sierra games that were at my fingertips was finite. That knowledge made the overall experience feel more like walking through a museum than consuming a piece of entertainment. A celebration of life, if you will."

Alastair's interests changed during his early teen years, but several years later his love of Sierra games was reinvigorated, thanks to two series he hadn't previously played.

"*Gabriel Knight* and *Quest for Glory* are both series I first experienced in my late teens, while I played through most of the other Sierra fare at a much younger age. I think that their greater emphasis on dialogue with branching trees compared to the simpler 'talk to person' of the Sierra games I was familiar with was what got me back into appreciating adventure games."

For those of us who found Sierra games when they were still new on the store shelves, it's great to know that younger people have been able to find and appreciate them as well.

Paul Marzagalli

Paul Marzagalli's career in game production was certainly influenced by Sierra, in particular the *Quest for Glory* series, although that wasn't the first name he mentions when asked what his influences are.

"The number one game that I cite as being the one that got me thinking about making games was the original *Bard's Tale*. One of the unique features of that series that I loved was the ability to port your heroes from the first game to the second to the third. The main reason I sought out the *Quest for Glory* series was because I learned that it featured that same element," Paul explains.

Growing up with a Commodore 64, Paul's only personal experience with Sierra had been *B.C.'s Quest for Tires* until a friend of his introduced him to *King's Quest I*.

"He hated the game because he was stuck. According to him, it was because the obvious solution wasn't working, and he had tried everything else. I had him show me where he was stuck. He typed in 'give rat egg' and, sure enough, it didn't work. I suggested that he try writing in 'give egg to rat,' which he begrudgingly did after I convinced him that it would make a difference. When it worked, he got angry at me instead of being relieved to be past the puzzle! Of course, please remember that we were eleven or twelve at this point," Paul laughs. "Sadly, there was no more playing *King's Quest* after that, at least not with him."

Sierra games did stay with Paul all throughout his school years, however.

"The first game that I ever finished in college was *Quest for Glory III*, just in time to pick up *Quest for Glory IV* when it came out a couple of months later. It was *Quest for Glory IV* and my general knowledge of vampires and horror in video games that got me involved in my first computer-based retail product, an interactive CD-ROM called *Dracula: Truth and Terror* that I worked on as a research assistant for a professor whose work was featured in it."

Paul has since worked on a number of games, but a definite highlight of his career so far was working on *The Bard's Tale* remasters with inXile Entertainment as a production coordinator.

His experience as both a consumer and a developer has helped him to see that adventure games are an important and unique part of the industry landscape.

"I hope adventure games stick around because there's nothing else like them in the gaming market. The gameplay is thoughtful and deliberate (despite all the times we scream at how arbitrary the logic of certain puzzles may be), and they let us think about situations and approach them in ways we might not normally, whether we're trying to be the best space janitor we can be or a cop trying to survive another day on the beat. There's such value to that kind of experience, and Sierra's games always delivered them.

"It kills me that the brand is currently languishing, because if my experience with our remastered *The Bard's Tale* trilogy taught me anything, [it's that] there's a dedicated market out there of gamers who want to revisit these games and a new generation of players who don't realize that this is the genre for them and just need the opportunity to discover it."

Stuart Feldhamer

"Some of the best times I've had in my life involved playing Sierra games and interacting with developers and other fans, and that still continues to this day," says Stuart Feldhamer, a lifelong gamer with a passion for collecting original boxed games. And it all started with his first glimpse of *King's Quest II*.

"A friend of mine had an IBM PC back when I was still using an Atari 800XL. He had a copy of *King's Quest II* and I was blown away by it. I used to try to make excuses to go to his house just so I could play the game. It didn't really work, though, because when he found out that's why I was there, he got angry," Stuart remembers.

It wasn't until he was in high school, several years later, that Stuart got two Sierra games for himself, 'copies' of *Police Quest 1* and *Space Quest II* from a friend at school. "I had no idea that there were so many of the animated *Quest* games out there! I had such a great time with both games that I begged my dad to take me to Electronics Boutique and buy me *Space Quest III*, which he did! Then I started buying the others whenever I could, and I never stopped!

"Back in the day I wrote a fan letter to Sierra, and asked for autographed photos of Ken and Roberta Williams, Jim Walls, Al Lowe, and the Two Guys from Andromeda. Much to my surprise, they actually sent me something in the mail. They were about the size and thickness of old baseball cards with press photos of those individuals, and what appeared to be preprinted signatures. I cherished those, but somehow they got lost over the years. I wish I still had them! I've never met anyone else who had anything like this."

In addition to playing and loving Sierra's adventure games in his younger years, Stuart created some of his best memories through the fan community. One of his first fan experiences was with Tierra Entertainment (the group that later renamed themselves AGDI) upon the release of their *King's Quest I VGA* remake.

"I wrote to them asking why they were not planning to include voice acting in the game. They responded that it would be difficult to find an actor who would not be divisive and whom people would accept as Graham. I asked, 'Why not ask Josh Mandel, who was the original voice of Graham in *King's Quest V*?' They thought that might be a good idea but didn't have a connection with Josh, so I made the introduction."

Josh ended up voicing King Graham in all three of AGDI's *King's Quest* remakes.

Stuart's love of Sierra has been a constant in his life, punctuated in 2019 when he had the opportunity to meet some of his heroes in person: Al Lowe, Josh Mandel, and Corey and Lori Cole.

"I even got Al and Josh to sign my *Leisure Suit Larry Reloaded* Kickstarter backer T-shirt, and Corey and Lori to sign a vintage *Quest for Glory* T-shirt," says Stuart.

"It's great to be part of a wonderful fan community, and to have the opportunity to interact with amazing game designers who are as humble as they are talented."

John-Thomas Foster

John-Thomas Foster and his mother have a close relationship. Over the course of his life, the two have set aside time to play Sierra games together, from the earliest *King's Quest* and *Space Quest* adventures to The Odd Gentlemen's recent *King's Quest* episodes.

"My first experience with Sierra games was playing through them with my mom, Meredith Foster," John-Thomas says. "My very first memories in life were going to local computer clubs with my mom when

I was three to five years old. Now, I am not saying that we pirated games back then at these clubs, but there were some ziplock bag games and that is how games were given out back then. There were a ton of games between Atari and IBM compatibles. It was a super fun time and I understood, oh, maybe 5% of what was going on, but my mom was there to make sure everything worked.

"So, the first memories I have with Sierra games are a mixture of *Donald Duck's Playground, Black Cauldron, Mixed-Up Mother Goose, King's Quest I, and Space Quest I*. I am pretty sure that I played through *The Black Cauldron* more than I ever watched the movie! I also learned my nursery rhymes through *Mixed-Up Mother Goose* and not through storybooks."

John-Thomas credits his love of reading to those early years playing Sierra games with his mother, and believes the games are partly responsible for inspiring him to pursue a career in law. After all, he says that most of what his job entails is "telling stories with an eclectic set of facts in a way that is easy to understand. Being able to move ideas around on the fly and to combine different ideas and facts together makes each case like its own little adventure game. Sierra taught me there is always a solution to any puzzle, if you just have the patience to see it."

For John-Thomas, "The Sierra *Quest* games will always hold a special place in my heart, because to me they were my childhood. I will never forget playing them with my mom. Spending hours moving through the vine maze in *Space Quest II*, hunting down the items of the dwarfs in *King's Quest VI*, ducking Sequel Police in the mall in *Space Quest IV*, meeting the Two Guys in *Space Quest III*, saving King Graham in *King's Quest IV*, dying in *Police Quest 1* for failing to follow police procedure, and even meeting Cedric were all amazing memories.

"When the narrator pointed out we were now in *Space Quest XII* [that] was the first time I ever really understood what was possible in fiction, how the creator can play with the audience, and how amazing it is when you are in on the joke. Even more exciting was that my mom saw that these were teaching tools and it really was one of the best ways to learn about life. How to overcome adversity, how to do the right thing, and when all else fails, look at the hint book!

"King Graham and Roger Wilco will always be a part of the family. No matter what happens in life, I can fire up any *Space Quest* or *King's Quest* game and immediately I am six again, playing through them with my mom."

Jeremy Hedges

Although he currently lives in Ottawa, Canada, Jeremy Hedges moved around a lot when he was young. His father was initially in the Navy, where he would often be reassigned to a new town, and later was forced to move for new job opportunities. During his formative years, Jeremy saw a lot of the United States, including Connecticut, Washington, Virginia, Tennessee, Ohio, and Pennsylvania, but there were a few constants in his life, both as a child and as a teenager.

"Computer games, and in particular Sierra games, were a consistent source of familiarity when I was growing up and moving to new places every few years," Jeremy remembers. "The characters in those games were my friends as a kid. It took months if not years to complete some of the games, especially when I was young and still learning the language required for the early parser games, so from one location to the next, books, movies, and games were the things that were always there.

"Many of my memories from growing up revolve around those games: learning to think critically and solve often convoluted puzzles; becoming engrossed in the stories and characters and details of the worlds; extending the worlds with my own imagination in writing my own episodes of those adventures while waiting for the next official chapter."

One unique experience for Jeremy occurred when he was ten, when he wrote two letters to Sierra, one to Scott Murphy and one to Roberta Williams, expressing his joy at the games they had created. He posted the letters only to discover that some neighborhood kids had taken the one addressed to Scott and ripped it up. Fortunately, the letter addressed to Roberta was sent and he quickly received a reply from Ken and Roberta's personal assistant.

"I received a letter on official Sierra letterhead a few weeks later from Kristy Welton, who worked for Ken and Roberta," Jeremy recalls. "Thus started a years-long correspondence between us. We talked about Sierra, but also about what was going on in our lives, the books we were reading, etc. She was sometimes able to send me hard-to-find goodies like the Roger Wilco comic book, the newest edition of *InterAction* magazine, and even autographed photos from Ken and Roberta! I looked forward to her response on that letterhead in the weeks following each of my letters. It was such a special connection to have with someone at the actual company, and it added this very personal touch to the magic of the Sierra experience."

As for the games themselves, Jeremy says he "can't really explain why they left such an impression on me. Perhaps because it was like a book or movie that I got to be a part of rather than just an observer. Like a lot of others who grew up with these games, I wanted to be a game designer like Roberta Williams or the Coles or the Two Guys. It didn't work out that way, but those games gave me a passion for critical thinking and solving puzzles that still exists today, for great storytelling and characters which led to a degree in English literature, and for interaction and experience design that is part of my career in user experience today.

"I can't say enough how much those games meant to me, but it was that added layer of the personal, the kindness, the thoughtfulness that speaks to how special Sierra was for fans like myself who grew up living in the worlds they shared with us."

Brad Herbert[*]

"Look in stump," "Get pouch," "Open pouch." "You open the pouch and discover many sparkling diamonds." That was it. I was hooked. *King's Quest* will be forever etched in my memory at age six, as will the company that created it.

Sierra quietly influenced my childhood, and my career. I keep peeling back layers of this proverbial onion to discover so many facets it touched.

Sierra challenged me. My grandfather also showed his young grandson how to program in the BASIC language on the same computer that ran *King's Quest*. How could I write code that made bright colorful characters walk across the screen smoothly, and with no flickering? My young programming mind couldn't figure it out to the same level, but it made me dig deeper into the language, the hardware, the creative theories on how to be more efficient with code, and think beyond standard ways of doing things.

Sierra inspired me. Four times a year I would get a quarterly newsletter from Sierra in the mail, and inside were articles and stories of all the designers, programmers, musicians, and business folks that worked hard and created entertainment out of essentially nothing but their own minds.

---

[*] I loved the way Brad put this together, showcasing how Sierra has affected his life in different ways, so I decided just to reprint what he sent me.

Sierra taught me how to solve problems. The very nature of a large portion of their games was to fix things, and to figure out how to solve a difficult situation. The skill to step back, calmly assess the moment, to map out the risks/rewards of any task, and how to extend an olive branch in hopes of creating an outcome that works for everyone is a trait that will be ingrained in me forever.

Sierra made me witty. I've had the privilege to talk with many Sierra employees over the years. One night I was chatting with Josh Mandel – he and I were crafting some incredible puns and poking fun at one another and the reality of the situation slapped me up the side of the head. I felt embarrassed that I hadn't realized until twenty years later that the writing in many of the games was laced with puns, humor, and sarcasm. Why did it take so long to realize that my dry sense of humor was heavily shaped by Sierra as well?

Sierra made me a better artist. The computer is a stage – camera angles, composition, music, movement, lighting, dialogue, special effects – they all come together to create emotion for the viewer. For over the last twenty years I have worked in the video production world, creating moments and emotions for my viewers. No doubt, the talent under the roof of Sierra was a monumental influence on how to not only create those individual components, but how to layer and time them for maximum impact.

Sierra made me a better person. From some of their earliest days in Oakhurst as they took on new team members, I watched them grow, and expand, and work together. I watched how they loved their own employees as much as they loved their customers. While hundreds of miles apart, they had this way about them where they could reach out and connect with you, pull you into their circle, and make you feel special – you did feel like part of their family. Now, of course every family has its struggles and is in no way perfect, but their underlying character and love could be felt by almost everyone that played and worked on their games. I hope that people I meet today feel that same love and warmth that Sierra afforded me.

Even to this day, I am still feeling the Sierra love as I work on my own tribute projects to this company. My journeys have taken me across the United States visiting in person with much of the Sierra family, and they have shown not only to me, but to my wife and kids who travelled there as well, the true character and kind hearts they possessed then and now.

Sierra was at the crossroads of a very important part of our human history. They brought to the surface many ideas and innovations that are still extremely relevant today. One might argue that there were lots of companies and people doing the same thing at that time, and it was bound to happen anyway. While on the surface that might be true to a degree, what isn't accounted for is the way they did it – the way they made a connection with people, the way they set an example both on and off the court.

Those secondary interactions, and the positive influence they had on myself and countless others, might just exceed the impact they had on the gaming world. I might argue that this influence by those that gave their blood, sweat and tears for Sierra On-Line is truly the greater accomplishment, as its reach went far beyond the keyboard.

To everyone that created such fantastic memories, taught me how to observe everything, and to pick up that which is not nailed down, I want to thank you for contributing to the person I am today.

Konstantin Grusha

Konstantin Grusha was born in 1983 in the large industrial city of Rostov-on-Don. Before the dissolution of the Soviet Union at the end of 1991, personal computers were mainly confined to schools and the corporate and government sectors. While some private citizens owned computers, the cost was out of reach for most people, who instead turned to building their own.

"Having a computer at home in the eighties was prohibitively expensive, if next to impossible," Konstantin says.

"There was demand, though, so a number of hobbyist designs were published, and many people started making their own computers. My father was a computer and electronics engineer in the eighties, and he built our first computer back in 1989. That one was an 8080-based original design, but ZX Spectrums were also quite popular and he built that one, too."

As was common in former Soviet states, copyright laws were lax and most people got their games through piracy.

"Most of the games at the time were either original designs, or unofficial adaptations/ports of the games that people had seen elsewhere. Then of course more and more pirated games started to appear, as the borders started to open up. The games would often be distributed on tape or sometimes as a hex code listing, usually free of charge or for a symbolic price. Nobody really knew about and definitely didn't care for copyright laws at the time. When the PC era began for us in the early nineties, we swapped games on floppies all the time! It was only in the late 1990s, early 2000s that the tide started to change," Konstantin remembers.

In early 1993, Konstantin's family got their first IBM-compatible computer and a friend soon gave him a copy of *Space Quest I*, translated into his native Russian. He was captivated by the game and when he completed it he went in search of similar games. In junior high, Konstantin found such games through some older friends he met in his computer lab.

"It turned out they were big fans of Sierra games and had *lots* of them. I really wanted to play all the games, and they gladly made copies for me, but every single game was in English. This made me go out there and buy two dictionaries, and then spend countless hours playing *Space Quest II* and *III*, painstakingly translating the story, one word at a time."

These same school friends had managed to successfully reverse engineer Sierra's SCI engine, and by then had translated the *Leisure Suit Larry 1* VGA remake into Russian, and were working hard at translating *Space Quest IV* while also working on *Space Quest V*.

"They called themselves Taralej & JaboCrack SoftWare. In May 1994, they gave me my very own copy of the freshly translated *Space Quest V* for my birthday, and I was extremely happy! I was hanging around for about two more years with these guys. We played lots of games, shared stories and experiences, and I am forever grateful to them for being kind to a random kid who just loved great stories in the form of video games," Konstantin says.

Meeting these friends who localized his favorite games into Russian caused Konstantin to change the course of his studies.

"Before I met the Taralej & JaboCrack guys, I was 100% sure that when I finished school I would go on to get my degree in maths and computer science," he recalls.

"Then I saw what they did, how they were able to take a story written on the other side of the planet, for people with a very different cultural background, and bring it to our side – masterfully and with great love and care. I remember being lectured on how *Space Quest V* parodied *Star Trek* among other things, which was completely unknown to us at the time. The guys learned about it from reading FAQs and email exchanges with overseas students.

"I still had to work hard on my English to be able to play all the other games, and I put in an immense amount of work and dedication, especially for a seventh grader. So instead of going to study computer science, I went on to study English language and literature, and even worked as a translator for a couple of years, all because back in 1994 I just wanted to be able to play great games in a language I didn't understand then!

"Playing Sierra games was a turning point for everything meaningful in my life!"

PushingUpRoses[*]

My very first experience with Sierra, and with computers in general, was playing *King's Quest III* with my aunt. I was at her house one night, and she had just gotten a new Tandy 1000 from RadioShack. I remember her being fascinated by the machine; she had gotten all of these programs for it including an address book, which took up a LOT of space on the computer, DeskMate [the Tandy operating system], and a couple games. I distinctly remember the 3.5-inch floppy disks, which were blue and had a white sticker with the *King's Quest III* logo on it. My aunt booted it up and I was amazed. She started controlling the main character with the arrow keys and I couldn't believe what I was seeing. Then she did something astounding; she typed "take cup" when we came across a dining room table with a silver mug on it. And the character took it. He took the cup. I saw my score turn from 0 to 1 and felt this incredible thrill.

Even though I was only four or five years old, I would spend hours trying to figure out this game. I would reread the manual; I would make my OWN handwritten list of inventory items I had found. Years later, when I had my own computer in my room, I found the key to a cabinet that held a magic wand, and I was so excited to finally progress that I hopped up, ran to my dad and exclaimed, "I FOUND THE KEY, I MIGHT BEAT THIS GAME NOW."

King's Quest III was not only my introduction to computer games, but also my introduction to fantasy and adventure. Unlike my nerdy friends who gravitated towards Tolkien and the King Arthur stories for their fantasy-related needs, I felt drawn to fairy tales, and *King's Quest* always had those elements in their games. I felt intrigued by the many fictional characters: the evil wizard Manannan, King Graham, the wizard

---

[*] I'm a huge fan of PushingUpRoses. As one of her quarter million followers on YouTube, I've watched many, *many* hours of her playing through the Sierra games that we both love. It was suggested that I contact her about sharing her experiences for this epilogue; I loved the idea and reached out. I've decided to publish what she sent me verbatim, because it's awesome and there is nothing that needs to be changed.

Mordack, even Cedric the Owl. Over the years as I discovered and played through the entire *King's Quest* series, I got more and more into adventure games.

My aunt also had *Space Quest* for her Tandy, and I enjoyed playing that one as well. I knew that the games had to be related somehow, due to the similar mechanic and aesthetic, but I was so young I didn't even understand that there were more just like it.

One Christmas, my aunt got me my own computer with Sound Blaster. It came with a bundle of applications, things like Compton's Encyclopedia and *DOOM*. One of the CDs had that logo on it, that logo I had noticed on the *King's Quest III* floppy disk when I was young. This one was *King's Quest V*, and I was over the moon to have another title from the same series. The game had a profound effect on me because it was a talkie, and the old parser command had been replaced with an easier to use point-and-click interface. I was in love. I had never played anything like it.

Over the next few Christmases, I kept asking for the *King's Quest* and *Space Quest* collections, which my family lovingly bought me. I played *King's Quest VI* early into the mornings, and was also introduced to a few games I hadn't heard of: *The Colonel's Bequest* and *The Dagger of Amon Ra*.

While a friend and I were hanging out at my house one day, I decided to boot up *The Colonel's Bequest*. We were both around twelve years old, which isn't *too* young, and yet we were both pathetically frightened of this damned game. I had never played a murder mystery game before and was *so lost* by the mechanic. When we finally beat the game, which we spent *all* night doing, we got the lowest rating possible because we were too scared to explore. And don't even get me started on *Dagger*; that game presented itself as a cheeky, wacky adventure game with a bright art style and a bubbly protagonist. I didn't realize it would have such grisly murders, so when I came upon one in-game, I freaked out, shut down the game, and didn't revisit it until years later. Both of these games are now in my top favorite titles of all time.

While I was in junior high, my dad got very sick, and was eventually diagnosed with cancer. We did what we could, but eventually we couldn't do anything more for him, and I had to come to terms with the fact that he would pass. To distract myself during this time, I played *Space Quest VI*. I remember my time with the game in a visceral way; I can even recall the exact setup of my room. I would play during the night with my lights off, because I had a beautiful blue and purple lava lamp that I enjoyed having on while I was at my computer. Sometimes I would play the Cars' *Greatest Hits* [album] while I aimlessly wandered around Polysorbate 60 as the bumbling protagonist, Roger Wilco. I remember being sad, thinking about what I was about to face, but having that routine gave me comfort. Playing by the light of the lava lamp, listening to the Cars, and wondering how the fuck I am going to get that crazy [homing] beacon device in the game working helped me in some bizarre way.

After my dad passed, things got difficult. I fell into a heavy depression. During this time I was desperate for anything to distract me, and that's when I started discovering games outside of the *King's Quest*, *Space Quest*, and *Laura Bow* franchises. Enter *Gabriel Knight: Sins of the Fathers*.

This was a game I couldn't put down; up until this point I hadn't played anything that could be categorized as a thriller, so this was new territory for me. I didn't know that adventure games could have such detailed, dark story lines and it really opened me up to games that were more plot-oriented, versus the more adventuresome ones I was used to. Not only that, but I also realized that video game plots could be serious; they didn't always have to be whimsical, or have bumbling, corny protagonists. They could be eloquent and well performed.

As technology advanced, I found I was unable to play some of these games on my newer, more powerful computers. There was a long spell where I had forgotten all about them; emulation wasn't as known as it is now, and I had gotten busy with college and trying to find a career, etc. It wasn't until around 2008 when my boyfriend made a GOG account for me, filled with adventure games. That spark was back; I could not WAIT to revisit my favorite games.

Then I found a community on YouTube doing retro game reviews, and I felt that I had so much love for them that I could create videos that showed my appreciation. I wanted them to be introspective, funny, and critical where necessary. Since 2010, I've made hundreds of videos about adventure games, with a huge chunk of them being Sierra. I never thought in a million years that these games would come back to me and I'd make something I'm truly proud of with them.

I think Sierra games have that way of sticking with you, especially if you discovered them in childhood. They feel magical. I have such fond memories of discovering and playing these games, and now I feel fortunate as heck to be able to talk about them on YouTube and encourage other people to give them a go. Sierra has always been a big part of my life and it continues to be. I will always, always have a great fondness for them, and I will even defend some of the ridiculous puzzle design, because so many of those titles were innovative with their technology. They deserve to be remembered, and I know that many indie developers take inspiration from some of the things Sierra accomplished over the years.

And you will be happy to know that I got over my fear of *The Dagger of Amon Ra* and have played it about fifty times in the last few years.

Hell yeah.

Acknowledgments

Thanks to all the hundreds, if not thousands, of people who worked at Sierra and created the games that I continue to love. Of those, I especially want to thank the dozens of people who agreed to be interviewed for this book. Whether I've quoted you directly or not, I can't express enough how amazing you've been. Simply put, without your help this book wouldn't have happened.

One person who deserves a special mention is Josh Mandel – not only for being the first person I interviewed, and not just for the brilliant foreword he wrote and the videos he recorded for the Kickstarter campaign, but for being a friend and willing to answer my random emails that usually started with, "Hey Josh, do you know how to get in contact with [insert any number of former Sierra employees here]?" And most especially for making *Freddy Pharkas* and *Callahan's Crosstime Saloon*, the latter making me yet another fan of Spider Robinson's amazing books.

To the Kickstarter backers, all of you are amazing. Thanks! Each and every one of you contributed to the book you are now holding, from the higher-tier backers who got their own Sierra stories recorded, to all those who chipped in even a few dollars with no reward, just to help out. From the bottom of my heart, it humbles me and brings me great joy to have finished this book and to see it in print, and that is completely because of you.

To Jack Allin for editing the manuscript. Your expertise has made my words shine. You managed to get the bits that I wrote in the middle of the night to make sense! I got to the point where I couldn't see the forest for the trees, so your perspective was magnificent. A big thanks also to Emily Morganti for her editing support, particularly in looking at the big picture and making sure the whole thing flowed, as well as her extensive knowledge of Sierra that caught a number of things I'd missed.

A special mention also to Josh Henry and Stephen Emond who helped me by letting me know about a number of missing games (those late-90's Hoyle releases are numerous and hard to track down!) as well as correcting a few of the details in the game appendix. Thanks also to everyone else who picked up the occasional mistake throughout the text – happily nothing major but they're all certainly worth correcting.

I'd be remiss not to mention my most excellent friend Steven Alexander, my co-founder at Infamous Quests. We might have grown up on different sides of the planet, but our shared love of Sierra games (and the fact that we're both amazing people) makes us a great team and great friends! We made *Quest for Infamy* (shameless self-promotion: if you don't have this game, you really should get it) because we both love *Hero's Quest* and we had some dumb conversations way too many years ago about how cool it would be to be a bad guy in that game. Over a decade and a half later, I still enjoy our random and daily conversations.

To my boys, Oliver, Alexander and Ezekiel, you three are the most important people in my life and I love you more and more each day as I see you all growing into amazing and unique young men. Ollie, you're my favorite. Bear Bear, you're my favorite. Zeke, you're my favorite. Don't tell your brothers.

Finally, and most importantly, to my wonderful, beautiful, and loving wife Lisa. You are incredible. You encourage me when I'm down. You kick my ass when I need it. You love me unconditionally. You help me grow as a person, as a Christian, as a husband, and as a father to our three sensational little men. I'm so glad I went to the pub that night. Without you, I wouldn't have written this book and I wouldn't be anywhere near as happy as I am today.

Shawn
May 2020 / December 2020

Kickstarter Backers

A Delvecchio
Aaron Tuller
Adam J Luptak
Adam Niedzwiedz
Adam Perfrement
Adam Postalian
AdventureGamer
Ahmed Riaz
Al Lowe
Alan Danzis
Alan Ralph
Alastair Mclellan
Alek Rzeszowski
Alex Kain
Alexander Peterhans
Alexander Polson
Alexander Schaubeck
Alexander Schultz
Alexander Wörndle
Alexandra Guyker
Alfred Guell
Alisha Gleeson
Alp Torun
Amar Sabeta
Amy Tant
Anatoly Shashkin
Anders Svensson
Andrea Brin
Andreas Adolf
Andreas Wiklund
Andrew Barton
Andrew Hubbard
Andrew J Dowden
Andrew McCarthy
Andrew Nicolle
Andrew Roach
Ano
Anthony Innaurato
Anthony Micari
Anthony Miller
Anthony Nicholson
Anthony Ryan Peterlin
Antonio Larrosa Jiménez
Arthur B
Axel Kothe
Bagofrats

Baldur Brueckner
Balog Gergely
Bård
Ben Galbraith
Benjamin Herzog
Benjamin Ragheb
Bertrand Fan
Bevan
Bil Kanawati
Bill Capella
Blake Wright
Bob Michiels
Bobby Dennett
Bolko Rawicz
Brad Herbert
Brandi Guidroz
Brandon "Link" Copp-Millward
Brandon Vidler
Brenda Romero
Brett Silk
Brian Cheng
Brian Cole
Brian Connors
Brian Dobberpuhl
Brian Hubel
Brian Robinson
Brock Wilbur
Browncoat Jayson
Bruce Brenneise
Bruce Walters
Bruno Copes
Bruno Fonseca
Byron
Caleb Parnell Lampen
Carey Martell
Carl Brich
Carlo Artieri
Carlos Duarte Do Nascimento
Casey Nordell
Cédric Leburton
Chad Armstrong
Chance Davis
Charles Irwin
Chelle Destefano

Cho Ki-Hyun
Chris Cuddy
Chris McGee
Chris Vandergrift
Chris Warren
Christiaan
Christian Harms
Christian Hudon
Christian Schmidt
Christina
Christine Clarkson
Christoph Licht
Christoph Reichenbach
Christopher Brendel
Christopher Galbreath
Christopher Lefevre
Christopher Munoz
Christopher Olewicz
Claes Argårds
Claire Dore
Clinton Smith
Cody Konior
Colin Mountfort
Corey Nash
Corinna Vigier
Cornelius Hardenbergh
Cowan Young
Craig Evans
Craig Harman
Craig Hulett
Craig Lemas
Craig Ritchie
Cris "Kurdt" Skelton
Crom
Cranberry
Curtis Myers
Cyrus Nemati
D. Russom
D.K. Rehn
Dan Peled
Dan Sutherland
Daniel Fernandez
Daniel Osers
Daniel Q. Van Wagenen
Daniel Ravipinto
Daniel S

Daniel Wolf
Dave Oshry
Dave Petrie
Dave Ross
David Bitton
David Guiot
David Ng
David Peake
David Richier
David Youd
Davie C. Fraga
Dean Thrasher
Dennis Spreen
Dennis Tollaksen
Derek Warren
Devon Brent
Domenico De Re
Dominik Reichardt
Don White
Donald Parsons
Douglas Baxter
Edward Hobbs
Edward J Schmidt
Edwin Keur
Edwyn Y Tiong
Elvin Liow
Emilie Roberts
Emily Morganti
Emma Rollinson
Emrecan Ozen
Eric Francois
Eric H Krieger
Eric Jensen
Eric Lin
Eric Pomerleau
Eric Starker
Eric Sten
Eric Wilkinson
Erico Mendonca
Ernst Krogtoft
Espen Terjesen
Evan Dickens
Fabrizio Pedrazzini
Faehnrich
Falko Loeffler
Federico Elli
Foone Turing
Francois Vander Linden
Fred Chagnon

Fredrik Liljeblad
FT
Gabe Schnerch
Gábor Tóth
Gabriel Sanmartín Diaz
Gaetan Cyr
Gareth Coster
Gareth Paterson
Gary Einstein
Gary Graybill
Gavin Greene
Gideon Hornung
Giovanni Stanta
Goatmeal
Gordon
Grady Haynes
Graham Laverty
Grant Wagner
Guillermo Useros Herrero
Gustavo Meza De Lama
Gwen Swierczek
Harald Eide-Fredriksen
Heath Phillips
Henrik Eriksson
Herman Choi
Hope Kodman
Herron Family
Hunter Scallion
Hylke Witjens
Ian Camaclang
Ian Cogill
Ichiro Ota
Ido Gordin
Ido Wodnizki
Iker Del Campo
Ingix
Ivo Teel
Jaap Jansen
Jackson Ng
Jadira Wolff
Jake Weisfeld
James Holmes
James Latzer
James Matuszak
James Wakelin
James Wang
Jameson Boyce
Jan E Hanssen
Jan Modrák

Jan-Hendrik Willms
Jani Hartikainen
Janne Virkkula
Jared
Jarek
Jari Avelin
Jarno Koskinen
Jarno Mielikäinen
Jason Broadley
Jason Chau
Jason Crase
Jason Goodier
Jason Hartwig
Jason Luke
Jason Nicholas Mical
Jason Penney
Jason Scarlett
Javier Fernández-Sanguino
Jeff Hillary
Jeff Ward
Jeff Witt
Jeffrey A Kline
Jennifer
Jennifer L.
Jenny Rouse
Jeremiah Nellis
Jeremy
Jeremy Blum
Jeremy Douglass
Jeremy LaMont
Jesper Hammarbäck
Jess Haskins
Jess Lai
Jessica Blank
Jim Ferguson
Jim Monteau
Joanie Rich
Joanna MacCarthy
Joaovargas
Jochen Fosselmann
Joe
Joe A Roth
Joe Mastroianni
Joe Sousa
Joel Mayer
Johan Driessen
John Caruthers
John Durnall
John Hanold

John Hnatowych
John Taylor
Johnny Angelo da Silva Vila
Jon & Beth Breisnes
Jon Magnus Stavik Vold
Jon Piornack
Jonas Jacobsson
Jonas Stjernström
Jonathan Casper
Jonathan Duffer
Jonathan M Davis
Jonathan Mulcahy
Jonny Karlsson
Joonas Linkola
Joost Peters
Jørgen Karlsen
Jørn Inge Frostad
Jose Couto
Joseph Moore
Josh Duff
Josh Lauber
Josh Mandel
Josh Markiewicz
Joshua Henry
Joshua Sutter
Joshua Van Ess
Jouko Mikkolainen
Jouni Heinonen
JT Foster
Juan Alcover
Jude Gore
Judy McMullan
Juha Sorva
Justin Archey
Justin Swart
Kai Engelbrecht
Karl Mok
Katie Hallahan
Katherine S
Keith Mercik
Keith Mogensen
Kelsey R. Marquart
Ken Burwood
Ken Gagne
Kenny Ketner
Kevin Clark
Kevin Foss
Kevin Griffin

Kevin Hanley
Kevin Ng
Kevin Savetz
Kimberlee Stiens
Kimmo Hassinen
Király Botond
Kisai
Klaus Foerster
Koen Heltzel
Konstantin Grusha
Kristopher Kwilas
Kyle Mack
Laurence Tailby
Lawrence Makin
Lee Hickin
Leif Romme Thomsen
Leon Schuurbiers
Les Waters
Liana Kerzner
Liegeois Alexandre
Liz Calkins
Lorenzo Perugini
Lucas Bloss
Lucas Mills
Lucian Lam
Luis Carrasco
Luis Gustavo de Moura Brasil
Luiz Rocha
Luke Jensen
Luke Rideout
M van der Ploeg
M van Schendelen
Mads Rasmussen
Magne Dyrnes
Marc Noel
Marco Sowa-Israel
Marek Kastelovic
Mariano Cribani
Marijn Hubert
Marina Müller
Maris Gabalins
Mark Goninon
Mark Newheiser
Mark Sztainbok
Marko Pilkkakangas
Markus Leptien
Martin Beijer
Martin Erhardsen

Martin Metzler
Martin Ottowitz
Mathias Albertsson
Mathias Luzius
Matt Andrysiak
Matt Flinton
Matt Hargett
Matt Heffernan
Matt Katinas
Matthew Beckham
Matthew Kerr
Matthew Montgomery
Matthew Resnick
Matthew Taylor
Matthew Taylor
Matthew Wee
Matthias Lamm
Matthias Mormino
Maus Merryjest AGL589
Max Sprauer
Mehron Kugler
Melissa Stenson
Michael
Michael Bailey
Michael Bates
Michael Bishop
Michael Crawford
Michael Della Pia
Michael Feldstein
Michael Gorton
Michael Hartmann
Michael Klamerus
Michael Martin
Michael Sharpe
Michael Street
Michal Nowakowski
Michelle Sorge
Michiel Graat
Michiel Willems
Mike B.
Mike Clark
Mike Wright
Mitch Johnson
Nabeel M. Al-Haider
Neil Matz
Nicholas A Chaimov
Nicholas Bryan
Nicholas Dahlman
Nicholas Reynolds

Nick Cottini
Nick Driver
Nick Sfakis
Nick Walton
Nikola Kotarov
Nina Shanafelt
Niv Steingarten
Norti
Nostalgia_Chaser
Nurot
Occam Aldanis
Oh Young Wook
Olivier Debonne
Pablo Mompart
Pabter
Panagiotis Pileidis
Panayotis Pantazis
Paolo Marco Bertoldi
PaoloSpaziosi
Pascal Vanhoecke
Pascal Welsing
Patrick Becher
Patrick Johnston
Paul Edwards
Paul Glinker
Paul Kautz
Paul Korman
Paul R. Miller (Rev.)
Paul Marzagalli
Paul Southerington
Paul Thomas
Paul Wilson
Paula Bruce
Paweł Krakowiak
Peter
Peter Krogtoft
Peter Liesenfeld
Petter Holmberg
Phil Waalkes
Phil White
Philipp Hamerski
Phillip Suttkus
PickledDog
Pieter
Pjotter Tommassen
Rainer Poser
Randy Pratt
Raoult Noel
Ravi Shah

Ray Schmidt
Richard Campbell
Richard Cobbett
Richard Houle
Richard Libera
Richard Moss
Richard Pickles
Richard Wade
Rick Budd
Rick Reynolds
Ricky Derocher
Riku Iso-Markku
Ritchie Le
Rob de Snoo
Rob Niederhoff
Rob Rooney
Robert Cox
Robert Kety
Robert Masterson
Roberta Vaughan
Robin Ward
Rodney Lelah
Roger Noguera Arnau
Rolf Scheimann
Ronnie Dark
Ross
Ross Specter
Ross Verschelden
Roy Martin Kristiansen
Roy Wagner
RoyBY
Rud B Sorensen
Rudy Marchant
Russell Hasenauer
Ryan Barnard
Ryan Jackson
Ryan Lynch
Ryan Middleton
Ryan P Buckland
Ryan Palmer
Ryan Rawson
Sam Gaus
Samuel Lucas
Sarah Conte
Sarah Kelley
Sarina Benn
Scheucher Nikolaus
Scott Duensing
Sean Beck

Sean Fredrick
Sean Kindley
Sean Sicher
Sean Teegardin
Sebastian Eriksson
Serena Nelson
Sergio
Seth A Robinson
Seth Marinello
Shamus Kelley
Sharad Cornejo Altuzar
Shaun Harvey
Shawn Jones
Shay Canfield
Shayne Lebrun
Siddhartha Barnhoorn
Simon Mok
Simplex
Slug
Snabbott
Stefan Schneider
Steffen Baier
Stéphane Lapie
Stephanie Stevens
Stephen Couch
Stephen Hammack
Stephen Walker
Steve Duane
Steve Lefebvre
Steven Pedrosa
Steven Que
Steven Vincent Savage
Stuart Butterly
Stuart Feldhamer
Stuart Lofthouse
Subq
Suzene   M   Campos
    del Toro
Sven Camrath
Sven Oesterle
Sven A Schäfer
Sylvain Rousseau
Szymon Łajszczak
Tania Liebowitz
Ted Kremenek
Teemu
Terrence Crossley
Terry Roehrig II
ThePhantom

Thomas Damgaard
Thomas Domdey
Thomas Hansen
Thomas Koehre
Thomas Williams
Tieg Zaharia
Tim Dennie
Tim Rocheleau
Tim Sweeney
Tim Willis
TJ Hollis
Todd
Todd M Estep
Tom Hammerheart
Tom Simpson
Tom Smith

Tom Veldran
Tomas Quintana
Tommy Knutsen
Tony Anjo
Tony L Page Jr
Tore Brede
Troels Pleimert
Tyler Drinkard
Tyler Kieft
Tyson Cote
Uldis Bojars
Unai Herrán
Urbanc
Vasilis Papaioannou
Vassilis Beglis
Vesko Gavrilov

Vincent Verhoeven
Warbird Games
Wayne Sung
Wes Raven
Wilcoweb
Xavier Bodenand
Xlynx
Y. K. Lee
Yannick Boudreau
Yodahome
Zac Maynard
Zachary Lee
Zack L
Zaina Alrujaib
Zivago Lee

Appendix 1: Systems Developed For

Company	System	Years of Release	Technical	Additional Notes
Apple	Apple II	1977–1990	8-bit	
	Macintosh (Mac)	1984– Current	8-bit 16-bit 32-bit 64-bit	*Introduced graphical interface and mouse to personal computing*
	Apple IIGS	1986–1992	16-bit	
Atari	2600	1977–1992	Console	
	400/800 (a.k.a. Atari 8-bit)	1979–1992	8-bit	*Officially the Atari 400/800 range; "Atari 8-bit" is a common though unofficial term*
	ST	1985–1993	16-bit 32-bit	*Replacement for the 8-bit Atari range*
Coleco	ColecoVision	1982–1985	Console	*Cartridge-based console*
Commodore	VIC-20	1980–1985	8-bit	
	Commodore 64 (C64)	1982–1994	8-bit	*The highest selling computer model of all time, selling 12.5 million units[46]*
	Amiga	1985–1996	16-bit 32-bit	
Fujitsu	FM-7 / FM-77	1982–1984	8-bit	*Mostly sold in Japan; PC compatible*
	FM-Towns	1989–1997	16-bit	*Mostly sold in Japan; PC compatible*
IBM	PC	1981–1987	8-bit	*IBM compatible became the standard in the 1980s / 1990s*
	PCjr	1984–1985	8-bit	*PC Junior, nicknamed Peanut*
Phillips	CD-i (Compact Disc Interaction)	1990–1998	Console	*CD-based format mostly used by Phillips, but compatible across a number of consoles; similar to Tandy Memorex VIS*

Company	System	Years of Release	Technical	Additional Notes
Microsoft	MS-DOS	1981–2000	Operating System	*The standard PC operating system until Windows 95*
	MSX	1983–1993	8-bit 16-bit	*An attempt by Microsoft and ASCII to create a computer standard; mostly sold in Japan*
	Windows	1985–Current	Operating System	*Windows 3 versions required MS-DOS; Windows 95 and later are standalone*
Nintendo	NES Famicom (Japan)	1983–1995	Console	*Nintendo Entertainment System*
	Game Boy Color	1998–2003	Console	*Handheld system*
Nippon Electric Company	PC-88	1981–1989	8-bit	*Mostly sold in Japan*
	PC-98	1982–2003	16-bit 32-bit	*Mostly sold in Japan*
Sega	Master System	1985–1996	Console	*3rd gen console*
	Sega CD	1991–1996	Console	*A CD-ROM drive for the Sega Genesis 4th gen console*
	Saturn	1994–2000	Console	*5th gen console*
	Dreamcast	1998–2001	Console	*6th gen console*
Sharp	X1	1982–1988	8-bit	*Mostly sold in Japan*
Sinclair	ZX Spectrum	1982–1992	8-bit	
Sony	PlayStation	1994–2006	Console	*5th gen console also known as PS1*
Tandy	TRS-80	1977–1991	8-bit	*Sierra developed for the Model III released in 1980, and the Model 4 released in 1983.*
	Tandy 1000	1984–1993	8-bit 16-bit	*IBM PC & PCjr compatible*
	Memorex VIS	1992–1993	Console	*Similar to Phillips CD-i*
Texas Instruments	TI-99/4A	1981–1984	8-bit	
Thomson	MO	1984–1986	8-bit	*Mostly sold in France*
	TO	1984–1986	8-bit	*More powerful version of the MO*

Appendix 2: Internal Development Systems

System	Notes
ADL (Adventure Development Language)	Written by Ken Williams in assembly language for *Mystery House*, ADL was later adapted into a game engine for other games in the Hi-Res Adventure Series. Primarily developed for the Apple II, which had only 4 colors, it was updated to allow a dithering pattern that created the illusion of 20 colors.
AGI (Adventure Game Interpreter)	AGI was developed for *King's Quest* and used a resolution of 160x200 in 16 colors. The graphics were vector-based, with coordinates stored in the code and backgrounds drawn in real time. It utilized the internal sound capabilities of the systems it was ported to and had a parser interface. AGI contained a separate runtime engine that allowed porting of the engine to other systems while keeping the game code intact.
SCI0 (Sierra's Creative Interpreter)	SCI was a completely new engine that utilized the higher 320x200 resolution, although still at 16 colors with vector-based graphics. External sound cards were supported (specifically the Roland MT-32 and AdLib), while mouse support was also added.
SCI0.1	The only variation from SCI0 was a different compression routine and the ability to store digital sounds.
SCI1.0	SCI1.0 utilized the same 320x200 resolution but allowed for 256-color VGA graphics, while a separate version of the engine allowed for 16-color graphics. It enabled graphics to be scanned in and displayed as a picture instead of the vector system previously used, added CD-ROM support and voice acting, and removed the parser, replacing it with a point-and-click interface.
I1.1	SCI1.1 removed the native 16-color version of the engine. Instead, the 16-color version was created on the fly using an algorithm extrapolated from the 256-color backgrounds. Support to play video files was also added, as was the ability to scale sprites.
SCI2/SCI3	SCI2 and SCI3 were collectively known as SCI32, a 32-bit version of the SCI engine. SCI2 added support for an enhanced 640x480 resolution utilizing SVGA graphics and enhanced video support. SCI3 included native Windows 95 support.

Appendix 3: Games

Games developed by Sierra – does not include subsidiaries except where noted. EGA versions of early SCI VGA titles were produced but have not been listed.

Release Year	Title	System	Engine	Additional Notes
1980	*Hi-Res Football*	Apple II		
	Mission Asteroid (Hi-Res Adventure #0)	Apple II, Atari 8-bit, C64, FM-7, PC-88, PC-98,	ADL	*Numbered zero as it served as an introduction to Hi-Res Adventures*
	Mystery House (Hi-Res Adventure #1)	Apple II	ADL	*First graphic adventure game*
	Skeet Shoot	Apple II		
	Trap Shoot	Apple II		
	Wizard and the Princess (Hi-Res Adventure #2)	Apple II, Atari 8-bit, C64, FM-7, MS-DOS, PC-88, PC-98, PCjr	ADL	*IBM version was renamed Adventure in Serenia*
1981	*Cranston Manor* (Hi-Res Adventure #3)	Apple II, FM-7, PC-88, PC-98	ADL	
	Crossfire	Apple II, Atari 8-bit, C64, VIC-20, PCjr, MS-DOS		*Not developed by Sierra but published as a PCjr launch title*
	Gobbler	Apple II		
	Hi-Res Cribbage	Apple II		
	Hi-Res Soccer	Apple II		
	Jawbreaker	Apple II, Atari 8-bit, Atari 2600		*Apple II version is an update of Gobbler, the Atari versions were different again – but all sold as Jawbreaker.*
	Missile Defense	Apple II		
	Pegasus II	Apple II		
	Sabotage	Apple II		
	Softporn Adventure	Apple II, Atari 8-bit, MS-DOS		*Only text adventure released by Sierra*

1981 cont...	*Threshold*	Apple II, Atari 8-bit, Atari 2600, ColecoVision, C64, Thomson MO, Thomson TO, VIC-20		
	Thrilogy of Games	Apple II		*A compilation of three arcade games:* Smashup, Bustout, *and* William Tell
	Ulysses and the Golden Fleece (Hi-Res Adventure #4)	Apple II, Atari 8-bit, C64, FM-7, MS-DOS, PC-88, PC-98	ADL	
1982	*Cannonball Blitz*	Apple II, TI-99/4A, VIC-20		
	Frogger	Apple II, Atari 8-bit, C64, Mac, MS-DOS, VIC-20		*Sierra-developed port of Konami's classic arcade game*
	Golf Challenge	Atari 8-bit		
	Marauder	Apple II, Atari 8-bit, Atari 2600		
	Laf Pak	Apple II		*A compilation of four arcade games:* Creepy Corridors, Mine Sweep, Apple Zap, *and* Space Race
	Lunar Leeper	Apple II, Atari 8-bit, C64, VIC-20		
	Mouskattack	Apple II, Atari 8-bit, MS-DOS		
	Pest Patrol	Apple II		
	Time Zone (Hi-Res Adventure #5)	Apple II, FM-7, PC-88, PC-98	ADL	

1982 cont...	Ultima II: The Revenge of the Enchantress	Apple II, Atari 8-bit, Atari ST, C64, Mac, MS-DOS		Developed by Lord British (Richard Garriott) and published by Sierra prior to his founding of Origin Systems
	WallWar	Atari 8-bit		
1983	Apple Cider Spider	Apple II, C64,		
	Aquatron	Apple II, Atari 8-bit		
	B.C.'s Quest for Tires	Apple II, Atari 8-bit, ColecoVision, C64, MSX, ZX Spectrum		
	Bop-A-Bet	Apple II		Originally released by Sunnyside Soft before Al Lowe sold to Sierra
	Creepy Corridors	VIC-20		
	The Dark Crystal (Hi-Res Adventure #6)	Apple II, Atari 8-bit	ADL	
	Dragon's Keep	Apple II, Atari 8-bit, C64, MS-DOS		Originally released by Sunnyside Soft in 1982 before Al Lowe sold to Sierra.
	Flip N Match	VIC-20		
	Jawbreaker II	Apple II, Atari 8-bit, C64, TI-99/4A, Vic-20		
	Learning with Leeper	Apple II, Atari 8-bit, ColecoVision, C64, ZX Spectrum		
	Mr. Cool	Apple II, Atari 8-bit, C64, MS-DOS		
	Oil's Well	Apple II, Atari 8-bit, ColecoVision, C64, MS-DOS, MSX, Sharp X1		
	Sammy Lightfoot	Apple II, ColecoVision, C64, FM-7, PC-88		MS-DOS port was announced but then cancelled.

1983 cont...	Troll's Tale	Apple II, Atari 8-bit, C64, MS-DOS		*Originally released by Sunnyside Soft before Al Lowe sold to Sierra*
	Ultima I	Atari 8-bit		*Port of the original Ultima Game.*
	Ultima: Escape from Mt. Drash	VIC-20		
1984	B.C. II Grog's Revenge	ColecoVision, C64, MSX		
	Donald Duck's Playground	Amiga, Apple II, Atari ST, C64, MS-DOS, PCjr, TRS-80	AGI	
	Hi-Res Learning Adventure: Story Maker	Apple II, C64, MS-DOS, PCjr		
	King's Quest	Amiga, Apple II, Apple IIGS, Atari ST, Mac, MS-DOS, PCjr, Sega Master System	AGI	*Renamed King's Quest: Quest for the Crown in later releases.* *Commonly held to be released in 1983, a demonstration version was released to stores in 1983 but it was not sold at retail until 1984.*
	Learning with FuzzyWOMP	Apple II		
	Mickey's Space Adventure	Apple II, C64, MS-DOS, TRS-80		
	Mine Shaft	PCjr		*Launch Title for PCjr.*
	Winnie the Pooh in the Hundred Acre Wood	Amiga, Apple II, Atari ST, C64, MS-DOS, TRS-80		
	Wizard of Id's WizMath	ColecoVision, C64		
	Wizard of Id's WizType	Apple II, Atari 8-bit, C64, MS-DOS		

1985	King's Quest II: Romancing the Throne	Amiga, Apple II, Apple IIGS, Atari ST, Mac, MS-DOS, PCjr, Tandy 1000	AGI	
1986	The Black Cauldron	Amiga, Apple II, Apple IIGS, Atari ST, MS-DOS, Tandy 1000	AGI	Final game developed under the Disney license
	King's Quest III: To Heir Is Human	Amiga, Apple II, Apple IIGS, Atari ST, Mac, MS-DOS, TRS-80	AGI	
	Space Quest: Chapter I – The Sarien Encounter	Amiga, Apple II, Apple IIGS, Atari ST, Mac, MS-DOS	AGI	
	Wrath of Denethenor	Apple II, Commodore 64		Published only
1987	3-D Helicopter Simulator	MS-DOS		
	Leisure Suit Larry in the Land of the Lounge Lizards	Amiga, Apple II, Apple IIGS, Atari ST, Mac, MS-DOS, TRS-80	AGI	A.k.a. Leisure Suit Larry 1
	Mixed-Up Mother Goose	Amiga, Apple II, Apple IIGS, Atari ST, Mac, MS-DOS	AGI	
	Police Quest: In Pursuit of the Death Angel	Amiga, Apple II, Apple IIGS, Atari ST, Mac, MS-DOS	AGI	
	Space Quest II: Chapter II – Vohaul's Revenge	Amiga, Apple II, Apple IIGS, Atari ST, Mac, MS-DOS	AGI	
1988	Gold Rush!	Amiga, Apple II, Apple IIGS, Atari ST, Mac, MS-DOS	AGI	
	King's Quest IV: The Perils of Rosella	Amiga, Apple II, Apple IIGS, Atari ST, MS-DOS	AGI SCI0	Developed in two separate versions using both the AGI and SCI engines
	Leisure Suit Larry Goes Looking for Love (in Several Wrong Places)	Amiga, Apple IIGS, Atari ST, MS-DOS	SCI0	A.k.a. Leisure Suit Larry 2

1988 cont...	Manhunter: New York	Amiga, Apple IIGS, Atari ST, MS-DOS, Tandy 1000	AGI	*Although developed by Evryware, the game was sold to Sierra and published under the Sierra label*
	Police Quest II: The Vengeance	Amiga, Atari ST, MS-DOS, NEC PC-9801	SCI0	
1989	The Colonel's Bequest	Amiga, Atari ST, MS-DOS	SCI0	
	Hero's Quest: So You Want to Be a Hero	Amiga, Atari ST, Mac, MS-DOS, NEC PC-9801	SCI0	*Later rereleased as Quest for Glory*
	Hoyle's Official Book of Games: Volume 1	Amiga, Atari ST, MS-DOS, Mac	SCI0	
	Leisure Suit Larry 3: Passionate Patti in Pursuit of the Pulsating Pectorals	Amiga, Apple IIGS, Atari ST, MS-DOS	SCI0	
	Manhunter 2: San Francisco	Amiga, Atari ST, Mac, MS-DOS	AGI	*Final game to use the AGI engine; although developed by Evryware, the game was sold to Sierra and published under the Sierra label*
	Space Quest III: The Pirates of Pestulon	Amiga, Atari ST, Mac, MS-DOS	SCI0	
1990	Codename: ICEMAN	Amiga, Atari ST, MS-DOS	SCI0	
	Conquests of Camelot: The Search for the Grail	Amiga, Atari ST, MS-DOS	SCI0	
	Hoyle's Official Book of Games: Volume 2	Amiga, Atari ST, Mac, MS-DOS	SCI0	

1990 cont...	Jones in the Fast Lane	MS-DOS	SCI1	Only game developed internally using an idea submitted from outside Sierra
	King's Quest I: Quest for the Crown	Amiga, MS-DOS	SCI0	(SCI remake)
	King's Quest V: Absence Makes the Heart Go Yonder!	Amiga, FM Towns, Mac, MS-DOS, NEC PC-9801, NES, Tandy Memorex VIS, Windows	SCI1	
	Mixed-Up Mother Goose	Amiga, Atari ST, MS-DOS	SCI0	
	Oil's Well	MS-DOS	SCI1	(VGA remake)
	Quest for Glory II: Trial by Fire	Amiga, MS-DOS	SCI0.1	
1991	Castle of Dr. Brain	Amiga, Mac, MS-DOS, NEC PC-9801	SCI1	
	Conquests of the Longbow: The Legend of Robin Hood	Amiga, MS-DOS	SCI1	
	Hoyle's Official Book of Games: Volume 3	Amiga, MS-DOS	SCI1	
	Leisure Suit Larry in the Land of the Lounge Lizards	Amiga, Mac, MS-DOS	SCI1	(VGA remake) A.k.a. Leisure Suit Larry 1
	Leisure Suit Larry 5: Passionate Patti Does a Little Undercover Work	Amiga, Mac, MS-DOS, Windows	SCI1	
	Mixed-Up Fairy Tales	MS-DOS	SCI1	
	Mixed-Up Mother Goose	Amiga, FM Towns, MS-DOS, Windows	SCI1	(VGA remake)
	Police Quest III: The Kindred	Amiga, MS-DOS	SCI1	
	Space Quest 1: Roger Wilco in the Sarien Encounter	Amiga, Mac, MS-DOS	SCI1	(VGA remake)
	Space Quest IV: Roger Wilco and the Time Rippers	Amiga, Mac, MS-DOS, NEC PC-9801, Windows	SCI1	

1992	*Crazy Nick's Software Picks: King Graham's Board Game Challenge*	MS-DOS	SCI1.1	
	Crazy Nick's Software Picks: Leisure Suit Larry's Casino	MS-DOS	SCI1.1	
	Crazy Nick's Software Picks: Parlor Games with Laura Bow	MS-DOS	SCI1.1	
	Crazy Nick's Software Picks: Robin Hood's Games of Skill and Chance	MS-DOS	SCI1.1	
	Crazy Nick's Software Picks: Roger Wilco's Spaced Out Game Pack	MS-DOS	SCI1.1	
	EcoQuest: The Search for Cetus	MS-DOS	SCI1	
	The Island of Dr. Brain	MS-DOS	SCI1.1	
	King's Quest VI: Heir Today, Gone Tomorrow	Amiga, Mac, MS-DOS, Windows	SCI1.1	
	Laura Bow: The Dagger of Amon Ra	MS-DOS, Windows	SCI1.1	
	Police Quest: In Pursuit of the Death Angel	MS-DOS	SCI1.1	(VGA remake)
	Quest for Glory: So You Want to Be a Hero	Mac, MS-DOS	SCI1.1	(VGA remake)
	Quest for Glory III: Wages of War	MS-DOS	SCI1.1	
1993	*Lost Secret of the Rainforest*	MS-DOS, Windows	SCI1.1	*A.k.a.* EcoQuest 2
	The Fates of Twinion	MS-DOS		

1993 cont...	*Crazy Nick's Software Picks: King Graham's Board Game Challenge*	MS-DOS	SCI1.1	
	The Shadows of Yersbius	MS-DOS		*Originally online through* The Sierra Network, *standalone edition was sold with* The Fates of Twinion *as an expansion.*
	Freddy Pharkas: Frontier Pharmacist	Mac, MS-DOS, Windows	SCI1.1	
	Gabriel Knight: Sins of the Fathers	Mac, MS-DOS, Windows	SCI1.1	*A.k.a.* Gabriel Knight 1
	Hoyle Classic Card Games	Mac, MS-DOS, Windows	SCI1.1	
	Leisure Suit Larry 6: Shape Up or Slip Out!	Mac, MS-DOS, Windows	SCI1.1 SCI2	
	Pepper's Adventures in Time	MS-DOS, Windows	SCI1.1	
	Police Quest: Open Season	Mac, MS-DOS, Windows	SCI1.1	*A.k.a.* Police Quest 4
	Quest for Glory: Shadows of Darkness	MS-DOS, Windows	SCI2	*A.k.a.* Quest for Glory IV
	Slater & Charlie Go Camping	Mac, MS-DOS	SCI1.1	
	Space Quest V: Roger Wilco – the Next Mutation	MS-DOS	SCI1.1	*Developed at Dynamix using Sierra's internal SCI engine*
1994	*King's Quest VII: The Princeless Bride*	Mac, MS-DOS, Windows	SCI2	
	Outpost	Mac, MS-DOS, Windows		
1995	*Gabriel Knight: The Beast Within*	Mac, MS-DOS, Windows	SCI2	*A.k.a.* Gabriel Knight 2
	Hoyle Classic Games	Mac, Windows	SCI2	

1995 cont...	Mixed-Up Mother Goose Deluxe	Mac, MS-DOS, Windows	SCI2	(SVGA Remake)
	Phantasmagoria	Mac, MS-DOS, Sega Saturn, Windows	SCI2	*Sierra's first full motion video game*
	Police Quest: SWAT	Mac, MS-DOS, Windows	SCI2	
	The Ruins of Cawdor	MS-DOS		*Originally online through* The Sierra Network, *standalone edition was sold as an expansion to* The Shadows of Yersbius
	Shivers	Mac, MS-DOS, Windows	SCI2	
	Space Quest 6: Roger Wilco in the Spinal Frontier	Mac, MS-DOS, Windows	SCI2	
	Torin's Passage	Mac, MS-DOS, Windows	SCI2	
1996	Hoyle Blackjack	Windows		
	Hoyle Bridge	Windows		
	Hoyle Casino	Windows		
	Hoyle Children's Collection	Windows		
	Hoyle Solitaire	Mac, Windows		*Remake of* Hoyle Official Book of Games Vol. 2
	Leisure Suit Larry: Love for Sail!	Mac, MS-DOS, Windows	SCI3	*A.k.a.* Leisure Suit Larry 7
	Lighthouse: The Dark Being	Mac, MS-DOS, Windows	SCI3	
	Phantasmagoria: A Puzzle of Flesh	MS-DOS, Windows	SCI3	
	Rama	Mac, MS-DOS, Windows, PlayStation	SCI3	*Developed at Dynamix — one of two games to use Sierra's SCI system*
	The Realm Online	Windows		

1997	Betrayal in Antara	Windows		Uses an updated version of Dynamix' Betrayal at Krondor engine.
	Hoyle Casino	Windows		
	Hoyle Classic Board Games	Windows		
	Hoyle Classic Card Games	Windows		
	Hoyle Poker	Windows		
	Shivers Two: Harvest of Souls	Windows	SCI2	
1998	Half-Life	Linux, Mac, Windows		Last game signed by Ken Williams, only published by Sierra
	Hoyle Board Games	Mac, Windows		
	Hoyle Battling Ships and War	Windows		
	Hoyle Bridge and Euchre	Windows		
	Hoyle Card Games	Game Boy Color, Mac, Windows		
	Hoyle Casino	Windows		
	Hoyle Classic Card Games	Windows		
	Hoyle Hearts and Spades	Windows		
	Hoyle Poke	Windows		
	Hoyle Solitaire	Windows		
	King's Quest: Mask of Eternity	Windows		A.k.a. King's Quest 8
	Leisure Suit Larry's Casino	Windows		
	Police Quest: SWAT 2	Windows		
	Quest for Glory V: Dragon Fire	Mac, Windows		Final adventure game developed at Oakhurst studios

1999	*Gabriel Knight 3: Blood of the Sacred, Blood of the Damned*	Windows		*Final adventure game developed by Sierra*
	Hoyle Backgammon and Cribbage	Mac, Windows		
	Hoyle Board Games	Mac, Windows		
	Hoyle Casino	Windows		
	Hoyle Craps and Blackjack	Windows		
	Hoyle Slots and Video Poker	Windows		
	Hoyle Solitaire and Mahjongg Tiles	Windows		
	Hoyle Word Games	Mac, Windows		
	Sierra's Complete Chess	Windows		
	SWAT 3: Close Quarters Battle	Windows		
2000	*Hoyle Board Games 2001*	Mac, Windows		
	Hoyle Bridge	Windows		
	Hoyle Card Games	Windows		
	Hoyle Casino	Game Boy Color, Mac, Sega Dreamcast, Windows		
	Hoyle Crosswords	Mac, Windows		
	Hoyle Kids Games	Mac, Windows		
	Hoyle Mahjongg Tiles	Mac, Windows		
	Hoyle Solitaire	Windows		
	Hoyle Solitaire and Mahjongg Tiles	Windows		
	Hoyle Slots and Video Poker	Windows		
	Hoyle Word Games	Windows		
	SWAT 3: Elite Edition	Windows		

1 *1983 Strategy Outline*, On-Line Systems, 1982.

2 Josh Mandel, "R.I.P. Sierra," The Sierra Help Pages (February 25, 1999), http://www.sierrahelp.com/Misc/History/SierraEulogy.html.

3 *King's Quest Collection Series* manual (Sierra On-Line, 1994), 11.

4 *KQ Collection Series* manual, 14.

5 *Tenth Anniversary Catalog* (Sierra On-Line, 1990), 34, https://archive.org/details/Sierra10thAnniversaryCatalog.

6 *Tenth Anniversary Catalog*, 34.

7 *Tenth Anniversary Catalog*, 35.

8 *Thexder* box cover, Sierra On-Line, 1987.

9 "Behind the Disk: Jim Walls – *Police Quest* Designer," *Sierra Newsletter* 1, no. 2 (1987): 4, https://archive.org/details/Sierra_Newsletter_The_Volume_1_Number_2_1987_Sierra_On-Line_US.

10 "Product Spotlight: *Police Quest* – Review of a Patrol Simulation," *Law and Order* (October 1988), reprinted in "*Police Quest* Used in Real-Life Police Officer Training," *Sierra Newsletter* 2, no. 1 (Spring 1989): 5, https://archive.org/details/Sierra_Newsletter_The_Volume_2_Number_1_Spring_1989_1989_Sierra_On-Line_US.

11 *Space Quest II: Chapter II – Vohaul's Revenge*, Sierra On-Line, 1987.

12 *KQ Collection Series* manual, 21.

13 *KQ Collection Series* manual, 21.

14 Al Lowe, "The Death of Adventure Games," Al Lowe's Humor Site (March 19, 1999), http://allowe.com/al/articles/death-of-adventures.html.

15 Nancy Smithe, "Roberta Williams: The Storyteller Who Started It All," *Sierra News Magazine* 2, no. 2 (Autumn 1989): 3, https://archive.org/details/Sierra_News_Magazine_The_Volume_2_Number_2_Autumn_1989_1989_Sierra_On-Line_US.

16 Smithe, "Roberta Williams," 3.

17 *KQ Collection Series* manual, 25.

18 Troels Pleimert, "The 10th Incarnation of the Increasingly Misnamed Official *Space Quest* FAQ," accessed January 2, 2020, https://wiw.org/~jess/SQFAQ20.txt.

19 Bridget McKenna, "Jim Walls Q&A," *Sierra / Dynamix News Magazine* 4, no. 2 (Summer 1991): 11–12, https://archive.org/details/Sierra-Dynamix_News_Magazine_Volume_4_Number_2_Summer_1991_1991_Sierra_On-Line_US.

20 McKenna, "Jim Walls," 12.

21 Lowe, "Death of Adventure Games."

22 Elon Gasper, "When You Wish Upon a Bright Star," *InterAction* 5, no. 3 (Fall 1992): 41, https://archive.org/details/InterAction_Magazine_Vol._V_Number_3_Fall_1992_1992_Sierra_On-Line_US.

23 Kurt Busch, "A Game Designer Designs the Future," *InterAction* 5, no. 2 (Summer 1992): 41, https://archive.org/details/InterAction_Magazine_Vol._V_Number_2_Summer_1992_1992_Sierra_On-Line_US.

[24] Rich DeBaun, "The Quest for *King's Quest VI*," *InterAction* 5, no. 2 (Fall 1992): 21, https://archive.org/details/InterAction_Magazine_Vol._V_Number_3_Fall_1992_19 92_Sierra_On-Line_US/mode/2up.

[25] Lowe, "Death of Adventure Games."

[26] Nancy Smithe Grimsley, "Decisions Behind the Scenes of *Police Quest: Open Season*," *InterAction* 6, no. 3 (Holiday 1993), 14, https://archive.org/details/InterAction_Magazine_Vol._VI_Number_3_Holiday_199 3_1993_Sierra_On-Line_US.

[27] Richard DeBaun, "Putting the Police in *Police Quest*," *InterAction* 6, no. 1 (Spring 1993), 23, https://www.sierragamers.com/wp-content/uploads/2019/12/017_InterAction_Volume_6_Number_1_June_1993.pdf.

[28] Pat Bridgemon, "Preview: *Police Quest 4*" *InterAction* 6, no. 2 (Summer 1993), 29, https://archive.org/details/InterAction_Magazine_Vol._VI_Number_2_Summer_199 3_1993_Sierra_On-Line_US.

[29] Lorelei Shannon, *King's Quest VII: The Princeless Bride – The Official Hint Guide* (Sierra On-Line, 1994), 5.

[30] Shannon, *KQVII Hint Guide*, 4.

[31] Peter Lewis, "CUC Will Buy 2 Software Companies for $1.8 billion," *The New York Times* (February 21, 1996), https://www.nytimes.com/1996/02/21/business/cuc-will-buy-2-software-companies-for-1.8-billion.html.

[32] John Romero, "I've Made a Lot of Mistakes, And You're Not My First One," February 19, 2017, in *Back Seat Designers* (season 4, episode 6), produced by Frederik Olsen, Gareth Millward, and Troels Pleimert, podcast, MP3 audio, http://www.backseatdesigners.com/2017/02/19/s4e6-ive-made-a-lot-of-mistakes-and-youre-not-my-first-one.

[33] Andrew Ku, "The Top 15 Best-Selling PC Games of All Time," *Tom's Hardware* (March 21, 2012), https://www.tomshardware.com/picturestory/587-best-selling-game-list-2.html.

[34] "Sometimes, a Husband Must Battle the Queen," *Philadelphia Inquirer* (March 9, 1997), https://web.archive.org/web/20160304091723/http://articles.philly.com/1997-03-09/living/25570956_1_roberta-williams-new-game-sierra-on-line.

[35] Roberta Williams, "Roberta Williams Speaks Out," *Just Adventure* (March 1999), https://web.archive.org/web/20071224080507/http://www.justadventure.com/Inter views/Roberta_Williams/Roberta_Williams_Interview_3.shtm.

[36] Lowe, "Death of Adventure Games."

[37] John Sauer, "King's Quest: The Mask of Eternity," *InterAction* (Fall 1996), 96, https://archive.org/details/InterAction_Magazine_Fall_1996_1996_Sierra_On-Line_US.

[38] Ken Williams (kenwilliams), "Roberta asked me to post the following," Phoenix Online Studios forum post, August 29, 2011, https://www.postudios.com/blog/forum/index.php?topic=10982.msg328576#msg32 8576.

[39] Roberta Williams, "I have been reading with interest all of the various comments that everybody has had about KQ8," Sierra On-Line forum post, July 7, 1997, as quoted by Baggins, "I'm reminded Roberta criticized the fans who criticized the more violent version of the game," Phoenix Online Studios forum post, August 28, 2011, https://www.postudios.com/blog/forum/index.php?topic=10982.msg328520#msg32 8520.

[40] Roberta Williams quoted by Baggins.

[41] Celia Pearce, "The Player with Many Faces: A Conversation with Louis Castle," *Game Studies* 2, no. 2 (December 2002), https://web.archive.org/web/20030627220215/http://www.gamestudies.org/0202/pearce/.

[42] Ken Williams (Ken W), "At the time we were acquired, the company wasn't for sale," SierraGamers forum post, February 22, 2010, https://www.sierragamers.com/forums/topic/email-you-fell-off-kenny-boy-you-fell-off-continued-from-12-08-2003/#post-25942.

[43] Ken Williams, SierraGamers forum post.

[44] Ken Williams, "Ken Williams' Official Letter to all Former Sierra Employees," The Sierra Help Pages, accessed May 25, 2020, http://www.sierrahelp.com/Misc/History/KenWilliamsLetter.html.

[45] Neil Druckmann, *The Game Awards 2014 (Full Show)*, December 5, 2014, produced by Geoff Keighley, archived video of YouTube livestream, 2:23:48, https://www.youtube.com/watch?v=KILvCLP2h84.

[46] Michael Stiel, "How many Commodore 64 computers were really sold?" *Pagetable* (February 2, 2011), https://www.pagetable.com/?p=547.

www.ingramcontent.com/pod-product-compliance
Lightning Source LLC
Chambersburg PA
CBHW070524220526
45467CB00003B/834